The Alternative Defence Commission is an independent body s̶
in 1981 by the Lansbury House Trust Fund in conjun̶
the S̶ of̶ S̶
have
to Br̶

ALTERNATIVE DEFENCE
COMMISSION

The Politics of
Alternative Defence:

A Policy for a Non-nuclear Britain

PALADIN
GRAFTON BOOKS
A Division of the Collins Publishing Group

LONDON GLASGOW
TORONTO SYDNEY AUCKLAND

Paladin
Grafton Books
A Division of the Collins Publishing Group
8 Grafton Street, London W1X 3LA

A Paladin Paperback Original 1987

ISBN 0-586-08580-7

Printed and bound in Great Britain by
Collins, Glasgow

Set in Baskerville

Contents

Members of the Alternative Defence Commission

July 1986

Viv Bingham, President of the Liberal Party, 1981–82

April Carter, writer and lecturer, former Politics Tutor, Somerville College, Oxford

Owen Greene, Researcher on nuclear weapons issues at The Open University, Author of *Europe's Folly: The Facts and Arguments about Cruise* (1983)

Malcolm Harper, Director, United Nations Association

Isobel Lindsay, Member of the National Executive of the Scottish National Party; lecturer in Sociology at Strathclyde University

James O'Connell, Professor of Peace Studies, University of Bradford

Rev. Paul Oestreicher, British Council of Churches, member of the Church of England Working Party which produced the report, *The Church and the Bomb* (1982)

Michael Randle, Research Fellow, University of Bradford, Co-ordinator

Paul Rogers, Senior Lecturer in Peace Studies, University of Bradford, Chair

Elizabeth Sigmund, Co-ordinator of the Working Party on Chemical and Biological Weapons; author of *Rage Against the Dying* (1980)

Dan Smith, Independent research worker on UK defence policy, member of the Labour Party Defence Study Group; author of *The Defence of the Realm in the 1980s*

Walter Stein, former Senior Lecturer in Literature and Philosophy, Department of Adult Education and Extra Mural Studies, University of Leeds; editor of *Nuclear Weapons and Christian Conscience* (1961; 1981)

Jonathan Steele, Chief Foreign Correspondent of *The Guardian*; author of *World Power: Soviet Foreign Policy Under Brezhnev and Andropov* (1983)

Dafydd Elis Thomas, MP, Plaid Cymru; Member of Parliament for Meirionnydd

Andrew Wilson, Associate Editor, and former Defence Correspondent of *The Observer*; author of *The Disarmer's Handbook* (1983)

Commission Researchers: Howard Clark, Lisa Foley

Abbreviations

ABM Anti-Ballistic Missile
ADM Atomic Demolition Munition (mine)
ASAT Anti-Satellite Weapon
CBMs Confidence Building Measures
CDE Conference on Disarmament in Europe
CDU Christian Democratic Union (FRG)
CSCE Conference on European Security and Co-operation
CSU Christian Social Union (FRG)
CTB (T) Comprehensive Test Ban (Treaty)
EC (EEC) European Community (European Economic Community)
EURATOM European Atomic Energy Community
FCO Foreign and Commonwealth Office
FDP Free Democrat Party (FRG)
FOFA Follow-On Forces Attack
FRG Federal Republic of Germany
GCD General and Complete Disarmament
GDR German Democratic Republic
GIUK Greenland-Iceland-UK gap
GLCM Ground-Launched Cruise Missile
IAEA International Atomic Energy Authority
ICBM Intercontinental Ballistic Missile
IEPG Independent European Procurement Group
INF Intermediate-Range Nuclear Force
JCS Joint Chiefs-of-Staff
MAD Mutual Assured Destruction
MBFR Mutual Balanced Force Reduction
MIRV Multiple Independently Targeted Re-Entry Vehicle (RV= warhead)
MOD Ministry of Defence
NATO North Atlantic Treaty Organization
NFU No-First-Use

NPT Non-Proliferation Treaty

NWFZ Nuclear Weapons-Free Zone

ODA Overseas Development Administration

OECD Organization for Economic Cooperation and Development

OPEC Organization of Petroleum-Exporting Countries

PII Pershing II missile

PGM Precision-Guided Munition

PTBT Partial Test-Ban Treaty

R&D Research and Development

SALT Strategic Arms Limitation Talks

SDI Strategic Defense Initiative

SEATO South East Asia Treaty Organization

SED Socialist Unity Party

SIOP Single Integrated Operational Plan

SLBM Submarine-Launched Ballistic Missile

SPD Social-Democratic Party (FRG)

START Strategic Arms Reduction Talks

UNCTAD United Nations Conference on Trade and Development

UNESCO United Nations Educational, Scientific and Cultural Organization

URENCO Uranium Enrichment Company

WEU West European Union

WTO Warsaw Treaty Organization (Warsaw Pact)

Foreword

The Alternative Defence Commission is an independent group set up in October 1980 to explore the range of defence options that would be open to Britain if it abandoned nuclear weapons and refused to have such weapons based on its territory. Its membership comprises a core of fifteen to twenty people from a variety of backgrounds and political persuasions, including many who are involved professionally in peace and conflict research. All share the conviction that Britain should renounce nuclear weapons and refuse to have such weapons based on its territory.

The Commission is sponsored by the Lansbury House Trust Fund, and the University of Bradford School of Peace Studies funding comes entirely from charitable and educational trusts and from individuals. We would like to take this opportunity to thank all those who have made donations to our work. We are particularly grateful to the Joseph Rowntree Charitable Trust, the Barrow and Geraldine S. Cadbury Trust and the Mertz-Gilmore Foundation who have continued to provide the basic funding for the Commission.

The Commission's first report, published in 1983 under the title *Defence Without the Bomb* (Taylor & Francis, £4.45), focused specifically on non-nuclear defence as such and aroused considerable interest and discussion. The present study shifts the main focus to the political aspects of security and to the foreign and arms control policies a non-nuclear Britain could pursue to promote European and global security.

Work on this new study commenced towards the end of 1983 and was completed in June 1986. Over the first year the Commission held a number of meetings at which specialists in international relations, arms control and foreign policy attended and gave us the benefit of their thinking. We are grateful to those who assisted us at this stage and to those who commented on sections of the drafts, and we would like in particular to thank Malcolm Dando, who was a frequent attender at the meetings, Wolf Mendl, Anthony McGrew, Julian Perry Robinson, and Nicholas Sims; they are not, of course, committed to the conclusions and recommendations of the report for which the Commission itself is solely responsible.

Clearly with a report of this kind, which considers and comments on a wide range of issues, unanimous agreement by Commission members on every detail was not conceivable. Nevertheless all Commission members are in accord with the main lines of the argument.

The drafting of this report was mainly done by four Commission members: Michael Randle, April Carter, Owen Greene and Dan Smith, with a fifth member, Walter Stein, undertaking an especially careful reading of the drafts at all stages and providing invaluable critical commentary. Lisa Foley acted as research assistant throughout the period of preparation of both the earlier and present reports, and the Commission would especially like to thank her and also Howard Clark who did research and drafting work for the Commission from 1981 until taking up his appointment as Secretary of War Resisters International in the Spring of 1985. A vital editing job in the later stages was also undertaken by Adrian Howe and Patrick Burke.

I would also like, on behalf of the whole Commission, to express special thanks to April Carter, and to the co-ordinator, Michael Randle, both of whom worked with commitment and dedication to ensure the successful completion of both reports.

The debate on how to rid the world of the menace of nuclear destruction remains the most important one in our time. All of us who worked on this report hope that it will make a useful contribution to that debate and will be read both by those who accept the need for Britain and Western Europe to reject any reliance on nuclear weapons, and those who are not yet convinced that this is the right course of action but accept the need for a critical reassessment of British and Western policies.

Paul Rogers, Bradford, June 1986

Introduction

1. BACKGROUND TO THE PRESENT REPORT

Rethinking Britain's Foreign Policy

Will the 1980s prove to be the turning point in the long struggle to rid the world of nuclear weapons? There are at least some reasons for hoping that it could be so. The decade began with major protests across Western Europe against new missile deployments in the region. It saw the spread of anti-nuclear weapons sentiment far beyond the boundaries of the traditional peace movement, encompassing scientists, doctors, other professional and trade union organizations, the women's movement, and religious bodies.

In the USA the Freeze Movement which sought to halt and then reverse the nuclear arms race won support across a wide spectrum of opinion. In Britain the Labour Party adopted a policy of British nuclear disarmament and the removal of US nuclear weapons and bases from this country. In several other European countries too, social democratic parties adopted policies that would at least move NATO away from its present degree of reliance on nuclear weapons. And many entirely orthodox strategists on both sides of the Atlantic also began to question aspects of NATO strategy and the assumptions that underlay them – such as deploying battlefield nuclear weapons and being prepared in some circumstances to be the first side to use nuclear weapons.

But while all this is hopeful, it is clearly not enough. Indeed much of the opposition to nuclear weapons is itself a response to destabilizing developments in technology and shifts in strategic doctrine which have left the traditional theory of deterrence in disarray. If a stage is to be reached where individual Western governments, or the NATO alliance as a whole, reject reliance on nuclear weapons, credible alternative policies have to be worked out and presented to the public.

It was in an attempt to begin meeting this challenge that the Alternative Defence Commission was set up in 1980. Its first report, published in April 1983 under the title *Defence Without the Bomb*, considered the defence options that would be open to Britain if it gave up its own nuclear weapons and refused to allow such weapons to be stationed on its territory.[1] That report focused on defence as such – on the implications of Britain's renunciation of nuclear weapons for its future relations with NATO, on the possibilities of non-nuclear defence for Europe as a whole, on what Britain might do by way of defence preparations if it left NATO, and on the scope for guerrilla warfare or non-violent civil resistance in this context.

But the security of a country or region depends also on factors over and above the defence preparations it makes and the alliances it forms to strengthen its position militarily. These include its success in settling differences with both nearby and more distant states, in fostering good relations within the region of which it forms a part, and on the stability of the international system as a whole. Some of these factors may be largely or even entirely outside its control; this is especially true for those states which are not superpowers.

At other levels, however, a country like Britain can make a direct and important contribution towards diplomatic and political initiatives. Moreover by acting in concert with other states it may be able to extend its influence – contributing, for instance, to the resolution of crises outside the region, or exerting pressure on the superpowers to desist from provocative actions or to enter into serious negotiations for arms control and disarmament. It is on this political dimension of security that the present report focuses. In doing so it elaborates, and occasionally modifies, some of the particular recommendations made in the first report.

The thrust of the new foreign policy which we recommend for Britain is summed up by the notion of dealignment. The objective of this approach is to support and strengthen the forces that are tending to break up the bi-polar structure of global politics dominated by the two superpowers. In the Third World, a commitment to dealignment implies resisting interventionist policies by the superpowers and their habit of imposing East-West rivalry on local and regional conflicts.

In Europe, the long-term goal of dealignment is to secure the dissolution of both military alliances and the withdrawal of superpower forces from both Eastern and Western Europe. In the case of the Soviet Union, this implies withdrawal to behind its own frontiers. Clearly such a fundamental restructuring cannot happen overnight, and the term dealignment is intended to denote the *process* of reducing superpower political and military dominance and creating by stages the conditions that would permit the dissolution of the alliances. Thus dealignment in Europe is a process that can begin within the existing alliance structures even though its longer term goal is to secure the dissolution of the alliances.

The notion of dealignment is closely associated with that of *disengagement*. Disengagement, in one common usage of the term, is the superpower end of the dealignment process. It clearly would not make sense to speak of the Soviet Union dealigning itself from Eastern Europe, or the USA dealigning itself from Western Europe, but they can reduce their military presence and political dominance; disengagement is an appropriate term to denote this process. The term, however, can also refer to a drawing back by the superpowers, or the rival blocs they have formed, from confrontation with each other. Thus the scaling down of superpower forces in Europe, the creation of nuclear-weapon-free zones and of zones from which major offensive forces have been withdrawn would involve disengagement in a double sense: the superpowers, and the two military alliances, would no longer be massively confronting each other in central Europe; and simultaneously the superpowers would be reducing the size of their military presence in the territories of their allies.

We argue in this report that a non-nuclear Britain would be well placed to promote dealignment both in Europe and in the Third World. At the European level it could exert pressure on NATO to denuclearize its defence, work with other European states to re-establish détente, and, in the longer term, seek to construct an alternative political and security framework.

We offer a range of suggestions concerning Britain's particular role in this process. Thus we indicate how the very process of British nuclear disarmament could provide a test experience for verification and control procedures and suggest how a non-nuclear Britain could work to strengthen the safeguards against the proliferation of nuclear weapons. We also suggest how Britain could go about changing its own relationship, and that of other Western industrialized countries, with the Third World.

Defining a Non-Nuclear Defence

The term 'non-nuclear Britain' is often used in different senses; it is important to distinguish between these and to make clear in what sense it is being used. First, it may be used to mean simply that Britain would decommission its own nuclear weapons. Second, it can mean that, in addition, Britain would require the US to remove its nuclear bases from British territory. Third, it could extend to a further commitment to denuclearize NATO strategy in Europe, without, however, an end to the US nuclear guarantee to Europe as a safeguard against Soviet nuclear escalation or blackmail. Finally it can mean a total rejection of any reliance on nuclear weapons. This rejection implies not only that Britain would scrap its own nuclear weapons and insist on the removal of US nuclear bases, but a repudiation of a 'nuclear umbrella' of any kind either for Britain itself or for Europe as a whole if Britain were to remain a member of NATO.

It is in this last and most radical sense that the Commission advocates the adoption of a non-nuclear approach by Britain and the report is aimed most directly at exploring the policies that a government adopting such a position might pursue. Many of the policies we advocate would, however, be relevant for any government that was non-nuclear in one of the above senses of the term or was simply committed to the serious pursuit of nuclear and conventional disarmament, the restoration of détente, and changing the basis of North-South relations.

Since the present work follows on from the first report, a summary of the conclusions and recommendations of the latter will be useful at this point. The recommendation that impinges most directly on the political domain – and on the concerns of the present report – has to do with the approach a non-nuclear Britain should take to NATO. Clearly a Britain that had taken a principled absolute stand against nuclear weapons could not remain indefinitely in an alliance which not only deploys nuclear weapons but is prepared to use them first under certain circumstances. Nevertheless *Defence Without the Bomb* recognized there were both negative and positive reasons to avoid a precipitate withdrawal from NATO. The negative reasons were that withdrawal could create a dangerous crisis in Europe, could be interpreted as a selfish and isolationist move, and could leave Britain vulnerable – not so much to a consequent opportunist attack from a hostile power, as to economic and political sanctions from its former allies. The main positive reason was that if Britain could persuade NATO to adopt a non-nuclear strategy this would have much greater political impact than if Britain on its own gave up nuclear weapons.

Accordingly the majority of the Commission recommended that a non-nuclear Britain should remain in NATO but on the strict condition that the Alliance would move step by step within a specified time period to the adoption of a totally non-nuclear strategy. These steps were, first, the adoption of a no-first-use policy; second, the withdrawal of battlefield nuclear weapons; third the removal of other nuclear weapons, thereby creating a nuclear-free Western Europe. At each stage every effort would be made to secure Warsaw Pact reciprocation, but if necessary the steps would be taken unilaterally. Finally the Commission recognized that as long as the US remained a nuclear power, a truly non-nuclear strategy for Western Europe would require a public commitment on the part of the US and the European NATO states that in future the US defence commitment to Europe would be strictly confined to the conventional level; in other words Western Europe would reverse the policy it has pursued since the formation of NATO and deliberately seek to decouple West European defence from the US nuclear deterrent at every level. If NATO continued to reject these conditions, Britain would in the first instance withdraw from NATO's military command structure, and if this failed to bring about the necessary changes, would withdraw altogether from the Alliance.

At the strategic level, we advocated the adoption of a clearly defensive and non-provocative posture. This concept of 'defensive deterrence' is at the opposite end of the spectrum from the offensive deterrence epitomized by a nuclear strategy which seeks to deter opponents by threatening the devastation of their societies. Defensive deterrence does not, however, imply that there would be no offensive capability whatever at the conventional level or that no weapons would be deployed that could be used for tactical counter attack. It does imply that military forces would be armed and deployed in such a way that a major strategic offensive against other states could be discounted. Long-range bombers and missiles, for instance, would be phased out, and the numbers of tanks deployed would be limited.

At the European level NATO would seek to achieve a position of what we termed 'defensive balance'. Though the Alliance would have only a limited offensive capability, it would be sufficiently strong in the defensive mode to make any Warsaw Pact conventional attack a highly risky gamble. Defensive strength has long been an achievable goal at the conventional level because of the inherent advantage of the defence. One could seek to establish defensive strength at the European level by such means as the erection of barriers, preparations for in-depth defence, greater reliance on anti-tank and anti-aircraft precision-guided munitions (PGMs), and building up the strength of reserve and territorial forces.

If Britain felt obliged to leave NATO it could not of course hope to achieve the same level of defensive strength. But by maximizing the advantages it possesses as an island, and by preparing for both coastal and in-depth defences, it could aim to achieve a posture analogous to a Swedish or Swiss 'high entry price' strategy likely to dissuade any foreign power from attacking it in most circumstances and probably to defeat most levels of attack.

We recognized that in the last analysis any conventional system of defence must reckon with the possibility of nuclear escalation by a nuclear-armed opponent. We stressed, however, that there are weighty political constraints on such use of these weapons; indeed one of the arguments against possessing nuclear weapons, or allowing them to be deployed on one's territory, is that this is likely to erode these political constraints and thus make the country concerned more rather than less likely to experience a nuclear attack in the event of war. Nevertheless, partly because of the ultimate vulnerability of *any* form of military defence in the nuclear age, at any rate in the context of an East-West conflict, we also stressed the importance of 'anti-occupation strategies' – namely guerrilla warfare and non-violent civil resistance – in our time. We concluded that in highly urbanized industrial countries, guerrilla warfare was likely to be of only limited effectiveness, to be extremely bloody and divisive, and to lead to severe repression, but that the possibilities of non-violent civil resistance merited serious consideration.

2. POLITICAL DEVELOPMENTS SINCE THE PUBLICATION OF THE COMMISSION'S FIRST REPORT

Developments at the International Level

Since the Commission's first report was published there have been several developments both at the international level and within Britain which have a bearing on its recommendations and concerns.

First, 1983 saw the deployment of cruise and Pershing II missiles in Europe despite massive public protests. This clearly represents a serious setback to the efforts to achieve a nuclear-free Europe. On the other hand in so far as these deployments had the political aim of strengthening the unity of the Western Alliance under US leadership, they have not succeeded. Controversy continues to surround the deployment programme, and in West Germany the SPD, following its defeat in the 1983 elections, reversed its position on the issue, mainly as a result of public pressure generated by the peace movement and the Greens. This raises the possibility that there could be a West German government opposed to the Euromissile deployments in 1987 or 1988. If this were to happen side by side with a Labour victory in Britain, the whole programme could be called into question. Moreover the majority of social democratic parties in Europe now advocate a policy that would move NATO some distance in the direction of a non-nuclear strategy, even though a US nuclear guarantee is still deemed necessary in the background.

Second, the Reagan-Gorbachev summit at Geneva in November 1985 seemed to promise an improvement in East-West relations and the possibility of progress in arms control negotiations. These hopes soon faded. Progress regarding strategic nuclear weapons remains unpromising – especially in view of the US insistence on pursuing the Strategic Defense Initiative.

The prospects for some kind of agreement on Intermediate Range Nuclear Forces (INF) in Europe seem slightly better. But one obstacle here is the apparent reluctance of some European governments, including those of Thatcher and Kohl, to accept a deal to remove all Cruise and Pershing II missiles in return for the removal of Soviet SS20s and other INF missiles aimed at Western Europe. Britain and France also rejected a proposal from Gorbachev that their nuclear weapons could be disregarded in an INF agreement in Europe provided they undertook not to increase the present size of their arsenals.

An early resumption of negotiations on a Comprehensive Test Ban Treaty is now also virtually ruled out following the US decision to continue testing during the period of a Soviet test moratorium, and the new US declaration that as long as nuclear weapons remain central to deterrence, testing must continue. The one concrete achievement in the period under review was the agreement at the Stockhom CDE conference in September 1986 on new and more extensive Confidence Building Measures.

Third, there has been the US bombing of Libya in April 1986 using planes attached to the US Sixth Fleet in the Mediterranean and F-111 fighter-bombers based in Britain. The raid, in reprisal for terrorist attacks which the US maintains were ordered by the Libyan government, represents a dangerous escalation in aggressive superpower behaviour. It cannot be justified as an act of self defence under international law not only because US territory was not under attack but because it occurred several days after the terrorist outrages in question and was not an immediate defensive response to an attack. It is likely to cause an escalation rather than a reduction in terrorist violence. And the consequences if such reprisal bombings became an established US practice could be disastrous.

The raid will certainly have helped to confirm the Soviet view of the US as an aggressive interventionist superpower and thus contributed further to the deterioration of East-West relations. It has been condemned not only by all the Arab states but by the whole Third World Non-Aligned Movement. But perhaps more significant in the longer term is what it has done to US-European relations. As Lord Carrington, the former British Foreign Secretary and now Secretary General of NATO, observed, the raid has led to what is probably the most serious rift within the NATO Alliance since its inception.

Finally, as this report was nearing completion, the disaster at the Chernobyl nuclear power plant in the Ukraine took place. The major repercussions of the disaster will no doubt be in the field of civil nuclear energy. But the arms control process could also be affected if the West, as some commentators are predicting, now insists on even stricter verification and controls to accompany any arms agreements. However, the extent of the fall-out from one accident at a nuclear power station may also increase awareness of how catastrophic an all-out nuclear war would be, and this could strengthen opposition to nuclear weapons.

Political Developments in Britain

In Britain, 1983 saw the election of a Conservative government firmly committed to maintaining Britain's own nuclear weapons and to the nuclear strategy *in toto* of the NATO alliance. One implication of that was that the programme of alternative defence proposed by the Commission had no possibility of being implemented until after another general election. Moreover the Commission's report came too close to the election to influence Labour Party thinking on the defence issue at that time. Yet the need for a well-thought-out policy of alternative defence was highlighted during the election campaign when the Labour Party failed to put forward a convincing policy and almost certainly lost votes as a result. Internal divisions within the party over nuclear disarmament, which surfaced in a highly damaging way during the campaign, added to Labour's embarrassment.

However, the Labour Party at its 1984 conference adopted a policy statement, *Defence and Security for Britain*,[2] which plugs many of the holes that became evident during the 1983 campaign and indeed is close to the policy recommended by the Commission in its first report. Thus the Labour Party is committed not only to British nuclear disarmament and the removal of US nuclear weapons and bases, but to the promotion of a new approach by NATO 'based on a non-provocative, no-first-use strategy of defensive deterrence'. (p.21) It also supports the creation of a 'continent wide' nuclear weapon-free zone in Europe and 'a new European-wide security system, leading to the ultimate replacement of the present division of Europe into NATO and the Warsaw Pact by the dissolution of the two blocs'. (p18)

The implementation of Labour's policy would constitute a radical break with the bi-partisan approach to defence and foreign policy of the post-World War II period. The dismantling of British nuclear weapons, and the removal of US nuclear weapons and bases, would itself mark a major change of direction. If the efforts to promote a nuclear weapons-free Europe, and to persuade NATO to move towards a defensively oriented and largely non-nuclear strategy were successful, this could transform the security situation in Europe and open up new political opportunities.

The Labour Party policy, nonetheless is not identical to the Commission's and it contains ambiguities and weaknesses. The main ambiguity concerns its attitude to a continuing US nuclear guarantee to Europe. The policy document does not address the issue directly, and subsequent statements by senior Shadow Cabinet spokespersons indicate continuing uncertainty over the issue. However, by the time of the 1986 Labour Party Conference, he leadership seemed to be moving in the right direction of rejecting outright any reliance on a US nuclear guarantee for Britain or Western Europe, partly on the grounds that the US 'nuclear umbrella' was anyhow incredible. But the Labour leadership has made it clear that it is committed to continued British membership of NATO even if the alliance is unwilling to make any moves whatever towards a non-nuclear strategy. This removes a crucial lever for changing NATO and could mean that Britain remained embroiled in a nuclear strategy in Europe.

The other opposition parties, with the exception of Plaid Cymru and the Scottish National Party, are less radical in their critique of existing nuclear strategy. The attempts of the Liberal/SDP Alliance to agree a common platform on defence ran into major difficulties in June 1986 when the SDP leader, David Owen, rejected the central recommendation of a joint SDP-Liberal commission on defence which left open the future role of an independent British nuclear deterrent and simply proposed extending the life of Polaris by ten years. A subsequent joint policy worked out between the leadership of the two parties for a Franco-British European deterrent was endorsed by the SDP conference but subsequently rejected by the Liberal conference. Finally in October 1986 the SDP and Liberal leaders agreed that the Alliance should support a continued British nuclear deterrent pending a comprehensive agreement on nuclear weapons between the superpowers. Both the Alliance parties, however, are opposed to Trident. Neither supports British withdrawal from NATO or making Britain's continued membership conditional on NATO denuclearisation.

The differences between the Alliance and Conservative positions on nuclear weapons, however, could be important for the promotion of arms control. The Alliance rejection of Trident would mean that a major increase in Britain's nuclear arsenal would be avoided and this could facilitate agreement on INF in Europe. David Owen has been particularly strong in his support for a Comprehensive Test Ban Treaty, and both the Alliance parties oppose the plans for providing NATO with new chemical weapons. The SDP-Liberal defence commission report also called for the adoption by NATO of strategies and weapons that are 'self-evidently defensive', and for the withdrawal of battlefield nuclear weapons from a zone stretching 150 km on either side of the East-West divide; it favours the inclusion of British nuclear weapons in arms control negotiations and a moratorium on British nuclear testing.

3. EXTENDING THE DIALOGUE

It is evident from this brief survey of the positions taken by the main opposition parties in Britain, that none will present at the next general election a non-nuclear policy in the full sense defined earlier and advocated by the Commission. We have nevertheless maintained the brief of considering the policies that a thoroughgoing anti-nuclear government could pursue assuming the domestic support for such a government existed. It is important to demonstrate that an anti-nuclear policy could be consistently maintained by a British government and to show how such a government might attempt to change the nuclear commitment of NATO, to promote arms control, and to bring about other political changes in Europe and elsewhere. Unless this is done, a truly non-nuclear policy will continue to be dismissed as utopian.

Demonstrating the viability of a non-nuclear policy is all the more important because nuclear deterrence, whatever adjustments are made to doctrine and strategy, cannot provide a rational or morally acceptable system of security. The dilemmas and contradictions at the heart of nuclear strategy mean that reforms which left the system itself intact are likely sooner or later to be overturned. Thus as long as the US insists that it must retain nuclear weapons to deter a possible Soviet nuclear attack upon itself, some of its European allies (unless they have rejected the whole concept of nuclear strategy) are bound to argue that the same logic applies to them and that either they must develop nuclear weapons of their own or be guaranteed US nuclear 'protection'. If the former solution is adopted the world moves towards the nightmare of general nuclear proliferation. If the latter concept is accepted the credibility of the US guarantee is again likely to be questioned by some European governments in the absence of nuclear weapons *in situ* in Europe. And if US nuclear weapons are retained in Europe all the doubts and debates about the possibility of a nuclear war confined to Europe are unavoidable.

The notion that there can be a sufficiently reliable stability in any form of nuclear deterrence is, in our view, an illusion; either one will be forced to a total rejection of nuclear weapons or towards concepts of extended deterrence and a qualitative arms competition, and probably also to war fighting strategies.

But while the task of developing defence and foreign policies for a consistently anti-nuclear government remains central, we nevertheless believe that much of our analysis is relevant to any government seriously committed to the pursuit of arms control and disarmament and the re-establishment of détente.

Much common ground in relation to changes in military

strategy and doctrine has been established in recent years as a result of a dialogue between those who reject nuclear deterrence and those who simply criticize key aspects of current policy. It is important, however, that this dialogue should not be confined to the area of defence strategy but should now be extended to the broader political issues which affect European and global security.

We hope therefore that this report will be studied and discussed not only by those committed to nuclear disarmament but by individuals, groups and political parties who believe that the time has come to review the foreign as well as defence policies of Britain and of Western Europe as a whole.

1. Why we need new policies for Europe

I. INTRODUCTION

The end of the 1970s witnessed a crisis of confidence in the policies of the Western Alliance for several reasons. First, shifts in strategic doctrine occurring in parallel with technological innovations, plus the controversy over cruise and Pershing II deployments, brought home to many people the ambiguities, risks, and moral indefensibility of nuclear strategy. Second, détente virtually collapsed. Little was left of it by the time the Soviet Union invaded Afghanistan in December 1979, thereby ending for the time being any faint hope that it might be revived. However, the Reagan Administration not only rejected the détente approach altogether but reverted to a rhetoric reminiscent of the first period of Cold War in the 1940s and early 1950s. Third, the Reagan Administration was more openly interventionist both in its rhetoric and actions than any of its predecessors since the end of the war in Vietnam and there was growing unease in Western Europe over the character of US foreign and military policy. Finally arms control which had aroused hope that the arms race could be kept under some kind of control virtually ground to a halt.

Whilst there is a sense across quite a wide spectrum of political opinion in Western Europe of the need for some change, there is considerable disagreement about the possible direction to take. The second part of this chapter sets out the policies and goals we recommend within both a European and a world context. First, however, we examine in more detail the causes of the crisis in the Alliance.

The Crisis of Nuclear Strategy
In the course of the 1970s there was a shift in strategic nuclear doctrine which meant that warfighting was emphasized at the

expense of deterrence. All nuclear strategies do of course envisage the use of nuclear weapons in war under some circumstances. But there is an important difference between regarding nuclear weapons as a deterrent whose actual use would bring disaster to both sides and seeing them as weapons with which a war could be fought to some purpose.

Since the early 1960s when the Soviet Union became a major nuclear power, Western policy has oscillated uncertainly between an emphasis on warfighting and deterrence. The doctrine of mutual assured destruction (MAD), largely predominant in the sixties and early seventies, at least as declaratory US policy, emphasized the deterrent aspect of nuclear weapons and rested upon the notion of mutual vulnerability. If it had been fully accepted it would have ruled out attempts to develop 'counter-force' weapons – i.e. weapons designed to destroy the nuclear capability of the opponent – or to end the vulnerability of one's own society by creating a defensive shield against missile and bomber attack. The SALT I ABM Treaty of 1972 formalized the partial acceptance of the fact that mutual vulnerability could contribute to the stability of deterrence and enable it to be maintained at lower levels of nuclear deployment.

Not surprisingly, however, the notion that mutual vulnerability could enhance security was never fully accepted on either side, and the military and strategic implications of mutual assured destruction were never consistently pursued. The Soviet Union did not officially accept the doctrine of MAD. And in the West, even when the SALT I agreements were being signed in the early 1970s, the US was already beginning to deploy MIRVed warheads (Multiple Independently Targeted Re-entry Vehicles) on its ballistic missiles, and Kissinger was justifying this develop-ment in terms of the superiority of a counterforce strategy which he claimed was 'more humane' than one based on assured destruction.

The MAD doctrine does of course draw attention to the morally outrageous implications of relying on nuclear weapons since it makes no attempt to disguise the fact that the civilian population would be the principal target in nuclear war. But in strategic terms too it is flawed since it rests upon a threat which it would be irrational and irresponsible ever to carry out; a state that had suffered a nuclear attack would gain nothing and simply add to the scale of global disaster if it retaliated in kind. McNamara, while US Secretary of Defense, acknowledged the dilemma. At the *Hearings on Military Posture for Fiscal Year 1964*, he maintained that some US nuclear forces would survive a Soviet first strike. 'But,' he continued, 'it exceeds the extent of my imagination to conceive of how those forces might be used *and of what benefit they would be to our Nation at that point*' (italics added).[1]

A counterforce doctrine, however, provides no escape from the dilemma. It represent a false solution to the moral problem since millions of civilians would also be killed in a counterforce nuclear war[2]. Moreover a counterforce doctrine is destabilizing in so far as it arouses fears that a first strike capability is being sought. In reality the likelihood of either side having a full first strike capability in the foreseeable future is remote. But a counterforce strategy nevertheless encourages the deployment of larger numbers of nuclear weapons to make up for those likely to be destroyed by the opponent's weapons, increases the risk of a pre-emptive strike in a crisis and imparts a momentum to the technological arms race.

It is also true, however, that technological developments can influence the formulation and emphasis of strategic doctrine, and it appears that this is indeed what occurred during the 1970s. The increasing accuracy of missiles, the development of MIRVed warheads which dramatically increased the damage that could be wrought by the same weight of nuclear explosive, improvements in surveillance and tracking abilities with both 'spy' satellites and new submarine detection technologies, the development of anti-satellite weapons (ASAT), are examples of this technological impetus which pushed both sides towards a counterforce approach.

On the US side, the drift away from MAD can be seen in the assertion in 1974 by the Defense Secretary, James Schlesinger, of the need for the US to have the option of fighting limited and controlled nuclear wars, and it was formalized in 1979 with President Carter's Directive PD59 which stated that in the event of a Soviet counterforce attack the US response would be aimed not at Soviet cities as such but at military targets such as missile sites, submarine depots, command centres and so on. However the Reagan Administration turned its back even more decisively on the doctrine of MAD. At one level it envisaged the possibility of fighting a geographically 'limited' nuclear war in Europe or elsewhere. At another level it proclaimed that US forces could 'prevail' in a protracted strategic nuclear war with the Soviet Union.[3]

The notion of fighting a limited war in Europe is bound up with the problem of extending nuclear deterrence to cover allied states. The credibility of a US nuclear guarantee to Western Europe declined as the vulnerability of the USA to Soviet retaliation became more evident. The SALT I accords, which acknowledged the approximate strategic parity of the super-powers, increased the anxiety of several European NATO governments that Western Europe might in effect be 'decoupled' from the US strategic deterrent, and this anxiety was further heightened in the later 1970s as the Soviet Union began to deploy improved intermediate range SS20 missiles (not covered by the SALT agreements) aimed at targets in Western Europe. It was due in part to such anxieties on the part of several West European governments that NATO took the 'twin track' decision in December 1979 to deploy cruise and Pershing II missiles unless agreement could be reached with the Soviet Union on INF deployments in Europe.

The decision aroused mass protest throughout Western Europe and more than any other single factor was responsible for the resurgence of the anti-nuclear campaign and for the revived debate on the whole rationale of Western strategy. The contro-versy was intensified when Reagan suggested in October 1981 that he could envisage a war involving the use of tactical nuclear weapons in Europe which did not escalate to all-out nuclear war between the superpowers. He partially retracted these remarks, but they nevertheless caused consternation in Europe and under-lined the fact that the same weapons that West European governments saw as guaranteeing nuclear coupling could also be used in a superpower nuclear war fought on European soil.[4]

At the strategic level the move away from mutual assured destruction was dramatically underlined by the Strategic Defense Initiative (SDI) plans unveiled by Reagan in March 1983.[5] By then, of course, the debate in both Europe and the USA over Western strategy was well under way. But it did point up the immorality and contradictions of a nuclear strategy which, despite inconsistencies and shifts of focus, had formed the cornerstone of Western policy for around twenty-five years. In particular Reagan's criticism of the morality of threatening the mass destruction of civilians radically undermined the case for any reliance on nuclear weapons.

There has in fact been a slowly maturing debate, especially within the churches, on the morality of either using, or threatening to use, nuclear weapons, and this too has contributed significantly to the reappraisal of nuclear policy in the 1980s. Some of the important developments in the debate on the moral issue have been: the speech of Pope John Paul II in Hiroshima in February 1981, the Statement by the Catholic Bishops in the United States in 1983, and the publication in this country in 1982 of *The Church and the Bomb*, the report of the Church of England Working Group which was discussed – though not adopted – by the Church Synod the following year.[6] Church and religious groups have played a significant role in the revived anti-nuclear campaign of the 1980s, most notably in Holland where the Inter-Church Peace Council (IKV) was particularly active in opposing cruise and Pershing II deployments. For many non-religious people, too, the moral issue constitutes the bedrock argument against reliance on weapons of mass destruction.

As for Reagan's proposed solution, the creation of an invulnerable shield that would make nuclear weapons 'impotent and obsolete', neither the US Defense Department nor the overwhelming majority of scientific and strategic specialists take that notion seriously. The claim cannot be sustained, not only because a hundred per cent success in destroying the opponent's ballistic missiles is unlikely ever to be assured, but also because the system cannot even in principle deal with the threat of nuclear weapons delivered by planes, cruise missiles, or other means.

The negative effects of developing SDI are only too clear. It will be enormously expensive. If the USA pursues it, the Soviet Union is bound to intensify its own researches. (The Soviet Union has already started research into space-based anti-missile technology, and thus there is an element of propaganda in some of its pronouncements on SDI; however it almost certainly lags behind the USA, and it has at least pressed for an agreement to ban further development of this kind). It will increase fears that a first-strike capability is being pursued. It will encourage the multiplication of nuclear weapons and the development of new technologies to overwhelm or defeat any SDI system that may eventually be deployed.[7] Finally SDI is likely to foster other forms of militarization in space, including improved ASAT weapons.

SDI also poses a direct threat to arms control. The most immediate challenge is to the 1972 Anti-Ballistic Missile Treaty; testing components of the new technology may well breach this.[8] Other treaties which might be breached by testing SDI technology are the Outer Space Treaty, which forbids nuclear weapons in orbit (nuclear explosions would be required to power X-ray lasers), and the 1963 Partial Test Ban Treaty which forbids nuclear explosions in the air or outer space. In addition, the opportunity to explore the seriousness of Gorbachev's offer to negotiate a Comprehensive Test Ban Treaty has for the present been thrown away, not because of the technical problems of verification which it may now be possible to resolve, but because of the US determination to continue nuclear testing related to new types of nuclear weapons and to the SDI programme. Thus in April 1986 scientists at the Los Alamos National Laboratory stated that more than 100 underground nuclear tests may be needed to perfect devices for use with the SDI programme.[9]

One reason the Reagan Administration has pursued strategic nuclear dominance is its belief that nuclear superiority confers political advantage. Influential conservative theorists like Richard Pipes argue that Soviet assertiveness in the Third World during the 1970s arose out of increased Soviet nuclear strength, and the Reagan Administration has set out to reverse the global balance of military and political forces by a major build-up of nuclear arms and development of the Rapid Deployment Force, which is to be equipped with nuclear weapons. Whether any kind of lead in the nuclear arms race, in terms of the numbers of nuclear weapons deployed or targeting accuracy, really confers global political advantage can be questioned.[10] But in the USA, increased nuclear strength has been associated with a psychology of greater assertiveness and willingness to intervene in the Third World through use of military force.

The Reagan nuclear programme and the doctrines associated with it are therefore closely linked to two important political issues of concern to Europe: the breakdown of détente and an increased willingness to intervene wherever its interests are seen to be at stake.

The term 'détente' is used in two distinct senses. First, it is understood broadly as the opposite of Cold War, denoting that the USA and USSR, despite their superpower and ideological conflicts, need not engage in all-out ideological warfare, and can recognize certain common interests in avoiding nuclear war and in entering into serious negotiations on political or arms control issues. In this sense they were gradually moving away from cold war confrontation towards détente in the period from 1954 to 1962. However, this progress was interrupted by a series of crises in Eastern Europe and the Middle East, and by conflicts over the role of the United Nations in the Congo. From 1963 to 1968, after the sobering shock of the Cuban missile crisis, the USA and the USSR entered a phase in which a series of bilateral and multilateral arms control agreements were reached. Most people viewed this as a form of détente at the time. However, détente is now often used in a more specialized sense, denoting the period from 1969 to the late 1970s, and is associated more specifically on the US side with Kissinger's strategy for managing the superpower relationship. Due to both Soviet and US actions, détente in this sense was being eroded by the late 1970s, although the SALT talks, often viewed as a symbol of this détente process, did result in the SALT II Treaty in 1979. It was the election of Reagan in 1980 that ensured the demise of détente in both senses. It entailed the specific repudiation of SALT (though in practice the US has observed its limits up to 1986), a general unwillingness to reach arms control agreements on terms which could be acceptable to the USSR, and a revival of fundamentalist anti-communist rhetoric.

What was involved in détente and why did it break down? When it began to evolve in the late 1950s, Khrushchev espoused an explicit doctrinal change in Soviet ideology, abandoning the thesis of the inevitability of war between the capitalist and socialist systems, and arguing that, with the threat of nuclear annihilation, peaceful coexistence was necessary and possible. But coexistence did not preclude continuing political, economic and ideological struggle, which the forces of socialism would eventually win. On the US side there was a more generalized sense that nuclear war must be avoided and that détente would mean acceptance by both sides of existing spheres of influence and respect for the status quo, which at that time greatly favoured the West, though decolonization was beginning to create a third force of newly-formed states.

The second phase of détente, which emerged at the end of the 1960s, reflected a significant change of emphasis on the Soviet side, and a much more elaborate and sophisticated policy from the USA. Brezhnev had replaced Khrushchev in 1964, and his conception of détente was less concerned with ideology and political competition than with the establishment of Soviet superpower interests by building military strength. After the 1962 Cuba crisis the Soviet Union had embarked on a military programme designed to achieve nuclear and naval parity with the USA and thus avoid a repetition of the humiliating retreat forced on Khrushchev. By the end of the 1960s it was close to achieving military parity, and the global political balance had altered as a result of change in Asia and Africa. The Soviet Union's main goals appeared to be formal recognition of its equal status, in both the military and political spheres, as a superpower, and acceptance by the USA of its right to act as such in the international community. The Soviet government also wished to reduce the risks and costs of a spiralling nuclear arms race by reaching arms control agreements, and to make economic and technological gains by trade and co-operation with the West.

The US interpretation of détente after 1969 included a willingness both to accept Soviet parity at the strategic level and to recognize the USSR as a superpower on the world scene. Thus the emphasis shifted from nuclear superiority to nuclear sufficiency. This did not prevent the USA from continuing to develop a new range of missiles; nor did it preclude the Nixon

33

Administration from exploring options for tactical and limited nuclear war. But détente, as envisaged by Kissinger and Nixon, did mean a significant shift from reliance solely on military strength to much greater emphasis on diplomatic, political and economic pressures on the USSR. Arms control was a central strand of this policy, but agreement was conditional on Soviet good behaviour. The US aim was to constrain Soviet behaviour by linking arms control negotiations to wider political and economic issues and, by offering economic and arms control gains, to encourage the Soviet Union to accept Western conceptions of how to promote international stability. The Nixon/Kissinger policy included limiting US global military commitments to allies and friends, reduced reliance on 'negotiations from strength', and a playing down of ideology in US-Soviet relations, including less stress on human rights in the Soviet bloc.[11] The new guidelines of the Reagan Administration – a drive for nuclear superiority, open-ended US military intervention around the world, a stress on negotiating with the Soviet Union from strength, and a high focus on ideology – all marked a break from the era of détente. The break was much more decisive than it had been under the Carter Administration, when there were conflicting tendencies.

However, in the early 1970s there were ambiguities in the US conception of détente and the way US foreign policy was conducted. In 1973, during the Arab-Israeli war, Kissinger was prepared to make political use of nuclear weapons by ordering a nuclear alert to ensure that Soviet troops did not enter the Middle East. The guidelines for superpower activity in the Third World were far from clear, since both sides hoped to make gains in this area.

There were three major reasons for the breakdown of détente. First, as the superior power, the USA seemed to be giving up more and gaining less than the USSR by accepting the principles of parity and co-operation. There was, therefore, always opposition in the USA to the principles of détente and arms control and, more specifically, to the SALT treaties. Prominent political and military figures, who were deeply distrustful of Soviet actions and goals, propagated the myths that during the 1970s the USA ceased to build up its own nuclear arsenal whilst the Soviet

Union relentlessly increased its missile force, and that the USA also ceased to promote its influence and interests in the Third World.[12]

Second, from the perspective of Washington the USSR breached the rules of détente when it established military presences in Ethiopia and, indirectly through the Cubans, in Angola. When the USSR sent its troops into Afghanistan in December 1979 there was widespread concern in the West that this denoted a new willingness to risk military action in order to extend Soviet power. Soviet actions therefore lent support to those who feared Soviet expansionism, and delivered a major blow to what was left of détente.

Third, the nuclear build-up on both sides, channelled but not seriously constrained by SALT I, created mutual anxieties. US strategists have expressed constant concern about the fact that some Soviet ICBMs can carry so many or such heavy warheads and fear that their own equivalent force is vulnerable to a first strike. The USSR has been particularly concerned about the enormous expansion of the US cruise missile programme, covering air- and sea-launched as well as ground-launched weapons. These fears provide powerful arguments for further research and for the development and deployment of new missiles.

2. THE FAILURE OF ARMS CONTROL

The breakdown of détente is linked to the failure of the USA and the USSR to reach any arms control agreements since Carter and Brezhnev signed the SALT II agreement in 1979. That agreement itself was never ratified by the US Congress, though both sides had agreed to abide by its provisions. However Reagan made it clear from the first that he did not consider the US under an obligation to abide by its provisions and in May 1986, citing alleged violations by the Soviet Union, he announced US abandonment of both SALT treaties as from the autumn of that year. This turning away from arms control by the US, coupled with the Soviet Union's decision to walk out of the START and INF talks in 1983, created a widespread and deep pessimism about the prospects for agreement on intermediate range or strategic missiles, and about arms control possibilities in general.

In early 1985, following Reagan's re-election, the USA and USSR began a new series of Geneva talks, purportedly designed to end the arms race both in space and on earth. This was initially greeted with a measure of public optimism, but by the first recess in the talks most observers thought any agreement unlikely, partly because of Soviet hostility to the continuing US SDI programme. And the record of negotiations in the post-World War II period shows that, despite some modest successes in the field of arms control, there are grounds for extreme caution concerning what can be expected from bilateral and multilateral negotiations – short at any rate of some fresh approach capable of achieving a breakthrough.

In considering the problem, it is important to distinguish between disarmament and arms control. International negotiations prior to World War II and in the first decade and a half after the war were mainly focused on disarmament proposals, i.e. programmes for the progressive elimination of weapons and armed forces, or at least for their drastic reduction to what was considered an irreducible minimum. Negotiations aimed at disarmament, or major reductions in military forces, have so far completely failed to achieve progress towards their objectives.

The last major reaffirmation of the goal of 'General and Complete Disarmament' (GCD) by the two superpowers was the McCloy-Zorin declaration of 1961. In general, however, the Kennedy years saw a shift away from the disarmament endeavour in favour of the more limited, and, it was argued, more realistic, goal of arms control. Arms control theory rejects the possibility of disarmament in the foreseeable future, seeking instead to stabilize and manage the military competition – to set limits on the arms race and to achieve agreements that would reduce the destructiveness or inhumaneness of war, should it occur. Closely related to arms control are confidence-building measures, such as the setting up of the telephone 'hot-line' between Moscow and Washington in 1963, aimed at reducing the risks of war by accident or miscalculation, or more generally at avoiding misunderstandings that could create friction or antagonism between East and West. Clearly confidence-building and war prevention measures serve the interests of both super-powers, and it is noteworthy that the only successful negotiations recently have been are those at the European Disarmament Conference at Stockholm where the strengthening of such measures was agreed in September 1986.

But arms control too can claim a number of successes during the 1960s and 1970s, some more significant than others. The Partial Test Ban Treaty (1963) and the Threshold Test Ban (1974) placed at least some restrictions on nuclear weapons testing, though the efforts to agree a Comprehensive Test Ban – a measure that could have a significant impact on the nuclear arms race – came to nothing. The Non-Proliferation Treaty (1968) was a critical element in the establishment of a non-proliferation régime which has helped to restrict the spread of nuclear weapons to other countries, while the Treaty of Tlatelolco (1967) barring nuclear weapons from Latin America is an important non-proliferation measure in its own right and also provides a model for the establishment of nuclear-weapon-free zones in other regions. In addition nuclear weapons have been prohibited from certain environments under the Outer Space Treaty of 1967 and the Sea Bed Treaty of 1971; these agreements did not challenge any current programmes but had some value in restricting possible future developments. There has been some success too in the efforts to prohibit non-nuclear weapons of mass destruction, notably the Geneva Protocols of 1925 on Chemical Weapons and the Biological Weapons Convention of 1972.

None of the above agreements was aimed at seriously con-straining the nuclear arms race between the two superpowers. This was the province of the SALT process. The ABM Treaty (1972) restricted the number of anti-ballistic missile systems on each side to a maximum of two (later restricted to one by a protocol signed in 1974), while the SALT I Interim Agreement (1972), the Vladivostok Accord (1974), and SALT II (1979) were all concerned with setting ceilings on the numbers of strategic nuclear weapons on both sides. Of these the ABM Treaty was the most significant in that it headed off a technologi-cal race that would have been astronomically expensive and almost certainly have stimulated more extensive deployment of

37

offensive ballistic missiles and other strategic systems. As we noted earlier, it was also significant in that it amounted to an acknowledgement that while nuclear weapons continued to be deployed, mutual vulnerability could have a stabilizing effect.

However the agreements reached under the SALT process have had an entirely inadequate impact on the momentum of the nuclear arms race and the development of destabilizing new technologies: even the achievements of the ABM treaty are now being put at risk by the SDI programme. Moreover, by the latter part of the 1970s, even before the election of President Reagan, progress in arms control had slowed down and it was clear that the endeavour was running into major difficulties.

The obstacles to successful arms control – or disarmament – negotiations have been extensively analysed and we need only mention some of the principal ones here. States are inevitably cautious where matters of security are concerned and thus wary about entering into agreements which might limit their freedom of action in some way, especially where provisions for verification and control are weak. The differences in the size, population and geography of states, and the asymmetries of forces and weapons systems, make the task of reaching agreement inherently difficult. The negotiations themselves may be cynically manipulated to gain propaganda advantages; but even when they are conducted in good faith, the practice of deploying new weapons as 'bargaining chips' can result in an escalation of the arms race. Internal divisions within a state or alliance frequently hamstring negotiations or reduce the effectiveness of any agreements that are reached. In general the agreements that are reached tend to have little or no impact on the military systems that each side regards as strategically central.

During the 1970s three factors were of particular importance in bringing arms control between the superpowers to a standstill and consequently a widespread sense of disillusion over future possibilities. First, arms control is much better at dealing with major capital items of strategic hardware which can be counted and monitored without intrusive inspection than with qualitative improvements in weapon systems. In a sense the SALT agreements of the early 1970s dealt with the easier end of arms control between the superpowers – restricting ABM deployments and setting ceilings on the deployment of strategic missiles; after that the going was bound to get more difficult.

Second, and closely related to this, the pace of technological change in the 1970s made the qualitative arms race that much more significant and tended to undermine the agreements that had been reached. The SALT I Interim Agreement, for instance, relating to the numbers of ICBM launchers and SLBMs to be deployed on each side, was largely by-passed by the development of MIRVed warheads – just as today the ABM Treaty is threatened by the SDI programme.

Third, the decline of détente and the slowdown in arms control reinforced each other. Failure to prevent a continuing arms race contributed to mutual suspicion regarding motives and intentions. And the deterioration in political relations, which occurred for a variety of reasons, added to the difficulties of reaching agreement on arms control and strengthened the hand of those – certainly influential on the US side and probably also on the Soviet side – who regarded the whole process as largely a waste of time.

In a later chapter we consider the role that a non-nuclear Britain could play in helping to regenerate the arms control and disarmament process. A breakthrough in controlling the strategic nuclear systems of the superpowers, however, may well require that one, or preferably both, of them, if they cannot be persuaded to renounce nuclear weapons, do at least accept the notion of minimum deterrence and firmly reject a counterforce strategy. The rejection of nuclear weapons by Western Europe could remove one major obstacle in the path of a US acceptance of this approach and encourage significant reductions in the Soviet nuclear arsenal.

3. THE WIDENING GAP BETWEEN THE USA AND EUROPE

Recent strategic developments, combined with the breakdown of détente and arms control, have created a considerable gap between Europe and the United States. For example, even conservative European governments are deeply sceptical about the SDI project, though the constraints of Alliance solidarity and insistence from Washington that they give public support have made them reluctant to say so loudly. Large sections of public opinion have been appalled by the fact that, since 1979, Europe has been the theatre of a deadly new missile race, and the Belgian and Dutch governments, who concurred in the NATO decision to deploy cruise and Pershing II missiles, have only maintained their willingness under intense US and NATO pressure. The British Labour Party and the German Social Democrats, both of whom had some responsibility for the 1979 decision, have repudiated that policy in opposition. Most sections of opinion have been worried by the breakdown of détente.

The gap between the USA and Western Europe was widened by the fact that, parallel to the détente process between Washington and Moscow, the West Europeans evolved their own policy of détente towards the USSR and Eastern Europe, and had no wish to abandon it. The evolution of this European-centred détente dates from 1969, spearheaded by Willy Brandt's *Ostpolitik*, and culminating in the 1975 Helsinki Agreement. The purpose of the German Social Democrats' policy was to lay the ghost of World War II and remove the threat of German revanchism; it involved explicit German recognition of Polish frontiers and limited recognition of the German Democratic Republic. The process of *Ostpolitik* coincided with diplomatic attempts by the Soviet Union to secure full recognition of the Yalta frontiers and strengthen East-West trade. These attempts came to fruition in the Helsinki Agreement, which recognized existing frontiers, stressed the importance of arms control in Europe, and pledged closer economic and cultural contacts. But this European détente did not exclusively favour Soviet interests; the West German intention was to create greater political space for East European governments and to strengthen their economies through western trade. A further effect of this relaxation of East-West confrontation, a changed perception of West Germany, and the promise of the human rights 'basket' agreed at Helsinki, was to strengthen the potential for internal political opposition in Eastern Europe, especially Poland. European détente also benefited West European interests, and resulted in strong economic links with Eastern Europe and the USSR which were symbolized by the Soviet gas pipeline.

When, therefore, a new cold war developed between the USA and the Soviet Union, Western Europe did its best to maintain its own détente – for political, security and economic reasons. The two Germanys have been particularly active in maintaining close ties – an ironic reversal of the position when Adenauer and Ulbricht were intransigent Cold War exponents, partly kept in check by their superpower allies. By 1983, when the USSR broke off the Geneva talks following the first deployments of cruise and Pershing II missiles in Western Europe, the Soviet leadership appeared as hostile to détente as did Reagan's Administration. They installed SS22s in East Germany and Czechoslovakia and put pressure on Honecker to cancel his official visit to Bonn in 1984. But West European governments displayed an interest in maintaining détente despite both Washington and Moscow. Even Mrs Thatcher's government, although ideologically in sympathy with Reaganism, resisted US pressure to implement economic sanctions after martial law was imposed in Poland, and tried to promote links with one of the more 'liberal' and independent members of the Warsaw Pact through an official visit to Hungary in 1984.

The divisions between the USA and Western Europe which have opened up since Reagan became president are not confined to differences over nuclear strategy and technology, or arms control and détente. Other trends in US foreign and domestic policy have underlined the divergence in interests. Most sectors of European opinion are unhappy about Washington's reversion to a policy of both covert and open military intervention in other parts of the world. They see this tendency as dangerous, since a world war is most likely to be sparked off by confrontation in the Third World, and they believe that in many cases US intervention is wholly unjustified. There is, for example, strong opposition to the attempts by the Reagan Administration to topple the government of Nicaragua by a combination of economic isolation and military force. There is also widespread concern that the USA has shown open contempt for international law – refusing to ratify the Law of the Sea Treaty, for example, and ignoring the International Court of Justice's judgement against the mining of Nicaraguan waters – and a tendency to bypass the United Nations. On these issues there are divisions in the USA and Western Europe: Democrats in Congress have opposed the President on Nicaragua, and the British government has followed the US example in refusing to ratify the Law of the Sea Treaty and leaving UNESCO. Nevertheless, Reagan's policies have the effect of strengthening the alienation from the USA of many Europeans, and of worrying others who were previously committed to the Atlantic Alliance.

There are discernible trends in US domestic and foreign policies that are more long-term than the specific impact of Reaganism. For example, a shift in the economic and political centre of the United States from the North East to the South West sunbelt is linked to a tendency for Americans to be less interested in, and sensitive to, European concerns. This trend could encourage US isolationism, which has always primarily meant isolation from Europe, not the rest of the world. There has been evidence of continuing unrest in Congress about the commitment of large numbers of US troops to Europe. The Mansfield Amendment of 1971, which would have reduced by half the US commitment to NATO, almost got through the Senate. Congressional pressure was defused by setting up the Vienna talks on Mutual Balanced Force Reductions, to which Brezhnev agreed at the opportune moment. The Nunn Amendment of June 1984, which also proposed cuts in US troops, was designed to spur European members of NATO to greater economic commitment. Although it was headed off by the US Administration, the extent of support for it did suggest the continuing popularity of reducing the United States' European commitments.[13]

Even within the accepted framework of NATO policy there are grounds for reassessment. There has been evidence of greater West European interest in strengthening both the European contribution to the Alliance and its voice within it. Proposals to strengthen the West European Union, which represents the core European members of NATO, might be seen in this light. European governments are also resentful of the dominance of US arms firms in the production of equipment for NATO forces. Through the EEC European countries have begun to enunciate foreign policy goals which are at variance with those of Washington, for example in supporting Palestinian representation at talks

42

on the Middle East. There have also been strong economic differences between Western Europe and the United States, centering recently on the high level of US interest rates.

4. The Geneva Summit and its Implications

The summit between Reagan and Gorbachev in November 1985 held the promise of an end to the second cold war and its accompanying deadlock on arms control. It was surrounded by a good deal of media hype and wishful thinking and achieved very few immediate results, so it is difficult to assess how far it heralds a new era in US-Soviet relations. So far it represents a thaw rather than a coherent policy of détente. There has been a welcome change of rhetoric and there are promises of closer cultural cooperation. On the other hand, the change in rhetoric on the US side is only small: shortly before the summit Reagan accused the USSR of aggression in various parts of the world, including Nicaragua, and Defense Secretary Weinberger repeated charges of Soviet violation of previous arms control treaties. The actions of the USA show no evidence of a willingness to renounce global ambitions, to cease direct and indirect military intervention designed to topple communist régimes in the Third World, or to halt its military build-up.

If the summit held out tentative prospects of an improvement in overall relations between the superpowers, it did nothing to increase the likelihood of any major arms control agreement. President Reagan stressed to Congress that he had not made any concession on SDI research, and Secretary Gorbachev stressed to the Supreme Soviet that without such a concession no progress in limiting nuclear arms was possible. It is clear, moreover, that sections of the Reagan Administration, in particular Weinberger and Perle at the Defense Department, remain committed to their military programmes and adamantly opposed to any kind of arms control agreement. For example, the Administration has fought with Congress for authorization to start a new programme of binary nerve gas production, although at Geneva it is engaged in one of the more promising disarmament negotiations – on the abolition of chemical weapons.

By taking steps towards a resumption of normal relations with

43

Moscow, the US Administration has removed one source of conflict with its West European allies. No doubt this was a factor in Reagan's decision to seek a summit, and NATO unity was displayed in its aftermath. But the spirit of Geneva alone will not remove the numerous other sources of tension between various political groupings in Europe and the USA. US alliance diplomacy in relation to the summit underlined Washington's supremacy; West European leaders were summoned to the White House at short notice to coordinate a common NATO policy. President Mitterrand was sufficiently angry at the imperious nature of the summons to refuse to go. Afterwards both NATO and the Warsaw Pact were informed by their respective leaders of what had happened at Geneva: a symbol of the fact that the destiny of Europe is effectively controlled by Washington and Moscow, though the Europeans retain some right to formal consultation.

If a Democratic US Administration is elected in 1988, it is possible that US policy will be less hostile to left-wing régimes, less intolerant of the UN and the precepts of international law, and less inclined to use military force as an instrument of policy. If so, it would reduce the ideological gap that has developed between Washington and most West European governments and political parties. A new Administration might also be willing to seek a more solid basis for détente and give priority to arms control, and thereby come closer to most West European opinion. It is unlikely that such measures would result in an end to the conflict between the Soviet Union and the United States, but arms control and a revived détente are likely to encourage stronger ties between Eastern and Western Europe, and between Western Europe and the Soviet Union, creating conditions conducive to seeking a new basis for peace in Europe.

In the short run the most that can be hoped for is the revival of détente, a reconstruction of a sense of common interest, and development of forms of rational cooperation between Moscow and Washington. At best we can hope that by the early 1990s arms control measures may be agreed which will prevent the nuclear arms competition running totally out of control. But in a longer perspective it is essential to change the role of the superpowers and the basis of their relationship. In particular, we believe it is necessary for the USA and USSR to reduce their global military commitments, end military intervention in other parts of the world, and reject reliance on weapons of mass destruction. At present the widespread discontent in Western Europe about the military and political situation is leading to widely varied prescriptions for change. The purpose of this report is to argue for what we believe is the most creative approach, and this requires a radical break with many of the assumptions and policies of the last thirty years.

5. THE CASE FOR DEALIGNMENT

In this report we argue that both Britain and Western Europe should try to promote a process of dealignment which, as we defined it in the Introduction, incorporates military disengagement – the withdrawal of military bases and personnel with the eventual aim of dissolving military blocs – but also has a broader connotation. A policy of dealignment also implies withdrawal by the superpowers from more loosely defined spheres of military influence and less formal military agreements. It implies that countries which now give automatic political adherence to either the USA or the USSR should be free to adopt a more independent position. A fully dealigned region would be wholly independent, which may be an improbable outcome in many areas. But if dealignment is seen as a process, then varying degrees of superpower withdrawal or regional independence might be achieved, even within the context of some continuing military or political ties. It is possible to favour the dealignment of Western Europe from the USA because one opposes specific US military, political and economic policies. But our aim here is to argue for the general principle of dealignment as a desirable model for international politics.

The case for dealignment rests in part on objections to attempting to form a superpower condominium and on the inadequacies of the 1970s form of détente. It should be recognized, however, that the USA and USSR find the possibility of cooperating to impose order on an unstable world an attractive goal, and it was one which was being entertained by some US theorists in the heyday of détente. Superpowers are seen as having special responsibility for world order, and they can sometimes stabilize their spheres of influence. There is also a school of thought which argues that the best way to prevent the spread of nuclear weapons is for the existing nuclear powers to extend their nuclear protection to all their allies and friends. This implies maximizing the global scope of superpower military deployments. If, therefore, the USA and USSR could agree on each other's sphere of influence and legitimate interests, and could cooperate to impose settlements in volatile areas like the Middle East, recognizing that nuclear weapons make a war between them impossible, the prospects for peace would be good.

There are, however, powerful arguments to suggest that this goal is neither realistic nor desirable. It is not realistic because it does not take account of aspiring great powers being unwilling to accept superpower hegemony – the pressure to acquire nuclear weapons has been in part a claim to great power prestige. It is also unrealistic because neither the USA nor the USSR is able to impose control over many areas of the world; for example, neither can do anything about Iran. Moreover, it is inherently unlikely that two powers in confrontation will agree to cede to each other areas where neither is yet in control. The lack of agreement about activities in the Third World, which undermined détente, is therefore likely to weaken any attempt at closer co-operation. The difficulty of agreeing new spheres of influence would be greatly exacerbated by the fact that the conflict between the USA and USSR is not only an old-fashioned confrontation of great power interests, but also an ideological conflict. Ideological considerations may be muted in times of détente, but neither side can wholly ignore them. The Soviet government's concern about ideology has been considerably eroded, but it cannot be discarded altogether because socialist goals are an element in the domestic and international legitimacy of the USSR. The US government is subject to strong ideological pressures: Reaganism has demonstrated the continuing power of bible-belt fundamentalism and populist anti-communism in US politics. Finally, superpower diplomacy is easily undermined by domestic pressures. There is some evidence that this is true in the Soviet Union, but the very virtues of the US system of government – its openness and the influence of Congress and popular opinion –

make it especially unsuited to managing a cooperative super-power relationship with the Soviet Union. For example, Kissinger's secret diplomacy prompted strong hostility in Congress, and the US government has to react to events in Eastern Europe in terms of its own declared principles and for electoral reasons, though, from a strictly 'realpolitik' standpoint, what the USSR does to control its own sphere of influence is not a matter for US concern.

Any policy which rests on the maintenance by the USA and USSR of far-flung military alliances and a global military presence, including nuclear and conventional bases, is both unrealistic and undesirable. It implies a very high level of military investment and preparedness by both sides, and is therefore almost certain to promote the mutual fears and techno-logical momentum which now characterize the arms race. Global nuclear deployments maximize the likelihood of a clash between the two superpowers which could lead to all-out war.

Finally, acceptance of superpower spheres of influence in areas where the peoples concerned are often hostile to the ideology and political or economic interests of the power concerned results in suppression of national independence, democracy and human rights. There is ample evidence that US involvement in Central America and Soviet power in Eastern Europe has these results. So long as both the USA and USSR are competing for influence there is the added problem that popular dissent is often seen as covert intervention by the other side, which may lead to greater repression.

If it is accepted that the USA and USSR could not agree permanently on extended spheres of influence, and that their global ambitions bring them into inevitable and potentially disastrous conflict, then the goal of limiting the military involve-ment of both powers becomes extremely desirable. As a first step, a reversion to some of the principles of 1970s détente – accepting parity between the USA and USSR, downgrading the role of strategic nuclear weapons in international politics, and laying more emphasis on political and economic aspects of both conflict and co-operation – would be a great improvement. But unless this is followed by military disengagement and by real nuclear disarmament measures on both sides, it will not stabilize the relationship between the USA and USSR. If a policy of disengagement is to be acceptable, evidence of military withdrawal by both sides – in terms of both direct military intervention and indirect support to armed groups – is probably necessary. But one side could, of course, take the initiative. Where both are already enmeshed in a region there may well be an important role for direct US-Soviet cooperation in the near future – most obviously in the Middle East – but the most desirable goal is co-operation in the context of international institutions. The principle of respect for international peacekeeping operations might also provide a face-saving device for superpower withdrawal in certain circumstances, as it did for the British and French after the 1956 Suez fiasco.[14]

6. REDUCING NUCLEAR ARMS

So long as the USA feels compelled to extend some form of nuclear deterrence to allies round the world, it will necessarily seek to maintain a network of nuclear bases and the right to port facilities for nuclear-armed ships. It will also feel under pressure to develop an extensive nuclear arsenal and to elaborate ideas of a limited nuclear war, in order to escape the risk of devastation on behalf of an ally. A crucial step, therefore, is to encourage a freeze on nuclear weapons technology and cuts in missile numbers, and to reduce the role of the US nuclear force to deterrence of a nuclear attack on the United States. In this context it is strategically possible to envisage a nuclear force designed as a minimum second strike deterrent, which seems the most realistic interim goal, although the only satisfactory outcome would be full nuclear disarmament. Moreover, limiting nuclear bases to the USA is likely to generate greater awareness among Americans of the risks of nuclear weapons and so make real cuts, and ultimately nuclear disarmament, more likely.

The possibility of reducing the nuclear arsenals of the USA and USSR does not, however, depend solely on the nature of their mutual confrontation, or on the extent of their nuclear commitments to allies. It also depends on whether there are any other nuclear powers. At present the Chinese nuclear arsenal is an additional threat to the USSR, and in the past it has figured in justifications for US anti-ballistic missile deployments. A multilateral nuclear arms race is potentially extremely dangerous, and this is the situation that is developing in the Pacific, where the USSR has been building up its conventional and nuclear forces to the alarm of both China and Japan, and the USA has also been developing its military potential. Under US pressure and in response to certain internal forces Japan is being pushed towards becoming a major military power, despite the limits on its defence forces enshrined in its constitution after World War II. A world in which there were half-a-dozen major nuclear powers would require each to plan to deter attack by several possible opponents; and proliferation of nuclear weapons to twenty or thirty smaller states would require the major powers to engage in complex multiple targeting and an expansion of their arsenals.[15]

We do not believe that a world of several major nuclear powers or many smaller nuclear weapon states is yet inevitable. Western Europe has a considerable responsibility to resist political groupings who are urging a degree of independence from the USA combined with development of a West European nuclear force and, as smaller nuclear powers, Britain and France also carry a burden of responsibility. A great deal also depends on the willingness of the USA and USSR to cut back their nuclear arsenals and demonstrate that they do not place supreme value on nuclear weapons for military, power-political or prestige reasons. To some extent a multi-polar world already exists, but it is possible to envisage power in economic and political rather than military terms. Since Mao died, China has shown cautious interest in limiting arms – but only if the superpowers first reduce their very much larger arsenals. Japan and Western Europe are not yet nuclear powers and both could still settle for an economic and political role. Preventing the spread of nuclear weapons to countries engaged in local conflicts is difficult, but it is the one issue in which the USA and USSR have, since 1967, shown a strong common interest. It is also a goal to which a non-nuclear Britain could make a contribution.

7. NEW DIRECTIONS FOR WESTERN EUROPE

There is some impetus from political groupings within the USA, who may be able to gain some support from the Democratic

Party, for turning US military and foreign policies towards curbing intervention and reducing military commitments. There are also economic and domestic pressures on the Soviet government that could possibly encourage similar developments. At present, however, it seems improbable that either superpower will renounce its ambitions, unless the initiative is taken by third parties. Potentially, Western Europe has a very important role to play in altering its own relationship with both the USA and the USSR. It also has a particular responsibility to reduce the dangers of military confrontation in Europe and encourage a reduction in nuclear arsenals. Western Europe could also reduce the dangers of nuclear proliferation, curb the arms trade and change its economic relationship with Third World countries.

In the past, West European members of NATO have actively encouraged US nuclear commitment to Europe, and have been happy to rely on US nuclear weapons to counterbalance Soviet conventional forces. The build-up of battlefield and theatre nuclear weapons since the early 1950s has occurred partly at the instigation of the US military, but European governments have promoted the process by their concern to ensure the 'coupling' of the US strategic nuclear force to Europe. US nuclear weapons have been seen as both a guarantee against Soviet conventional attack and a safeguard against nuclear attack. In return for West European loyalty and acceptance of its leadership, the USA has declared its willingness to risk nuclear attack by intervening on behalf of Western Europe. The risks to the USA of this bargain grew as the USSR built up its strategic missile force during the 1960s and 1970s. Indeed, it is debatable whether the US nuclear guarantee to Europe really exists – Kissinger once stated publicly that in reality it would not operate[16] – though the whole of NATO strategy still hinges on it. The risks to Europe have also grown, due to developments in missile technology which encourage fears of a first strike. Popular awareness of these risks, and of the possibility of Europe becoming a battlefield for a supposedly limited nuclear war, has also grown. SDI reflects this tension between the USA and Western Europe. As long as SDI seems to make possible a new invulnerability for the American people, US officials will not be greatly influenced by West European objections.[17] But the West European military fear that space defence will lead to the decoupling of Europe from the USA. There are therefore good reasons for both parties to rethink the bases of their military relationship.

One obvious and attractive goal, espoused by many European peace movements, is the creation in a nuclear-weapons-free zone throughout the whole of Europe, East and West. This would end direct nuclear confrontation between the USA and USSR, and should therefore, in the event of war, reduce the risks of immediate escalation and mass destruction of the European battlefield. But the case for nuclear weapons-free zones does not rest on this, for both superpowers could still reintroduce nuclear weapons or use their long-range missiles. The main benefits of such zones is that they reduce the danger of war through accident or miscalculation in a crisis and, above all, that they encourage reductions in both sides' nuclear arsenals. Establishment of a nuclear-weapons-free zone may set in train political processes which will encourage forms of conventional arms limitation or political agreement on sources of conflict. There are particular objections that can be made to nuclear weapons-free zones in Europe, arising out of the geographical position and numerous conventional forces of the USSR. There are, therefore, supplementary measures which would be desirable if even a limited zone were introduced in Europe. These issues are discussed in detail in Chapters Three and Four.

However, a European nuclear-weapons-free zone is not likely to result from negotiations between NATO and the Warsaw Pact. At present, proposals for more limited zones are part of Soviet propaganda in negotiations, and they are ritualistically rejected by NATO. There are good reasons to believe that East European governments are not particularly happy with the siting of nuclear missiles on their territory, and there have been quite widespread popular protests in Czechoslovakia and the GDR about Warsaw Pact nuclear and other military policies.[18] But given the much greater freedom of action available to governments and popular movements in Western Europe, it is from the West that an initiative can realistically be expected. West European countries can act unilaterally to change NATO nuclear policies if they agree on the measures needed. They might well secure US cooperation on at least some shift away from reliance on US nuclear weapons in NATO strategy, but if necessary they should be able to insist that the USA alters its military policies in Europe.

At this point it is essential to distinguish between two separate concepts of unilateral action designed to promote mutual reductions in arms. First, there are unilateral initiatives which are designed to demonstrate a serious desire for arms control or disarmament measures, to promote greater trust and to put pressure on the other side to reciprocate. They are usually seen as the prelude to a negotiated agreement. The object of a strategy of such unilateral initiatives is the promotion of military restraint and improvement of the political atmosphere without altering significantly the existing nuclear or conventional balance.[19] This approach is usually recommended as a lever in relations between the USA and the USSR, but it could also be used at a NATO/ Warsaw Pact level.

This book is primarily concerned with the second, and more radical, concept of unilateral action, which involves making real changes in one's own military dispositions with the aim of bringing about fundamental strategic and political shifts in the nature of the existing military confrontation. Here we are concerned with the arguments for NATO progressively dismantling its nuclear armoury, and doing so unconditionally.

West European measures of nuclear disengagement would result in a safer defence policy for both Western Europe and the USA. They would also have a powerful impact on Soviet military strategy and foreign policy, and promote a change in the political relationship between Western Europe and the USA. Western Europe would be pursuing a safer and more rational strategy by agreeing to no-first-use of nuclear weapons, and by removing in stages all battlefield and European-based theatre nuclear weapons, even if the USSR did not reciprocate. The risk of war starting in Europe through miscalculation, and of rapid and uncontrolled nuclear escalation once war had broken out, would be removed. Many strategic analysts would accept the desirability of a radical reduction in the number of nuclear weapons in Europe, but most would probably wish to retain some to deter the USSR from using theirs. While this consideration does have real weight, it is necessary to set against it the very high probability that, so long as they have nuclear war-fighting weapons, both sides will be under strong pressure to launch pre-emptive nuclear strikes. A number of groups studying European defence agree with the Commission that a non-nuclear policy in Europe would, on balance, be a safer basis for defence; this possibility has received particularly detailed scrutiny in West Germany, which would suffer the most immediate devastation if nuclear war broke out in central Europe.[20]

A consistent non-nuclear policy requires the severing of West European reliance on the US strategic nuclear force: that is, the 'decoupling' of Europe from the US nuclear force as deliberate policy. This proposal is controversial, even among those who advocate removal of all war-fighting nuclear weapons from Western Europe, because it runs counter to the basis of NATO policy and long-standing defence orthodoxy, and could leave Western Europe vulnerable to nuclear attack or blackmail in a major conventional war with the USSR.

The strategic case for such 'decoupling' is that so long as nuclear retaliation is part of NATO strategy there would be pressure to reintroduce battlefield nuclear weapons into Western Europe in the event of war, and Washington and Moscow might feel compelled to launch pre-emptive nuclear strikes against each other. Even more important would be the tendency to view as nuclear any crisis or confrontation in Europe. Denuclearizing Western Europe would not in itself end the dangers of nuclear confrontation between the superpowers. But it would remove some of the existing strategic pressures on the USA to create bigger and more threatening nuclear arsenals, and if most West European governments concluded that it was more dangerous to be part of US nuclear strategy than to be independent of it, there might be a major re-evaluation of deterrence within the USA. The fundamental case for renouncing reliance on US nuclear weapons is that the theory of nuclear deterrence is inherently flawed and long-term nuclear stability an illusion. As we have seen earlier an apparently stable nuclear balance is vulnerable to technological developments, and there is always a risk of accident and miscalculation leading to war – a risk which can be reduced by such measures as the 'hot line', but never eliminated.

Although a prudential military case can be made for Western Europe abandoning reliance on US nuclear weapons even if the USSR does not modify its own nuclear policies, the goal would be to achieve a scaling down of the Soviet arsenal and formalize agreement on a European nuclear-weapons-free zone. NATO would be in a strong position to press for appropriate Soviet responses – what kind of measures might be looked for and their probability, is assessed in detail in Chapter Four. But the general case rests on the logic of reversing the arms race and the political leverage that unilateral measures could offer.

If decisions about weapons are affected significantly by fears of the reactions of the other side, and are at least in part a response to their research and deployment, then it is reasonable to expect that a scaling down of NATO's nuclear arsenals will affect Soviet strategic planning. This does not mean that there will be automatic reciprocation – for example, cuts in missiles. While all major developments in nuclear arms have been matched by the other side, there have always been strategic asymmetries between the USA and USSR which might be expected to influence a Soviet response. The logic of reversing the arms race will, of course, be modified by the fact that several factors affect military policy, including the desire to maintain spheres of influence. But if NATO removed its nuclear bombers and intermediate range missiles, then the military justification for present Soviet missile deployments would be considerably reduced.

The pressures on the Soviet leadership to respond to NATO measures would not, however, be confined to altering perceptions of the strategic threat. Soviet concern to avoid a nuclear war would encourage reciprocation of some kind, as would awareness of the impact of Western nuclear disarmament measures on international opinion. The USSR has always been at pains to promote the view that its own nuclear preparations are a purely defensive response to the USA. It is also anxious to prevent the spread of nuclear weapons and would hesitate to give the impression that it plans to use such weapons against countries that have renounced them. Moreover, the burden of arms on the

Soviet economy would encourage a response. The real problem would not be whether the USSR would respond, but how satisfactory any response would be in terms of Western military perceptions.

Another element in the argument for systematically loosening and finally severing the nuclear links between Western Europe and the USA is that it is a condition for any genuine political independence for Europe. Presently the price of the nuclear 'guarantee' to Western Europe is that NATO countries fall into line behind the USA on military and political issues.

There are, of course, more general pressures for alliance solidarity in bargaining with the USSR, but the USA is dominant in defining the terms of NATO policies. The other direct lever of US influence on NATO is the presence of US troops in Europe. Whether the USA would seek to maintain that influence if West Europeans pressed for changes in NATO strategy, or whether it would reduce or even withdraw conventional support, is unpredictable. In the long run, a much looser alliance seems probable. The Commission's proposals envisage in the short term a US conventional presence in Europe, but in the longer term look to a dissolution of military alliances.

The potential for Western Europe to promote dealignment is therefore linked to decreasing and eventually ending its reliance on US nuclear weapons. One natural result of greater West European political autonomy would be to take further the process, already begun by *Ostpolitik*, of extending links with Eastern Europe and developing a separate relationship between the USSR and Western Europe on political and economic issues. The fear that has long cemented Western Europe to the USA has been that a loosening of ties would leave the USSR the dominant power on the European continent and lead to some form of 'Finlandization'. But, given the political influence, economic strength, and actual and potential conventional military strength of Western Europe, it is not certain that the USSR would be dominant in a new relationship. Of course, there are questions to be asked about political arrangements that might obtain within Western Europe, the role of Germany, France and Britain, and how far Western Europe relates as a whole or as a group of diverse countries to the USSR. We pursue these problems, and the related question of possible future relations between Western and Eastern Europe, in Chapter Five.

However, focusing on West European interests in dealignment runs the risk of creating a very simplified picture. It may underplay the extent to which West Europeans' have been, and in many cases still are, committed to close ties with the USA and to reliance on US nuclear weapons. In addition, it may fail to distinguish between West European interest in changes within Europe and their attitudes to the rest of the world. So far the behaviour of major West European states – exporting, with inadequate safeguards, nuclear reactors which may later be used in a nuclear weapons programme, and selling arms to developing countries – has been no better than that of the USA. Indeed, at times it has been worse: for example, undermining President Carter's efforts to impose strict controls on the export of nuclear plants by moving into markets left open by US self-restraint. Commercial pressures to sell nuclear reactors and surplus armaments abroad would still exist in a Europe free of nuclear weapons. In their relations with the Third World, European countries still enjoy economic dominance. If, therefore, Western Europe is to promote changes in international relations, it will have to change internally.

2. A new role for Britain

In Chapter One we analysed the need for a new policy for Europe and new approaches to peace and disarmament. But ideal goals need to be translated into reality, and it is in attempting to achieve aims such as dealignment and disarmament that problems of a most daunting complexity arise. In this chapter we explore the specific role that Britain could play through nuclear disarmament and the adoption of new defence and foreign policies.

1. BRITISH FOREIGN POLICY SINCE WORLD WAR II

Despite the fact that Britain's world role has altered significantly, there have been three basic assumptions underlying the foreign policy of Labour and Conservative governments ever since 1945: the importance of the special relationship with the USA, the need to link Western Europe to the USA, and the need to counteract the perceived threat from the USSR. When thinking about future foreign policy it is necessary to consider whether these forty-year-old guidelines remain valid. First, however, we should look briefly at how they evolved.

The 'special relationship' between Britain and the USA was a product of World War II. Its essence has been that Britain recognized that the USA had become the major Western power and so relied on a unity of British and US interests to promote Britain's own goals. In the inter-war years Britain and the USA were still rival powers, and the predominant isolationism of US foreign policy excluded close ties with either Britain or Europe. The economic support given to Britain early in the war by Roosevelt's government, and the later military cooperation which culminated in the Allied landings in Europe, created an economic, political and military relationship which carried over into the Cold War of the late 1940s. It was a partnership in which, after 1945, Britain was necessarily subordinate in terms of economic and military power. Moreover, there were elements of conflict in it: the USA was determined to see the dismantling of the British Empire, both for ideological reasons and in order to open up new markets and access to raw materials. But there was also a genuine coincidence of political beliefs and values which shaped their views on the future of Western Europe.

The explicit goal of British foreign policy under Ernest Bevin was to link the USA to Europe in military as well as economic terms. The British government, impoverished by the war, was unable to maintain its great power role in Europe and invest resources in combating Communist movements and Soviet influence. At the beginning of 1947, Britain handed over this task in Greece and Turkey to the USA. As the Cold War developed, Bevin's diplomacy was geared primarily to strengthening US ties with Europe. First, he promoted a rapid and coordinated response to the Marshall Plan, whereby a sixteen-nation group formulated a four-year plan for European economic recovery to make good use of US aid. Second, he helped to build in stages a combined European and US military alliance against the USSR. The first stage was the Brussels Treaty of March 1948, which brought France and the Benelux countries into an alliance with Britain. The second stage was the linking of the USA and Canada to the new Brussels Treaty Organization, a goal increasingly favoured by US policy makers, worried about possible Soviet pressure on Western Europe, and by the US military, who wanted a ring of forward bases and advocated a US-led military force in Europe. Therefore the linkage of North America to Western Europe was wished for by governments on both sides of the Atlantic, and it was achieved when the isolationism of the US Congress was overcome by apparent evidence of Soviet aggressive designs in Europe, in particular the Berlin blockade and Communist takeover in Czechoslovakia early in 1948. The outcome was the North Atlantic Treaty of April 1949, which incorporated not only the United States and Canada but also a wider range of West European countries in a military alliance. The central purpose of NATO has always been to commit US military power, and especially its nuclear arsenal, to the defence of Western Europe.

Why Britain soon perceived its other major World War II ally, the Soviet Union, as a serious threat is examined in more detail in the next chapter. Given Conservative hostility ever since the Bolshevik revolution, and a history of imperial rivalries between Britain and Russia, it is not surprising that Churchill was bitterly suspicious of the USSR. That a Labour government should be active in enlisting US support for military containment of the Soviet Union needs explanation. Before the Hitler-Stalin Pact was signed, many on the left had favoured an anti-fascist alliance with the Soviet Union; and many distrusted the economic and political role played by the USA in Europe in the aftermath of the War, a role which seemed designed to ensure US economic dominance and to bolster right-wing governments against the leftist groups which had won mass support during the Resistance. It can be cogently argued that as Foreign Secretary, instead of pursuing socialist goals, Bevin followed policies almost indistinguishable from those of the coalition government led by Churchill, and did so with the support of the majority in Attlee's Cabinet. But in view of Stalin's ruthless domestic policies and his equally ruthless extension of Soviet territory to its pre-1914 boundaries during the war, there were powerful reasons for distrusting the Soviet leader's intentions, even in 1945. Western democrats were now also extremely sensitive to the dangers of appeasing dictators. By 1948, the imposition of Stalinist régimes on Eastern Europe gave good cause for alarm, even though these moves may have betokened consolidation of the Soviet sphere of influence rather than aggressive designs against the West.

After Stalin's death, with the resulting partial liberalization of the Soviet régime and its relations with Eastern Europe, and the easing of the Cold War in 1955, the Labour Party, then in opposition, did indicate unease about the permanent division of Europe into military blocs. However, belief in the necessity of remaining strongly armed to deter Soviet aggression has remained a central tenet of British defence and foreign policy, espoused by both parties alike when in office and by civil service orthodoxy. The concept of the Soviet threat has become detached from its original historical context and is now a largely unexamined premise; belief in it is strengthened by the very fact of NATO membership and by pressure to explain and justify high defence expenditure. The Soviet Union's own military build-up has been interpreted as clear proof of the necessity of NATO, and the Soviet threat has been understood and projected in terms of assessments of Soviet conventional strength or missile deployments. It is also used as a handy rhetorical weapon against all critics of Britain's military policies. The ideological usage of the concept of the 'Soviet threat' does not preclude the possibility of a real threat; but it prevents objective reassessment, which is now clearly needed.

The Commission examined in detail the nature of the Soviet threat in its first report, and argued that the predominant motives in Soviet policy appear to be pursuit of equal superpower status with the USA and fear of external aggression.[1] These motives do not always have reassuring consequences. The former has led to direct and indirect military involvement in Africa during the 1970s and is one of the reasons for the consolidation of Soviet power in Eastern Europe, including military intervention to maintain control. Determination to avoid a further war on Soviet territory has also been a strong incentive to keep forces in Eastern Europe, and nervousness about stability on Soviet borders encouraged the sending of troops into Afghanistan. Soviet defence concerns have also led to a dangerous pre-emptive military strategy in Europe.

However, superpower ambitions and over-insurance against the possibility of attack do not mean a desire for global conquest. It is often assumed that the Soviet Union is committed to the creation of world communism, but the available evidence does not suggest that Soviet policy has been decided primarily on the basis of ideology. This does not mean, however, that ideology is irrelevant. Where possible, the USSR is still anxious to assert its authority in relation to other Communist parties. It naturally tends to ally itself with other socialist states and the legitimacy of its own régime is linked to the maintenance of Communist Party rule in Eastern Europe.

Fear of Soviet intentions and determination to oppose extensions of Soviet power have, perhaps, constituted the main bond between the United States and Western Europe. Of course, there are genuine historic and cultural ties, common liberal-democratic beliefs, and close political and military cooperation over nearly forty years. But without the underlying effect of the perceived 'Soviet threat', the latent tensions between the United States and Western Europe would have become more overt.

While some central elements of British foreign policy have remained relatively unaltered since the 1940s, there have been two major changes: decline in political influence and decline in economic strength. Britain emerged from the war greatly weakened, but as one of the victors with an unchallenged claim to be one of the Big Four powers in the new world order. Forty years on Britain is clearly a secondary power and economically near the bottom of the league table of industrialized countries. This changing world role has led to a reassessment of British relations with Western Europe.

The most obvious change is that Britain no longer has an empire. A major impetus was given to the process of decolonization when India became independent in 1947 and, although at first Britain tried to retain its African colonies, the independence of Ghana in 1957 signalled that change was inevitable. By the mid-1960s Britain was no longer a colonial power and appeared impotent against the unilateral declaration of independence by Southern Rhodesia's white government. As Britain withdrew from its overseas colonies the need for so many bases and troops abroad declined and the government reduced its military forces, in particular the navy.

Even after decolonization, however, British military deployments still reflected a vestigial conception of Britain as a world power, with the navy seen as an instrument of power and prestige, British garrisons quartered in the Middle and Far East, and Britain still aspiring to influence and to safeguard its oil supplies and trade through military means. Moreover, in the 1950s Britain had joined two more military alliances, SEATO in the Far East and CENTO in the Middle East, both designed to strengthen pro-Western régimes. Although neither alliance involved explicit military commitments, membership reflected

Britain's belief in its great power status during the 1950s.[2] By the late 1960s this aspiration seemed wholly unrealistic. The Labour government under Harold Wilson bowed to economic necessity and declared in 1967 that it would withdraw from most of its commitments East of Suez.

The second factor in Britain's diminishing power was its increasingly obvious economic weakness in the 1960s and 1970s. Britain's economic problems are part of a long-term trend of relative industrial decline which can be traced back to the late 19th century. World War II also inflicted great economic damage on Britain, but this was true of all the major combatants except the United States. During the 1950s Britain, together with the rest of the industrialized world, appeared to enjoy a remarkable economic recovery and a period of new affluence, but by the early 1960s the weakness of Britain's international trade position and currency was being exposed.

The contrast between Britain's imperial past and its post-war acquiescence in a secondary status has created certain psychological strains which manifest themselves in political life. Decolonization was achieved without acute crisis in domestic politics, and Suez marked the last attempt by a British government to act like a great power. But nostalgia and unwillingness to relinquish some of the accessories of world power still contend with political and economic realism. Mrs Thatcher has consciously evoked this nostalgia, most effectively at the time of the Falklands War, and since then British defence policy has been framed in terms of a continuing, if residual, world role. An attempt at realism was made by John Nott when, as Defence Secretary, he proposed to cut the navy and limit Britain's defence role to NATO, an attempt scuppered by the Falklands campaign and the celebration of Britain's ability to conduct a war 8000 miles from home. Continuing economic pressure on a costly defence budget is, however, likely to prevail. Since the war, British defence costs have outrun economic capacity, but as Britain's economic position worsens it becomes more imperative to tailor expenditure to available resources.

A general reassessment of Britain's ability to act as an independent world power was the main factor in persuading British governments in the 1960s to reconsider their relations with

Western Europe. What Britain could not do alone it might still achieve as part of a European entity. After the war British governments remained aloof from the proposals for a federation of Europe. Britain still saw itself as a world, not a European, power, and policy makers were still distrustful of, and hostile to, continental Europe, especially France. In the defence sphere Britain did overcome its historic prejudice against continental entanglements, even committing itself under the Brussels Treaty to maintain a large number of troops in Europe. But British governments promoted European defence cooperation because it appeared to be a condition of US military commitment to Western Europe, not out of enthusiasm for European connections. The Coal and Steel Community and, later, the EEC were created without British participation.

However, in the early 1960s, awareness of economic weakness and greater willingness to recognize that Britain could no longer claim to be a world power propelled official opinion in favour of joining the European Community. This was a strongly-held Foreign Office view and was accepted by the leaderships of the Conservative and Labour parties, though both parties contained passionate opponents of such a move. Britain still tended, however, to give priority to the relationship with the USA, which led de Gaulle to veto Britain's first attempt at entering the EEC. Even now Britain remains an uneasy member and is hesitant to see itself as a purely European power, as its unwillingness to attach its currency to Europe demonstrated. The anti-EEC stance in its 1983 Election Manifesto showed that the Labour Party is still beset by political doubts about the desirability of membership.

A number of reasons are given for opposing British involvement in the EEC, including fear that membership will restrict the freedom of a British government in its economic policies (one cause for socialist doubts) and suspicion that the Community may become a vehicle for narrow West European interests, excluding a genuine all-European perspective or true internationalism. Whether the EEC can promote political disengagement in Europe is discussed below. But there is clearly a continuing distrust of European entanglements and a tendency for popular opinion either to seek a world role or retreat into 'little Englandism'.

2. The Central Case for Abandoning British Nuclear Weapons

The detailed military arguments for and against British nuclear weapons have been rehearsed many times elsewhere, including in the Commission's first report, which also looked carefully at the moral arguments for renunciation. The purpose here is to look briefly at the position of Britain's 'independent deterrent' in the context of the historical evolution of British foreign policy, and to summarize the main arguments for a unilateral renunciation of nuclear weapons which are relevant to promoting wider measures of nuclear arms restraint and disarmament.

The British Labour government acquired its own atomic bomb after the war almost automatically, both because British scientists (including many emigrés to Britain) had played a central role in developing the bomb during the war, and because Britain still counted itself a great power and took for granted that it should have this frightening and formidable new weapon. British determination to go it alone was hardened when the US Congress ended the close nuclear cooperation Britain had initially enjoyed by passing the McMahon Act.[3] During the 1950s the Conservative government decided to build the H-Bomb. Britain's great power status was now visibly declining, and possession of the bomb became a symbol of and a substitute for the reality of major economic or military power. The nuclear bomb also commended itself as a strategic weapon in the emerging theory of nuclear deterrence, and promised to be fairly cheap: the 1957 Defence White Paper presented it as an alternative to maintaining conscription and a high level of expenditure on conventional weapons.

During the 1950s nuclear weapons also found favour in Whitehall because they became a key element in forging the special relationship between Britain and the United States, as the USA relented and allowed the British closer access to its nuclear know-how and technology. Britain also began to make its own plutonium available to the USA for civil and military use. The independent deterrent thus bound Britain into closer dependence on the USA, a process which went a step further in the early 1960s when the British government discovered that the soaring cost of missile technology meant that nuclear weapons were no longer so cheap an option, and Macmillan committed Britain to buying its missiles in future from the United States.[4] This has meant that Britain has had to accept what is available from the USA rather than have a missile force tailored to its own defence needs. It has also seen its original choice of missile scrapped by the US government for domestic reasons and been forced to accept a substitute.

As missile technology costs have also risen, and the pound has declined against the dollar, buying US technology has ceased to be cheap. (All these factors are illustrated by Britain's present commitment to buy the Trident D5 missile, which was accepted when it became clear that the original choice, the C4, would be phased out by the time Britain was ready to switch to its new submarine weapons system. Trident D5 represents a counterforce capacity and magnification of the British nuclear armoury that most commentators regard as provocative and unnecessary, whose costs have risen, between 1982 and 1985, from an estimated £7.5 billion to a probable minimum of £11 billion. As a result there is a growing lobby, even in military and Conservative circles, to abandon Trident. Some look to cheaper alternatives like cruise missiles based on submarines, but others see a strong economic and strategic case for abandoning British nuclear weapons altogether.)

Until the 1980s, the leaderships of both the Labour and Conservative parties have supported an independent British nuclear force, despite strong opposition within the Labour Party. Nye Bevan was prevailed on to cast his weight against the Labour Left when, at Brighton in 1957, he said that a British foreign secretary who was deprived of the bomb would be 'going naked into the conference chamber'. One of the chief arguments for Britain's nuclear force has been that it gives us more influence in disarmament negotiations – a 'seat at the top table'. This argument had greatest validity from 1958 to 1961, when Britain made a third at the Test Ban Treaty talks and did, while strongly supporting the US line, attempt a number of initiatives and compromises to secure agreement. During 1962, eight non-aligned nations were admitted to disarmament talks for the first time, and they put pressure on the USA and USSR for a test ban treaty. In 1963 deadlock was finally resolved by the bilateral diplomacy of Kennedy and Khrushchev, with Britain playing a supportive but minor role. Ever since, the pattern of arms control negotiations has been a mixture of multilateral talks and bilateral talks between the USA and USSR from which the UK has normally been excluded – as it was from SALT I and II, INF and START, and is now from the new Geneva talks. The only exception has been the 1977-80 talks on a comprehensive test ban, where Britain was centrally involved, although bilateral CTB negotiations have also been taking place at the Geneva Committee for Disarmament. The case for British nuclear weapons as a ticket to the top table is now, therefore, extremely weak.

However, the argument for British nuclear disarmament is not only the negative one that many of the original justifications for British nuclear weapons no longer carry any conviction. There are a number of more important positive arguments, of which the central political one is that it could promote the cause of general nuclear arms limitation. It would simplify negotiations between the USA and USSR since the British and French forces have further complicated the delicate problems of 'nuclear balance', and created difficulties during the SALT and INF talks, especially as the British were not prepared for their missiles to be officially 'counted in'. Furthermore, British nuclear disarmament could be used as a valuable test case for verifying the destruction of a nuclear arsenal and bomb-making capacity, thus serving the long-term goal of wider nuclear disarmament.

British renunciation of its independent bomb is particularly relevant to preventing the future spread of nuclear weapons, for their possession by a secondary power with no immediate threats to its security is 'propaganda by deed' for proliferation. In addition, one of the main public justifications for a British nuclear force – that in thirty years' time we may live in a world where almost all states are nuclear – is a clear invitation to other governments to pursue the same logic. If they do, we will indeed be faced with the nightmare world of multiple nuclear-armed states.

The principal safeguard against proliferation is widespread recognition that mutual restraint will make the world safer for all. Independent nuclear disarmament would demonstrate Britain's commitment to this approach, even though it would not have instant and dramatic results and might not influence some countries with acute security needs or strong ideological commitments. But it would have indirect influence in future debates about acquiring the bomb, and would put Britain in a strong diplomatic position to press for strengthening of the Non-Proliferation Treaty, which is the main bulwark against the spread of nuclear weapons. How a British government could maximize the value and effectiveness of its own nuclear disarmament is discussed in detail in Chapter Seven.

Some distinguished political and military commentators who have concluded that Britain should cease to be a nuclear power still resist the idea of unilateral nuclear disarmament. They would prefer to bargain our nuclear bombs and missiles away as part of a US-Soviet deal. They oppose unilateralism on the often unargued assumption that it is politically ineffectual, and in the belief that a negotiated renunciation will require the USSR to give up some of its missiles in return. But there is a strong case for believing that a coherent strategy of unilateral nuclear disarmament would be much more effective than leaving British nuclear weapons to be bargained away as a relatively minor item in a US-USSR strategic arms limitation agreement. The timing and presentation would be in the hands of a British government, which could plan to maximize its international impact and minimize domestic dislocation. If British nuclear weapons were put into US-Soviet talks, assuming that such talks were taking place, then their final abandonment would depend on the negotiations being successfully completed by an agreement. Britain might also find itself in the absurd position of trying to update a nuclear force which it intended to dismantle, in order to present it as a credible 'bargaining chip'. If US-Soviet talks failed, Britain would still have to act unilaterally if the government intended to cease being a nuclear power, but its action would lack conviction.

The argument that a negotiated renunciation of the British nuclear weapons would have more impact on Soviet nuclear missile strength than unilateral action is also questionable. If US-Soviet talks were in progress at the time of Britain's abandonment of its nuclear force, then the USA would certainly expect the Soviet Union to take account of British action in the terms of an agreement. Moreover, the Soviet Union might well find itself under pressure to reciprocate immediately by reducing its planned or existing missile strength. The Soviet leadership did give a very public pledge to Neil Kinnock and Denis Healey in November 1984 to respond to British nuclear disarmament by dismantling or destroying an equivalent number of missiles.

3. The Limited Case Against US Nuclear Bases

The arguments against US nuclear bases in Britain fall into two categories: there are limited and specific arguments about their dangers and disadvantages, and there is a much more general and fundamental criticism of involvement in US and NATO nuclear strategy, which we examine in the next section. The limited objections are that the bases make Britain a major nuclear target, that they undermine British sovereignty, and that the most recent weapons – the ground-launched cruise missiles now at Greenham Common – are part of a provocative nuclear deployment.

US bases make it likely that Britain would be an early target for a major Soviet nuclear attack in the event of war. British Defence Ministry calculations of likely nuclear targets take account of major US nuclear bases and facilities. This argument has some weight, for Britain is a relatively small and densely-populated country which, under present policies, seems to invite total devastation in the early stages of any nuclear war. But so long as Britain belongs to a nuclear alliance, or is in danger of being involved in a major European war, non-nuclear military installations may also become nuclear targets; and even if there were no direct nuclear attacks on British territory, a mass release of radioactive fallout over Europe and the effects of a 'nuclear winter' after a major war could prove deadly. Britain incurs extra vulnerability from hosting so many US nuclear bases, but the main threat comes from the nature of the NATO-Warsaw Pact nuclear confrontation.

The argument that US nuclear bases infringe British sovereignty needs no qualification, although successive British governments have acquiesced in this erosion of national control. US bombers arrived in Britain during 1948, ostensibly as a temporary measure during the Berlin crisis but, as was always intended by the US Air Force, they have remained here ever since and US military facilities have multiplied. The Ministry of Defence has never given either Parliament or the electorate a full account of US bases in Britain, and British governments have never achieved a genuinely satisfactory agreement on the terms for hosting them. The most sensitive issue is whether a British government has any control over a US decision to launch nuclear weapons from British territory. Winston Churchill did achieve what had been refused the Labour government – a formal communiqué stating that use of nuclear weapons from British soil would be a 'joint decision'. About thirty years later, in response to widespread public opposition to cruise missiles, Mrs Thatcher received public confirmation of the 1952 agreement with Churchill, but leading figures in the US Administration avoided confirming her claim that this meant that the weapons could only be used with British agreement. A number of senior US defence experts, including Robert McNamara, have suggested that there may be consultation, but the USA is bound to make the final decision. Dual key arrangements can provide direct control over the firing of particular missiles, as they did for the Thor missiles which were based in Britain in 1958 and 1959; they have never, of course, applied to bombers.[5]

In practice, even promises of advance consultation are worthless. A US President on the brink of nuclear war, or in a fast-moving crisis which could become nuclear, is bound to act as Commander-in-Chief of the US armed forces and give primacy to US interests. In the event of a war in Europe, the NATO Council would be convened if time permitted, but the USA could delegate in advance to its own commanders the right to release nuclear weapons without cumbersome political consultation. Moreover, reports indicate that cruise missiles are to be fully integrated into US strategic nuclear planning, which suggests that the United States will have exclusive control over their use. If the threat of war is not in Europe but in the Middle East or elsewhere, then the USA might well alert its nuclear bases in Britain, as it has done in the past, for example during the 1973 Arab-Israeli war, when nuclear-armed bombers were put on a low level alert without even informing the British government. At best, on the brink of actual war, consultation is likely to mean the USA telling Britain and other allies what it intends to do. At worst, as the warning time available for deciding whether to retaliate against an incoming counterforce attack shortens to a few minutes, 'launch on warning' procedures may mean that the decision to launch US nuclear weapons will be made, effectively, by computer, without even the US President having a real choice.[6]

Vulnerability to nuclear attack and abrogation of sovereignty constitute quite significant arguments for reducing the number of US nuclear facilities and refusing to accept bases over which the British government has no control. These considerations would certainly justify refusal to have nuclear-armed bombers and might be good enough reasons to require removal of the Poseidon nuclear submarine base at Holy Loch. Additional strategic and technical arguments, associated with the current US counterforce strategy and the dangers of a first-strike nuclear policy, apply to the cruise missiles scheduled for Britain as part of the current European deployments. But uncompromising rejection of American nuclear bases requires a more comprehensive political and moral position.

4. IMPLICATIONS OF A TOTALLY NON-NUCLEAR POLICY

The more fundamental argument for requiring withdrawal of US nuclear bases is that it is a crucial step in trying to disengage Britain from involvement in the existing nuclear confrontation. The strategic and political case for not continuing to rely on US nuclear deterrence was discussed in Chapter One. Britain alone cannot change the nature of the nuclear confrontation between the USA and USSR, but it can force reconsideration of the whole basis of NATO strategy.

There are also powerful moral arguments against reliance on nuclear weapons, which were set out in detail in the first report. The essential points are that launching nuclear weapons, whether in a first or second strike, could never be justified in accordance with the principles of a just war, and that nuclear deterrence requires a declared willingness and strategic preparation to use nuclear weapons that is morally unacceptable. It is not politically possible to alter at once the entire basis of US and NATO policy, but there is a moral imperative to move away decisively from reliance on nuclear weapons, and Britain could opt for a wholly non-nuclear stance.

A British government committed to a non-nuclear policy could not only reject US bases where nuclear weapons are deployed, but also refuse to provide facilities for command, control and intelligence that are directly relevant to US nuclear strategy. A Britain that no longer asked for US 'protection' could also follow New Zealand's example in denying all port facilities to US ships carrying nuclear weapons.

Of course, adoption of a non-nuclear policy has important implications for British membership of NATO, which presently relies on nuclear weapons to repel conventional attack, plans extensive battlefield use of nuclear weapons and nuclear strikes against the Soviet Union as part of its war-fighting strategy, and relies on the deterrent effect of long-range US nuclear missiles. One approach, favoured by a majority of Commission members, is to use British membership of NATO to try and move the Alliance towards a non-nuclear defence strategy, and to make continued membership conditional on NATO responding. The other approach is to leave NATO and adopt a policy of neutralism or non-alignment. Both options are explored below.

Abandoning British nuclear weapons is intrinsically connected with reappraising Britain's status and goals in international politics, since it would mean renouncing finally any claim still to be regarded as a 'great power'. At the same time it would free a British government to adopt a more modest but also more constructive role which gave primacy to disarmament and non-military solutions to world problems. Ironically, as we have noted earlier, nuclear weapons, which are meant to make Britain more independent, actually bind it into close nuclear cooperation with, and dependence on, the USA for missile technology. If, therefore, Britain ceased to be dependent on the USA for its nuclear force it would have taken one step towards greater independence in its relations with Washington, and thus change the nature of the special relationship between them. Britain could then be free to stand back from such policies as SDI or Reagan's attempts to crush the government of Nicaragua.

If a government came to power with a mandate to remove all US nuclear bases and try to create a non-nuclear Europe, there would necessarily be a considerable shift in US-British relations and the United States' role in Europe. Foreign and defence policies are interlocked, and a change in defence priorities would influence broader attitudes. NATO's evolution has, as originally desired by Britain, tied the United States closely to Western Europe. It has also strengthened the power of the USA in relation to its allies, since the United States, by virtue of its conventional military contribution and the centrality of its nuclear force in NATO strategy, has become the dominant partner. The cost to Western Europe of this tie with the United States has been acceptance of a degree of subordination. European members of NATO have, on the whole, been willing to accept this in preference to dominance by another European power but, as we argued in the previous chapter, since the election of Reagan the disadvantages and dangers of this kind of relationship have begun to loom much larger. Through the plethora of over 100 US nuclear and other military bases Britain has become more tied to the USA than the rest of Europe, with the possible exception of West Germany.

The requirements of NATO cohesion and acceptance of US leadership have generally been reflected in foreign policy – in the stance adopted by the West at disarmament negotiations, at votes in the United Nations, and in hesitancy to criticize US action in other parts of the world such as South-East Asia or Central America. Britain has been particularly unwilling to break ranks in public, partly because of its close nuclear, military and intelligence ties with the USA and also because of its conception of a special relationship and belief in bringing influence to bear quietly behind the scenes. Whatever the nuances of this diplomacy, the public impression is that Britain is Washington's most acquiescent ally.

Asking the United States to withdraw its bases and disengage from its nuclear commitment to Europe would also mean a shift in its relationship with Western Europe, leaving both parties freer and the European countries more independent. The United States would be taking fewer risks on behalf of Western Europe, while the Europeans would be more equal partners and more likely to strike out independently in foreign policy. Of course, a change in the balance of contributions to conventional defence and in European willingness to accept US leadership in disarmament and other policies could occur within the present NATO framework, and to some extent it does. But given the central role played to date by the coupling of US nuclear weapons to Europe, moves to reduce the reliance of NATO strategy on nuclear weapons and phase out such weapons in Europe are bound to have far-reaching repercussions on the defence and foreign policies, and indeed the domestic politics, of European countries. (Some of these implications were explored in Chapter One, others are developed in Chapters Four and Five.)

Finally, moving towards a non-nuclear strategy for NATO should be linked to a public re-examination of the nature of the Soviet threat to Western Europe to disentangle the realities from ideoligical assertions. As the Commission argued in its first report, the case for unilateral measures of disarmament does not depend on trusting the intentions of the Soviet Union. Indeed, emphasis on non-nuclear defence suggests some concern about the potential superpower ambitions of the USSR. However, a major reassessment of the nature of NATO defence policy does imply thinking about its real purposes. Rethinking defence and exploring the possibilities of disarmament also means recognizing that an important element in the perceived threat from the USSR derives from the logic of the arms race. The West fears Soviet missiles, but the public is often encouraged to ignore the extent to which Soviet nuclear armaments have been a response to Western nuclear build-up, or part of a modernization process pursued autonomously by both sides. A non-nuclear defence policy would not only alter thinking in the West. It would also impinge on Soviet attitudes and strategy. How the USSR might respond is discussed in detail elsewhere in this report, but it is clear that a major reduction in the nuclear threat posed to the Soviet Union by the West must change East-West relations in some way.

5. THE ROLE OF A NON-NUCLEAR BRITAIN IN NATO

If Britain changed the emphasis of its defence and foreign policy it would have to promote its new goals through its alliances, through the international bodies to which it belongs, and through its relationships with particular countries. The Atlantic Alliance is central to this task.

There is a paradox in a British government promoting dealignment and the ending of military blocs through NATO, but success in changing its policy would lead in this direction. The political advantage of working through NATO would be the potential of mobilizing combined West European pressure to encourage a change of direction in US defence and foreign policy, and of promoting a strategy whereby a number of West European countries could act together to bring about change in Europe and its relations with the wider world. If it proved impossible to alter NATO policy from within, Britain could leave the Alliance and pursue non-alignment.

Britain has leverage in NATO because of its status as one of the major powers in Europe and its substantial contribution to NATO defence planning. Britain's contribution includes a permanent force of 55,000 troops based in West Germany, its naval role in the Eastern Atlantic, and its planned use as a staging post for US reinforcements in the event of war. All these forms of military support are compatible with a non-nuclear NATO defence, and indeed Britain's ability to offer considerable forces and facilities for conventional defence strengthens its position in arguing for a non-nuclear strategy. But if NATO decided to move towards a non-provocative strategy, or if US troop commitments were reduced, then the precise nature of Britain's contribution might change. Whether British nuclear disarmament would affect its influence in NATO is difficult to assess. Giving up nuclear weapons may be interpreted in some quarters as further evidence of British economic and political decline, but it is also likely to be widely welcomed in most European capitals as a sign that Britain is adjusting to its new status as a European power. Requiring removal of US nuclear bases strikes more directly at NATO's reliance on the US nuclear umbrella and is therefore likely to evoke mixed responses in European members of the Alliance. But it is closely linked to the non-nuclear strategy that Britain would be urging on its NATO partners, and has the advantage of a unilateral commitment which would indicate British seriousness and urgency. Unilateral action on bases may also prompt a popular response in Western Europe, where cruise and Pershing II missiles have been imposed against strong peace movement protests and much wider public disquiet.

How Britain should tackle the diplomacy of trying to bring about a radical change in NATO strategy, reversing one of its basic tenets – the need to harness US nuclear weapons to Europe – is open to considerable discussion. Orthodox diplomacy suggests a round of quiet governmental consultations preceding discussions in the NATO Nuclear Planning Group and NATO Council. But orthodox approaches may not suit unorthodox demands, and a British government might get more political mileage by publicizing its requirements as widely as possible and stressing its own commitment to act unilaterally, thus mobilizing opposition, peace movement or other forms of public pressure, even though this would also mobilize the political forces committed to retaining nuclear weapons and bases in Europe. Those who lobby for nuclear weapons are usually well equipped to work behind the scenes of government, while their opponents seldom have any option but to rely on popular pressure. But a public strategy need not exclude detailed consultation and negotiation.

The other, related, question is the scope of the demands made on NATO and the timetable attached to them. Here again there are two kinds of approach: to tailor demands to what might be acceptable initially to a broad range of political and military interests within a timetable which takes account of bureaucratic inertia and the slowness of NATO decision-making; or to make all-out demands in a tight timetable geared to the fact that British governments can only rely on about four and a half years in office. The first approach risks compromising too far with existing orthodoxy, failing to produce a momentum for change, and ending in the erosion of the government's non-nuclear commitments. The second risks presenting such impossible demands that the government loses all credibility and alienates the much-needed middle ground of opinion. How to steer between these two dangers and present a coherent set of policy proposals is discussed in detail in Chapter Four.

The most important NATO partner is, of course, the United States. Giving up British nuclear weapons would not in itself arouse anger influence in Washington. Indeed, it would probably be discreetly welcomed as removing the risk of the USA being forced into a nuclear war by an intransigent nuclear ally, and would help simplify nuclear calculations between Washington and Moscow. Cancellation of Trident might be a minor irritant, but could hardly be very significant to the US government.

However, requiring removal of US bases would almost certainly trigger a strongly hostile reaction, even if it can be argued that technological developments are removing the need for the Holy Loch facilities for Poseidon submarines. Any restriction on the use of the US base on the British-owned island of Diego Garcia in the Indian Ocean – a base which is probably designated for the Rapid Deployment Force – might be strongly resented. There would be a much more direct impact on the United States' nuclear capacity if the British government took over Fylingdales early warning system and restricted to conventional use the Brawdy submarine tracking station – steps which would be consistent with a total decoupling of Britain from reliance on US nuclear forces.

US reactions to pressure on NATO to move away from a nuclear war-fighting strategy would probably be mixed. Influential voices, including those of Robert McNamara and McGeorge Bundy, have argued for a Western 'no-first-use' commitment. Public opinion poll evidence suggests that most Americans do not want to risk an all-out nuclear war with the USSR by starting a nuclear exchange in Europe, but at present public fears do not translate into an effective lobby on this issue. A Democratic Administration would probably be more sympathetic to the case for reducing NATO dependence on nuclear weapons, but is still likely to be suspicious of a non-nuclear British government.

The reaction in Washington to Britain pursuing non-nuclear policies would not depend solely on the strategic impact of British moves, but also on the political symbolism and fear of further repercussions. The US government has automatic hostility to manifestations of 'neutralism' and 'pacifism' in Europe, and distrusts left-wing governments. It is also concerned that the example of countries which adopt anti-nuclear policies might spread. An interesting instance has been the strong pressure brought to bear on New Zealand in February 1985 for the relatively minor gesture of refusing to allow ships carrying nuclear weapons to use its ports. Washington orchestrated public attacks on New Zealand for breaching the Anzus Treaty (a claim which was not legally correct) and publicly threatened to withdraw military support or impose economic sanctions. The Administration seems to have reacted strongly in order to frighten off any other ally which might be inclined to become too independent. One dimension to the US response may have been concern about Belgium and the Netherlands fulfilling their commitment to take cruise missiles. Probably even more crucial was concern about Japan following the New Zealand example over nuclear-armed ships, and fear that the idea of a Pacific nuclear-free zone might gain ground. Washington's instinct might therefore be to demonstrate its unwillingness to tolerate non-nuclear moves by Britain, even though it did accept French withdrawal from NATO's integrated military command and rejection of US army bases in the mid-1960s.[7]

In the USA there is a constituency of liberal Congressmen, arms control and world order institutes, the Freeze Movement, and some church groups which would respond favourably to some non-nuclear actions by Britain, and who would argue the value of the United States retreating from some of its global commitments and limiting its nuclear arsenal and strategy. In time this constituency could be strengthened considerably by nuclear disarmament in Europe, but it is unlikely to have much direct influence on US government reactions, though it might moderate their severity. A British government committed to independent nuclear disarmament could therefore not expect to be listened to with great sympathy in Washington, and the normal cordiality of relations would be disrupted. Some of the practical manifestations of the 'special relationship', such as close cooperation in intelligence gathering and naval links via the NATO Channel Command Headquarters at Northwood, are also likely to be disturbed, but then a government which espoused dealignment might deliberately break these links. Whether economic ties between the two countries would be eroded outside the defence field is less clear: but in any case Britain's trading relationship with Western Europe is today a far more important factor than that with the USA.

As Britain would be likely to lose the leverage it has acquired as the United States' most reliable ally, remaining in NATO, at least for a few years, should be an advantage. It may mitigate the strength of US reactions to its non-nuclear stance, and give Britain some protection against overt US moves to destabilize a non-nuclear government. More positively, Britain might be able to exert influence via NATO which it could not exert alone, provided it found some real support in Europe. But it should not be assumed that a non-nuclear Britain would lose all its influence in Washington. An unreliable ally, likely to make awkward terms, may have to be heeded more seriously than a reliable one, so long as the USA sees any reason to maintain some kind of alliance. There is no reason why British diplomacy should be deliberately awkward; indeed there are strong reasons for taking reasonable notice of US difficulties when setting a timetable for withdrawal of bases, and stressing the advantages to the United States of nuclear disengagement from Europe. But it is prudent to assume that Britain should look for friends in Europe and elsewhere to counterbalance the probable hostility of Washington.

The most important European member of NATO, and the country which would have a decisive effect on how non-nuclear proposals might be received, is West Germany. If there were a Social Democratic government, which maintained present SPD commitments to alter NATO strategy, in power before a non-nuclear government was returned in Britain, the West Germans might already be raising the no-first-use issue and suggesting moves towards a non-provocative conventional defence strategy. But a Christian Democratic government in Bonn might strongly oppose moves to change NATO's reliance on nuclear weapons. The Scandinavian NATO countries, the Netherlands and Belgium might well respond favourably to such moves, even with predominantly conservative governments in power, though they might hesitate to alienate the USA too far. Canada, which adopted a formally non-nuclear position within NATO in 1969, modified in practice by US pressure, might give Britain support.

6. BRITISH LEVERAGE IN EUROPEAN ORGANIZATIONS

While the reception of British proposals to move towards a non-nuclear NATO strategy in Europe is uncertain, there are other European bodies within which Britain might be able to promote non-proliferation of nuclear weapons, encourage various measures of disarmament, and advocate a more independent political stance for Europe. The three predominantly West European organizations which represent political and economic interests, and are not so far involved in defence matters, are the European Economic Community, the Council of Europe and the Organization for Economic Cooperation and Development. Of these, the EEC is by far the most important, and also the most in danger of being conscripted as an economic arm of NATO.

The European Economic Community

Because of the overlap between EEC and NATO membership there have been a number of attempts to use the Community as a forum for defence planning and cooperation. After Mrs Thatcher's election in 1979 the British government put pressure on the EEC to promote collaboration in military procurement through the Community, a move opposed by Eire and Denmark. Political debates during 1984 calling for a stronger European pillar in NATO nominated the EEC, as well as the moribund West European Union set up explicitly for defence purposes, as a possible vehicle for West European military coordination; and early in 1985 EEC involvement in research connected with the SDI programme was proposed by some West European leaders. Therefore, although in practice the EEC has avoided direct linkage with NATO, or with proposals for a West European initiative on military cooperation, the pressure may grow. A British government committed to the long-term goals of arms reduction and European dealignment should clearly resist such pressures and block attempts to make the EEC an arm of NATO.[8]

The most important political question about the European Community is whether it can develop economic cooperation with Eastern Europe and the Soviet Union and so moderate the division of Europe, or whether it will become a more tightly integrated economic and political bloc with aspirations towards West European superpower status and military potential. During the early 1960s the Soviet Union displayed strong hostility to the EEC and some Europeans did look to a West European political federation. But by the 1970s, as part of the process of European détente, EEC countries were developing close economic ties with East European members of Comecon and with the Soviet Union itself, and Soviet opposition to the Community had been abandoned. The expansion of Community membership also effectively curbed the possibility of closer political union in the immediate future.

There are conflicting tendencies within the EEC. Moves towards closer Franco-German cooperation and the creation of an inner group, and the Italian initiative in 1985 to abolish the veto on the EEC Council and promote greater political unity, point to a greater integration. But the admission of Spain and Portugal in 1985 and the independent attitudes of Greece and of Britain itself, suggest that national interests are too diverse to allow the Community to become a unified power bloc. However, since the early 1970s it has evolved a form of consultation and cooperation in foreign policy which has begun to give it a distinctive voice, and this role could be developed. The EEC also has close ties with non-aligned European countries and economic links with a wide range of developing countries, and it does, therefore, have the potential to promote a policy of dealignment.

How much influence Britain now has in the European Community is perhaps open to differing interpretation. Reluctance to join, followed by a continuing ambivalence about membership and protracted haggling over budget contributions, have not accumulated a great deal of goodwill for Britain. This does not much matter when the main aim is to accrue maximum economic benefits from the Community's internal policies, and when all governments are driving hard bargains. Despite economic weakness Britain is still one of the more important members, with the power to assist or hinder the EEC in its goals. But if a future British government has more far-reaching aims in the EEC – for example to achieve a new Lomé Agreement with Third World countries on terms more favourable to them than in the previous Lomé Convention – it would require active support from other countries, not simply the power of veto and the sanction of withholding budget contributions or refusing to accept EEC regulations. In the past Britain has taken positive initiatives: a Labour government played a part in creating the Lomé Convention of 1975, which, though it remains controversial, has been widely interpreted as an improvement on previous EEC relations with the Third World.[9] To do so in the future Britain may need to show more positive commitment to the Community than it has so far. Whether or not this would be possible depends considerably on domestic economic policies and EEC attitudes to them. However, as suggested earlier, the political reassessment involved in nuclear disarmament might well tend to bind Britain more closely to Western Europe than in the past.

The Council of Europe
The Council of Europe was founded in 1949, the same year as NATO, but its emphasis has been political, legal and social rather than military. It was created at a time of enthusiasm for European unity, but Britain helped to block ambitious political goals. Sweden and Eire were among the ten original members, so it always included neutral countries, and upholding the principles of parliamentary democracy was one of its founding principles. This is a principle which the Council has taken seriously, unlike NATO which has never shown much concern about the dictatorships among its members. The Council of Europe expelled the Greece of the Colonels, and has debated the status of Turkey since the military takeover. The European

Convention on Human Rights was signed under the Council's aegis in 1950, and concern for human rights has been prominent in Council discussions. It has also been a forum for foreign policy debates, for example on the European Common Security Conference and the Arab-Israeli conflict. Therefore, although the Council of Europe cannot be regarded as an effective or, with the exception of the Human Rights Commission and Court, very significant body, it could be a helpful forum for a British government concerned to explore political alternatives in Europe. In fact, the West German government has already urged that the Council should act as a bridge between a divided Europe.

The Organization for Economic Cooperation and Development
This arose out of the moves in the late 1940s to promote European cooperation in order to receive Marshall Aid from the USA. Britain prevented it from becoming a vehicle for European economic unification, and later British attempts to promote it as a less ambitious alternative to the European Community were opposed by governments committed to the idea of the Treaty of Rome. The OECD has therefore played a rather minor role as a body concerned with economic issues. It has a wider membership than the EEC, including the European neutrals Austria, Finland, Sweden and Switzerland; and when it was recast in 1961 it was extended to North America. It is therefore one forum for discussion with the USA. Discussions in the OECD in the past ten years have concerned themselves with Soviet bloc countries and the Third World debt problem, as well as obvious issues such as oil, energy supplies, unemployment, inflation and trade. It could therefore be a useful consultative body for policy initiatives. Britain does not seem to have particular leverage, or any special disadvantages, in the OECD.

7. OTHER SOURCES OF FOREIGN POLICY INFLUENCE

The one organization in which Britain has a unique role as a European state is, of course, the Commonwealth. The earlier economic basis of unity, the system of Commonwealth preference which encouraged close trading links with Britain, has been ended by British EEC membership. What remains is a connection based on the British Empire. The way Britain has operated its immigration system since the early 1960s has underlined the gap between the old white Commonwealth and the newer Asian, African and Caribbean members, and diverse regional and ideological interests are exposed at the Commonwealth conferences.

Nevertheless, the very diversity of the Commonwealth is a potential advantage. It is a body within which Britain could explore such issues as non-proliferation and curbing the arms trade. It is also an obvious forum for discussion of North-South economic relations, though at New Delhi in 1983 Mrs Thatcher vetoed proposals for a conference to lead to a new international economic order. If there were agreement within the Commonwealth on particular issues it could be an organization capable of supplying its own peacekeeping forces on occasion, as Secretary-General Ramphal suggested in relation to Grenada. Commonwealth conferences have not usually had significant results – with the exception of the Lusaka Conference which opened the way to the independence of Zimbabwe – but they do bring together heads of government and attract some attention. Britain clearly can play a major role in the Commonwealth, and a government committed to nuclear disarmament and dealignment would be much closer to most of the other governments than has been the case in the past.

The Commonwealth could be a useful basis for mobilizing votes in the United Nations on certain issues. While the value of UN General Assembly resolutions is often limited, a British government committed to promoting measures of disarmament and enhancing respect for international law would have to be active in the available United Nations bodies. Britain's permanent seat on the Security Council could be particularly important in trying to promote the UN's peacekeeping role during crises, and in possible moves to change the procedures of the Security Council itself. At present the five permanent Security Council members all happen to be nuclear powers. There would be advantages in one of them having a non-nuclear status and perhaps even greater advantages in Britain moving towards independence of the USA in Security Council debates and votes.

The position of both Britain and France in the Council is due to their great power status at the end of World War II, but it is an historically created precedent which no state is now likely to challenge, and a non-nuclear British government could make good use of this diplomatic advantage.

It would, however, be a mistake to place too much emphasis on the organizational levers available to British diplomacy and ignore the role of cooperation or negotiation with individual countries. As Sir Geoffrey Howe's diplomacy towards certain East European countries has demonstrated, this currently plays quite an important role. A non-nuclear Britain could do a good deal by working with governments committed to nuclear-weapons-free zones, such as New Zealand, or with a record of taking initiatives in disarmament, such as Canada or Sweden. Britain could also oppose interventionist US policies in Central America by protests to Washington and by diplomatic and economic support for governments which claim reasonable democratic legitimacy and are being destabilized by the US Administration. A non-nuclear Britain would certainly need to engage in intensive diplomacy with the Soviet Union and East European countries, explaining its own measures and goals and encouraging political and arms-limitation responses to British or Western moves.

There may also be scope for more imaginative diplomatic and economic links with countries or regions not tied to Britain by any particular organizational connection. One interesting possibility is closer political cooperation between Japan and Western Europe, since Japan is a major economic power, and economic rival, and is closely bound to the USA. The Pacific is becoming the focus of a dangerous new nuclear and conventional arms race between the United States and the Soviet Union, with both China and Japan being drawn in. Although Japan is now arming itself more heavily, it inherits a commitment from the end of World War II to deploy military forces for defensive purposes only. As the country where the atomic bomb was used it also inherits an abhorrence of nuclear weapons, though the strength of anti-nuclear feeling is beginning to wane. Western European dealignment might encourage a similar move from

Japan, and political cooperation might be increased by institutionalizing consultative procedures, perhaps via a special secretariat.[10] Britain could take the initiative in establishing this kind of consultation.

Unilateral nuclear disarmament should put Britain in a much stronger position to pursue arms limitation or disarmament. Britain has a seat in all the existing multilateral forums that are negotiating arms control or disarmament measures: the forty-nation Conference on Disarmament meeting in Geneva; the thirty-five-nation Conference on Security and Cooperation in Europe that has existed since 1973 as part of the Helsinki process; the eleven-nation Mutual Balanced Force Reduction (MBFR) talks that began in Vienna in 1973; and the General Assembly of the United Nations. None of these bodies can achieve much unless the major participants have some real interest in an agreement. For example, as there has never been serious commitment by either the Warsaw Pact or NATO to reduce troop levels, the MBFR talks have remained ritualistic. In the 1970s the Helsinki process did play a considerable role in promoting European détente, but during the 1980s it has been bogged down in the antagonisms between the Soviet bloc and the West, though its offshoot the Stockholm Conference agreed to strengthen the confidence building measures first adopted in 1975. Strong pressure by Britain to alter NATO's nuclear and conventional strategy would, however, shift the political and military context in which these negotiations are taking place and might, in some circumstances, infuse new life into them. The Geneva Conference on Disarmament has been the focus of some serious negotiations, and has made significant progress on the detail of a treaty to ban chemical weapons. It is on this issue that the British government has played a most consistently constructive role.

If Britain gave up its own nuclear weapons, it would clearly try to maximize the value of this step in order to strengthen the Non-Proliferation Treaty (NPT) and encourage nuclear limitation by the superpowers. The immediate forum for the NPT is the five-yearly conference provided for under the 1968 Treaty. Britain could demonstrate its commitment by accepting more stringent international safeguards on its own civilian nuclear energy programme, and by taking steps to strengthen international inspection. Independent British action could be more potent than diplomacy in putting nuclear disarmament back on the international agenda. Britain would also be fulfilling Article VI of the NPT, which calls on the nuclear powers to reduce their arsenals, and might encourage renewed pressure on the USA and USSR to negotiate a comprehensive test ban. These possibilities are explored in detail in Chapter Seven.

8. WHAT BRITAIN OUT OF NATO MIGHT DO

So far the discussion of how a non-nuclear Britain might influence events has assumed that it would stay in NATO, though moving towards a position more independent of the USA. It has also assumed that Britain might find significant support in the Alliance for moving towards a non-nuclear strategy. If, however, the United States were implacably hostile, the result might be the break-up of NATO and the formation of a new, independent European defence association. If, on the other hand, key West European countries were also opposed to altering NATO's nuclear strategy, a British government that was serious about its non-nuclear commitments would have to leave the Alliance. Britain would then become non-aligned, which would mean a major break with the beliefs and policies of the last forty years.

Leaving NATO could, of course, be the chosen policy of a government committed to nuclear disarmament, on the grounds that it is the most clear-cut and consistent policy, both morally and politically, for a country that wishes to disentangle itself from reliance on US nuclear weapons and distance itself from US military and foreign policy. Many supporters of British unilateralism favour British non-alignment, and some Commission members took this position in our first report. But whether Britain left NATO as a preferred and deliberate policy or as a fall-back position if it were impossible to change NATO from within, the government would face some of the same choices about its foreign and defence policies.

In principle Britain would have a choice between neutrality and non-alignment. The former was evolved in Europe as a policy appropriate to small nations, and was respected as a legal as well as a diplomatic stance in the 19th century. Neutrality denotes a withdrawal from international commitments, and self-reliance – especially in national defence. Non-alignment, or positive neutralism, is associated with the rise of Third World countries since 1945 whose declared aim was to avoid involvement in the Cold War.[11] Non-alignment implies an active role in bodies like the United Nations, in disarmament talks and in peace-keeping, but less concern with legal status. In practice these distinctions are over-simple. Switzerland, for example, has a long tradition of successful neutrality, but demonstrates that it is compatible with playing a constructive role through hosting international bodies and negotiations and promoting humanitarian aid in war. Switzerland's international banking role may also underpin the legal and military defences of its neutrality. Nevertheless the concept of neutrality does imply greater isolation.

In Britain a policy of neutrality does have some potential appeal for groups on both the right and left of the political spectrum.[12] On the other hand it is a policy of limited efficacy in the nuclear age, when security must ultimately depend on preserving world peace. For Britain neutrality would also involve abandoning the international role that it has seen itself playing, and would require strict, and possibly unacceptable, conditions of non-involvement in international organizations: for example, withdrawal from the European Community. A more positive policy, of the kind usually labelled 'non-aligned', would therefore seem a more appropriate choice for a non-nuclear Britain, though this does not necessarily imply formal membership of the non-aligned group of nations. The most obvious model for a non-aligned foreign policy, and one which might influence Britain, is that of Sweden, which was for a long time a traditional European neutral but has moved, since the 1960s, towards a policy much closer to non-alignment. Sweden has played an active role in disarmament negotiations, been a frequent contributor of troops to UN peacekeeping forces, and shown concern about such problems as refugees (to whom it has given generous sanctuary) and Third World development. Sweden has also felt free to criticize the superpowers for military intervention in other countries and to promote the general principle of non-alignment. Of course, there have been some fluctuations and changes in the nuances of Swedish foreign policy, but since the early 1960s it has been a clearly non-aligned country which leans politically towards the West but is independent of the United States.

Non-alignment would require fundamental reconstruction of British defence policy. The Commission's previous report examined the defence arrangements of three European neutrals – Sweden, Switzerland and Yugoslavia – and concluded that Sweden came closest to providing a suitable model for Britain, although Britain's much larger population and the preferences of its professional armed forces might make conscription unnecessary.[13] Different force levels could be envisaged for a non-nuclear and non-aligned Britain, but the guiding concepts for a re-structured defence should be the ability to inflict a 'high entry price' on an attacker, and the adoption of a purely defensive stance in weapons deployment. The purpose of a strictly defensive strategy of the kind adopted by Sweden, Switzerland and Yugoslavia is to make clear that the country has no offensive intent and so reduce the danger of war through mutual preemption in a crisis, while at the same time demonstrating the resolve to defend tenaciously one's territory.

Discussion of British neutralism or non-alignment often assumes that if Britain withdrew NATO wuld remain in being – which is possible, particularly as, in practice, France under President Mitterrand has almost returned to the NATO fold. However, British withdrawal might be such a shock to the Alliance that it would split up – because the USA turned away from Europe in anger, or because several countries, already unhappy about NATO's nuclear strategy and US policies, also left, or because West Germany decided to seek new security arrangements. It is possible to imagine a number of different developments if NATO did dissolve – some promising to the cause of peace in Europe, others very dangerous. But whatever the outcome, Britain might find itself involved in new political or military groupings, and would not necessarily pursue an independent, non-aligned path. These possibilities are explored further in Chapter Six.

A non-aligned Britain would probably pursue diplomatic policies very similar to those which might be evolved by a government that promoted nuclear disarmament and dealignment from within NATO. But a Britain out of NATO could, of course, oppose US strategies or actions more forthrightly, and it would not be under the same pressures to compromise its criticisms or goals. On the other hand, its diplomatic leverage in Washington would be very limited – indeed it might be a target for extreme hostility – and relations with European governments still strongly committed to NATO would initially be poor. A non-aligned Britain would probably remain in all European organizations except NATO; there could be doubt about EEC membership, but unless the Community became more closely involved in military policies Britain, like Eire, could be a non-aligned member.

Much of the impact of a non-aligned Britain would not come from official diplomacy but from the pressure it put on other governments to adjust to a change in the European balance of power. British non-alignment would also be a potent example to other governments, to opposition parties and to peace movements as well as public opinion in other countries already opposed to aspects of Western nuclear strategy. New Zealand's refusal to allow nuclear-armed US ships to use its ports has shown how quite a modest gesture may have worldwide impact. A British government that required the United States to remove all its nuclear bases would have a much more significant impact in Europe and elsewhere, even if it stayed in NATO. But the uncompromising and dramatic nature of total non-alignment would have particularly strong reverberations throughout the world.

3. Background to security problems in Europe

1. INTRODUCTION

The purpose of this report is to explore ways of resolving the security and political problems facing Europe today. But before we think about the future, we need to understand how these problems arose at the end of World War II and to evaluate progress made in reducing them during the period of détente in the 1970s.

Our reason for analysing the events that led to the division of Europe and the Cold War is to clarify why the West felt under threat from the Soviet Union and to examine the Western responses. There are three questions underlying this historical analysis. Firstly, was the political and military division of Europe inevitable? Secondly, were these Western responses always appropriate? Finally, what lessons can be learned for the future in Western relations with the USSR?

But although it is necessary to understand the causes of the division of Europe (especially as a younger generation now has no memory of this period), lessons drawn from the post-war period have to be interpreted in the light of changes in the West and in the domestic and the international position of the Soviet Union since the death of Stalin.

The détente process of the 1970s resolved some of the political problems outstanding from World War II, improved East-West relations and saw the development of new economic and political ties between the two halves of Europe. But it left two basic problems in Europe unresolved. First, it did not alter the basic military confrontation between NATO and the Warsaw Pact, and this was one major cause of the breakdown of détente after 1979, as the deployment of new Euro missiles by both sides became a key issue. Second, it brought about no major change in the relationship between the great powers and their respective spheres of influence in Europe. Chapter One examined the diverging interests between Western Europe and the USA. The conflicts inherent in the Soviet role in Eastern Europe were demonstrated when the Soviet Union brought pressure to bear on the Polish government to suppress Solidarity. The declaration of martial law in 1981 impinged directly on East-West relations and increased the difficulties of restoring détente.

A lasting peace in Europe, then, will require significant measures of nuclear disarmament and military disengagement but also changes at the political level. In this chapter we re-examine some of the proposals for military disengagement and the creation of nuclear-weapon-free zones which were put forward in the 1950s and are arousing renewed interest today. Although the position has changed since the 1950s, it is useful to examine the ideas, possibilities and problems of that time as a prelude to assessing their relevance today. In a later chapter we consider in greater depth the major political problems that underlie the division of the continent.

Interpreting the Cold War

No account of the division of Europe after World War II and the rise of the Cold War can fail to be controversial, and nor can this summary analysis do justice to the complexity of the issues involved. These issues are at the heart of an historical and political debate which, if anything, became more intense as East-West relations deteriorated in the late 1970s and early 1980s, and gave rise to what is sometimes dubbed the 'New Cold War'.

'Traditionalist' historians, especially those writing in the late 1940s and during the 1950s, accepted, by and large, the Western account of the origins of the Cold War, attributing it to Stalin's expansionist ambitions in the post-war period and regarding Western actions, such as the institution of the Marshall Plan and the creation of NATO, as necessary defensive measures. This view was increasingly challenged from the 1960s onwards by the 'revisionist' historians on the left, partly in response to the US war in Vietnam and other US military and subversive interventions in the Third World which lent weight to the view that capitalist powers were intrinsically expansionist. For the revisionists, therefore, it was largely the West, and in particular the USA, which had nurtured expansionist ambitions in the post-war period and the Soviet Union which had reacted to aggressive Western moves in a defensive manner – even if some of these reactions took extreme and repressive forms.[1]

Some more recent accounts have struck a different balance, acknowledging the contribution of the revisionist historians, particularly to our understanding of the economic motives on the Western side, but maintaining that there were genuine and perhaps justifiable fears of Stalin's intentions that must be taken into account in evaluating Western policies.[2]

We focus here on the Soviet role in creating the Cold War and the Western response because we are concerned with the nature and correctness of the rationale behind Western defence policy. But this does not mean that we believe that Western policies were merely reactive. Western countries also sought strategic, economic and political advantages, at times in disregard of the democratic principles to which they were formally committed.

The European colonial powers, for instance, attempted in most cases to re-establish control by force over the parts of their empires lost during World War II.[3] Both the Truman and Eisenhower Administrations were frequently critical of the colonial policies of West European states, though from a mixture of motives, including concern to extend US influence. Occasionally the USA took action to halt colonialist intervention – as for instance in 1949 when it suspended Marshall Aid to Holland as a sanction against its continuing use of force in Indonesia. Its opposition to French policies in North Africa, and to the Anglo-French aggression against Egypt at the time of Suez, led to bitter rows and contributed to France's disenchantment with NATO and the eventual decision to withdraw from its military command structure. Yet the USA continued to maintain its own sphere of influence in Central and South America and in 1954 intervened militarily in Guatemala to secure the overthrow of the freely elected and moderately reforming Arbenz government. In the same year it also began to involve itself in South Vietnam.

In Europe too, US motives were mixed, and its policies were partly designed to ensure its influence in Western Europe. US leaders were disturbed by the strongly leftward swing of European politics in the immediate post-war period and alarmed at the strength of communist parties in several countries, France and Italy especially, and their participation in post-war coalition governments. Here too more was at issue than the fear that these communist parties would provide the basis for an extension of Soviet power; US influence and interests would also be affected by a strongly socialist Europe, however independent of the Soviet Union. During the liberation of Italy, for instance, US and British forces sought systematically to undermine the position of the left: Workers' Councils were disbanded, factory managers were encouraged to re-assert their authority, and local committees of liberation, invariably leftist, were replaced by military government for a few months.[4] Later, in 1948, the US made it clear in the run-up to the Italian elections that there would be no further economic aid if a Socialist-Communist government came to power.[5]

Economic considerations also influenced US policies, even if this factor is overstated in some revisionist accounts. Direct US interests in Eastern Europe, for instance, were small; but the USA was concerned to ensure the free exchange of goods between Eastern and Western Europe because without this the Western European economies, which were important for the US, might stagnate or face severe crisis. Outside Europe, the economic factor in the shape of oil was important to both the USA and the Soviet Union in the Iran crisis in March-April 1946. During the war the US government worked closely with US companies to gain oil concessions in the Middle East. Thus US insistence that Soviet forces withdraw from northern Iran in March 1946 in accordance with a wartime agreement[6] was motivated not only by alarm that the Soviet Union might renege on its previous undertaking to withdraw and might set up a client state in Northern Iran, but also by the wish to secure an Iranian oil concession for itself and to prevent threats to other US interests in the Middle East, particularly in Saudi Arabia.

2. STALIN AND THE FIRST COLD WAR

Stalin was, in one sense at least, expansionist. He was determined to incorporate into the USSR the Baltic states and Eastern

Poland (annexed during the Nazi-Soviet Pact), thereby substantially restoring the European boundaries of the Tsarist Empire as they had existed at the outset of World War I. The Soviet Union also acquired territory at the expense of Romania and Czechoslovakia, as well as part of the Finnish territory occupied in the Winter War of 1939. In addition it divided up the former German Baltic province of East Prussia between itself and Poland, and, in the Far East, incorporated into the USSR the Kurile Islands and Southern Sakhalin, territories which had been the subject of a long-standing dispute between Russia and Japan but which had been in Japanese possession since the Russo-Japanese war of 1904-5.

Nevertheless, it was not these territorial acquisitions which chiefly aroused fears of Soviet expansionism. In fact, at the Yalta conference in February 1945, Churchill and Roosevelt were prepared to cede Eastern Poland to the Soviet Union and in compensation to see Poland's western frontier expanded at the expense of Germany; they also agreed that the Kurile Islands and South Sakhalin should be ceded to the Soviet Union. Nor did they make an issue of the Baltic states, though they withheld final agreement to their incorporation by the Soviet Union.

The quarrel between East and West at the end of the war focused on two issues: first, the nature and extent of Soviet control of Eastern Europe, particularly in Poland, which figured prominently in the Yalta discussions; second, the future of Germany, to which attention mainly shifted in the immediate post-war period. However, Western anxieties were also aroused by a number of other Soviet claims and demands – territory at the expense of Norway (Spitzbergen and Bear Island), joint fortifications with Turkey in the Dardanelles, and Soviet trusteeship of Libya.[7] In fact the first major East-West showdown after the war was the Iran crisis.

To some extent both sides were motivated by security considerations and a determination not to repeat the mistakes of the 1930s. The Soviet Union would take whatever steps it considered necessary, including the use of political intimidation and manipulation in key East European countries, to avoid being vulnerable to attack from the West and to prevent the resurgence of a powerful German state. The Western powers were haunted by the spectre of Munich and feared allowing a totalitarian state again to make a series of incremental gains until it could dominate the European continent and threaten world peace.

However, this explanation, though necessary, is inadequate. Security concerns, however genuine, do not justify steps which put the security of other countries at risk or deny their fundamental political and human rights. Neither do they fully explain the actions and reactions of either side. Calculations of political, strategic and economic advantage also played a role. Ideology too was important, and continues to be so, however much ideological imperatives may be modified in particular instances by more immediate security concerns. The Soviet leaders saw themselves as engaged in a struggle with an inevitably hostile global capitalist system and this coloured their view of Western actions. Similarly, the United States viewed with suspicion the power of the left in European politics after the war and used its influence to end communist participation in post-war coalition governments.

Stalin's policies in the post-war period were characterized by a mixture of ruthlessness and caution. The ruthlessness had already found expression in the terror of the 1930s, in the mass deportations from Eastern Poland after August 1939, and in the other deportations of whole peoples within the Soviet Union in the latter part of the war. It was George Kennan's first-hand experience of this ruthlessness while serving with the US Embassy in the Soviet Union in the 1930s that led him to take an extremely pessimistic view of the possibilities of accommodation with Stalin after the war – and his views in turn were to strongly influence the Truman Administration.

Predictably, as US-Soviet relations deteriorated during 1946, the Soviet Union strengthened its control over Eastern Europe. In Hungary, for instance, from July 1946 onwards the Soviet Union intervened more and more directly in political life, demanding the resignation of some members of the National Assembly, measures against the Catholic Church and the dissolution of numerous organizations. By May of the following year the Premier, Ferenc Nagy of the Peasant Party, and his Foreign Minister Gyongyosi, were forced to resign as a result of Soviet and Communist Party pressure and were replaced by other smallholders subservient to Moscow's wishes.[8]

The political options in both Eastern and Western Europe narrowed still further from 1947 onwards when the Cold War began in earnest with the announcement of the Truman Doctrine in March 1947 and the Marshall Aid plan in July. On the Eastern side came the formation of the Cominform which coordinated, under Soviet leadership, the activities of the communist parties of Eastern Europe, France and Italy.

In the West, communists were forced out of coalition governments not only in Italy and Belgium, where they had received a substantial share of the vote in the post-war elections, but also in France where they were the largest single party in the Parliament – though without an overall majority. In Eastern Europe, the persecution of peasant and non-communist groupings was intensified. In Romania there was a wave of arrests including that of the Peasant Party leader Maniu who was sentenced to life imprisonment for conspiring with British and US agents to overthrow the government – a charge the substance of which remains in doubt. In Bulgaria, in April, shortly after the US Senate had ratified the Peace Treaty with that country, Petkov, leader of the Agrarian Party, which had polled almost a quarter of the votes in the 1946 election, was arrested and hanged. In Poland, in October, the Peasant Party leader Mikolajczyk, fearing for his life, fled the country. By March 1948, when communists seized power in Czechoslovakia, communist governments were firmly in control throughout Eastern Europe.

However, the split with Yugoslavia in mid-1948 was a clear warning that a communist government would not automatically toe the Soviet line, even in Eastern Europe. Stalin responded in two ways: by taking action against Tito, and by a series of purges throughout Eastern Europe aimed at eliminating all communists whose absolute commitment to Moscow was in any way suspect. Yugoslavia was expelled from the Cominform, and Tito subjected to a campaign of fanatical vilification, particularly during the trials of leading communists in Eastern bloc countries from 1949 onwards. Stalin's agents also plotted, though unsuccessfully, with elements in Yugoslavia, including high-ranking military officers, to secure Tito's overthrow.[9]

The purges in Eastern Europe lasted from 1949 to Stalin's death in March 1953 and did not spare those in the highest ranks of the communist parties and governments – starting with the former Hungarian Foreign Minister Laszio Rajk (sentenced to death in September 1949), Vice-Premier Kostov in Bulgaria (sentenced to death in December 1949 after unmasking the whole charade by withdrawing his 'confession' during the trial) and, some years later, the First Secretary of the Czechoslovak Communist Party, Slansky, who was executed with other leading Czech and Slovak communists in 1952. In Poland, Gomulka, First Secretary of the Polish United Workers' Party, was arrested and tortured but never brought to trial. One of the most terrifying aspects of these purges was the way in which most of the accused went into the dock and mechanically confessed to absurd and impossible crimes. Later, following Khrushchev's denunciation of Stalin at the 20th Congress of the Soviet Communist Party, it was acknowledged that, overwhelmingly, the charges had been groundless and the confessions extorted under physical and psychological torture.

The scope of the persecution was extensive, affecting both communists and non communists. In Czechoslovakia government investigations during the Prague Spring of 1968 revealed that the period of the purges 136 thousand people, out of a population of 12 million had been executed, imprisoned or interned.[10] Much earlier, however, mass deportations had taken place throughout Eastern Europe and the Baltic States during 1944–45;[11] in Hungary during this period an estimated 600,000 people were deported to Siberia.[12]

Nevertheless, there was also caution in Stalin's foreign policy. This expressed itself in an unwillingness to risk a direct confrontation with the West or even to give support to revolutionary movements where the vital interests of the West were judged to be at stake but Soviet interests were more marginal. Stalin refused to support Communist guerrillas in Greece, and advised the Chinese Communists to seek accommodation with the Kuomintang regime. When challenged by the West over the continued Soviet presence in Northern Iran, the Soviet Union withdrew, and it did not press claims for territorial concessions from Turkey or Norway, or for control of Libya. In Finland, where the threat to Soviet security from adjacent states was minimal, it was even prepared to conclude a treaty on relatively liberal terms.

In retrospect it is clear that in the post-war period the Soviet Union pursued a variety of goals of which some, as one would expect, were accorded greater priority than others. With regard specifically to Soviet expansionism, the considerations that appear to have influenced Stalin's thinking were the proximity of a country to the Soviet Union, its strategic importance for Soviet security, Soviet ability to ensure a favourable political outcome, notably through the presence of the Red Army, and the degree of Western interest in an area – and hence the likelihood of provoking a reaction that could put more essential goals in jeopardy.[13]

This implies that certain key aspects of Soviet policy were non-negotiable but others might have been influenced by diplomacy and bargaining, and by the overall state of international relations. The critical mistake of the Western, and especially the post-Roosevelt US, approach was that after a period of debate and uncertainty it settled for a view of the Soviet Union that virtually discounted the role of diplomacy and the possibility of accommodation.[14] And of course, as the battle-lines were drawn from mid-1947 onwards, the Soviet Union increasingly acted in just the ruthless and inflexible way that the theory predicted.

The priority for the Soviet Union, once it had established its new post-war frontiers, was to strengthen its security by the establishment of compliant governments in the immediately adjacent states in East-Central Europe: Romania, Bulgaria, and, most crucial of all, Poland. The history of Polish-Russian relations had been marked by conflict and antagonism, particularly during World War II. By the end of 1944 there were two Polish governments each claiming legitimacy, the Soviet-backed Lublin government within Poland, and the strongly anti-communist Polish Government in Exile that had operated from London since the beginning of the German occupation. Moreover, it was clear that any freely-elected government would not only be non-communist but was also likely to be distinctly anti-Soviet, and for this reason the elections that had been promised as part of the Yalta agreements were continually postponed.[15]

Poland was critical in the breach that developed between East and West in the closing stages of the war. For the West, Soviet conduct in Poland was something of a test case. After all, it was the Nazi invasion of Poland in 1939 that had led France and Britain to declare war on Germany, and at Yalta the Polish question took up more time than any other single issue. Roosevelt himself, though committed to achieving a *modus vivendi* with the Soviet Union, felt constrained, at the beginning of April 1945, to send a letter of protest to Stalin about Soviet conduct in Poland and Romania.

In Hungary and Czechoslovakia, however, partly perhaps because they were considered strategically less vital, Stalin was prepared at first to pursue more liberal policies, permitting free elections and the formation of genuine coalition governments. Here it is conceivable that if the Cold War had been avoided, a Finnish-style solution might have worked. Given Soviet security concerns in East-Central Europe and the nature of the Stalin régime, however, such an outcome may not have been likely. But certainly in Czechoslovakia there were occasions when US policies under the Truman Administration had the inadvertent effect of undermining the position of the non-communist forces in that country.[16]

The second major element in Soviet post-war policy related to Germany, where the priority was to ensure that it would never again be in a position to attack the Soviet Union. But though the goal itself was not negotiable, the means of achieving it were less certain. For much of the war the Soviet Union, in line with the Western Allies, insisted that a defeated Germany should be dismembered. But after Yalta this objective was abandoned on all sides except, for some time, by France. Instead, after the Four Powers failed to reach agreement, the country was divided on the present East-West lines. Yet at least until the mid-1950s the Soviet Union did seem prepared at various times to contemplate the possibility of a reunited Germany whose neutrality would be guaranteed after the manner of Austria.

Finally there is the question of whether Stalin hoped to achieve Soviet hegemony, if not direct control, over Western Europe. It is impossible to be certain about the answer, but on two points at least there is now a fair degree of consensus among historians.

First, whatever Stalin's hopes and ambitions may have been with regard to Western Europe in the post-war period, its subjugation was not, even according to the judgement of the Soviet Union's severest critics, a priority. Indeed, every indication, from Eden's first wartime meeting with Stalin in December 1941 to the Churchill-Stalin deal in Moscow in October 1944,[17] and the Yalta agreements, suggests that, at least in the short term, Stalin was prepared to settle for US-British dominance in Western Europe in exchange for a more or less free hand in Eastern Europe. However, from mid-1947 onwards, with the Cold War now under way, Moscow was prepared to use the newly-formed instrument of the Cominform to go more on to the offensive, as was shown by the wave of strikes, under communist leadership, in France and Italy in the winter of 1947.

Second, even if Stalin hoped that a US withdrawal from Western Europe might open up an opportunity for the Soviet Union to dominate the continent, it is unlikely that he was thinking, at least initially, in terms of military conquest. The opportunity to extend Soviet influence was much more likely to come from the collapse of economic and political life in Western countries which might then provide opportunities for local communist parties to seize power.

The most solid indication that Stalin harboured an ambition to establish Soviet control over Western Europe comes from the writings of the exiled Czechoslovak historian, Karel Kaplan.[18] According to Kaplan, in January 1951 Stalin assembled the Party Secretaries and Defence Ministers from Eastern Europe at a four-day secret conference in Moscow where he outlined plans for an invasion of Western Europe in order to drive out the Americans before they consolidated their military presence on the continent. A secret document signed at the end of the conference pledged the Ministers of Defence of the various governments to place their troops under direct Soviet command in the event of war.[19]

Assuming that Kaplan's testimony is reliable, there are nonetheless difficulties in interpreting the events he describes. If Stalin had ambitions from the immediate post-war period to extend Soviet hegemony across Western Europe, what steps was he prepared to take to achieve this goal? Kaplan's evidence is consistent with the judgement that while Stalin would probe the possibilities of extending Soviet power westwards and seize suitable opportunities if they arose, he was not prepared to take any serious risks to achieve a goal which was of relatively low priority.

Stalin was certainly conscious of US military and economic strength, and its commitment to Western Europe had been convincingly demonstrated by its participation in the recent war, and in World War I. Thus it seems unlikely that he planned to engage in any direct military, or even political, assault on Western Europe, at least in the early period after the war. When Stalin ordered Yugoslavia to end its support for the communist forces in the Greek civil war, he described the USA as the most powerful state in the world and said that the US and Britain would never permit their lines of communication in the Mediterranean to be broken. How much less likely was it then that they would countenance a communist take-over in France or Italy or anywhere else in Western Europe?[20]

The meeting in Moscow in 1951, though certainly sinister, could be seen as a response to the US military build-up in Europe and an indication of the fear of an eventual US attack, rather than final proof (as Kaplan himself interprets it) that Stalin's intention all along had been to subjugate Western Europe, by subversion if possible and, if not, by direct military conquest. Kaplan does note that, according to Khrushchev's account, there was a veritable war psychosis among the Soviet leaders by this time, with Molotov making urgent phone calls from international conferences to warn the Kremlin of the imminent risk of a new world war.[21]

Clearly, however, there were genuine uncertainties and dangers in this period which have to be understood in evaluating the policies of each side. Equally clearly they increased as the Cold War produced actions and reactions which tended to confirm each side's worst images of the other.

3. The West and the Cold War

The Western Role in Military Confrontation

There were four aspects of Western post-war security policy that had a crucial impact on East-West relations. The first was its diplomatic and negotiating strategy, which in turn was linked to a critical debate on the nature of Soviet society and its regional and global ambitions. The second, stemming from an increasing emphasis on a direct Soviet *military* threat to Western Europe, was the formation of NATO. The third was the decision to make nuclear weapons the central element of Western strategy, and finally there was the integration of West Germany into the economic and military system of the West.

Diplomacy or Confrontation: the Yalta and Riga Axioms
Towards the end of the war, and in the immediate post-war period, two broad approaches towards the Soviet Union contended for supremacy among top Western policymakers, especially in the United States. The first of these, based on what the American historian Daniel Yergin has dubbed the 'Yalta Axioms', saw the Soviet Union as essentially a great power. It had genuine fears and grievances which the West ought to take all reasonable steps to assuage, as well perhaps as ambitions and designs that would have to be kept in check. But it was a power that could be negotiated with and whose policies might be modified by diplomacy and accommodation.

The second approach, based on what Yergin calls the 'Riga Axioms', saw the Soviet Union as trapped – by its past history, its ideological commitment to Marxist-Leninism, and its totalitarian system – into pursuing a path of internal repression and external expansionism.[22] The man who was to be most influential in promoting this view was George Kennan. In his famous 'long telegram' in February 1946 from Moscow to the Office of European Affairs in the State Department in Washington, Kennan depicted the Soviet Union as an implacable enemy of the West. In compensation for a 'traditional and instinctive Russian sense of insecurity', he argued, the Soviet leaders were permanently on the attack 'in patient but deadly struggle for total destruction of rival power, never in compacts and compromises with it'. Here was a 'political force committed fanatically to the beliefs that with the US there can be no permanent *modus vivendi*, that it is desirable that the internal harmony of our society be disrupted, our traditional way of life be destroyed, the international authority of our state be broken if Soviet power is to be secure.'

It was a view that allowed little, if any, role for diplomacy and the give and take of negotiation, and indeed Kennan was sharply critical of the concessions that the US Secretary of State for Foreign Affairs, James Byrnes, had been prepared to make at the Foreign Ministers' Conference in Moscow in December 1945. The West, he argued, should be drawn together in a tighter bloc by the United States: the Soviet Union, though 'impervious to logic of reason, is highly sensitive to logic of force. For this reason it can easily withdraw – and usually does – when resistance is encountered at any point.'[23]

For a variety of reasons – not least, of course, Soviet actions in Poland and Eastern Europe – it was the Riga Axioms that gradually came to dominate US policymaking in the post-war period. The death of Roosevelt in April 1945 was itself a blow to the Yalta approach. Nevertheless, even under the Truman Administration the issue remained in contention throughout 1945. Truman, for instance, despite his aggressive manner from the outset in dealing with Soviet representatives, sent Roosevelt's former personal adviser Harry Hopkins on a diplomatic mission to Moscow in May 1945, and in December 1945, James Byrnes played an important role in reaching agreement with the Soviet Union on a number of outstanding issues at the Foreign Ministers' Conference in Moscow. As Yergin observes, 'In Russia, the Yalta strategy worked. The Moscow Conference was the one moment of accommodation and compromise in the otherwise bleak history of post-war polarization.'[24] Unfortunately it was to mark the virtual end of the Yalta approach at the official US level, and Byrnes returned home not to congratulations but to recriminations, and to reproaches from Truman himself, for having gone too far in making concessions to the Soviet Union.

NATO and Western Rearmament
The second development that had an important impact on East-West relations and contributed to the militarization of the confrontation between the two sides was the signing of the Brussels Treaty in 1948 and the formation of NATO the following year.

The received wisdom today is that the formation of NATO halted Soviet expansion and thus prevented a takeover of Western Europe, and that it has kept the peace for the last forty years. As we noted above, it was understandable, given the uncertainties about Soviet intentions in the post-war period, that the Western European nations should wish to group together in a military alliance, and to associate the USA in their defence. Yet despite fears of Soviet intentions, the fact remains that in the immediate post-war period the USA and Western governments generally thought a direct Soviet military attack against Western Europe was unlikely, at least for some time. Stalin acted with extreme ruthlessness in establishing Soviet control in Eastern Europe, but there was no military expansion westwards by Soviet forces after the end of the war against Germany. On the contrary, the Soviet Union withdrew, if under pressure, from northern Iran, from parts of Finland, and later, in 1955, from Austria.

At the end of the war, the Soviet Union, like the USA, Britain and other countries, undertook a major demobilization of its forces. It remained the predominant military power on the European mainland, but the size of its total forces, and in particular of its occupation forces in Germany and Eastern Europe, was actually lower than the US Joint Chiefs of Staff (JCS) had predicted – and considered reasonable – at the end of the war.[25] By 1948 the Soviet Union was deploying half the number of divisions in Europe, and altogether 700,000 fewer ground troops than the JCS had earlier considered appropriate for Soviet security needs in the first years of occupation.[26]

It was subversion, rather than military attack, that the USA and Western governments mainly feared in the late 1940s, and the first line of defence against this was to be the Marshall Plan announced in June 1947 to ensure European economic recovery and strengthen its political stability. The plan came into operation in March 1948, more than a year before the formation of NATO. Significantly, some of those who had been most vehement in the immediate post-war period in stressing the Soviet threat, Kennan in particular, were critical of the decision to create a Western military alliance and embark on rearmament. Kennan considered it a diversion from economic problems, and feared that it would lead to the final division of Europe and Germany. He was also concerned that a preoccupation with a threat which did not exist might bring that very threat into existence.[27]

It is true that Kennan's views of the Soviet Union had shifted, and that he had become in effect one of the foremost critics of the Riga Axioms which he had previously done so much to promulgate. Yet he was not alone in doubting that the Soviet Union seriously planned an invasion of Western Europe, and indeed the formation of NATO was not immediately followed by the setting up of a military command structure, or a substantial increase in Western military strength. It was not until after June 1950, with the outbreak of the war in Korea, that Western Europe embarked on a major programme of rearmament. Nevertheless the formation of NATO marked a significant step in the militarization of the East-West division in Europe.

Of course it is impossible to know how different things might have been if NATO had not been formed, and if Western rearmament, and the eventual inclusion of West Germany in the Alliance, had not occurred. It can be argued that these developments represented in sum a prudent insurance policy given the uncertainties over Soviet intentions. Nevertheless it is important to recognize that NATO and Western rearmament represented only one possible avenue for Europe in the post-war period – one that was challenged at the time by specialists of some weight, and has been questioned since by some historians on the basis of their analysis of Soviet policies and military potential.

Nuclear Weapons
The third factor which aroused deep and genuine fears in the Soviet Union and made cooperation in the post-war period very much less likely was the development, in the strictest secrecy, of the atomic bomb by the USA, and the failure even to inform the Soviet leaders of the project, much less share information with them. The psychological impact of the successful US testing of its first atomic bomb (which Molotov was obliquely informed of at the Potsdam conference), and of the subsequent bombing of Hiroshima and Nagasaki, has never been fully appreciated by

Western leaders or the general public. The Soviet reaction was, however, succinctly put by the British Ambassador in a letter to the Foreign Secretary in December 1945:

'The German invasion caught them still unready and swept them to what looked like the brink of defeat. Then came the turn of the tide and with it first the hope and then a growing belief that the immense benison of national security was at last within their reach. As the Red Army moved westwards belief became confidence and the final defeat of Germany made confidence a conviction. . . . Then plump came the Atomic Bomb. At a blow the balance which had now seemed set and steady was rudely shaken. Russia was balked by the west when everything seemed to be within her grasp. The three hundred divisions were shorn of much of their value.[28]

The fact that the Soviet leaders knew, through their espionage network, about the US project to build an atomic bomb, and had themselves in consequence embarked on a modest programme to develop their own in early 1943, did nothing to dispel Soviet anxieties and suspicions. US success in producing the bomb still came as a shock, and led to the Soviet project being given top priority. The use of atomic weapons by the USA against Japan may also have appeared to Soviet leaders as a kind of warning shot across the bows. There are historians in the West who argue that this was the US intention.[29]

The failure of the USA even to inform the Soviet Union of its atomic programme probably destroyed whatever slim hope there may have been of reaching agreement to put atomic power under international control at the end of the war. The historian Margaret Gowing has written: 'If Russia had been formally consulted about the bomb during the war . . . it might have made no difference. The fact that she was not, guaranteed that the attempts made just after the war to establish international control, which might have failed anyway, were doomed.'[30]

A Western initiative at an early stage to prevent the development of thermonuclear weapons whose power could be expanded almost limitlessly, might have avoided the amassing of H-Bombs by both sides. Truman announced in January 1950 that work on thermonuclear weapons would be speeded up – partly as a reaction to the successful testing of an atomic bomb by the Soviet

Union the previous August. The decision was controversial in the US scientific community, and in October 1949 the General Advisory Committee of the Atomic Energy Commission, chaired by Robert Oppenheimer, had recommended against an all-out effort, arguing that 'the extreme dangers to mankind inherent in the proposal wholly outweigh any military advantage that could come from this development'.[31] Since the Soviet development of a thermonuclear superbomb lagged two or three years behind the USA up to the mid-1950s (and the USSR did not obtain the capability to target the USA with large numbers of nuclear weapons until the mid-1960s), US restraint in 1950 would not have involved any serious risk to itself and might have opened up the possibility of mutual restraint by the two powers after the death of Stalin.

The USA also led in the development of miniaturized atomic weapons, and first deployed these 'battlefield' weapons in Europe in 1952. In principle they were supposed to compensate for western conventional inferiority levels, but they would certainly have appeared as particularly menacing to the Soviet Union when their own overall nuclear programme was still at an early stage.

German Rearmament

Finally, among the Western moves that caused deep concern in the Soviet Union, as well as in other countries in the Soviet bloc, was the incorporation of West Germany into the Western military alliance and the decision to allow it to rearm. This was especially worrying at a time when the Federal Republic did not recognize the existence of the German Democratic Republic, and insisted that the final delineation of Germany's boundaries to the East must await the conclusion of a Peace Treaty. It does appear that at one point in the early 1950s the Soviet Union contemplated military and political withdrawal from East Germany, and would thus have ditched the Ulbricht régime, if this could have brought about a reunited Germany whose neutrality would be guaranteed.[32] The East German workers' revolt in June 1953 was probably one factor that led the Soviet leaders to abandon this plan since a Soviet withdrawal from East Germany under popular pressure would have looked like a defeat. Nevertheless up to the Four Power Geneva Summit in mid-1955 the Soviet Union was still willing to explore the possibility of German reunification with appropriate guarantees.

4. The German Question

There are several reasons for devoting special attention to the problems of the two German states and Berlin. First, the problem of Germany has been central to the debate on European security. Second, the détente period in Europe, and particularly the *Ostpolitik* of the West German Chancellor, Willy Brandt, in the early 1970s, led to the alleviation of important aspects of the problem, though without finally resolving it. Any moves to end the division of Europe into blocs would have implications for both German states.

Division and Confrontation

East-West differences over Germany at the end of the war revolved around two issues. The first concerned the international frontiers of a post-war German state, particularly its frontiers with Poland. At Yalta it was accepted by the three powers that Poland would cede territory to the Soviet Union in the East but would receive territory in compensation at the expense of Germany. However, there was no agreement on where exactly the new German-Polish frontier would be drawn. At Potsdam it was agreed that Poland would administer the former German province of Silesia up to the line formed by the Oder and Western Neisse rivers and that a final decision on Germany's frontiers would await the outcome of a Peace Treaty.

The second issue concerned the composition of an all-German government with whom such a Peace Treaty would be signed. This rapidly became a problem as the occupation zones in Germany took on a political aspect, leading eventually to the creation, in 1949, of two separate German states. The two issues were obviously linked: without the formation of a German government recognized by both sides, there could be no Peace Treaty; and without a Peace Treaty the *de facto* post-war frontiers would continue to be provisional.

Early US initiatives to establish a united Germany whose

neutrality would be guaranteed by the Four Powers for twenty-five years were resisted by the Soviet Union for whom at that time the question of war reparations to build its shattered economy was more pressing. At this period France too was deeply suspicious of any scheme that entailed a unified Germany, and initially the USA and Britain regarded France rather than the Soviet Union as the chief obstacle to a settlement of the German problem.

Inevitably, the longer the separate occupation zones remained in existence the more they began to take on a political character, and the more difficult it became to agree about the procedure for reunification. During 1946, a degree of German self-government was allowed in all the occupation zones. But whereas in the Western zones a plurality of political parties emerged in a parliamentary system, in the Soviet zone the Communist and Social Democrat parties were fused, under Soviet pressure, and the resulting Socialist Unity Party (SED) totally dominated the political scene within a Soviet style system. All subsequent proposals for German reunification were to fall foul of disputes as to how it would be achieved and whether the legislative and executive bodies in the Soviet zone – and subsequently in the GDR – were genuinely representative.

Berlin added a further complication to the problem. It was subjected to Four Power occupation at the end of the war in accordance with war-time agreements. But when East and West failed to agree on the procedure now adopted to bring about an all-German government, the Western Sector became an exposed outpost some 100 miles inside the Soviet zone of Germany and, eventually, inside the German Democratic Republic. West Berlin has been a thorn in the flesh of first the Soviet and then the East German authorities, and has been used by the West as a showcase for demonstrating the advantages of the capitalist system. But its vulnerability also made it a target for Soviet pressure in times of East-West tension.

A series of measures consolidated the division of Germany: the closing, at the Soviet request, of the border between the Soviet and Western zones in July 1946, following the exodus from the East of a million and a half refugees; the fusion of the British and US occupation zones in the summer of 1946 and the later incorporation, in April 1948, of the French zone; and the inclusion of the Western zones in the Marshall Plan.

The introduction of currency reforms in the Western zones in the following year flowed naturally from this last decision. Rampant inflation had, in any case, made reform, delayed by the Soviet representatives on the Allied Control Council, long overdue. When the three Western powers announced a currency reform in their zones (but not Berlin), the Soviet Union responded by announcing that the whole of Berlin would be included in a currency reform for the Soviet zone. The Western powers then announced that the Western mark would also be circulated in West Berlin and on 25 June 1948, the Soviet Union began the Berlin Blockade, cutting off road and rail links between the Western zones and Berlin. In essence, of course, this was not a dispute over currency reform but a struggle for political influence and control. The reforms in the Western zones would integrate them politically (and eventually militarily) into the West, and this the Soviet Union was determined to prevent.

The Blockade, from June 1948 to May 1949 and the Western airlift in response, marked the most dangerous period in Europe in the immediate post-war period. The Western response was restrained. There were those, including some on the left, most notably Aneurin Bevan in the British Labour government, who advocated the sending of an armed convoy to test Soviet resolve, a course of action that could very easily have led to armed conflict and perhaps to a major war.[33] The blockade also consolidated the division of Germany. It was during it that plans for the creation of German governments were published in both the Eastern and Western zones, and the city of Berlin was divided politically as a result of undemocratic communist tactics in the Soviet sector.[34] In September 1949, the Federal German Republic, claiming jurisdiction over the whole of Germany, was established in the Western zones. This was followed a month later by the setting up of the German Democratic Republic in the Soviet zone.

Throughout the 1950s two hostile German states confronted each other, each claiming the sole right to speak on behalf of the German people, and each acting as a brake on any efforts to achieve détente in Europe which they thought were likely to

110

prejudice their position. A Peace Treaty to settle the post-war frontiers was never signed, and indeed when the GDR recognized the Oder-Neisse line as the frontier between Germany and Poland, the Western powers denounced the move as a violation of Four Power agreements, and the government of the Federal Republic again insisted that decisions regarding the German provinces east of Oder-Neisse could only be made in a Peace Treaty with an all-German government. Neither German state recognized the existence of the other, and from 1955 onwards the Federal Republic operated the 'Hallstein Doctrine' under which third parties which recognized the GDR could expect to face political or economic sanctions.

The critical developments during the 1950s and early 1960s in relation to Germany were first the failure of recurrent attempts to find a formula for reunification acceptable to East and West; second, the rearmament of West Germany and its inclusion in the Western military alliance; and third, the building of the Berlin Wall which put an end for the time being to hopes of reunification.

1952 saw an important initiative on the Soviet side. Stalin suggested that a new Four Power Conference should work out details of a Peace Treaty with Germany and put forward proposals for a unified Germany free of foreign troops and bases and forbidden to join any military alliance. It would, however, be allowed enough military forces for its own defence. The proposals envisaged a provisional German government, made up of both the Federal and Democratic Republics, which would organize elections. The West, however, insisted on free elections throughout Germany, supervised by an international body and leading to a new German government before a Peace Treaty could be discussed.

The other stumbling block was the question of whether a reunited Germany would have the right to join a military alliance. Soviet proposals insisted on guaranteed neutrality for a reunited Germany, or alternatively its inclusion in a wider European security pact based on the principle of collective security. The West rejected German neutralization as an unwarranted restriction of sovereignty and clearly expected a reunited

Germany to be included in NATO. Obviously the Soviet Union was never going to accept German reunification on these terms.

In fact plans for West German rearmament and its inclusion in NATO were also controversial in the West, particularly in France, and in West Germany itself where the main opposition party, the Social Democrats (SPD) vigorously opposed it in the early stages. In October 1954 the Paris Accords restored German sovereignty (subject to certain Four Power restrictions), extended the Brussels Pact to include West Germany and form the West European Union (WEU), and approved West German membership of NATO.

There was, however, a nationwide campaign within West Germany to oppose the ratification of the Paris Treaties. On 29 January 1955 over a thousand representatives of West German political, religious, industrial and economic life, met in Frankfurt to warn against the consequences of ratification and to urge the federal government to give priority to unification rather than participation in a military bloc. Despite this, and a warning from Molotov that the Treaties would make reunification impossible, they were ratified in the Bundestag on 27 February 1955.

The question arises whether the Soviet Union was genuinely interested, in the 1952-55 period (and especially after the death of Stalin in 1953), in a compromise solution for Germany. There are indications that it was, and that if agreement over Germany had been reached, it would have been willing to contemplate broader plans for disengagement in Europe. Western reticence was understandable in the aftermath of the Stalinist political manipulation and purges in Eastern Europe, as was the fear that proposals for German reunification without prior elections under international supervision might prove to be a device for extending Soviet influence. Nevertheless, the refusal by the West to contemplate any move that implied a degree of recognition of East Germany, and its rejection of proposals for neutrality for a reunited Germany, meant that an opportunity to explore alternative options for Germany and Europe as a whole was lost.

The building of the Berlin Wall in August 1961 set the final seal on the division of Germany. It came as the climax to the 'Second Berlin Crisis' which began in 1959 with Khrushchev's threat to conclude a separate Peace Treaty with the GDR, thereby handing over responsibility for arrangements in Berlin to the East Germans and putting a question mark against future Western access to West Berlin. The construction of the wall ended, for the time being, West German hopes for reunification and marked the beginning of a change in their foreign policy. The change gathered momentum when Willy Brandt became Foreign Minister in the 'Grand Coalition' government formed in December 1966, but it was not until he himself became German Chancellor in a new SPD/FDP coalition in December 1969 that his plans for a new policy towards the East could be put fully into effect.

5. BRANDT'S *OSTPOLITIK* AND DÉTENTE IN EUROPE

In a formal sense at least, Brandt's *Ostpolitik* was far removed from any concept of German neutrality or non-alignment. He himself put it firmly in the context of a parallel *Westpolitik* whose aim was to consolidate West German integration into NATO and the European Community. Brandt argued that an historic transformation was taking place in Europe in which constructive dialogue between East and West was replacing the propaganda monologue. The West German role should be to encourage and contribute to this process of détente, but the FRG would undertake nothing in its policy towards Eastern Europe which might undermine NATO, since the US presence in Europe provided the necessary balance of power without which a lasting détente with the Soviet Union would be impossible.[35] Nevertheless the wider aim of Brandt's policy was to create the conditions for the ending, not only of the division of Germany, but also of East-West military confrontation in Europe.

A key feature of Brandt's policy was the formal renunciation of force which permitted some of the touchier problems to be left open while at the same time taking out of them much of their sting.[36] He was also willing to be pragmatic in dealing with the question of German unity and recognition of the GDR, searching for formulations which would preserve continuity, in a formal legal sense, with the positions taken by previous West German governments, while allowing room for the development of a more constructive political and economic practice. Thus while the

FRG could not deal with the GDR as a fully independent state under international law, it could enter into agreements with it on the basis of 'states rights' (on the analogy of agreements between states within a federal system), and would no longer object to third parties giving the GDR full recognition.

The goal of eventual reunification was not abandoned. On the contrary, Brandt and his colleagues anticipated that the recognition of existing realities would remove some of the obstacles to achieving this goal and the conclusion of a Peace Treaty. But reunification, he recognized, was not a practical possibility for the foreseeable future, and he proposed to tidy up some of the loose ends left after Yalta and Potsdam and normalize relations with the FRG's eastern neighbours through a series of bilateral agreements. Again, however, it was made explicit that these were not intended to be a substitute for a Peace Treaty, and did not end Four Power responsibility for Germany as a whole, including, of course, Berlin.

The first of these agreements was the Moscow Treaty signed with the Soviet Union in August 1970. Among its provisions was an undertaking to respect the territorial integrity of all states within their present boundaries and regard all existing frontiers in Europe as inviolable, including the Oder-Neisse line and the frontier between the FRG and GDR. Both parties also declared that they would not make any territorial claims against other countries. But the West German commitment to the longer term political aim of reunification was made clear in the form of an accompanying letter.

The Moscow Treaty led to the conclusion of others along similar lines. In November 1970, the Warsaw Treaty was signed, at which the Oder-Neisse line was confirmed once more as the frontier between Germany and Poland. In December 1972, in Berlin, after difficult and protracted negotiations, the FRG and GDR signed the Basic Treaty under which, among other things, each side accepted the other's internationally independent status and agreed to exchange permanent representative missions. The following year both states were accepted as members of the United Nations. In December 1973, the Prague Treaty normalized relations between the FRG and Czechoslovakia and confirmed the renunciation by both parties of the 1938 Munich

Agreement. Almost immediately afterwards, full diplomatic relations were also established with Hungary and Bulgaria. Meanwhile a Four Power Agreement on Berlin in 1972 had recognized the rights of each Power and reduced the danger of future crisis over the city.

By the end of 1973, the principal goals in the first phase of Brandt's programme had been achieved. But Brandt was forced to resign in May of the following year, and the hope that these bilateral agreements, and the Four Power Agreement on Berlin, would open up the way to a more permanent solution to the German Problem, and lead to the signing of a Peace Treaty, has still not been realized.

The Conference on Security and Cooperation in Europe
The final element in détente, in so far as it affected Europe directly, was the Conference on Security and Cooperation in Europe (CSCE). The process, involving thirty-three European states plus the USA and Canada, began in 1973 and led to the Helsinki Final Act of 1975 and a series of follow-up conferences and consultations. Essentially, Helsinki confirmed at a multilateral level the agreements on post-war frontiers that Brandt had negotiated on a bilateral basis with the Soviet Union and other states in Eastern Europe. The Accords also covered the promotion of trade, cultural and other exchanges, respect for certain fundamental human rights and the implementation of a number of 'confidence building measures', mainly to do with prior notification of planned military manoeuvres over a certain size, as a means of reducing tension and the risk of accidental war.

The human rights issue was to prove the most contentious. Principle VII of 'Basket One' committed the participating states to 'respect human rights and fundamental freedoms, including the freedom of thought, conscience and religion', while 'Basket Three' attempted to give substance to this commitment in the form of undertakings on issues such as the reunification of families, the facilitation of travel, cultural and educational contacts between East and West, and the free flow of information. These human rights provisions gave independent and oppositional movements in Eastern Europe, such as Charter 77 in

Czechoslovakia, KOR and Solidarity in Poland, and the Helsinki Monitoring Group in the Soviet Union some leverage in their campaigns for human and political rights. But they have also led to many sterile sessions of recrimination and mutual accusation in the follow-up conferences. Nor has the commitment to refrain from the threat or use of force against the territorial integrity or political independence of any state inhibited either side from intervention or campaigns of subversion, whether by the US in Central America or the Soviet Union in Afghanistan.

The Helsinki process has, however, produced one new arms control and disarmament initiative – the Conference on Confidence and Security Building Measures and Disarmament in Europe which began in Stockholm in January 1984. The initiative came originally from France in 1978 at the First UN Special Session on Disarmament and was supported at the Madrid CSCE conference by France, Poland, Romania, Sweden and Yugoslavia. As the title of the conference implies, the emphasis is on extending the confidence-building measures agreed at Helsinki. However, wider issues can be raised, and at the opening session Gromyko for the Soviet Union argued that the most important goal for the conference should be to secure a no-first-use of nuclear weapons agreement and a pledge on the mutual non-use of conventional and nuclear force. Gromyko also reiterated his country's interest in making northern Europe a nuclear-weapon-free zone, and securing the removal of nuclear and chemical weapons from the continent.[37]

Unlike the MBFR Talks in Vienna, the CDE provided a forum for the neutral and non-aligned states of Europe to put their views forward, and agreement on further confidence-building measures was achieved in September 1986.

Assessing Détente

Détente reduced tension in Europe, virtually eliminating any sense of immediate peril on either side. It promoted trade and led to increased East-West contacts at various levels.

The dramatic increase in East-West trade was one of the most tangible results of the process. Thus between 1969 and 1974 economic exchanges tripled.[38] The trade benefited the West by opening up a new market for goods and investment – as well as holding out the prospect of new energy supplies from the Soviet gas pipeline. It also enabled Eastern Europe to avail itself of Western loans and modernize its industry through importing Western technology. Despite the debt problem which the high level of Western imports gave rise to, it is clear that in general Eastern European governments are keen to continue developing trading relationships with the West.

This increased economic interdependence also has a pay-off at the security level. A Soviet attack today on Western Europe, even if nuclear escalation could be avoided, would not only disrupt the economy of Western Europe but have devastating consequences for the whole of Eastern Europe, including the Soviet Union. Decisions about war and peace are not always made in accordance with a careful calculation of gains and losses. Nevertheless the economic interdependence of Europe is likely to prove a stabilizing factor, serving to discourage adventurism on either side.

The effects of détente on political developments in Eastern Europe are harder to gauge. It is difficult to decide for instance, whether détente encouraged liberalization in the East European régimes, as some of its supporters had anticipated. Economic reform and some political relaxation continued in Hungary, and presumably this would have been more difficult in an atmosphere of Cold War. On the other hand, there was no let-up in the repression in Czechoslovakia, and in Poland periods of granting concessions and introducing reforms alternated with the use of riot police and troops to crush popular unrest and culminated in the introduction of martial law in 1981. What is clear, however, is that the scope of political and intellectual dissent has broadened, giving rise not only to groups demanding human rights, but also to the independent trade union movements like Solidarity, and to unofficial peace groups prepared to challenge aspects of the foreign and defence policies of their governments.

Détente almost certainly has played a role here, not necessarily because the various régimes have become more tolerant of dissent, but because the removal of uncertainties at the international level and the reduced fear of war, has given independent-minded groups and individuals greater confidence. It has become less easy to silence them with the spectre of German revanchism or the likelihood of imminent NATO aggression.

Some of the limitations of détente have also been touched upon. In terms of arms control the achievements, aside from the two SALT treaties, were very limited. And even the SALT treaties did not prevent both sides from continuing to research and develop new generations of destabilizing weapons.[39] Détente did not, of course, achieve, or lead to, the disengagement of the two superpowers from Europe. Yet without that, the situation in Eastern Europe is certain to remain troubled and give rise to recurrent crises which could threaten the peace of the continent. It did not even reduce the level of armed confrontation in Europe – more massive here than anywhere else in the world. It ameliorated the German Problem but it did not resolve it. Finally, détente did not remove the danger of global nuclear war. Indeed, at the time of the Arab-Israeli war of 1973, at the high point of détente, the world probably came nearer to nuclear devastation than at any time since the Cuban missile crisis. Détente creates a more auspicious climate for East-West dialogue, but it does not solve the problems posed by the existence of nuclear weapons and the willingness of states under certain circumstances to use them.

6. THE SEARCH FOR DISENGAGEMENT

Some of the achievements of détente have survived the deterioration in East-West relations and the continuing row over nuclear missile deployments in Europe. The conservative-liberal CDU/ CSU-FDP government elected in the FRG in 1983, was not disposed to repudiate the Brandt government's recognition of the post-war frontiers in Europe, despite some pressure to do so from the right wing in the country. It has also showed its desire to maintain good relations with the GDR.

The question today, therefore, is what proposals might restore and strengthen détente in Europe so that it can provide the basis for an end to the rift in the continent? Clearly, the problem cannot be solved purely at the European level, for relations between the two superpowers, and the policies each pursues in other areas of the world, are important factors. But Europe remains critical, even if other areas have assumed increasing importance in the East-West struggle. Thus resolving the major problems within Europe could improve the prospects of a wider détente.

It is important that future proposals for détente in Europe should operate on both the military and the political fronts. They are closely linked, especially if one is considering major change. Thus, to take the extreme case, the dissolution of the military blocs is not conceivable without a resolution of the German question and a transformation of Soviet relations with Eastern Europe. On the other hand, agreements to reduce force levels or eliminate certain types of weapons need not affect political arrangements; and conversely some political agreements, such as those achieved in the early 1970s, may have little effect on arms control and military confrontation.

In considering the steps that might be taken it makes sense to review proposals that were widely discussed at an earlier period. The proposals of the 1950s may not be so viable today, but on the other hand the achievements of the détente period may have removed some of the obstacles to their acceptance and for this reason also they are worth re-examining.

For a number of reasons the mid- to late-1950s was a period particularly rich in terms of such proposals. First, there were major changes within the Soviet Union, following the death of Stalin in March 1953. The machinery of terror was largely dismantled and by 1956 when Khrushchev exposed and denounced the practices of the Stalin period, Soviet policies had been revised on a number of fronts.

Domestically, economic reforms were introduced, and there was a shift towards consumerism with the aim of raising living standards. This had repercussions elsewhere, notably on the arms budget. In external affairs there was a serious attempt to put both economic and political relations with Eastern Europe on a new footing, and to seek some kind of *modus vivendi* with the West. The 'mistakes' in Stalin's dealings with Eastern Europe were acknowledged; many victims of the purges were exonerated, and links with Yugoslavia were restored. The limits of these changes were dramatically underlined by the Soviet intervention in Hungary in October 1956 which claimed some 20,000 Hungarian lives. Nevertheless it remains true that, post-Stalin, East European states were able to exercise much greater freedom of action than before; in Poland, especially, significant reforms were undertaken in 1956 without provoking Soviet intervention.

Moreover the idea that war between capitalist and socialist systems was inevitable was replaced with the notion of 'peaceful co-existence'. This is the context in which Soviet proposals in the mid-1950s relating to Germany and European disengagement need to be seen. Soviet willingness, in 1955, to conclude a Peace Treaty with Austria under which its forces were withdrawn is another indication of changes in the Soviet approach.

The second reason that quite radical proposals for a European settlement were widely debated during the 1950s relates to the fluidity of the situation. Soviet proposals on Germany from 1952 to 1955, were aimed in large measure at preventing West German rearmament and its inclusion in a Western military alliance. NATO itself was still in the early years of its existence, and was not yet regarded as an almost inevitable feature of the European landscape. The Warsaw Pact only came into existence in 1955 in response to West German membership of NATO. It was thus easier at that time to envisage different political and security arrangements, such as the creation of a zone of disengagement in the centre of Europe as advocated by Hugh Gaitskell and Denis Healey in the British Labour Party.

The third reason was the alarm aroused by the events in East Germany in 1953, when Soviet tanks were used to put down demonstrations and strikes by workers, and Hungary in 1956. These events suggested that the situation in Eastern Europe was not as stable as it appeared to be, and there was concern that unrest there might spark off a European or global conflict. It was this anxiety that lay behind George Kennan's proposals in 1957 for the withdrawal of US forces from Europe in exchange for a Soviet withdrawal in the East. On the positive side, however, the rebellion in Hungary and the changes in Poland indicated that if Soviet forces were withdrawn the Soviet Union would not necessarily be able to manipulate, as it had in the past, the military and political decisions of Eastern European states.[40]

The proposals widely debated in the 1950s fall into three main categories. First, those for German reunification and neutrality favoured by the Soviet Union which we referred to in the previous section. These were resisted by the West, partly because of disagreement about how reunification would be brought about, and partly because neutralization was acceptable neither to the West as a whole nor to the West Germans themselves. Second, proposals for partial or total military disengagement by the United States and the Soviet Union from their respective halves of Europe, which were usually linked to proposals for a solution to the German question. Third, proposals for military de-escalation, including the removal of nuclear weapons from Europe and the scaling down of military forces. The most significant of these was the 'Rapacki Plan' (named after the Polish Foreign Minister Adam Rapacki who put it forward in 1957) for the removal of nuclear weapons and delivery systems from East and West Germany, Czechoslovakia and Poland.

Total Military Disengagement

Proposals for complete military disengagement by the USA and USSR were put forward at the official level only on the Soviet side, but records now available show that President Eisenhower also considered the option. In September 1953, the US Secretary of State, John Foster Dulles, sent a memorandum to Eisenhower suggesting a spectacular effort to end world tensions on a global basis by negotiating a mutual withdrawal of US and Soviet forces from Europe. Eisenhower replied that renewed efforts should be made to relax world tensions, and thought that mutual withdrawal of US and Soviet forces could be suggested.[41] There, unfortunately, the matter ended – in part because Dulles, believing that the Soviet Union was in a weak position, wanted to press its leaders even harder.

On the Soviet side Bulganin, at the Four Power Geneva Summit meeting in 1955, proposed mutual withdrawal as part of a plan which included German reunification and its guaranteed neutrality. In June 1956, he repeated this proposal and suggested that a start should be made with the progressive reduction of troops on German soil. In February of the following year, Khrushchev returned to the theme in an interview with the

American journalists Joseph Alsop and Chester Bowles, and again in a television interview in July.

Western reluctance to take up such proposals stemmed from various causes. First, they could not be negotiated, much less implemented, without an agreement on Germany, and this was blocked over neutralization and the method of reunification. Aside from the objections of the German government, there were fears on the Western side that a neutral Germany might fall under Soviet influence. Moreover, the concrete advantages of having substantial German forces to bolster NATO strength appeared more attractive than the uncertain fruits of the proposed political settlement. Second, there was the fact that the dissolution of the Warsaw Pact would not affect bilateral agreements between the Soviet Union and Eastern European governments. The fear was that once the USA had withdrawn from Europe the Soviet Union would become the dominant power and would ultimately be in a position to control the continent.

George Kennan's proposals for disengagement made in the BBC Reith Lectures in 1957, sought to meet West European fears by the suggestion that, following the departure of US forces, there should be an explicit threat of US nuclear retaliation to any Soviet aggression. But the Bonn government was hostile, and in the USA, Dean Acheson disclaimed all responsibility for the proposals on behalf of the Democratic Party.

Partial Disengagement
What, then, of the proposals for a more limited zone of disengagement in Europe? The most important of these, in terms of having the backing of a major political party, were those put forward by Hugh Gaitskell and Denis Healey, and supported also on the left by Aneurin Bevan, which formed the basis of Labour Party policy in the late 1950s. Gaitskell proposed a disengaged zone covering a reunited Germany, Poland, Czechoslovakia, Hungary, and if possible also Romania and Bulgaria. No foreign troops would be permitted in this area, and the indigenous armed forces would be subject to limitations and control. The scheme would be underpinned by a multilateral European security pact under which the states involved would have their territories guaranteed by the superpowers and by each other. Thus any

aggression in the area – including of course Soviet intervention – would be dealt with on an international level and would involve the two superpowers. US forces would not be withdrawn from Europe but would continue to be deployed beyond the frontiers of a reunited Germany.[42]

Denis Healey elaborated this plan in his Fabian pamphlet published in February 1958. He too insisted that US forces must have a foothold in Europe so that, in the event of Soviet aggression, the West would not be faced with the alternative of capitulation or all-out nuclear war. But he suggested that the neutral zone might be extended on a *quid pro quo* basis; for instance, Denmark to be included for Romania. The forces of the neutral area should be substantial enough to deter or deal with limited attacks but would be armed only with conventional weapons; it would, in other words, be a nuclear-weapon-free zone. But outside the zone, Western and Soviet forces would have tactical nuclear weapons which could be delivered by aircraft and missiles to deal with a major aggression, and would also retain the option of escalating to full-scale nuclear war if the need arose.

Clearly, the Gaitskell-Healey plan posed problems for both the Soviet Union and the West. The Soviet Union would be relinquishing its control over Eastern Europe and be threatened with war – including, very probably, war with atomic weapons – if it moved its forces back into the area. In exchange it would have obtained US military withdrawal from West Germany but not from Europe as a whole. It was probably considerations of this kind that Adam Rapacki had in mind when, a few years later, he wrote about his own plans for a nuclear-weapon-free zone and distinguished it from plans for disengagement 'about all of which we have, in any case, more or less fundamental reservations'.[43]

. The problems for Western security were analysed at the time by Michael Howard, though some of the factors he points to would have been at least equally as worrying for the Soviet Union and Eastern Europe.[44] There was the problem of how NATO would liaise with the states in the disengaged area. Without preliminary close liaison, he argued, guarantees of military aid would be ineffective, as the experience of both World

Wars had shown. Yet whatever plans for military coordination NATO might require could be equally well demanded by the Soviet Union. The inescapable dilemma was that 'if you observe neutrality strictly, you render yourself incapable of helping the neutral; while if you put yourself in a position to aid the neutral, you cast doubts on his neutrality'.

The other problem, he argued was how the forces in the zone would be organized. If they were integrated, along the lines of NATO, they would inevitably come to be dominated by Germany – a situation that would be unacceptable to the Soviet Union and Eastern European states as well as to those of the West. But if each state simply retained control of its own forces with no structure of supreme command, then in war this would be the equivalent of military suicide. A third alternative would be for NATO to retain close links with a reunited Germany while the Soviet Union maintained a similar relationship with the states in the Warsaw Pact. Even disengagement in this form, he argued, would raise problems of morale if the US commitment to Western Europe was thought to be on the decline.

Some of these objections were specific to the Gaitskell-Healey plan, others would presumably apply to many other proposals for US-Soviet military disengagement in Europe. But no political or military arrangements can provide absolute security, and given a progressive scaling-down of forces on both sides, and the strengthening of East European autonomy, alternative security arrangements, as we suggest in Chapter Five, could be devised.

Could there have been a breakthrough in East-West relations in the mid-1950s if the West had responded more positively to Soviet initiatives? It is impossible to be certain because, as we have seen, there were intractable problems, particularly in relation to Germany. However a Czechoslovak writer, Zdenek Mylnar, generally a severe critic of Soviet policy, argues that in the early Khrushchev period the Soviet leaders, because of weaknesses and problems within the Soviet system and sphere of influence, '*truly began to seek* a way out of their own isolation and from a situation in which conflict constantly dominated their action with other systems'. To this end they were willing to negotiate and compromise on issues affecting their superpower status, including the future of Germany. But the response from the USA and other Western countries was slow and suspicious – there was '*preventative mistrust* of the Soviet proposals, stemming from past experience but projected onto the future'.[45] (Italics in original.)

A change in US attitudes began to occur after the launching of the first Sputnik, and policy shifted soon after Kennedy took office. But about the same time Soviet willingness to cooperate even at the cost of major concessions began to diminish, as was evident from the building of the Berlin Wall and the installation of missiles in Cuba.

The change in the Soviet approach was signalled by a shift of doctrinal emphasis, within the overall concept of coexistence, away from competition between different socio-economic systems towards 'relaxation of tension' between them. On the face of it this might appear a positive shift, but what it meant was that, although détente would be sought, the arena of competition was now seen to be primarily in the military, rather than the economic and political, sphere. Thus the shift led to the military exercising greater influence, especially during the Brezhnev period beginning in 1964. It also led to a build-up of military forces, a move away from economic reforms at home, a tightening of the bloc discipline, and military rather than economic assistance as a way of extending Soviet influence in the Third World. As Mylnar puts it, the Soviet Union had decided that it 'had found a way out from its own crisis and was able to overcome it without risky steps in the direction of cooperation'.[46]

Thus an opportunity was missed in the 1950s to explore the possibility of a more radical solution for outstanding East-West problems in Europe. To cite Mylnar again:

'This *phase shift* (i.e. US willingness to cooperate coming at a time when the Soviet position was hardening) ... did not stem, in our opinion, from a "breach of faith" on the Soviet side and "naïve credulity" on the Western side. It was rather an example of the situation ... where the actions of a larger number of actors lead to results none of them actually wanted'.

Demilitarization and Nuclear-Weapon-Free Zones

Demilitarization represents a different emphasis in approaching the problem of military confrontation: the limitation of certain types of armaments within a given zone and/or the reduction of force levels by the parties involved; it may also, of course, be part of a process of disengagement or be seen as a way of leading to it. Most of the disengagement proposals of the 1950s did in fact envisage some limitations on armaments within the disengaged zone. But there were also proposals which focused specifically on demilitarization.

The most significant of these was the Rapacki Plan, already referred to, for a nuclear-free zone covering East and West Germany, Poland and Czechoslovakia. It was first outlined to the UN in October 1957 and presented as a formal proposal to Western governments in February 1958. Inside the zone there would be a ban on the production, transfer and deployment of all nuclear weapons. Nuclear delivery systems would also be prohibited, and states possessing nuclear weapons would undertake not to violate the status of the zone or to use nuclear weapons against any territory within it.

The Rapacki Plan aroused a great deal of interest. In December 1957, following the first presentation of the plan at the UN, Denis Healey speculated that it 'may mark a turning point in Soviet diplomacy'. Among NATO countries, Belgium and Canada welcomed the plan and both France and Denmark expressed cautious interest. But the USA, Britain and West Germany rejected it, arguing that it would upset the military balance in Europe since the Soviet bloc enjoyed a superiority in conventional forces. It might also lead to the withdrawal of US forces, and delay German reunification.

In an attempt to meet Western objections, Rapacki presented a revised version of the plan, in November 1958 – with further modifications in detail in March 1962. The revised plan proposed implementation in two stages. In the first stage there would be a freeze on nuclear weapons and bases, and the countries within the zone would also undertake not to produce any kind of nuclear weapon or delivery system. The transfer of nuclear weapons to states within the zone was also prohibited, a provision which reflected Polish, and Soviet bloc, concern at the possibility of West Germany being given access to nuclear weapons.[47] In the second stage, nuclear weapons and delivery systems would be eliminated altogether from the zone but, to meet Western anxieties, conventional weapons and forces would be simultaneously reduced to an agreed level. Verification was to take the form of strict international control and inspection on the ground and from the air and the establishment of control posts.[48]

In retrospect one can see that if negotiations on the Rapacki Plan ever had got under way a major difficulty would have been reaching agreement on reductions in conventional armaments and forces – ironically, the issue introduced to assuage Western fears. As it was, however, the negotiations never even started. The West continued to dismiss the plan as one which could threaten its security, and not even the Kennedy Administration in the USA, or, later, the Wilson government which took office in Britain in 1964, were prepared to give it serious consideration.

Rapacki himself made no extravagant claims for the plan. 'We know very well,' he wrote,

'that the problem of peace in Central Europe is not dependent only on decisions taken in Central Europe. We also knew only too well that recurrent tensions in Central Europe were caused not only by nuclear armament but also by a certain type of political phenomena and political tendencies. We realized no less that a non-nuclear zone in Central Europe could not be a barrier to long-range rockets between East and West. This is why, from the beginning, we saw in our plan only an initial or partial step towards the solution of at least two from among the few problems of world peace of the same rank of importance: the problem of disarmament and the German problem.'[49]

The two main benefits of the scheme, he argued, were, first, that it would remove the danger of a clash escalating, by chance or accident, to a global nuclear conflict, and second that it would reduce the danger of nuclear war in Central Europe 'caused by political controversies exaggerated and sharpened by strategical considerations'.

Relevance of Nuclear-Weapon-Free Zones Today
In recent years, thanks largely to the efforts of the peace movements in Europe, there has been a revival of interest in the Rapacki Plan and in the notion of other nuclear-weapon-free zones in Europe – in the Baltic and Balkan areas. Peace and

human rights groups in Eastern Europe, including Charter 77 in its important policy statement of March 1985, have also supported the idea of creating nuclear-free zones.[50] But the British government continues to dismiss these proposals, pointing out what everyone has known and acknowledged all along – that such zones in Europe, or a zone covering the whole of Europe, would still be vulnerable to long-range missile attack.[51]

Clearly, if there is an all-out nuclear war between the USA and the Soviet Union, Western Europe would be unlikely to escape attack, at any rate if it was still an important political and military ally of the USA. Moreover, even if it were to escape direct nuclear attack it could hardly expect to escape from the wider disaster caused by fall-out and possible climatic changes. But as leaders on both sides know that global nuclear war would be a disaster, it is not likely that either side will deliberately embark on such a war. It is, in fact, more likely to occur for the reasons listed by Rapacki: miscalculation or accident, or tensions getting out of hand and leading to an essentially irrational decision. Measures to prevent accidents and heightened tensions are therefore critical in the nuclear age for the prevention of war.

There is no doubt that missile deployments in Europe led to increasing tension, starting with the Soviet deployment of SS20s. Indeed, the Western reaction to Soviet deployment largely undermines the government argument that a nuclear-weapon-free Europe would be an irrelevance. Western Europe was vulnerable to nuclear attack before the SS20s were deployed, not only from the intermediate-range SS4s and SS5s, but from also from longer-range systems. This did not prevent the deployments of SS20s from being regarded as a threat or from heightening tension. Similarly the Western deployment of cruise and Pershing II missiles has increased fears on the Soviet side.

Just how significant the implementation of the Rapacki plan would have been would have depended in large measure on the policies pursued by Britain, France and the United States outside the zone. If US Polaris and Poseidon missiles had still been provided with a base at Holy Loch, and Britain and France had continued to build up their own nuclear forces, the Soviet Union might very well have developed and deployed new intermediate range missiles. It is, however, possible that successful negotiation of a nuclear-weapon-free zone in Central Europe could have encouraged other measures of nuclear restraint, if not nuclear disarmament.

The second main British, and Western, objection to a nuclear-weapon-free zone in Central Europe is that it would put NATO at a decisive military disadvantage, since it faces overwhelming odds at the conventional level.[52] There is a continuing debate about the balance of conventional forces on the Central Front. The judgement of the International Institute of Strategic Studies over the past several years has been that although the Warsaw Pact does indeed have an advantage, it is not of the magnitude that would make aggression other than a highly risky gamble.

But even if NATO conventional forces were dangerously under strength, this could only be remedied at the conventional level – for instance by reinforcing the front line, by more effective deployment of the forces now available, by increasing the strength of reserve forces, or whatever other steps may be appropriate, including, ideally, mutual negotiated reductions in forces. It could not be dealt with by the threat to use nuclear weapons first against a conventional attack.

In the late 1950s, when the West still had considerable superiority in nuclear weapons at every level, the threat to use tactical nuclear weapons to defeat a major Soviet conventional attack had at least a military rationale. Today, when both sides have massive arsenals at every level and thus when any use of nuclear weapons carries an enormous risk of escalation to all-out nuclear war, it makes no sense whatever. This is why a number of strategists on both sides of the Atlantic have been demanding that NATO accept a no-first-use of nuclear weapons policy and remove most, if not all, battlefield nuclear weapons.[53]

In the next chapter we consider in more detail proposals for introducing nuclear-weapon-free zones in Europe. In supporting the idea of such zones, we do not, of course, suggest that of themselves they solve the problem of European security. But they could make a significant contribution, especially if the Soviet Union could be persuaded as part of the deal to adopt a more defensive strategy at a conventional level.

The relative success of Brandt's *Ostpolitik* in the early 1970s owed much to the emphasis he put on advancing by a series of steps and being willing to accept interim arrangements provided they could be shown to be in keeping with the broader goals of the policy. The establishment of nuclear-weapon-free zones might operate in a similar way to achieve the goal of a nuclear-free Europe and, beyond that, nuclear disarmament by the superpowers themselves.

Yet the analogy with *Ostpolitik* contains an implicit caveat. That policy brought concrete and lasting improvements to East-West relations in Europe, but the momentum was not carried through to the point of resolving the German question as Brandt had hoped. And while it may be appropriate to think in terms of two or three decades for sorting out complex political arrangements, the moral imperative to renounce nuclear weapons demands more immediate action. Thus while an anti-nuclear British government should support efforts to establish nuclear-weapon-free zones in Europe, it cannot make the unequivocal renunciation of any reliance on weapons of mass destruction dependent on the outcome of complex negotiations with allies and potential adversaries to establish such zones. For this reason we have retained the recommendation, put forward in the Commission's first report, that Britain should not only get rid of its own nuclear weapons and secure the removal of US nuclear bases, but should make its continued membership of NATO dependent on the Alliance adopting a non-nuclear strategy within a specified period.

Disengagement and Demilitarization in the Post Détente Era
It remains to consider whether the achievements of the détente period have made the situation more favourable for the acceptance of proposals for disengagement and nuclear-free zones in Europe. In the centre of Europe matters are more settled than in the 1950s; the two German states are on talking terms, Berlin is less of a problem, and, by and large, the issue of Germany's frontiers with Poland and Czechoslovakia has been resolved. Moreover, the greater economic interdependence of the whole of Europe, and Soviet interest in maintaining some kind of reasonable relation with the United States, makes a Soviet invasion of Western Europe appear less likely. In principle this ought to make European governments more ready to explore new

approaches to security, perhaps even to take some calculated risks in terms of the military balance in order to achieve wider goals such as reducing the level of military confrontation or the removal of nuclear weapons from Europe. But the fact remains that the MBFR talks in Vienna have been bogged down since 1973, apparently immune to the spirit of détente. If there is a better prospect of nuclear-weapon-free zones being accepted in Europe today this stems largely from the groundswell of opinion in their favour, especially following the anger and alarm over new missile deployments.

The political changes brought about by détente and Brandt's *Ostpolitik* have a more direct bearing on prospects for military and political disengagement. In the 1950s one of the objections to such proposals – especially in the most radical form in which Soviet and US forces would be withdrawn altogether from the territories of their European allies – was that they might exacerbate the German problem. Thus Selwyn Lloyd, as Foreign Secretary, speaking in the Commons on 20 February 1958, argued that plans for disengagement must include provisions for German reunification, as the Eden Plan of 1955 had done. He described the Gaitskell-Healey plan for a neutral zone in Central Europe, where only the conventional forces of the states concerned would be deployed, but backed by nuclear weapons outside it, as 'a trail of gunpowder laid across the centre of Europe'.[54]

Clearly the German problem has not been finally resolved, and any plan for radical disengagement in Europe would have to address itself to this question. However, thanks to détente the problem is less acute. The *de facto* recognition by each state of the other's existence has opened up new possibilities for solving outstanding problems.

Other developments since the mid-1950s have probably made disengagement more difficult. The passage of time itself has created rigidities. Today, for instance, the Soviet Union may be much more reluctant than in the 1950s to contemplate withdrawal from Eastern Europe when there are clear signs that if it did so, several states would probably opt for a political system closer to that of the West.

The achievements of détente have more bearing on disengagement than on nuclear-weapon-free zones since the latter require fewer political adjustments and are an essentially less complex proposition. We turn our attention to them, and to the denuclearization of NATO strategy, in the chapter that follows, before returning to the problems of disengagement and dealignment in Chapter Five.

4. Creating a non-nuclear Europe

1. INTRODUCTION

The Commission's overall objectives for Europe are radical: to denuclearize European defence policies (East and West) and make them visibly defensive and non-threatening to neighbouring states, and to loosen and ultimately dissolve the two military alliances in the belief that this would promote long-term peaceful relations. However, it is one thing to analyse long-term goals, and quite another to identify the best strategy for achieving them. This chapter focuses on the short- and medium-term steps that an anti-nuclear British government could take to change the military situation in Europe.

Defence and disarmament initiatives cannot be divorced from decisions about foreign policy and international politics, and as far as possible these dimensions are integrated into our discussion. However, the dangers of the present confrontation between Warsaw Pact and NATO forces mean that our highest medium-term priority is to secure military changes. Military issues overlay political and economic relations between East and West Europe to such a large extent that little progress is likely to be made on our wider political goals without clear movement on nuclear and conventional arms policy. Nor could a British government with fundamental objections to nuclear defence policies remain in NATO for long without radical changes in Alliance strategy.

In practice the policies of any anti-nuclear British government would be greatly influenced by the domestic political situation. They would depend on the compromises reached within and between political parties, on other political and economic pressures on the government, and on the strength and direction of public opinion. The resulting configurations of policy and power are largely unpredictable. Attempts to take them into account would distract us from our primary objective, which is to identify the best strategy that a consistently anti-nuclear British government elected in the near future *could* pursue in the existing international context, if it were not diverted by domestic compromises. We therefore largely neglect domestic British politics.

Even modest attempts at limiting dangerous military trends and preserving détente have recently seemed ambitious. Many powerful political, military, ideological, and economic factors lock NATO and the Warsaw Pact into their present relationships and strategies. A radical British government could not expect to achieve much success by relying solely on those groups in Europe and North America that already fully support its objectives: alone they do not have sufficient influence. Broad alliances would have to be built around more limited proposals, which should be achievable and advantageous in themselves, while also helpful in creating favourable conditions for future progress towards our more ambitious objectives.

In choosing such limited proposals and building support for them, it is easy to lose sight of the longer-term objectives, or even to compromise them. The decoupling of the defence of Western Europe from US strategic nuclear weapons provides an example of this: in order to argue for the withdrawal of tactical nuclear weapons from Europe, it could be plausibly maintained that the US troops stationed in West Germany provide a sufficient guarantee of the US nuclear commitment to Europe. Yet this is not an argument that a government fundamentally opposed to nuclear defence policies can deploy without risking the basis of its entire policy.

Nor is it clear that our long- and short-term objectives will always be complementary. For example, urgently required steps to improve crisis stability and reduce the level of armaments may be most easily achieved if they are accompanied by policies which increase the stability of the blocs and reinforce the division of Europe. Such seeming contradictions are only to be expected in any process that aims at fundamental change.

134

2. Obstacles and Starting Points

Our objective of denuclearizing military policies in Europe and changing conventional defence postures is wide-ranging, and it would obviously be valuable to identify the main obstacles to starting the process. This would allow attention to be focused on these areas first. In summary, we believe, for reasons given below, that NATO would provide the greatest initial obstacle to the denuclearization process, while the Warsaw Pact is likely to present the greatest hindrance to changes on the conventional level.

On the nuclear level, although nuclear weapons are integral to the strategies of both military alliances, they are more central to NATO than to Warsaw Pact policy. NATO explicitly deploys nuclear weapons to deter conventional as well as nuclear attack: its 'first-use' policy threatens that the Alliance would respond to a conventional invasion with nuclear attacks. Additionally, although strategic nuclear forces are linked to the deterrence policies of both alliances, the supposed coupling of European defence to US strategic forces has immense symbolic and political importance for the Western Alliance. This is partly because the USA cannot impose unity on NATO to the same extent as the Soviet Union can in the Warsaw Pact, but it is mainly because of the ocean that separates North America and West Europe, which makes it harder to make this linkage credible. These difficulties with 'extended deterrence' have generated a requirement for many tactical and theatre nuclear weapons and arcane strategic doctrines. Thus nuclear weapons and the threat to use them in response to a conventional attack are central to NATO's conception of deterrence.

In contrast, the Warsaw Pact is less likely to oppose European denuclearization so vigorously, at least in its initial stages. Nuclear symbolism is less important to its unity, and the USSR has long given public support to nuclear-free zone proposals. Furthermore, although the asymmetry between NATO and Warsaw Pact conventional capability is often overstated, the Warsaw Pact's comparatively large conventional forces in Central Europe and relatively secure land lines of communication mean that it has less to fear than NATO (and especially the

FRG) from conventional attack. The major problem for an anti-nuclear British government appears to be to identify ways of pressurizing the USSR to make clear and tangible changes in its nuclear posture rather than simply to make declarations of intent or alterations in deployment that are difficult to verify.

French nuclear policy needs to be considered separately. The '*Force de Frappe*' commands broad popular support in France, and party political consensus on this matter seems, if anything, to be increasing.[1] An anti-nuclear British government would probably have little immediate influence on French nuclear policy, particularly since France, though a member of NATO, is not integrated into its military command structure. Although radical initiatives in the rest of Europe could stimulate a broader debate in France about nuclear policy, in the medium term this country must be excluded from our discussion. This does not mean that France can be ignored. On the contrary, it will become clear that France could greatly influence the achievement, or otherwise, of our objectives.

The other central aspect of European military deployments, and a matter of great concern, is conventional forces: European security would hardly be improved if the removal of nuclear weapons from the continent was accompanied by a rapid build-up of offensive conventional forces, with heightened fears of surprise attack and reduced crisis stability, especially since a major European war could well escalate to involve the use of Soviet and American strategic forces. Furthermore, because conventional and nuclear weapon policies are linked – vividly illustrated by NATO's first-use policy – it is unlikely that long-term reductions in the role of nuclear weapons in Europe could be achieved without important changes on the conventional level.

NATO's conventional land forces in central Europe are largely structured for the defence. However, if the Follow-On-Forces-Attack (FOFA) and Airland Battle doctrines are implemented by NATO, its offensive capabilities could substantially increase.[2] Certainly these developments are likely to be perceived as threatening by the Warsaw Pact. However, Warsaw Pact forces do appear to be more offensively structured than those of NATO.[3] This does not necessarily indicate offensive intentions.

There are obvious historical reasons why the USSR has chosen to try and fight any future war on enemy territory. In addition, effectively by attempting to hold West Germany hostage to Warsaw Pact attack, the offensive posture may be designed to deter the USA and its allies from exploiting any unrest in Eastern Europe.[4]

Nevertheless, this Soviet conception of security is unacceptable. It increases the chance of war arising from instabilities in Eastern Europe or confrontation with the USA. It increases West European fears of surprise attack or political coercion, and it undermines the political impact of peaceful initiatives. Just as NATO appears to be the prime obstacle to denuclearization, the Warsaw Pact is likely to prove the more resistant to the adoption of a defensively oriented conventional force posture.

This difference between the roles of nuclear and conventional forces in NATO and the Warsaw Pact means that changes in only one of these categories would involve greater concessions from one alliance than from the other. Since the process of change would be promoted if each alliance's prime security concerns were addressed at the same time, policy changes in each category of weaponry should be tackled together. The key task is to identify how a British government could most successfully help to exert pressure on NATO and the Warsaw Pact to make these changes.

Perhaps the most fundamental issue facing an anti-nuclear government would be whether to leave NATO to adopt an independent foreign policy like that of Sweden or to stay in NATO and try to change it from inside. As explained in the Introduction, the majority of the Commission believe that remaining in NATO would, on balance, put Britain in the best position to promote disarmament, reduce tension and break up the polarization of the Cold War and the military confrontation in Europe.[5]

3. DENUCLEARIZING NATO

If nuclear weapons are militarily and politically more central to NATO than Warsaw Pact policy, and if the Western Alliance can therefore be expected to be the main obstacle to starting the process of phasing out nuclear defence policies in Europe, then it is logical to focus first on the task of denuclearizing NATO. In any case, the UK can exert more direct influence on NATO than on the Warsaw Pact. Moreover, a British government with fundamental objections to nuclear deterrence policies would have an obligation either to work to remove NATO's reliance on nuclear weapons or to leave the Alliance.

Some NATO countries have already sought to distance themselves from nuclear weapons policies. Norway and Denmark have always refused to allow nuclear weapons to be based on their territory in peacetime, and Canada implemented such a policy during the 1970s.[6] However, although these countries illustrate the fact that it is possible to refuse to provide nuclear facilities and still remain a member of NATO, they are not good models for an anti-nuclear British government. They have gone to some lengths to avoid disrupting the Alliance over the issue, whereas one of the important reasons why we recommend that an anti-nuclear government should remain in NATO is precisely to change its defence policy.

Even to get NATO to adopt a no-first-use (NFU) policy would be an extremely significant achievement. It would amount to persuading it to change its conception of the strategic situation and of deterrence and to resolve in new ways a range of intra-alliance tensions and suspicions that many would prefer not to confront. Yet our objective of denuclearizing NATO policy includes decoupling US nuclear weapons from the defence of Europe. Clearly NATO could only be fully denuclearized over an extended period, during which more limited moves toward non-nuclear defence are made and the arguments for decoupling and other radical steps gain wider support.

As a 'core' member of NATO, the UK has a fair amount of influence within the Alliance to start this process of change. Up to now, the UK and its European allies have often abstained from playing a central role in the NATO decision-making process, and have allowed the USA even more influence than it would otherwise command as the most powerful member.[7] So a committed British government could hope to increase its influence simply by playing a greater role in the committee work of the Alliance. The UK is a member of NATO's Nuclear

Planning Group and of all the other key committees. As an anti-nuclear government would have a keen interest in NATO nuclear and conventional policy, it would want to retain its membership of these committees, and there is no mechanism by which it could be removed from them. Potential British leverage is enhanced because NATO's decisions are made unanimously rather than by majority vote. Once in power, an anti-nuclear government should probably call for a major review of NATO policy in NATO Council and other NATO assemblies and committees, in order to promote discussion and change, and to provide a focus for building alliances with potential supporters.

Britain's military contribution to the Alliance provides it with some more direct forms of leverage. For example, the UK could refuse to participate in naval or land exercises if it disagreed with the military strategy that was being rehearsed. Or it could threaten to withdraw the Royal Navy from certain maritime roles if it thought that they were integrated with nuclear policy or were unnecessarily provocative. These tactics could allow the UK to influence NATO policy on naval and battlefield nuclear weapons quite effectively.

Significant though they are, these sources of leverage are probably not powerful enough to achieve rapid changes. An anti-nuclear British government could not afford extended delays. It could only be reasonably sure of remaining in office for four or five years, during which time it must at least aim to ensure that a process of denuclearization of NATO had really started. However, the complexity and inertia of the present system and the tendency for muddle and misunderstanding during any reorganization would be bound to slow down the denuclearization process, even if there was broad agreement about the direction of the changes, which would certainly not be the case. This means that an additional source of pressure is necessary to force the pace of change. Otherwise NATO governments opposed to denuclearization or worried about rocking the boat could simply play for time and wait for a change of British government.

The most important such strategy, proposed in our first report, would be to threaten to withdraw from NATO unless certain minimum changes were made within a specified period of time. The strategy of conditional membership is designed to clarify to our allies the minimum acceptable rate at which the denucleariz-ation process must proceed for Britain to remain in NATO.

Nevertheless, conditional membership poses difficult choices. On the one hand, the UK would have to insist upon sufficiently far-reaching changes to ensure that a process of denuclearization had genuinely started in NATO within the lifetime of a single Parliament (i.e. 4–5 years). On the other hand, the timetable for these changes should be as realistic as possible and take account of the processes involved. If other NATO countries decided that the required changes were impossible within the timescale, they would have little incentive to support them. They would be resigned to the fact that either Britain would withdraw from NATO or the anti-nuclear government would fall (and would perhaps concentrate their energies on promoting the latter).

Unrealistically radical demands would constitute a politically astute strategy for leaving the Alliance rather than a serious attempt to change it. It would, however, be vital that the threat to withdraw from the Alliance if the demands for denucleariz-ation were not implemented was intended seriously.

The Initial 'Package' of Denuclearization Measures

The range of measures which Britain could insist upon range from the adoption of a no-first-use (NFU) policy, the creation of nuclear-weapon-free zones (NWFZs) and the withdrawal of types of nuclear weapons system (such as cruise missiles and battlefield nuclear weapons) to the removal of all nuclear wea-pons from Western Europe and a formal declaration that US nuclear weapons played no role in West European defence policy.

Since Britain could not hope to denuclearize NATO strategy on its own, the chosen package of measures must, as far as possible, be potentially acceptable to at least some other NATO member states. Later in this chapter we will show that this may not be as difficult as some think. One significant obstacle to acceptance, however, is that the UK would have to insist upon NATO implementing this package unilaterally. Otherwise continued British membership of the Alliance would be con-ditional only upon negotiations being started, with all of the loss of momentum and delay and confusion that this would entail. In any case, we believe that the denuclearization measures we propose would be beneficial to NATO countries' overall security even if the USSR did not immediately reciprocate (although it is clear that the process of changing NATO policy and deployments cannot, in practice, be expected to continue for long without significant reciprocation by the USSR and its allies).

However, most of the potential allies of an anti-nuclear UK prefer negotiations to unilateral approaches. This problem cannot be by passed, and so a coordinated effort must be made to persuade our potential allies of the appropriateness of unilateral approaches to improving security in Europe.

Such a task of persuasion could well prove to be effective, for the case is strong. It gives proper weight to the fact that negotiations in the past have made little impact on European nuclear or conventional forces or their associated policies, and that their future prospects for success seem poor, at least until significant progress has been made through other means. In addition to all of the usual difficulties with formal negotiations, the key security problems in Europe do not at present appear to be directly amenable to solution through this approach. In the main, NATO's objections to the adoption of a no-first-use policy, the creation of NWFZs, or the withdrawal of tactical nuclear weapons do not focus on worries about verification or about equivalent Warsaw Pact policies, but are mostly concerned with doubts about whether they would be good for NATO even if the Warsaw Pact agreed to take corresponding measures. These doubts stem from NATO's conceptions of what level of threat NATO needs to pose in order to deter the USSR effectively – an issue that the UK would want to debate explicitly with its allies, and arms control negotiations would probably only confuse this debate.

To the extent that NATO objections to the above measures focus on Warsaw Pact military forces, they centre on concerns about Warsaw Pact conventional capabilities.[8] But negotiations covering both the nuclear and the conventional forces in Europe, and discussing force structure and strategy as well as numbers, would be a nightmare. They would be so unlikely to succeed that it is best to rule them out from the start and to concentrate instead on unilateral processes.

We now briefly consider each of the elements of the package of unilateral measures on which we believe a country trying to denuclearize NATO should insist.

No first use: The attempt to persuade NATO fully to adopt a no-first-use (NFU) policy is the central element of the first stage of denuclearizing Alliance strategy. A decision to depend purely on conventional forces to deter a conventional attack by the Warsaw Pact would release NATO policy from a number of constraints and contradictions, and a range of other nuclear disarmament and disengagement proposals would become much more acceptable to it. An abandonment of the present first-use policy would have immense symbolic and political importance in the Alliance, and could only be associated with a fundamental reappraisal of defence policy and the problem of European security.

Since the USSR has already made a no-first-use commitment, a similar declaration by NATO could be seen as reciprocation to a Warsaw Pact initiative. However, unless it were associated with real changes in military strategy and weapons deployment, an NFU declaration can do little to raise the nuclear threshold in a crisis or war. As a confidence-building measure, a declaration alone is just as likely to generate scepticism and suspicion as it is to increase trust and stability. It must therefore be made clear from the beginning that an NFU policy must involve real, visible changes in military deployments and exercises as well as a declaration of intent.

In our view, the main value of a no-first-use policy arises from the possibilities it would present for further change in weapons deployment and strategy. However, because of the dramatic shift it would represent in NATO doctrine, the adoption of a no-first-use policy would in itself be a particularly powerful signal to the Warsaw Pact and the rest of the world that the Alliance was ready for serious initiatives to promote arms control and military disengagement.

Nuclear-weapon-free zones: Nuclear-weapon-free zone (NWFZ) proposals for areas of Europe have a long history, as described in Chapter Three, and are now focused on central Europe, the Nordic region, and the Balkans. If they were established, such NWFZs would be important confidence-building measures and, by securing the withdrawal of forward-based nuclear weapons, could improve crisis stability and raise the nuclear threshold in war. In the long term, NWFZs could promote the military disengagement of parts of Europe from their respective super-power, as these regions would be partially insulated from the superpower's nuclear weapon policies. However, the effectiveness of this aspect of NWFZs is often exaggerated.

Obviously, the larger the NWFZ, the greater is its military and political significance. A NWFZ covering both Germanys and perhaps even beyond would certainly have greater impact than the more limited zone stretching about 150 kilometres either side of the East-West German border, proposed by the Palme Commission.[9] The larger zone was widely discussed in the 1950s and it may be possible to achieve an agreement to establish it in the future. If so, then the Commission would support it.

However, the division of Europe into two military blocs (and in particular the place of East and West Germany in their respective alliances) has been consolidated since the 1950s, and political resistance to such a wide nuclear-free zone would now be intense. West German governments have traditionally been very sensitive to being singled out in NATO policy and, in the short term at least, would probably strongly resist any proposal for a NWFZ covering all of its territory. Although the German Green Party and small sections of the SPD would support such a NWFZ, they remain very much in the minority.

The Commission believes that an anti-nuclear UK should insist that a NWFZ in central Europe be established. However, in view of West German objections to a NWFZ covering all of the FRG (particularly if it were established unilaterally), a zone stretching at least 100-150 kilometres from the East-West German border would be acceptable. This zone should be established unilaterally, but, as discussed later in this chapter, we would hope that it would be reciprocated by the Warsaw Pact.

The proposal to create such a zone, though, through a unilateral rather than negotiated process, would at least command wider support than other NWFZ proposals for the region and has the advantage of being a well-known and well-discussed measure, so that misunderstandings and unnecessary fears are more likely to be avoided. Since NATO has few nuclear weapons stored within 100 km of the inter German border, the minimum zone would not involve much relocation of nuclear caserns.[10] More disruptively, satisfactory verification procedures should be established for dual-capable systems in the area, such as heavy artillery, in order to demonstrate adherence to the NWFZ policy.

There is strong support in the Balkans and the Nordic area for the establishment of NWFZs in those regions.[11] The Finnish and Swedish governments have supported a Nordic zone, but Norway's position has fluctuated according to the political party in power. If NATO were to adopt an NFU policy there would be fewer strategic and political obstacles to all-party support in Norway. In the Balkans the main barrier to the creation of an NWFZ seems to be Turkey. There are difficult questions about passage through the Bosphorus and Dardanelles and about how much of Turkey should be included within the zone. As denuclearization progressed, these problems would become much easier to resolve. In particular, Turkey's opposition to the proposal might be overcome if the USA came to accept a no-first-use policy, as at present the USA exerts considerable influence in the region, especially through military aid during this time of tension between Turkey and Greece.

If Balkan and Nordic NWFZs were established, strong pressure could be exerted on the USA and USSR to withdraw or relocate nuclear forces clearly intended to overfly the zones or allocated to targets within them. This could affect sea-launched cruise missiles in the Norwegian and Mediterranean Seas, GLCMs in Sicily, and medium-range missiles based in the USSR in areas adjacent to the NWFZs. If the zones were established by a negotiated treaty, then it is likely that it would guarantee the withdrawal of at least some of these forces.

A non-nuclear UK should provide support and encouragement for Nordic and Balkan NWFZs. However, the pace and manner in which they are set up must be primarily determined by the countries directly involved. We do not think it is necessary to include them in the initial package of denuclearization measures on which continued British membership of NATO would depend.

Pershing II and GLCMs: The withdrawal of PIIs and GLCMs

must be a top priority for any unilateralist British government. Their withdrawal would improve crisis stability and be a powerful signal of intent to the USSR, since they directly threaten Soviet territory. These missiles have acquired an enormous symbolic importance, and removing them from Europe would have a significance out of all proportion to its impact on crisis stability, great though this would be.

This measure is also likely to command broad support from amongst the European public. The campaigns against these missiles since 1980 have ensured that the issues have already been widely discussed and that people sympathetic to at least some limited measures for reducing reliance on nuclear weapons can be most readily mobilized in support of the withdrawal of cruise and Pershing missiles. On the other hand, European governments invested a great deal of political capital in the installation of these missiles, in most cases against majority opinion in their countries. They may therefore prove particularly resistant to reraising the issue now that the missiles have been installed. Whether or not an anti-nuclear British government and its allies could achieve this measure would be a sensitive indicator of the chance of getting started a wider process of NATO denuclearization.

Battlefield nuclear weapons: There is growing consensus in NATO that many of its battlefield nuclear weapons allocated to central Europe should be withdrawn. Many are seen as obsolete or as having no strategic or military value. In 1983, after a NATO meeting in Montebello, Canada, it was announced that some 1,400 battlefield nuclear warheads would be withdrawn over the following five years, although this was seen as part of a process of modernization of NATO's forces which could involve deploying longer-range and more effective nuclear systems in Europe in the future.[12]

In war, NATO's battlefield nuclear weapons (the atomic demolition mines (ADMs), nuclear artillery shells and short-range missiles like the Lance missile system) can only be intended for nuclear warfighting purposes. In peacetime their only plausible deterrent value is to threaten to escalate any war to a European or global holocaust. They make a tempting target for pre-emptive attacks in a crisis, encourage the delegation of the

145

authority to use nuclear weapons to battlefield commanders, and distract NATO's military tacticians from what should be their central task: to prepare for effective and purely conventional defences against attack.[13] Their withdrawal would greatly strengthen the credibility of a no-first-use policy. It would improve crisis stability, and would also improve the chances of limiting any war to the purely conventional level.

The withdrawal of these weapons should therefore be one of the conditions for continued British membership of NATO. Because of the existing scepticism about the role of such weapons in NATO, this might well prove to be the measure in our 'package' for which it is easiest to secure NATO agreement. However, the timescale over which these weapons are withdrawn may prove much more controversial. The Commission would certainly favour the withdrawal of all of them within four years, and a minority recommended that this be insisted upon. However, the majority believed that, provided that most such weapons had been removed, it would be unnecessary to threaten withdrawal from NATO if a few of them remained after four years. However, from the start of the anti-nuclear government's term of office, Britain should refuse to participate in exercises involving the simulated use of nuclear weapons.

The Commission recognized that the removal of all the remaining US nuclear weapons in Europe – bombs and naval tactical weapons – within the first five years would be even harder to achieve, although it would be desirable. Because there is no guarantee that a government committed to non-nuclear defence policies would be re-elected, deadlines for the removal of nuclear weapons from West Europe which extend beyond the lifetime of a single Parliament would have diminished force and credibility. However, the majority of the Commission reluctantly accepted that there was no alternative in this case. To insist on impossibly short deadlines would be against the spirit of trying to change NATO from within.

Longer Term Prospects
We therefore recommend that a NATO review conference should be held seven or eight years after the unilateralist government first comes to power (i.e. two or three years after the first term of

146

office is likely to finish). This conference would review all aspects of alliance policy, including the continued existence of NATO itself. It would provide a valuable focus for campaigning on NATO nuclear policy and a clear indication of whether the process of denuclearization was still underway. All battlefield nuclear weapons should be withdrawn from Europe by the time this conference is held. It is at this conference also that we would expect a decision to be made to withdraw all remaining nuclear weapons from Europe within the following two years.

The broad agenda for this review conference should be fixed before the end of the anti-nuclear government's first term of office. The governing political party in Britain would then include in its election manifesto a commitment to withdraw from the Alliance unless the above timetable were agreed at the review conference. If it were re-elected, it would carry through its manifesto promise. If defeated, it would argue for its policies in opposition, and campaign for withdrawal from the Alliance if the Review Conference indicated that NATO was likely to remain a nuclear alliance for the indefinite future.

Were NATO to agree to withdraw battlefield and tactical nuclear weapons, it would obviously be preferable if they were dismantled rather than just stockpiled or redeployed. Otherwise they could be flown back into Europe during a crisis. Furthermore, dismantling the warheads would increase the pressure on the USSR to reciprocate by scrapping or withdrawing its own tactical nuclear weapons in Eastern Europe.

If the USA did agree to dismantle these warheads, international verification procedures should be set up to monitor the process. This would not only increase the international impact of the changes in NATO policy, but also establish norms for the verification of any Soviet reciprocation. This issue is discussed in more detail in Chapter Seven. However, it is ultimately for the USA to decide what to do with the warheads withdrawn from Europe. NATO and Britain can advise, but they cannot dictate the final decision.

Decoupling: The final stage of the process of weaning NATO away from reliance on nuclear deterrence would be to sever the link between any US nuclear weapons and European defence-'decoupling'. This must necessarily wait until all US nuclear weapons have been removed from Europe. Even after that, so long as NATO remains in existence or the USA has any military links with Western Europe (or even close political relations), doubt about coupling is bound to exist in the minds of the Soviet leadership. Whatever NATO or US official doctrine would say, Soviet leaders would be likely to fear that war in Europe could escalate so that US nuclear weapons would be used against their country.

However, in this context we are not seriously concerned about reassuring the Soviet leadership. Their fears cannot be removed short of global nuclear disarmament. Our ethical and practical concerns are with the effects of coupling on the Alliance itself and on Britain's place within it.

If NATO deterrence policy continued to rest ultimately on US strategic nuclear weapons, there would be continual pressure to make the coupling more 'credible'. NATO doctrine would contain the seeds for the reintroduction of nuclear weapons to Western Europe. Furthermore, being fundamentally opposed to nuclear defence policies, we would want NATO doctrine to be purged of any role for nuclear weapons. Unless this could be achieved, we would recommend any consistent anti-nuclear government to withdraw from the Alliance.

The decoupling debate might seem very remote, given the immediate dangers of the military confrontation and the large numbers of nuclear weapons currently deployed in Europe. However, a unilateralist British government would probably have to confront this issue almost immediately after it was elected. Unless the government were consistent in its rejection of nuclear defence policies, its whole programme of denuclearization could be undermined. For example, if it accepted coupling, the UK would be under some obligation to grant facilities to US strategic forces.

In view of this, we believe that the incoming government should state from the outset that it does not need or want any US nuclear guarantee for itself, opposes any NATO reliance on such a guarantee, and will therefore not contribute facilities for US strategic nuclear forces. It should state openly that its goal is to persuade its European allies of the desirability of decoupling, but explicitly recognize that since this is a minority view at present it would be keen to work with governments that still valued nuclear coupling in order to achieve more limited steps away from nuclear policies.

NATO governments that sought to *guarantee* the link between European defence and US strategic weapons would probably be reluctant to support even these more limited denuclearization measures. They would regard the first-use policy and tactical nuclear weapons as a way of tying the survival of mainland USA to the security of any part of NATO Europe. However, the search for an absolute nuclear guarantee is in any case doomed to failure. Whatever the US promises in peacetime, in a crisis or war a US president can always decide not to launch nuclear retaliation against the USSR and other Warsaw Pact countries if they invade Western Europe. It must always be doubtful that the USA would choose to risk the total obliteration of its homeland in response to the invasion of an ally.

Our expectation is that most European governments could accept this reality and reconcile themselves to the deterrent effect of the mere, irreducible possibility of US nuclear retaliation in response to nuclear attack on Europe. Not only is this all that exists at the moment, but it can also be coherently argued that this possibility is a very powerful deterrent to any possible Warsaw Pact aggression. Acceptance of this position would open the way for these countries to support, or at least aquiesce in, the package of denuclearization measures described above.

How long could a government fundamentally opposed to nuclear deterrence remain in NATO if nuclear weapons remained part of its deterrence policy? A majority of the Commission believes, in line with our first report, that Britain should impose a strict time limit within which NATO should renounce any reliance on nuclear deterrence. NATO would be asked to agree to decoupling in principle at the review conference, and to establish this as Alliance policy as soon as all US nuclear weapons had been removed from European soil. If this was not agreed at the review conference, then Britain should prepare to leave the Alliance, though more in sorrow than in anger if substantial progress had been made toward reducing the role of nuclear weapons in Alliance policy.

It was recognized that agreement to decoupling would be very difficult to achieve. However, most of the Commission decided that if the deadline for this were extended beyond seven or eight years, it would be so weak as to have little meaning. With no effective deadline, the policy of working to denuclearize NATO from within could continue indefinitely, and there would be a great risk of being co-opted into long-term support for nuclear deterrence. A minority of Commission members, however, took a different view. They believed that Britain should continue to work within the Alliance so long as the denuclearization process was going forward, even if the review conference failed to commit itself to the final stages of the denuclearization process.

Summary of Recommendations

To summarize the discussion of this section, in addition to implementing its own nuclear disarmament programme for British nuclear weapons and attempting to change NATO by argument, committee work and leverage through military exercises, the Commission recommends that an anti-nuclear British government should seek to change NATO policy by making its membership of the Alliance conditional upon the implementation of the following set of measures:

- the adoption of a no-first-use policy (within two years)
- the removal of all Pershing II missiles and GLCMs from Europe (within two years)
- the establishment of a NWFZ at least 100 kilometres wide in the FRG along the East-West German border, with adequate international verification procedures to reassure outside observers that NATO had removed nuclear weapons from the zone (within three years)
- agreement to hold a NATO review conference about seven or eight years after the election of the British anti-nuclear government to review fundamentally all aspects of NATO policy
- the withdrawal of most US battlefield nuclear weapons from Europe within about four years, with the remainder being removed by the time the NATO review conference was held
- a decision to be made at the review conference to phase out

the remaining US nuclear weapons in Europe within two years and formally to decouple European defence from US nuclear weapons as soon as all these nuclear weapons had been withdrawn from Europe.

A minority of the Commission took the view that the last deadline should not be strictly enforced provided it was judged that the process of weaning NATO away from nuclear deterrence was still going forward.

If the anti-nuclear British government and its supporters could not persuade NATO to adopt these measures within the given timetable, then it would start the process of leaving NATO – first by suspending British membership and then, after a gap of up to two years, by withdrawing completely. By suspending membership as soon as a deadline is missed, the government would be showing resolve and exerting strong pressure on other NATO governments to agree to the denuclearization measures. If this worked and the measures were implemented before Britain had completely withdrawn from the Alliance, then the UK could immediately resume its participation in Alliance activities.

We considered the possibility of withdrawing from NATO's military command structure instead of suspending all Britain's Alliance activities (as was recommended in our first report). However, there would be a great deal of popular confusion about what this meant (note for example the widespread uncertainty about whether or not France is a member of the Alliance), whereas suspension is a much more easily comprehended and vivid step.

These are our recommendations to an 'ideal' anti-nuclear British government. In practice, an anti-nuclear British government may be unwilling to adopt them in full. To our mind this would either compromise the government's opposition to nuclear deterrence or reduce its effectiveness in changing NATO policy (or both). Nevertheless, such a government could still greatly improve the situation in Europe even if it only took up elements of our approach.

We now consider the possibility of our NATO allies agreeing to our recommended measures. We focus on the initial stages of the denuclearization process. The longer-term possibilities are even harder to predict, since they depend a lot on the progress achieved in the first years.

4. PROSPECTS OF CHANGING NATO

Although Britain's leverage in NATO would be significant, especially if the strategy of conditional membership is handled well, it is nevertheless limited and certainly less than that of the USA and FRG. There is little chance of forcing NATO to accept even part of the initial package of denuclearization measures outlined above in the face of determined opposition from both the USA and FRG. The opposition of only one of these countries would mean the package would require the support of several NATO governments and of strong popular movements to have any prospects of success. An anti-nuclear British government would clearly have to seek allies and do all that it could to neutralize or weaken opposition.

This consideration has already affected our choice of minimum denuclearization measures. A number of social democratic and other parties in Europe already support several elements of the package outlined above. However, as yet, most of these put their hopes in negotiated solutions rather than in unilateral approaches, and there is still relatively little support for the complete denuclearization of NATO strategy. The obstacles to success are great, and even if the international situation were favourable to progressive change, an anti-nuclear British government would require considerable tactical skill, and luck, to succeed in winning NATO over to the denuclearization process.

Each country, in or out of NATO, to which we might look for support, has its own traditional foreign and defence policy objectives, its own special sensitivities, and a relatively autonomous agenda for internal political debate. The presentation of the British proposals should try to take this into account.

Since states rarely like being dictated to, the strategy of making a set of demands on NATO will make it easier for opponents to isolate Britain politically. This disadvantage can be partially overcome by making joint proposals with other countries wherever possible. This requires prior preparation, involving discussions and coordinated policy statements in the period before the anti-nuclear British government is elected.

The UK need not simply lobby for support among governments. If conditions were right, a well argued and principled stand by the UK could mobilize substantial public support in Europe, the USA, and elsewhere. This could help to pressurize hostile governments into moderating their opposition or bolster the position of sympathetic governments.

Though such public support would be very important to our prospects for success, it is of course the government of the day in each country that would ultimately take the decisions about foreign and defence policy. These decisions can be greatly influenced by public opinion and campaigns, but the strength and timing of mass movements depend upon many domestic as well as international political conditions and we cannot expect such movements to be in phase with each other or to be most influential in each country at the most critical times. Furthermore, in spite of the activities of the peace movements over the last few years, the majority of people in Europe and the USA are not radical nuclear disarmers awaiting effective leadership. Opinion polls in most NATO countries indicate overwhelming public support for NATO and for at least a minimum Western nuclear retaliatory force.[14] Even in Spain and Greece, whose publics are much more ambivalent about NATO membership, parties that have questioned NATO membership during their election campaigns have proved to be reluctant to leave the Alliance when actually faced with the decision.

This imposes important constraints on the way in which campaigns for radical change should be conducted. The fact that there is widespread concern about the dangers of the nuclear arms race, and broad public support for components of the denuclearization package, means that popular pressure and opposition parties are potentially very important to our strategy for denuclearizing NATO. But this potential will only be fully realized if, in the initial stages at least, measures like no-first-use or the withdrawal of tactical nuclear weapons are put at the top of the agenda of public debate, rather than nuclear deterrence *per se* or the continued existence of the Alliance. We now consider each NATO country's likely reactions to the initial denuclearization measures in more detail.

The USA has always been the dominant power in NATO and has usually set the political and military agenda of the Alliance. Its commitment of conventional forces to Europe and the crucial role that US nuclear weapons play in NATO strategy gives it enormous leverage. Its economic and financial strength allows the US to cajole, coerce, or provide incentives to influence European governments. Furthermore, some NATO governments prefer US leadership because they find it politically convenient to allow the USA to take major public responsibility for NATO policy, either for reasons of domestic politics or because any alternative system of leadership might bolster the position of a European rival. So even as Western Europe's combined economic and conventional military power has grown to match that of the USA, the USA has retained its position of political leadership.

However, Europeans also have several sources of leverage over the USA. The United States has never had the power to impose a programme on NATO without making compromises with its European allies. One striking difference between NATO and the Warsaw Pact is that US dominance over its European allies is unlikely to be backed up by direct military force. On several occasions European governments have been able to force major compromises or alterations in US proposals for NATO policy or arms control negotiations.[15]

Europe is important to the USA's policy of containing Soviet power and influence. US bases in Europe have always been important to US strategic policy as well as to NATO European strategy.[16] The US values European naval facilities for its operations in the Norwegian and Arctic seas, the Mediterranean, North Africa, and the Near East. Crucial intelligence-gathering facilities are sited in the UK and elsewhere in Europe. The threat of losing these military bases and facilities provides Europe with influence.

The USA also has a keen interest in preserving pro-US West European policies and the freedom to invest in, and trade with, Europe. Whether the US takes seriously the threat of Warsaw Pact invasion or military coercion of Western Europe, or sometimes simply finds the 'threat' useful in tying Western Europe to the USA, it has a clear self-interest in contributing to NATO.

Even as the focus of military confrontation has spread from Europe to the Third World, Middle East, and Far East, political and ideological support from Western Europe is of great value to the US world position. Its growing economic strength also provides Europe with its own influence in the USA, and West European nations are increasingly coordinating their foreign and defence policy positions.

US influence over NATO policy is therefore strong but not unshakeable, and the US has numerous reasons for making concessions in order to preserve NATO. With this in mind, we now assess likely US reactions to our denuclearization package, and the impact that US government decisions could have on its adoption by the Alliance.

There are several reasons why the USA is likely to be very reluctant to agree to the package. Even if it could accept the proposals themselves, it would be deeply suspicious of the implications of making concessions to the new foreign and defence policy of the UK and its anti-nuclear allies. The very act of proposing the package would be a challenge to US leadership. It could be interpreted in the US as a move towards 'neutralism' and a potential defeat in its superpower competition with the USSR.

The denuclearization measures would remove any US leverage arising from its theatre and tactical nuclear weapons. The 'problem of decoupling' (i.e. worries about the credibility of the US 'guarantee') has caused West European NATO governments continual anguish, and has provided the US with an easy source of influence which could be reduced if NATO adopted a no-first-use policy. However, US conventional forces in Europe have always been the more potent source of US influence in NATO, and the importance of these would, if anything, be enhanced by the denuclearization process. So the proposals in themselves need not greatly reduce sources of US influence in NATO and therefore might not be opposed on these grounds.

In fact, several influential groups (both liberal and conservative) in the USA already advocate the strengthening of 'the second (European) pillar' of NATO, in order that Europe bear a greater proportion of the political responsibility and economic and military burden of NATO policy.[17] Support for this argument seems partly to be based on an assumption that such a development would tend to favour the Right: once Europeans were more directly confronted with the responsibility of 'standing up to the Soviet threat' they might increase their military spending and take a tougher attitude.[18] But it also indicates that the US establishment is not always jealous of its position as undisputed political leader of NATO, provided it believes that the West Europeans will not take a non-aligned or pro-Soviet position.

Moreover, the USA has often urged NATO to place less reliance on the early use of nuclear weapons in central Europe. This was one of the main sources of controversy during the formulation of the flexible response strategy in the mid-1960s, and it was the European governments (especially the FRG and UK) that were most concerned to retain the threat of the early use.[19] Similarly, there have been times, during the Carter Administration for instance, when the US government has been more sceptical than many European political leaders of the need for certain US theatre nuclear forces in Europe.[20] Given the growing consensus in NATO that many tactical nuclear warheads should be withdrawn from central Europe, a European demand to withdraw nuclear artillery shells, and other battlefield nuclear warheads may well be acceptable to the US government.

The removal of Pershing II and GLCMs would meet much stiffer opposition. Some senior US officials regard them as strategically important, and would resist their removal because of their deterrent and nuclear-warfighting capability. Moreover, as we argued earlier, the deployment of these missiles acquired enormous symbolic value, representing the unity and resolve of NATO under US leadership. A great deal of political capital was invested in securing deployment and most of the European countries in which the missiles are based would have to support their removal before the US government is likely to be convinced that the political costs for NATO of retaining the missiles outweighed the political and strategic costs (as they would be seen in the USA) of withdrawing them.

There could be fears in the USA (and elsewhere in NATO)

that a no-first-use policy would radically undermine the US policy of containing Soviet influence. Because of the standard NATO belief that the Warsaw Pact conventional forces are greatly superior to those of the Alliance, many Americans would be worried that a no-first-use policy would open the way for Soviet military coercion, or even invasion, of Western Europe and other countries adjacent to the Soviet bloc. Proposals to reorganize NATO conventional forces along more clearly defensive lines would fuel such suspicions further unless NATO continued to aim to repel a WTO attack rather than just to exact a 'high entry price'. However, since defensive deterrence in NATO will probably involve an expansion of reservists or the Territorial Army, there may be some compensating symbols of our 'will to resist' available.[21]

Nevertheless, there is increasing support in the USA for a no-first-use policy. Many senior and experienced military and political people now advocate it.[22] Hopefully, if these people were supported by several European governments (and particularly by the FRG), the US Administration might be persuaded to adopt a global no-first-use policy. It is more likely, though, that the USA would be reconciled to a no-first-use policy in Europe while retaining the option of first use in areas like the Middle East or Korea where the spheres of influence are less well established. While such a partial change in policy would be unsatisfactory, it may be the best that can be achieved in the medium term: European NATO governments cannot insist on changes outside the NATO area.

If the USA became reconciled to a NATO no-first-use policy, agreement in principle to the establishment of nuclear-weapon-free zones in Europe would probably be relatively easy. However, the unilateral aspect of our proposals could make it difficult to secure US agreement in practice. At present there is little understanding or support in the USA for unilateral approaches, even in the arms control community. However, even if Americans could not be convinced of the advantages of a unilateral approach to arms control in Europe, they should be prepared to accept this approach if the NATO European governments insisted that the relevant measures be implemented. The weapons affected by our denuclearization package are, after all, supposedly deployed for the defence of Europe.

In practice, although US government resistance to the denuclearization package should be expected for strategic and political reasons, whether or not it would ultimately accept it would depend upon the unity amongst European governments. If the major European NATO countries were divided, and especially if the FRG opposed the British proposals, then the USA could be expected to exploit these divisions. In this case, the denuclearization process in NATO is unlikely to get very far. If, however, the UK and FRG were in broad agreement and joined by several other members of the Alliance, and if the price of restoring some consensus in NATO were a shift of political power towards Europe, then the USA could well acquiesce in the implementation of the proposals. There would almost certainly be retaliatory moves by the US Congress to reduce the US conventional forces in Europe. But it is unclear to what extent these would actually be implemented. In the medium term, many US forces are likely to remain based in Europe because, as outlined above, it is probably in the USA's national interests to retain a significant military presence in Europe. In fact the reductions could well be no more than symbolic.

There are at least two European defence institutions that might play an important role in sustaining and moulding European unity against US pressure. They are the Western European Union (WEU) and the Eurogroup in NATO.

WEU includes France and all of the most powerful European NATO countries. It was recently revived to strengthen European joint military development and procurement programmes and to provide an institution within which France could discuss defence coordination with European members of NATO.[23] As far as we are concerned, the WEU's main disadvantage is that it excludes potential supporters of measures to reduce reliance on nuclear weapons, such as Greece, Denmark, Norway, Spain, and Portugal. It could also promote unwelcome discussions about how to involve French nuclear weapons in West German defence.

The Eurogroup in NATO was founded in 1968 to promote European influence in NATO.[24] It excludes France and has no permanent secretariat. It would obviously be important for the

UK to argue its case and gain support in this group, and there may be a case for increasing the resources allocated to it. However, while both the Eurogroup and the WEU could prove to be important, it is clear that normal diplomacy and sensitivity to each country's concerns will be critical in building broad European support for denuclearization. Of all European countries, the position taken by the West German government would be of greatest significance.

The Federal Republic of Germany (FRG)

Most of the measures in the denuclearization package bear directly on deployments and strategy in the FRG. West German security concerns dominate much of the debate about NATO strategy, and the FRG's influence in the Alliance is second only to that of the USA. Furthermore, anxieties about possible West German reactions if the UK left NATO are one of the main reasons why a majority of the Commission favours trying to change NATO from within. The UK must be sensitive to West German security problems.

As outlined in Chapter Three, West German policy is broadly characterized by attempts to strengthen military deterrence while at the same time seeking to improve political and economic relations with Warsaw Pact countries, and particularly with the German Democratic Republic.

Preventing war is of overriding importance to the FRG, since its territory would be devastated by any major war between NATO and the Warsaw Pact, whether nuclear or conventional. At the centre of West German deterrence policy is the joint commitment by the NATO allies to defend it against attack, mainly expressed through the peacetime presence of the allies' conventional forces in the FRG. None of our proposals for the reform of NATO are designed to change this, at least until Soviet troops are withdrawn from the GDR.

However, the package would greatly affect another traditional aspect of West German deterrence policy: the coupling of US nuclear forces to the defence of the FRG against both conventional and nuclear attacks from the East. As described earlier in this chapter, the main NATO rationale behind its first-use policy is that its conventional forces are inadequate reliably to deter a conventional offensive by the Warsaw Pact. Tactical and theatre nuclear weapons are intended to demonstrate that any war in central Europe could lead to the obliteration of Europe (including European Russia) and, by providing a link with US strategic nuclear forces, to global holocaust. The first stage of the proposed denuclearization process is to change West German and NATO policy so that nuclear weapons aim to deter only nuclear attack, and then only by the very existence of US strategic forces rather than by tactical weapons based in Europe.

The credibility of a US commitment to risk its own survival by responding with nuclear weapons to a successful conventional attack on West Germany has already been questioned in this chapter, and it is now widely questioned in the FRG. Support for NATO policy has further diminished as the existing policy of flexible response and counterforce deterrence has been seen as destabilizing.

There is already widespread support in West Germany for rejecting GLCMs and PIIs and reducing the battlefield nuclear weapon stockpiles.[25] The SPD party conference of May 1984 rejected these weapons and supported a no-first-use policy and the establishment of a NWFZ in central Europe, though through negotiations rather than unilateral measures.[26] This means that an SPD government may well support the denuclearization package but, unless the party can be persuaded to change its position on unilateralism, it would resist the crucial proposal that it be implemented independently. The Green Party would probably wholeheartedly support the whole package, and indeed would argue for even more radical measures. If they still held seats in the Bundestag, the Greens could bolster SPD resolve to see the package through.

In the middle ground of West German politics, there would be fears that the proposed change in NATO policy was putting all of the risks on the FRG. Britain's own nuclear disarmament programme would demonstrate that the UK was not asking the FRG to move away from nuclear policies alone. But it would be vital to good relations between the two countries that the level of British conventional forces in the FRG were, at least, maintained.

If the FRG government supported changing NATO strategy, some in the USA might well try to stimulate West German fears by threatening to remove US troops from Europe if the measures were implemented. West German reactions to this are hard to predict, but it must be recognized that such threats could well prove very effective. The UK could do little to replace withdrawn US divisions, and would have to argue that the denuclearization process should proceed even if NATO conventional forces are weakened by US troop withdrawals. A West German government would have to be strongly committed to the proposed alternative strategies to maintain its support for them in this situation. However, if East-West relations were good and its European allies in North Europe all supported change, there is a possibility that it would resist US pressure. US forces in Germany are substantial, but nevertheless they constitute only a minority of the forces in place. The West Germans may not believe that the USA would actually withdraw a significant number of its forces, and would also have to take the possibility of the complete withdrawal of Britain from NATO into account.

In comparison with the SPD, the conservative parties (CDU/CSU) and liberals (FDP) officially oppose every element of the minimum package, though they would support a 'no-early-use' policy.[27] Unless the West German defence debate shifts ground radically, a CDU-dominated government would be very unlikely to support any of the proposals – except perhaps the withdrawal of some battlefield nuclear weapons – unless the proposed changes had unexpectedly strong support from the USA and most of the less powerful European NATO countries. It is more likely that the UK would have to reconcile itself to building up support for its proposals and hoping for a change of government in the FRG. If after two years this still had not happened, then it would have to start the process of withdrawal from NATO.

Other NATO Countries
There is a real possibility that most of the remaining NATO countries would accept the package and that several could actively support it. A number of these countries – for instance Greece, Canada and Denmark – have a history of opposition, or at least reservations about aspects of US or NATO policy.[28] However, because these reservations have been uncoordinated and unsupported by any 'core' NATO country, they have

generally been consigned to 'footnote status' (whereby the reservations are noted but given little serious consideration and have no impact on policy). If they acted together, and in coordination with countries more centrally important to NATO military strategy, such countries could greatly improve the prospects of starting the denuclearization process.

Toward the north, Canada, Norway, Denmark and Iceland do not permit nuclear weapons to be stationed on their territory in peacetime, and expressed concern when it was recently discovered that the USA had plans to deploy tactical nuclear weapons in some of them in a crisis. They are likely to see some merit in the implementation of the denuclearization package. However, they may still oppose the package (or at least fail to support it) if it seemed to threaten the NATO Alliance itself. For example, they have been unwilling, largely in the interests of NATO's political unity, to vote at the UN in favour of no-first-use.

At times, however, these countries have broken ranks with NATO policy. There have been abstentions on the issue of a freeze, Denmark suspended its contribution to the INF infrastructure programme, and the Nordic social democratic parties support a Nordic NWFZ.[29] If social democratic governments were in power in these countries, there is a good chance that they might give positive support to the denuclearization package, especially if they believed that one or both of the FRG and the USA could be persuaded to accept it.

In central Europe, there is potential support for the package in both Belgium and Holland. Their role in NATO strategy and the bases on their territory make them middle-ranking NATO powers. Both countries delayed making a final decision to deploy GLCMs, though coalition politics makes it difficult to predict government policy. The Dutch Labour Party (PvdA), the Flemish Socialist party, perhaps the Belgian (Walloon) Socialist Party, and the parties to the left of these, could be expected to support at least some of the package.[30] It is even possible that sections of the Belgian Christian Democratic Parties (CVP and PSC) and the 'progressive minority' of the Dutch Christian Democratic Appeal would also give some support. However, as in the FRG, none of the social democratic parties have policies which support unilateral measures (except the Dutch Labour Party for the withdrawal of GLCMs), so discussions on unilateral approaches before the anti-nuclear British government came to power would be important. Luxembourg's position would probably be similar to that of Belgium.

In Spain, the referendum, held in March 1986, endorsed Spain's membership of NATO, but only on condition that nuclear weapons were banned from Spanish territory and that there be a 'progressive reduction' of the US military presence in the country, as well as no integration into NATO military structures.[31] Almost 40 per cent of the population voted against even this limited involvement in NATO. In Greece, the PASOK government in 1981 was elected on a platform involving withdrawal from NATO, though its 1985 manifesto changed this policy to one of changing at least some of NATO's policies from within.[32]

For both these countries, therefore, a possible break-up of NATO would not be so potent in bringing them back into line behind the USA. If socialist parties were in government, both countries could be expected to support the denuclearization package. PASOK, for example, is committed to support a Balkan nuclear-weapon-free zone and a change to no-first-use. The main opposition parties – the Spanish Centre Democratic Union and the Greek New Democratic Party – are both pro-NATO, but they lack a strong commitment to nuclear policies and favour close ties with Western Europe, so their position could depend upon the weight of opinion amongst their European allies.

In Portugal, the 1983 agreement with the USA that no nuclear weapons are to be stored on the Azores or elsewhere on Portuguese territory indicates at least tacit support for denuclearization proposals.[33] However, nuclear issues have yet to be widely debated in Portugal.

In Italy, the situation is different. As an important member of NATO, both politically and because of its naval facilities and GLCM base, Italy would be a particularly valuable ally for an anti-nuclear British government. Warsaw Pact forces in Hungary are not thought to pose a great threat, which means that the tactical nuclear warheads for Lance missiles and artillery based in north-east Italy are widely regarded as unimportant. No

Italian government seems likely to resist strongly a proposal for their withdrawal as part of a change in NATO strategy. Neither is it likely to object to a no-first-use policy and NWFZ in West Germany, provided that these were acceptable to the FRG (though the Italian Navy may oppose a no-first-use policy for the Mediterranean).

However, both the Christian Democrats and Craxi's Socialist Party strongly supported the deployment of GLCMs in Italy. Only a government dominated by the Italian Communist Party (PCI) is likely to be sympathetic to the unilateral withdrawal of cruise missiles. But such a government would probably be so concerned about internal destabilization that it would be extremely wary of taking a lead on anti-nuclear issues: even in opposition the PCI does not support the unilateral withdrawal of GLCMs. It appears that no likely Italian government can be expected to give more than tacit support to the denuclearization package until either the changes have secured strong European backing or the USA accepts the change.

France

Although the denuclearization package would not directly affect French nuclear policy, France's political and economic importance in Europe, and its military strength, mean that French reactions to an anti-nuclear British government and to the proposed changes in NATO policy cannot be ignored.

At present there seems to be little hope that the anti-nuclear policies of a UK government and its allies would be widely understood or sympathetically received in France. All the major political parties support the *Force de Frappe* and oppose no-first-use or NWFZ agreements. Only the Communist Party supported the nuclear freeze proposal and opposed the deployment of cruise and Pershing missiles. However, France does support the development of a West European bloc to balance US influence, so it may also see advantages in the attempt to alter NATO policy. The position of the West German government would be a key influence on any French decision, but France is unlikely to participate in any sanctions that might be imposed if the UK becomes isolated.

The Neo-Gaullist Party (RPR), Giscard d'Estaing's UDF

party, and the Mitterand government all favour the development of a 'Euro-defence system', either within NATO but with the USA playing a much less dominant role or, in the long term, in place of NATO.[34] The system would be based largely on Franco-German cooperation backed up with French and British nuclear forces. As mentioned earlier, it was with this in mind that the WEU was resuscitated. The military consultation procedures of the Franco-German mutual defence treaty (the 1963 Elysée Treaty) have recently been reactivated, and a standing defence commission has been set up by the two countries.[35] There is little doubt that the FRG welcomes the opportunity to increase French support of its defence, but at present it would resist any moves which tended to reduce US commitment to West German defence. However, if NATO policy were in flux and the USA was threatening to withdraw some or all of its troops, the FRG could go along with French plans much more than it presently intends.

The Commission does not oppose in principle the development of closer military ties between France and the FRG, at least in the medium term. On the contrary, these might help the FRG to resist any US pressures to abandon the NATO denuclearization programme. But any integration of French nuclear weapons into West German defence policy would be highly undesirable, and it should be a high priority for British foreign policy to prevent this.

Conclusions

There would be great obstacles to a British government which tried to force important changes in NATO policy. However, the strategy does have some chance of success.

What is clear is that a great deal would depend on preparation before the anti-nuclear government's election, and on the politics of the first year or two after it came to office. If the UK antagonized potential European allies or became isolated, or if opponents managed to shift the focus of the debate away from the initial measures to the question of support for NATO and minimal nuclear deterrence, then the chance to change NATO from within could slip away.

Full discussions between social democratic, socialist parties,

165

and other potential supporters of a move away from reliance on nuclear deterrence, must take place well before an anti-nuclear government in the UK, or elsewhere, comes to power. Once elected, the value of an anti-nuclear UK government making joint proposals wherever possible is clear. The importance of widespread comprehension of, if not support for, the objectives of the denuclearization package in the USA makes it imperative that similar discussions are held with US groups. It is also of key importance to persuade potential allies of the important role of unilateral measures: at present there is little support or understanding of these approaches in either the USA or mainland Europe.

5. DISENGAGEMENT OF CONVENTIONAL FORCES: DEFENSIVE DETERRENCE IN NATO

If the denuclearization of NATO strategy were to begin, the Alliance's policy on conventional forces would inevitably be reassessed. It is therefore important for the UK and its allies to have a policy for conventional forces as well as for nuclear deployments: Europe's security would not be greatly improved if the withdrawal from Europe of a proportion of the nuclear weapons were accompanied by an intensified conventional arms race. Since NATO concern focuses mainly on central Europe, we will also concentrate on this region.

Our discussion will be based on NATO's present conventional force posture. However, it is worth noting that the struggle in NATO over denuclearization could severely limit or alter the available choices. For example, the USA may withdraw a proportion (or conceivably all) of its present divisions from Europe, or the French may become more deeply involved with the forward defence of West Germany.

If these struggles resulted in large reductions in NATO forces in central Europe, then NATO conventional force policy could not aim to repel a determined conventional attack on the FRG by the Warsaw Pact. It would have to settle for a high-entry-price policy instead. The deterrent effect of such a policy would be judged adequate if one believes (as we do) that there is no foreseeable situation in which the USSR would choose to start a costly and enormously destructive war simply to occupy or destroy the FRG. A high-entry-price policy would be a sufficient deterrent if the main risk of attack were to be during a political crisis, perhaps in Eastern Europe, when the Soviet leaders might consider an attack on the FRG to be a less costly course of action than any of the other alternatives. The high-entry-price policy would aim to ensure that there was no realistic situation in which this judgement is likely to be made.

The conventional force postures that might be involved in such a high-entry-price defence policy are discussed in some detail in *Defence Without the Bomb*. A strong argument could be made that this policy would be both perfectly adequate and desirable, because it would reduce military tension in Europe and allow resources to be diverted to more socially useful ends. However, in the near future, this argument is likely to be acceptable neither to the FRG nor to the USA; the denuclearization process is most likely to begin if the West Germans and others can be reassured that NATO policy in Central Europe aims to repel an all-out Warsaw Pact conventional attack. Of course, attempting to *guarantee* that NATO forces could achieve this would in fact be a guarantee for an arms race: war is a highly uncertain enterprise and the search for guarantees leads to worst-case assumptions. But this is well understood in the NATO establishment (even if sometimes conveniently forgotten) and should therefore be acceptable, at least in principle.

Assuming that the NATO armed forces in central Europe remain roughly at their present levels, the Alliance's conventional strategy could develop in one of three ways. First, there could be a major strengthening of NATO's offensive capability. Demographic trends make it unlikely that this would involve major increases in troop levels: the Bundeswehr, for example, will have severe difficulties even maintaining its present levels over the next decade.[36] Instead it would involve the implementation and extension of the FOFA and Airland Battle doctrines, using new weapons and communication and intelligence systems based on emerging technologies. This option would probably decrease crisis stability, fuel a conventional arms race, increase tension and undermine the denuclearization initiatives. It also promises to be very expensive. Any Soviet fears that NATO might intervene in any uprisings or crises in Eastern Europe would be exacerbated, and would bolster the legitimacy of Soviet forces in Eastern Europe. From the Soviet point of view, the integration of nuclear weapons into NATO battlefield strategy does at least act as a self-deterrent against Western interventions.

A second choice would be to retain NATO's present strategy with its mixture of offensive and defensive elements, and to seek to bolster it. This would be much less destabilizing than the first option, and is widely agreed by well respected analysts that present conventional forces are sufficient to deny the Warsaw Pact any assurance of victory in even an all-out conventional war.[37] There are several measures that could be taken to improve present capabilities without significant increases in NATO's offensive capabilities: for instance by increasing stocks of supplies, ammunition and spares; by making fuller use of better trained reservists and Territorial Armies; and by increasing use of obstacles along the East/West German border.[38]

The third choice would be to reorganize NATO conventional forces into a more visibly defensive posture.[39] This would aim to make even fuller use of the tactical advantages of the defence over the attacking force, to deliberately decrease tensions by making it clear that aggression is not intended and would be relatively impractical and, by making it clearer where the aggression actually came from, to increase the political constraints against aggression. It could also reduce NATO fears of surprise attack: since mobilization would be less threatening and destabilizing, NATO political leaders could be more willing to authorize it at an early stage (in contrast to the present situation where fears of triggering further escalation are more likely to encourage delays in responding to intelligence warnings of impending attack). It should be noted that this option is largely a matter of reorganization and would not necessarily involve any overall reductions in force levels.

The political constraints against aggression could also be increased by advance preparations for defence by civil resistance on a national level. The Greens in the FRG favour such a policy and some military strategists in West Germany and elsewhere in Europe have advanced proposals in which preparations for civil resistance in the towns and cities would complement military defence in the countryside, thereby enhancing the overall strategy of defensive dissuasion.[40]

Although the Commission believes that the first, offensive, option should be vigorously opposed, it does not recommend that an anti-nuclear government should absolutely insist on the third, instead of the second, option. The UK should insist that the FOFA programme be either abandoned or modified to concentrate only on shorter-range weapons, but otherwise it should be willing to accommodate to its allies' wishes about how to implement options two or three. Recalling the asymmetry discussed earlier this chapter, it is the Warsaw Pact that has the most political and military room for manoeuvre to make concessions on conventional force levels. Initially at least, attention should be focused on NATO's nuclear weapon policy rather than on its conventional forces.

Nevertheless, to choose option two would be to miss an important opportunity to change the basis of conventional deterrence in Europe at an early stage. A clear change of NATO policy towards 'defensive defence' policies would allow the maximum political pressure to be exerted on the Warsaw Pact to reciprocate with a change in its own offensively-oriented force posture. In doing so, NATO could open up an alternative route to reductions in the military confrontation in Europe to the still fruitless MBFR talks. It may also help to delegitimize the present level of Soviet forces in the GDR, Poland, and Czechoslovakia, and create favourable conditions for the development of a greater degree of autonomy in Eastern Europe.

The MBFR talks appear to be deadlocked. There are occasional hints that a breakthrough is imminent, but it seems clear that neither side has much interest in the success of the talks. Though the USSR does probably want reductions in armed forces in central Europe, this objective seems to have a lower priority than preserving secrecy about the details of its force levels and locking the US and other troops into the FRG to restrain any West German temptation to intervene in the GDR. At the same time, the USA and its allies clearly have no sense of urgency either. The argument about the existing force levels seems eminently resolvable if there were political will to make progress. Since this disagreement has continued for almost a decade, it is highly unlikely that the talks will make a real impact on European security unless the political and military situation changes significantly.

However, even if the MBFR talks were successful and a small reduction in the forces in central Europe took place, NATO's prime security concerns would hardly even have been addressed. Changing the absolute number of troops based in the area would have little effect on the offensively-oriented forces of the Warsaw Pact or on fears of surprise attack.

The confidence-building measures agreed in 1986 at the CDE conference in Stockholm touch on these security problems by focusing on exchange of information and achieving greater 'transparency' of force deployments and exercises. However, what is really needed is an approach that could achieve something more basic: a restructuring of force deployments to reduce the capability for surprise attack and increase the advantages of the defence.

However, to approach this problem by trying to negotiate for changes in force structure is likely to be even less successful than the MBFR talks: there is even more scope for bogging down negotiations in arguments about force structure than there is in counting troops. Furthermore, most of the concessions would have to be made by the Warsaw Pact, and so there would be haggling about offsetting concessions on other arms issues.

If NATO were unilaterally to reorganize its defence along more visibly defensive lines, its capacity to resist attack would not necessarily be reduced. Yet crisis stability would be improved and the USSR could be placed under intense political pressure to reciprocate. This approach seems more likely to succeed in securing a significant change in the character of the military confrontation than do the MBFR talks.

Though the details of how NATO forces could be reorganized into more defensively-oriented force structures still need much more work, the principles are reasonably clear: the changes should result in a militarily coherent posture, and it should be clear, even to the non-expert, that they entail a significant move toward a more defensive capability.

One promising approach is based on the creation of a 'disengagement zone': a zone from which categories of offensive forces such as heavy artillery, battle-tanks, and other heavy armoured forces would be withdrawn to behind a line some distance from the East/West German border.[41] Only lightly armoured forces would be permitted to operate inside the zone. A combination of static and highly mobile forces, armed for instance with mines, anti-tank and anti-aircraft precision-guided munitions (PGMs), could be stationed in the zone. These would be able to respond quicky to any minor incursion, and, in the case of major attack, would aim to slow down and disrupt the invading forces to give the heavy armoured divisions time to respond effectively. Obstacles and 'pipe mines' of explosives might also be used.

A standard objection to such proposals is that the FRG might be worried about the implied abandonment of the principle of forward defence. In fact the important aspects of that principle would hold for such a disengagement zone as much as they do for the present set-up. The scheme outlined above would still mean that the forces of West Germany's allies would be engaged in combat from the beginning of any war, thereby increasing deterrence and helping to ensure that the allies would not renege on their commitments if war occurred. Furthermore, it is virtually certain that present NATO strategy is also based on the assumption that a certain amount of West German territory would have to be conceded before a WTO attack could be halted.

The size of the disengagement zone, as for the NWFZ, should depend on political as well as military considerations. A 150 km-wide zone would include most of the FRG territory and cities such as Frankfurt, Nurenberg, and Munich and would use up a large proportion of NATO's tactical depth. So it would probably be unacceptable. It is also worth noting that if reciprocation is intended, Prague, Berlin, Leipzig and Dresden are also all within 150 km of the border, making mirror-image-like reciprocation unlikely. Even a 100 km-wide zone would include about 30 per cent of the West German population and 25 per cent of the country's industrial capacity. However, the zone cannot be too narrow, or it would lose most of its value. An acceptable zone width in the FRG would seem to be somewhere between 60-100km. If such a zone were reciprocated by the Warsaw Pact, the resulting disengagement area could be expected to allow the heavy armoured division of each side at least three or four days' preparation, after an attack began, for heavy battle with the adversary's land forces, although air attack could obviously be expected much sooner.

There are still many unresolved military issues associated with reorganization along more defensive lines and disengagement zones. Which categories of weapons, forces, and facilities should be withdrawn? When and how should the light forces in a disengagement zone be reinforced once the adversary's heavy armoured divisions were unambiguously advancing through its side of the zone (assuming that the initiative had been reciprocated)? What range of missiles and heavy artillery should the main forces possess (bearing in mind that light forces are very vulnerable to artillery bombardment)? There is, however, no reason to suppose that militarily satisfactory answers cannot be found to these questions.

One should also consider how best to increase the political constraints on attack. A disengagement zone – as with the adoption by NATO conventional forces of a defensive posture – would increase these substantially by making it much clearer to the world which side was the aggressor. There might be additional advantage if international representatives were permanently established in the zone. These could be justified by the need to verify that the disengagement zone and the wider NWFZ were being respected.

Naval disengagement could also be important. NATO has a legitimate interest in being able to secure, in war, the sea lines of communication across the Atlantic and Mediterranean. Control of these seas is of little defensive importance to the USSR. However, US and NATO plans to take the war into the Barents Sea, though militarily understandable, are highly provocative.[42] The UK, as the major contributor to NATO naval forces in the north-east Atlantic, could have sufficient influence to change NATO naval strategy in that area. For example, NATO strategy and exercises should not involve threats to Soviet strategic missile submarines in the Barents Sea, because of the dangers of rapid escalation such threats pose in times of crisis or conventional war.

Formal agreements on naval disengagement would, however, be difficult to achieve. This is partly because naval forces are inherently mobile and it would be very difficult to monitor the activities of submarines. It is also because neither side is going to accept constraints on its right to navigate anywhere in international waters. In this area, therefore, tacit restraint would be most appropriate. The importance of naval disengagement could further increase in the near future: for example, in addition to the military importance of the Norwegian and Barents Seas, the economic rights over the western part of the Barents Sea are disputed by Norway and the USSR. Up to now this has not been a major source of tension, but this may change as the oil fields of the Norwegian Sea are developed further northwards.[43]

6. WARSAW PACT RECIPROCATION

Although we believe that the denuclearization of NATO should not be made conditional on satisfactory reciprocation by the WTO, the political and military realities are such that the denuclearization process in NATO would have little chance of making much progress unless there were significant reciprocation by the Soviet Union and its Warsaw Pact allies. Recalling the asymmetry in threat perceptions in the two alliances, changes in Warsaw Pact conventional force postures could be even more important to NATO's, and particularly West Germany's, attitudes towards denuclearization than Soviet nuclear reductions would be.

There are several reasons why the USSR might be willing to reciprocate and to encourage the denuclearization of Europe, at least in its initial stages. It has traditionally supported the creation of NWFZs in central Europe, and has recently declared a no-first-use commitment. The Soviet leaders seem to be genuinely alarmed at the danger of nuclear war in Europe or elsewhere. They are also concerned to reduce the levels of damage inflicted on Soviet territory in the event of such a war.

However, the signs are not all good. Soviet support for NFU and NWFZs could be seen as part of a strategy to undermine present NATO strategy and to aggravate well-known sensitivities in the Western Alliance. This would be an easy way for the

USSR to gain the moral high ground, while remaining fairly sure that its offer would not have to be implemented. Its enthusiasm could diminish once the proposals have a good chance of implementation.

Though the Soviet no-first-use declaration was welcome, there has been little firm evidence of subsequent changes in Warsaw Pact deployments or strategy. There is debate among Western analysts about whether tactical changes identified in WTO exercises (relating to the so-called Operational Manoeuvre Group) imply greater or lesser integration of Soviet tactical nuclear forces with conventional operations. The forward basing of SS21, SS22, and SS23 nuclear missiles in East Germany and Czechoslovakia casts further doubt on whether the USSR has seriously tried to change its military plans in line with the no-first-use commitment. So long as NATO itself has a first-use policy, perhaps the forward deployment of Soviet nuclear forces is not too surprising, but it does raise the suspicion that the NFU declaration is regarded by some in the USSR as a propaganda coup rather than a serious initiative requiring significant changes in operational plans.

Nevertheless, the positive indications of the USSR's willingness to work for the denuclearization of European strategies do give grounds for hope about Soviet reciprocation to the NATO initiatives discussed earlier, especially as it probably perceives that, by itself, denuclearization ultimately works to Warsaw Pact military advantage.

As far as Soviet willingness to reduce or restructure its conventional forces in Europe is concerned, the clear links between Warsaw Pact concessions on the conventional level and the chances for NATO denuclearization could provide an important incentive for change. If NATO further emphasizes the defensive orientation of its conventional forces, and especially if this were to involve highly visible changes such as the creation of a disengagement zone, then the rationale behind the size and posture of the present Warsaw Pact forces will have been publicly undermined. This kind of unilateral action is less open to misunderstanding than Western proposals for negotiated reductions which are often suspected of being biassed against the Soviet Union. Fears of NATO intervention in Eastern

Europe would recede, creating an atmosphere in which the defence budget could be squeezed. The economic costs of maintaining large forces in Europe would then provide a strong incentive for reciprocation.

Unfortunately, the costs of maintaining large conventional forces are unlikely to prove automatically decisive. If they were that powerful, Warsaw Pact forces would be smaller than they are now. The Soviet military appears to be deeply attached to the importance of tactical surprise and offensive capabilities; a change to a defensive posture would appear to most of it as being against all military good sense. Moreover, as in any country, the defence ministry is likely to resist cuts in its budget. Even if the budget were reduced overall, it is hard to identify reasons why Soviet ministers and managers outside the defence ministry would have an interest in challenging the Soviet military's preference for preparing for the offence; these people would be interested in expenditure, not tactics.

The military resistance to reciprocating to a NATO initiative could be overruled by the Soviet Politburo, and it would be a prime objective to create an atmosphere in which a favourable decision is likely. There are some grounds for being optimistic, but it should be remembered that there may be more than institutional obstacles to reciprocation. The members of the Soviet government appear convinced of the political utility of military power. They could be tempted to retain the present offensively structured forces in Eastern Europe in the hope that they might prove politically useful in the future. Large Soviet forces in Eastern Europe might also be regarded by many in the USSR as important for retaining a decisive political influence in Eastern Europe.

There are therefore reasons to doubt that substantial reciprocation to NATO unilateral initiatives would follow automatically. It could be blocked or diluted by a number of bureaucratic or political obstacles. However the UK or NATO could exert significant leverage over Warsaw Pact and Soviet decisions, which could significantly increase the possibility that these obstacles could be overcome.

The most telling source of pressure on the USSR to reciprocate

175

is that it knows that the process of denuclearizing NATO can always be reversed. Failure to respond to NATO initiatives would strengthen the 'hawks' in every country in the Western Alliance and make more likely the defeat of the anti-nuclear British government and its allies in NATO. The USSR would be fairly sure that any unilateral gains achieved by resisting reciprocation are likely to be short-lived. Since the USSR would probably prefer a process of denuclearization and reductions in tension to a renewed arms race, it may well decide to reciprocate fully.

Secondly, NATO countries should be able to mobilize significant international political pressure on the Warsaw Pact. It would be extremely embarrassing for the USSR to reverse its position on NWFZs and to be seen to be unwilling to participate in the denuclearization process and in moves towards more defensive force structures. Even in the USA and Western Europe, where the USSR is used to getting a bad press, it would almost certainly prefer to avoid loss of credibility as a country of peace. It would be rather more worried about losing its credibility in the non-aligned countries and national liberation movements. Though it would be unwise to exaggerate the influence of international opinion on Soviet decisions, it would nevertheless be an important consideration for the USSR and its Warsaw Pact allies.

A third source of pressure could come from political pressures in the Warsaw Pact and the USSR itself. The pressures on the Soviet defence budget have already been noted. There is also the matter of political legitimacy: 'issues of world peace' are always on the tongues of Soviet government representatives and the Soviet media, and it would be very hard to misrepresent such clear initiatives as those we are recommending to NATO. Although the leadership of the USSR has no worries of electoral defeat, it does seem to be increasingly sensitive to internal public opinion.

In Eastern Europe, the NATO initiatives, if they were implemented, would undermine the rationale both for the present large numbers of Soviet troops in these countries, and for the forward deployment of tactical nuclear missiles. Some East European governments may pressure for reciprocation, partly for reasons relating to East-West relations and security, and possibly also because they want reductions in the Soviet forces stationed in their country in order to increase their own room for manoeuvre. Soviet refusal to reciprocate at all on the conventional level would be widely perceived as tantamount to a public admission that its forces were primarily intended as an army of occupation. For whatever reason, the USSR would have an incentive to reduce its forces somewhat, especially as lower levels of force would probably still be quite adequate for maintaining political control.

It must be admitted that the second and third sources of pressure are indirect, and that much of the above discussion is rather speculative. However, the first source of pressure we discussed is likely to be strong, and in practice the costs for the USSR of not reciprocating at all are likely to ensure some sort of response. A more likely problem is that the reciprocation might be relatively insubstantial or difficult to verify – a public relations exercise rather than a real attempt to promote denuclearization and military disengagement throughout Europe. This danger is inevitable in any strategy involving the mobilization of international and public opinion. Success in the propaganda battle does not always go to the most deserving side. Our problems would be compounded by the likelihood of continuing dissension and debate within NATO itself, even if the measures we recommend were being implemented. However, these measures generally have the advantage of being clear and radical, and so it would be hard for the USSR to convince international opinion by purely nominal responses even if it wanted to do so.

We now discuss in more detail the particular forms of reciprocation that might be expected to each element of our recommended denuclearization and conventional force reorganization programme.

Direct reciprocation to British measures: During the INF negotiations, the USSR argued that part of its intermediate-range missile force was a counterbalance to French and British missiles. A natural way of reciprocating to the withdrawal of British Polaris missiles would therefore be for the Soviet Union to scrap a similar number of SS20s. It has already indicated a willingness to do this, though it did not refer to the SS20 specifically.[44] If, instead, the USSR chose to scrap its obsolete SS4 missiles (which are being withdrawn anyway), it would be a sign that the USSR was playing the game of unilateral advantage rather than showing political imagination. A sign of real imagination would be for the USSR to scrap a much more substantial number of SS20s than the number of British missiles being withdrawn: since the USSR would retain thousands of warheads that could be targeted on Europe, it would not weaken itself militarily, and the action would have a dramatic impact on the debate inside NATO countries.

It would make strong political sense for the USSR to withdraw the same number of SS20s as the number of GLCMs withdrawn from the UK, since it would encourage other NATO countries to follow the UK's example. Some reciprocation to the withdrawal of US nuclear bombs and warheads from bases such as Upper Heyford and Machrihanish might also be forthcoming; this could be an opportunity for more creative reciprocation involving logically unconnected aspects of Warsaw Pact forces of concern to the West.

Pershing II and GLCM: If these were withdrawn from Europe, one could hope for the withdrawal of all or most of the SS20s within range of Europe. Furthermore, as the forward deployment of SS21, SS22, and SS23 missiles was justified as a response to the cruise and Pershing deployments, it would be hard for the USSR not to withdraw these missiles to Soviet territory. Its allies would probably exert strong pressure for this: some of them were reported to be unhappy about having to accept the missiles in the first place. If the USA were to dismantle the missiles it had withdrawn, then the USSR could hardly refuse to do likewise, although it may allow only very limited independent verification of this.

The Soviet Union also presented the forward deployment of missile submarines close to the US coast as a response to the Pershing II, which directly threatens its own command and control centres. NATO could remind the USSR of this rationale and pressure for the withdrawal of Soviet missile submarines from patrol close to the USA. If implemented by the USSR, many Americans' attitudes to the unilateral approach could change substantially: crisis stability would be improved and, since Soviet missile submarines have patrolled those regions for years, the USA would have got a good deal.

NWFZ: The reciprocation invited by the unilateral declaration of a 100-150km-wide NWFZ in West Germany is obvious: it is to declare a zone of equal width in East Germany and Czechoslovakia. The USSR has publicly supported for a long time the creation of a wider zone, to include the whole of Germany. Although the narrower zone would not serve the same political purposes, the USSR is unlikely to reverse its support for NWFZs and refuse to reciprocate.

However, there is a danger that the USSR would not accept the verification procedures necessary for the zone to succeed in building mutual confidence and improving crisis stability. It may simply declare that it has no nuclear weapons deployed within 100-150km of the West German border and refuse to allow any independent verification or to redeploy dual-capable systems. This would probably result in an increase, rather than a decrease, in tension. Europeans will know of US State Department claims[45] that some 4,000 nuclear warheads are deployed in Eastern Europe and will be aware of reports that Soviet nuclear-capable artillery have been deployed in Eastern Europe since 1978.[46] At the very least NATO would want any SS21, SS22, and SS23 and other nuclear or dual-capable missiles withdrawn from the zone, and some assurance that heavy artillery and other potentially dual-capable systems in the zone were not collocated with any nuclear warhead depots. Ideally, the dual-capable systems should be removed from the zone.

There would be enormous advantages for NATO in establishing suitable verification procedures in its own section of an NWFZ – ideally involving international expert bodies – as soon as it is established. This would establish norms for the verification of such zones and would allow maximum and consistent pressure to be exerted on the Warsaw Pact to adopt very similar measures itself after reciprocation. Moreover, seeing the system work in practice could reassure the USSR that satisfactory verification need not expose it to spying. If NATO declared a disengagement zone, this would exert further pressure on the USSR to withdraw dual-capable systems, such as heavy artillery, some distance from the border. The withdrawal, and public dismantlng, of

NATO's battlefield nuclear weapons could also be useful in creating an atmosphere in which the USSR would allow reliable verification of the NWFZ and disengagement zone.

The Commission believes that an anti-nuclear UK should refuse to recognize the East European zone as a full NWFZ unless some provision for verification is made. We regard as very important for the prospects of further denuclearization and a shift to defensive postures that the Warsaw Pact becomes more open. The Soviet penchant for secrecy, in particular, is one of the main generators of suspicion, and could undermine the political momentum towards further denuclearization. The NWFZ is probably the most convenient focus for pressure on this issue. By its own radical actions, the UK government would have earned the right to criticize the USSR strongly where it threatens to undermine the denuclearization and disengagement process, and NATO would have earned the same right if it implements the policies discussed in earlier sections of this chapter. However, the criticisms (and in this case, the issue of verification) should not get so much emphasis that NATO's own denuclearization process gets bogged down.

If the verification problems related to the NWFZ are resolved, then the whole NWFZ (East and West) should be confirmed by formal treaty. Indeed, once a reciprocal unilateral process has been implemented satisfactorily, it is in general advisable to confirm the changes by treaty. This makes it less likely that the changes would be reversed during a crisis or as a result of a change of political power.

Reducing the Offensive Capabilities of Warsaw Pact Conventional Forces
Changes in deployment of Warsaw Pact conventional forces are of great importance to the whole process. If NATO were to declare a disengagement zone, it would clearly hope for a similar move from the East. The obstacles to Soviet reciprocation have already been noted. However, after a period of successful denuclearization and of cooperation between the two alliances, it is quite possible that the Soviet leadership would override all obstacles and decide to adopt a less threatening posture and agree to some sort of disengagement zone.

In conclusion to this whole chapter, the obstacles to the success of our strategy for an 'ideal' anti-nuclear British government are clearly very great. Success in persuading NATO to accept even the minimum package of denuclearization measures would depend on some of the following factors: good preparation before the anti-nuclear government comes to power, involving discussions and understandings with potentially sympathetic political parties in Europe and in the USA; whether the governments in several European countries, and especially in the FRG, are dominated by social-democratic or socialist parties; mobilizing mass popular support for the denuclearization package; withstanding political and economic pressures from the USA and other likely opponents of the denuclearization programme; avoiding the development of closer nuclear links between the FRG and either France or the USA. Even then success would still be very uncertain: many events could still undermine the denuclearization process, and there is no guarantee that NATO conventional strategy would not move toward a more offensive orientation. Finally there is the problem of Warsaw Pact reciprocation.

Nevertheless, the majority of the Commission believe that this strategy is the best available for any anti-nuclear British government to attempt to denuclearize NATO policy and promote military disengagement in Europe while maintaining a policy of consistent rejection of nuclear deterrence. There is a real chance that the approach described in this chapter could work. If the process got started it could develop its own momentum. The process of denuclearization and military disengagement would then promote an environment in which creative action on some of Europe's underlying military and political issues might be possible. Together with more immediate political issues, this is the subject of the next chapter.

5. Unfreezing the Blocs

In Chapter Four we put the case for NATO adopting a non-nuclear and defensive strategy, seeking reciprocation at various levels from the Soviet Union and attempting to break the deadlock on arms control and disarmament in Europe. In this chapter we examine broader political and military solutions to the underlying problems.

1. DESIRABLE GOALS FOR EUROPE: DÉTENTE, DISENGAGEMENT AND THE DISSOLUTION OF THE BLOCS

The short-term objective can be summed up as the re-establishment and strengthening of détente at the European level.[1] The implementation, or even partial implementation, of the programme outlined in Chapter Four, should contribute to this goal.

The medium-term objective – which could be realized in conjunction with détente – would be the partial military and political disengagement of the superpowers from their allied or client states in both parts of Europe.[2] We later discuss the extent to which partial superpower *military* disengagement – a reduction in the size of their forces, coupled with the removal of nuclear and chemical weapons – would reduce superpower leverage on both East and West Europe. In so far as it does so and strengthens the autonomy and bargaining power of the non-superpower European states it contributes to the process of dealignment in Europe. (Political disengagement by the superpowers by definition implies an increase in the freedom of action of European states.)

However, in the longer term the goal must be more ambitious

– to secure European non-alignment and with it genuine autonomy for all European states. This implies the *total* withdrawal of superpower armed forces from their present spheres of influence in Europe, and the ending of the system of rival military blocs: the 'dissolution of the blocs'. In a sense this is the process of dealignment taken to its ultimate logical goal. In this chapter we suggest in broad terms the kind of political settlements that eventual superpower withdrawal would require and which we believe an anti-nuclear British government should raise and be prepared to explore.

Problems of Détente, Disengagement and Bloc Dissolution
It cannot be taken for granted that détente and the weakening of superpower dominance will necessarily lead to the dissolution of the blocs. Indeed, in one sense the détente of the 1970s served to legitimize and consolidate the bloc system. When the Soviet Union, for instance, agreed, after an initial objection, to the participation of the USA and Canada in the Helsinki Conference, it effectively acknowledged a US and Canadian role in Europe for the foreseeable future and, by implication, a continuing role for NATO in the European security system. Chancellor Brandt's *Ostpolitik*, as he himself insisted, was predicated on West Germany's integration into the Western military and political system. Similarly, as far as the Soviet side was concerned, the agreements of the détente period brought international recognition of the GDR (and of post-war European frontiers), and a tacit acceptance that the Soviet Union would continue to be the dominant power in East and East-Central Europe.

The difficulty about moving beyond détente (which essentially seeks to normalize relations between the blocs) and beyond partial disengagement to the goal of dissolving the blocs is that this would be perceived as a threat by both superpowers and, as matters stand, would be opposed by many governments in both Eastern and Western Europe – though doubtless the populations in most East European countries at least would support it. The United States would fear that its strategic position in the global struggle against the Soviet Union would be seriously weakened and that Western Europe would be in danger of falling under Soviet influence, thereby also putting US economic interests at risk. The Soviet Union would feel even more threatened if it thought its military and political hegemony in Eastern Europe was being called into question. In other words, the task of re-establishing détente and securing measures of nuclear and conventional disarmament in Europe may be made more difficult if there is the suggestion from the start that the long-term goal is the dissolution of the blocs.

Nevertheless the question has to be raised, if only because, so long as the bloc system and superpower dominance in Europe continue, the process of re-establishing détente and of denuclearization – and, in some circumstances, peace itself – will be at constant risk. The bloc system brings with it the danger that Europe could be dragged into a war between the superpowers that began elsewhere and was unrelated to the politics of Europe as such. It means that, to a great extent, the progress of détente (and probably arms limitations) in Europe is at the mercy of the vagaries of superpower relationships. It is also questionable whether détente could survive, in any recognizable form, another major Soviet military intervention in Eastern Europe, even if the ultimate disaster of war could be avoided.

The Commission recognizes, therefore, that, while the move from détente to partial superpower disengagement in Europe is a natural progression, the step beyond that to the actual dissolution of the blocs requires initiatives of a different kind and raises problems that sit uncomfortably with the détente process. In particular, ending the bloc system, which implies withdrawing superpower forces, would mean resurrecting and resolving the whole German question, which has, in a sense, been pushed to one side in a half-resolved state during the détente years.

Possible Timetables

The question of when and how the difficult issue of bloc dissolution should be raised is one of the key issues in the debate about the future of Europe. On the Commission there were differing views. The argument against raising the matter explicitly at an early stage, *at any rate at government level*, is that to do so could frighten off the superpowers, particularly the Soviet Union, and thus hinder progress in nuclear and conventional disarmament. Proponents of this argument may acknowledge that, were future unrest in Eastern Europe to lead to yet another Soviet military intervention, this could have a disastrous effect on détente and arms limitation; but they point to the relative stability of the situation in Eastern Europe and argue that the strengthening of détente and the effects of partial military disengagement by the two superpowers could significantly reduce the likelihood of Soviet intervention. The argument in favour of raising the issue and outlining proposals for the dissolution of the blocs at an early stage is that it is better at the outset to face the fact that measures of radical nuclear and conventional disarmament in Europe will at some point involve tackling the political dimension of the problem. A British government that had demonstrated its good faith by getting rid of its own nuclear weapons would be well placed to raise the contentious political issues involved in dismantling the bloc system. Moreover, even if the situation in Eastern Europe is judged to be relatively stable, any further crisis that once more led to Soviet intervention, could still gravely endanger détente and any arms limitation programme that had been set in motion.

The prospects of an early end to the bloc system are minimal. Thus Europe probably has to go on living with the risks inherent in the bloc system for the time being. However, détente and disengagement can reduce such risks significantly. A future anti-nuclear British government would have to devote its major efforts in its early years of office to promoting the denuclearization of NATO strategy, the re-establishment and strengthening of détente, and fostering disengagement and dealignment in Europe. At the same time such a government should raise the wider political issues and begin exploring ways in which the problems could eventually be solved. This approach reflects both the cautious and hard-headed expectation that dealignment will be a lengthy and piecemeal process but also the recognition that at some point a bold package of measures will be called for if progress is not simply to peter out or be reversed.

In the near future, however, the main campaigning effort to achieve such radical change may have to come from non-governmental groups – especially the West European peace movements, and the independent peace and human rights campaigns in Eastern Europe.

Whatever the likely pace of change – and this can never be predicted with certainty – Western governments have to decide what combination of foreign and military policy to pursue. In doing so they must simultaneously bear in mind the reasonable needs of Western security and the possibility of unfreezing the bloc system and re-establishing European security on a new basis. It is on the balance to be struck between these two goals that the debate on defence and foreign policy should now be concentrated. Inseparable from this is the wider discussion of the circumstances most likely to encourage the Soviet leadership to reassess the relationship with Eastern Europe and reinterpret the requirements of Soviet security in the area.

Obstacles to Soviet Withdrawal

In this chapter we focus principally on the problems on the Warsaw Pact rather than the NATO side in securing the end of the bloc system because, although securing US agreement to withdrawal from Western Europe is likely to be a complex and problematic task, Soviet withdrawal from Eastern Europe raises additional specific problems which need to be recognized.

In Western Europe the US military presence has been sanctioned and legitimized by elected governments and, despite some opposition, enjoys majority support among the population in all NATO countries except possibly Greece and Spain at present. However, in Eastern Europe Soviet-type governments were imposed during the Stalin period and the background threat of Soviet intervention prevents fundamental change. The existence of NATO is compatible with the sovereignty of Western European states (although it limits political options in Europe), whereas political autonomy in Eastern Europe would threaten the Warsaw Pact. If any Eastern European state were now to choose a radically different path from that of the Soviet Union this would not only pose a political challenge to the Soviet system, but would probably also be seen as a challenge to the doctrine of the irreversibility of history: that once a country had taken the socialist path there can be no going back.

However, although we devote much space to considering how governments and populations in Eastern Europe might attain greater freedom of action in their dealings with the Soviet

Union, including the freedom to develop more open and pluralist political systems and install representative governments should they so wish, our concern is not primarily with the concept of a just political and social system as such. Our primary focus is on inter-state relationships, especially those between the super-powers and their allies, and how these might affect the prospects for détente and peace. However, because the nature of the present Soviet relationship with Eastern Europe precludes many political and social choices, and because this has been a basic cause of unrest and instability in Eastern Europe – which in turn has caused Soviet military interventions since World War II – it is relevant and necessary to consider possible models of political and social development in Eastern Europe which the Soviet Union might tolerate and which, apart from their intrinsic merits, would extend the choices open to Eastern European countries.

Another, more crucial, respect in which internal policy impinges directly on the defence and foreign policy of states is that inaccessibility of information to the citizens and a ban on open critical debate prevents the citizenry from acting as a restraining influence on governments. In its first report the Commission was critical of the secrecy and lack of open debate that accompanied the British decision to manufacture nuclear weapons in the late 1940s, and of the Labour government's secret decision, in the 1970s, to spend one billion pounds on the Chevaline programme to update Polaris. Consistency demands that we criticize the much greater degree of secrecy and manipulation of information, and the lack of an open debate on defence and foreign policy, in Soviet bloc countries, or at any rate the fact that it takes place only at great risk to those concerned. The small independent peace movements in the Soviet Union and Eastern Europe have faced harassment on a scale that has no parallel in Western Europe – with the exception of Greece under the Colonels and Turkey under military, or highly militarized, rule. However hesitant one may be, in a report such as this, to comment in detail on the internal policies of governments, it is necessary to stress the relevance to peace issues of the plea that a government's foreign and defence policies ought to be publicly available, and dissent from those policies be permitted. Not only is this desirable in terms of basic human rights, it can also have an important, sometimes critical, bearing on the whole range of peace politics.

Such a change in the Soviet approach would seem to require two complementary circumstances: first, the removal, as far as possible, of anything that could reasonably be regarded as a major external military threat aimed at forcing changes in the Soviet system; second, pressure for change from below, and from East European states in the Soviet bloc, that might lead the Soviet leadership to question whether the present relationship was not chronically unstable and in need of a radical overhaul.

Western governments neither can, nor should, attempt to control movements for change in the Soviet Union and Eastern Europe. But the West can pursue foreign and defence policies calculated to produce a favourable atmosphere for constructive change in the Soviet bloc.

The programme of nuclear disarmament by Britain and Western Europe and the move towards a defensive conventional system which we advocate would certainly signal that Western Europe had no intention of trying to alter the status quo in Europe through military pressure. We do not claim that ours is the only programme that might achieve this. We do contend, however, that the central elements of any such programme must be the re-establishment of détente and substantial progress on nuclear and conventional disarmament in Europe.

We shall now consider how the process of superpower disengagement from both parts of Europe might develop; first, in Western Europe, and second, in the Soviet bloc. We shall then return to a consideration of the kind of political settlement that would permit the dissolution of the blocs and the total withdrawal of superpower forces.

2. WESTERN EUROPE: THE DECLINE OF US DOMINANCE

During the late 1940s and the 1950s the USA wielded enormous power in Western Europe because of its economic and military dominance and the European desire for US military protection after the onset of the Cold War in 1947. It exercised this power most dramatically at the time of Suez in 1956, when Britain was forced to agree to a cease-fire, partly as a result of US pressure on the pound and the decision by the International Monetary Fund, at the instigation of the USA, to block Britain's attempt to withdraw funds.[3] In this instance, however much one might regret the fact that the USA had that degree of political dominance in Europe, it did use its power positively; indeed, it is one of the few occasions when economic and fiscal sanctions were immediately effective in contributing to the halting of an act of blatant international aggression. However, US influence has operated in more subtle and frequently less positive ways to limit the political options in Europe. Even today calculations of US reactions to a particular course of action, of the allies which it could hope to muster in support of its views, and of the pressure it could bring to bear play an important part in determining the agenda of mainstream political debate in Europe, on the Left as well as the Right.

Nevertheless, as we argued in Chapter One, US leverage in Europe in both the economic and political spheres has declined markedly in the past fifteen years and to this extent Western Europe's freedom of action has increased. Thus in terms of production and trade the strength of the EEC now rivals that of the USA. One consequence of this has been increased economic competition together with strains and divergencies between the USA and Western Europe on economic and fiscal matters.[4] As we noted in Chapter One, there has also been a degree of disenchantment with the US approach on the political front, and even at the official level Western Europe has tended to distance itself from aspects of US policy, particularly over Central America, the Strategic Defense Initiative and the Reagan Administration's hard-line foreign policy and rejection of détente. At the non-government level, there has of course been widespread popular opposition to the deployment of cruise and Pershing II missiles and, more generally, to NATO reliance on nuclear weapons.

In fact it is now mainly as a result of its critical role in the military/strategic sphere that the USA continues to exercise a dominant influence in Western Europe. Its allies still look to the USA to provide a military counterbalance to the Soviet Union, which they fear would otherwise dominate the continent and threaten their independence and security. Despite the 'independent' nuclear systems of Britain and France, it is through the nuclear guarantee and the deployment of nuclear weapons in Europe that the USA makes its most singular and powerful contribution to the military system of the Western Alliance.

There are, however, certain broad political and economic developments taking place that could increase the likelihood of governments eventually coming to power in Europe which would reject reliance on nuclear weapons and reassess the security problem in Europe. For instance, the economic interdependence of the two halves of Europe may diminish the apparent rationality, and hence the assessment of the likelihood, of a deliberate attack by one side upon the other. The problems facing the industrialized capitalist countries (some, though not all, of which they share with the centralized economies of the Soviet bloc) – including chronic unemployment, disparities of wealth, destruction of the environment and pauperization of the Third World – could strengthen those political forces in various countries that are prepared to re-examine the whole spectrum of domestic, foreign and military policies.[5] The political advances of the Greens in West Germany, which no-one predicted a decade or so ago, is a case in point.

3. Problems and Possibilities of Soviet Disengagement in Eastern Europe

Soviet disengagement in Eastern Europe would require a fundamental readjustment in Soviet perceptions and attitudes. We begin, therefore, by considering Soviet reasons for wanting to retain a sphere of influence in Eastern Europe.

Soviet Interests in Eastern Europe: the Strategic Factor

As noted in Chapter Three, strategic and security considerations were paramount in the immediate post-war period when Stalin established client régimes in Eastern Europe and masterminded extensive purges to root out any possible opposition to Soviet control.

Today, strategic considerations alone do not determine Soviet policy in Eastern Europe; it is even questionable whether such considerations are the most central. But neither should their importance be underestimated. They explain, at least in part, Soviet opposition to any internal development in Eastern European states which could challenge the control of communist parties and governments in political life. In the circumstances of continued East-West confrontation, such political developments are certain to be regarded as the possible beginning of political pluralism and the eventual defection by the state or states in question to the West, something the Soviet leadership is unlikely to allow unless it were part of a wider bilateral process.

It is true that in both East and West there is no longer the fear of imminent war. Moreover, the détente period of the 1970s saw the confirmation of post-war frontiers in Europe and a partial regulation of the German situation. But this does not mean that either side could contemplate with equanimity the loss of a strategically important ally, whether the state in question adopted a neutralist stance and thereby created a gap in the chain of defence, or actually joined the opposing alliance. In either event the strategic balance would have been altered.

A negotiated settlement in Europe involving the dissolution of the alliances is in principle one context in which the Soviet Union might be prepared to accept genuine autonomy in Eastern Europe. It is perhaps also conceivable that, with a breakthrough in East-West relations and major force reductions in Europe, a deal for the simultaneous withdrawal of one or two of the strategically less vital states from the two alliances – for instance Romania from the Warsaw Pact and Denmark from NATO – would be acceptable. Clearly, at present an overall settlement, or more limited deals of this kind, is hardly imaginable. The crucial question in relation to the recommendations of the Commission is whether bold Western initiatives, especially nuclear weapons' reductions together with a NATO move towards a clearly defensive strategy, would improve the chances of agreement. We return to this question later in this chapter.

The Ideological and Political Dimension of Soviet Insecurity
The political and ideological element in the East-West confrontation complicates the search for a *modus vivendi* and eventual agreement to end the bloc system. There are two areas of

191

particular concern for the Soviet leadership here: first, the prestige, standing and influence of the Soviet Union in the outside world; second, the stability of the Soviet system itself.

If, as the result of the withdrawal of Soviet forces from Eastern Europe, one or more states opted for some kind of democratic pluralist system, this would represent a humiliating political and ideological defeat for the Soviet Union. Whether some régimes maintained themselves in power with the introduction of Hungarian- or Yugoslav-type economic and political reforms, or became more repressive along Romanian lines, it is likely that eventually some, if not all, would develop genuinely pluralist politics, though perhaps retaining important characteristics of a socialist system. Such a possibility could not but be important to the Soviet leadership. The development of alternative political models, perhaps especially those of a genuinely democratic socialist nature, in what had been part of the Soviet bloc, could lead to demands for similar reforms and radical restructuring in the Soviet Union itself. Thus, even if there were no military threat from Western Europe, the development of such models could, by threatening to undermine the rigidly authoritarian structures on which the legitimacy and stability of the system depend, pose an acute security problem to the Soviet Union.

Studies of events leading up to the invasions of Hungary in 1956 and of Czechoslovakia in 1968, and to the Soviet-backed clampdown in Poland in 1981, suggest that the Soviet concern was not simply strategic, relating to the East-West confrontation, but also political and ideological. The virtual lifting of political censorship in Czechoslovakia during the Prague Spring, for example, was extremely worrying for the Soviet leaders, especially as it resulted in material being printed which had been censored in the Soviet Union.[6] Although the Soviet leaders, in their discussions with the Czechoslovak government, stressed the strategic aspects of the situation and although this was doubtless a factor in Soviet thinking,[7] it is clear that the ideological and political implications of the Prague Spring were of grave concern to them.

Though it is, in present circumstances, nearly impossible to disentangle Soviet political and ideological motives from strategic ones, it is clear that they will not automatically disappear if there is no longer a military confrontation between East and West. This conclusion is not encouraging for the prospects of an early breakthrough in East-West relations: first, because, however genuine the desire of the Soviet leaders to avoid an armed conflict with the West, they may be tempted to maintain a certain level of confrontation in order to justify the continued Soviet presence in Eastern Europe (just as the US government has an interest in keeping the situation simmering in Europe to help ensure the continued loyalty of its European allies); second, because it suggests that not only a nuclear-disarmed, but even a totally disarmed Western Europe might be regarded as posing a threat to Soviet security.

The imposed ideological orthodoxy in the Soviet bloc affects not only politics but also intellectual and cultural life. One is struck, for instance, when reading accounts by Soviet historians of the interventions in Hungary and Czechoslovakia, by the rigid ideological framework within which events have to be interpreted if they are to be published in the Soviet Union.[8]

In some Eastern European states the situation is less rigid, and particularly in film, theatre, and the arts in general more unorthodox views can be expressed and new artistic avenues opened up. The Kadar government of Hungary, for instance, allows its artists some latitude, and on a number of counts is more tolerant than other East European governments. It is therefore worth considering whether any Soviet bloc countries provide models of how the boundaries of free discussion and political participation could be extended, and thus serve to reduce the likelihood of dangerous political crises.

Although the development of genuinely democratic structures would pose a severe political and ideological challenge to the Soviet leaders, they might be able to cope with it and might reach the view that they should. A great deal is likely to depend on the progress of reforms within the Soviet Union itself – including purely economic reforms – on whether the Soviet authorities felt they could count on the loyalty of the majority of their population, and on whether they could control any similar tendencies that did arise in the Soviet Union. These issues are never completely cut and dried: even over the Soviet intervention in Czechoslovakia in 1968 there were divisions in the Soviet hierarchy, with Prime Minister Kosygin opposing military action as late as July 1968.[9] At another time, in a wholly different international climate, the decision might go the other way and a firm precedent be established for political change in Eastern Europe.

The Dynamics of Change in the Soviet Bloc

In considering how the situation in Eastern Europe could change, one needs to take account of the dynamics of change at both intra- and inter-state level.

At the intra-state level, the governments and ruling parties have to take some account of the wishes and demands of the populations they seek to govern. With the present exception of Poland, human rights, trade unions and other openly critical organizations do not enjoy large-scale active support among the population. Yet the speed at which the Solidarity movement grew in Poland, and the ties it had with intellectual dissent both at home and in other East European countries, must serve as a warning to the authorities that at the right moment small centres of dissent may play a crucial role in the creation of a mass opposition. (The Czech playwright and Charter 77 activist Vaclav Havel has argued that it is not that the dissidents have a different view from the majority of the population of the realities of Eastern Europe, but rather that they refuse to go along with the official pretence; it is for this reason that they pose an unacceptable threat to the authorities.[10])

The authorities have also to be concerned with the reactions of the bulk of the population which has no close attachment either to the ruling Communist Party or to any kind of organized opposition but whose acquiescence is essential to the smooth running of the system. With the notable exception of Hungary, where Party membership has been rising since the early 1970s and where the government's emphasis on consumerism and economic reform appears to enjoy considerable popular support, there is evidence of disaffection with governments among large sections of the population, especially among younger people.[11]

The demands of the non-Party majority might be expected to be transmitted by means of the Party and official trade unions working at the base to the régimes' decision-making centres. To some extent, no doubt, this does occur: in Poland, for instance, the officially-sponsored trade unions which were introduced to replace Solidarity have now themselves come under official attack for supporting 'unrealistic' demands.[12] One difficulty, however, is that during the early 1970s there were mass expulsions of reformists from the ruling communist parties: indeed it was the extent of these purges which partly accounts for the growth of centres of criticism and opposition outside the parties. It thus becomes more difficult for the governments to introduce the very reforms which those they expelled had been demanding.[13]

Despite this, the need to improve economic performance may lead to the adoption of at least some of the economic changes the reformers had been demanding. Gorbachev's accession to power, and his drive to eliminate corruption and improve economic efficiency in the Soviet Union, may create an atmosphere more conducive to certain kinds of reform throughout the Soviet bloc. So far, however, Gorbachev's reforms have focused on making existing structures more efficient rather than on any extensive decentralization of decision-making along Yugoslav or Hungarian lines – though his government has indicated its provisional assent to the continuing reforms in Hungary.[14]

Many analysts of Soviet-type economies argue that while the system is economically effective during an initial period of extensive industrialization – the introduction of heavy industry and the raising of gross industrial output – it is far less effective for the subsequent phase of *intensive* industrialization – the production of a wide range of high-quality goods – which requires greater specialization, flexibility, and responsiveness to consumer needs. What may be required, therefore, if economic reform is to be successful, is not simply a tightening up of efficiency within existing structures, but the sort of devolution of decision-making and the extension of consumer choice that is being attempted in Hungary and, in a still more radical way, in Yugoslavia. For the moment, however, it remains an open question whether the demands of the situation will lead in time to the introduction of more far-reaching measures of economic decentralization in the Soviet Union and, if it did occur, what impact this would have on the prospects for political change.[15]

The response of Eastern European governments to pressure from their own populations, whether these are demands primarily for economic change, or for greater recognition of human and political rights, may be the introduction of reforms which they think the Soviet Union will tolerate; or repression; or, of course, a combination of reforms and repression and an emphasis on the risks of Soviet intervention if the reforms are too radical. But whatever the immediate response, changed expectations at the base, and continuing pressure for change, can be expected to alter the nature of the relationship between the régimes and the populations they govern.

At the inter-state level, the most important relationship is that between individual East European states and the Soviet Union. The examples of the GDR in 1953, Hungary in 1956, Czechoslovakia in 1968 and, in a different way, Poland in 1981, indicate the limits of change in Eastern Europe that the Soviet Union has been prepared to tolerate. Nevertheless, military intervention is a last resort, entailing consequences the Soviet Union would much rather avoid. East European governments, therefore, if they are genuinely concerned to pursue a reformist path, or face pressure from below to do so, are given some leverage by the argument that changes are necessary in order to keep the situation under control. The room for manoeuvre may not be very great, but it could be enough for limits of permissible reform to be gradually extended.

Eastern European governments also have a stake in the maintenance of détente among other things because this facilitates the importation of Western goods and technology. In fact, the economic consequences of the increase in Western imports in the 1970s were ambiguous: technology imports, for instance, at their highest in the early 1970s, did not solve the structural problems of East European economies, and at the same time rapid inflation in Western Europe led to several Eastern European countries falling heavily into debt, most notably Poland. As a result there was a severe cut-back in the imports of Western machinery in the late 1970s.[16] Despite this, in the 1980s Eastern European governments have been keen to maintain a high level of trade with the West and, partly for this reason, to maintain détente. Individually or collectively, therefore, East European

196

governments could exert a moderating influence on Moscow, even urging the Soviet leaders to make concessions on arms control and disarmament or, at the level of foreign policy, to meet genuine Western fears and strengthen détente.

Of course, there have been instances when an individual East European government has taken a harder line than Moscow: in the late 1960s, the Ulbricht government in the GDR was highly suspicious of Brandt's *Ostpolitik* and of the moves towards European détente. The insecurity of individual governments may also mean that they feel particularly threatened by reforms in neighbouring Soviet bloc states: it was the Husak government in Czechoslovakia that was among the most vehement in its condemnations of events in Poland in 1980-81.

If a situation were to arise in which the Soviet Union found itself faced with unanimous opposition from East European governments to military intervention, with perhaps several states in the region simultaneously introducing very similar reforms, this might tip the balance against intervention in a future Prague Spring or other political crisis in Eastern Europe.

This is more likely to be the case if there is a period in which the régimes involved, and the Soviet Union, become accustomed to a kind of *de facto* pluralism established by the non-violent struggle of people insisting on their basic human and political rights and if a series of reforms, partly in response to that pressure, has resulted in some devolution of power in the Soviet-type systems, including the Soviet Union itself.

With this in mind we consider now some political models which the Soviet Union might eventually be willing to live with in Eastern Europe.

Possible Models in Eastern Europe

The most hopeful precedent is Finland: independent, though with the restriction that peacetime neutrality and friendly relations with the USSR be maintained. Critics of Finland point to its unwillingness to criticize Soviet policies in public; yet its political system is democratic and pluralist and it enjoys a freedom of action that does not exist anywhere in the Soviet bloc. Yugoslavia, a one-party state committed to Marxist-Leninist principles, might be more attractive to some East European states as a model for the conduct of domestic politics. What is important, however, is that they would be free to make that choice without the threat of Soviet (or Western) intervention.

A solution which would change the situation in Eastern Europe, so that, as far as foreign policy and independence are concerned, it was analogous to that of Finland, is worth striving for. However, because it would represent a major concession for the Soviet Union and entail hazards of various kinds for the Soviet system, it is only conceivable in the context of a wider East-West settlement in Europe.

Are there any intermediate models that would accustom the Soviet Union to the extension by East European states of their autonomy and which might gradually shift the balance of power in favour of Eastern Europe – similar to the way the balance of power in the West, at the political and economic level, has shifted away from the USA in favour of Western Europe?

Three very different models suggest themselves: Romania, Hungary and the Prague Spring. Romania has, since the mid-1960s, pursued a highly independent foreign and defence policy and has been prepared publicly to criticize Soviet policies, for instance the invasion of Czechoslovakia. However, there are several reasons why Romania would be neither a desirable nor a viable model for other East European countries. The régime is one of the most repressive in the Eastern bloc, and because of this, its long-term stability is in doubt; if, as has been suggested, the Soviet leaders were contemplating an invasion of Romania in 1968, how much less likely is it that they would allow any of the states of the main region of East-West confrontation – the GDR, Czechoslovakia and Poland – the same degree of latitude in foreign policy as Romania enjoys?

Hungary is a more promising example. The Kadar government was imposed on Hungary following the Soviet invasion of 1956, but from all accounts it has won widespread support with a programme of economic reform, raising living standards, and with the pursuit of a relatively tolerant internal policy. Not that there is anything close to political pluralism, as the harassment by the authorities of the nascent peace movement indicates; but the atmosphere is freer than elsewhere in Eastern Europe and cultural life is less restricted.

For at least some East European states the Hungarian model, or something approximating to it, would be a welcome improvement for the population. The introduction of Hungarian-type reforms could thus help stave off the kind of crisis that can lead to Soviet intervention. How far the Hungarian model could be followed in other countries is debatable: in Poland, for instance, the widespread disaffection with the military-backed régime and the Communist Party do not make it a real option at present and it would take many years of patient work and genuine reform for the Polish régime to regain public confidence.

The third possible model which, however unpromising at the moment, cannot be altogether ruled out for some future date, is that of the Prague Spring. Its defining characteristics are that the Communist Party and the government, supported and driven by pressure from below, introduce both economic reforms and wide-ranging political reforms and in effect change the nature of the system. The model is unpromising for the time being, not least because of the fate that befell Czechoslovakia in 1968. But, as we argued earlier, in a different configuration of circumstances, which would include a Soviet leadership that felt more assured of its own position, and a more favourable international climate, one could not altogether rule out, for instance, a 'Budapest Spring'. If there is to be significant political change in the Soviet Union itself – which could well prove to be the necessary condition of change in Soviet-East European relations – the initiative may have to come to some extent 'from the top', in the manner of Czechoslovak reforms.

Finally, a possible alternative to the gradual 'liberalization' of Eastern European régimes, based on either a Hungarian or a Prague Spring model and leading to a Finnish – or Yugoslav – type solution, would be the spread of pluralism from below, instituted by movements like Solidarity, accompanied by increasing alienation between state and society. It is possible that the Soviet Union will eventually face a situation in Eastern Europe in which the more 'liberal' governments, enjoying a good deal of popular support, will be wanting to introduce reforms that Soviet leaders are reluctant to tolerate, while others will be more hard-line and repressive but, as in Poland today, confronting an alienated and largely defiant population. Such a situation would be highly unsatisfactory from a Soviet perspective and, with the appropriate international circumstances, could lead it to reconsider its needs and goals in Europe and accept the desirability of a new European settlement.

4. The Process of Ending the Bloc System

Given the above analysis, are the elements of the programme for Europe advocated by the Commission – including NATO denuclearization, adoption of a defensive strategy and initiatives to restore and strengthen détente – likely to further the long-term goal of ending the bloc system, involving the withdrawal of superpower forces from the territories of their present European allies? We address this question under three headings:

a) The dynamics of European nuclear disarmament and force reductions and their impact on internal relations in the alliances.

Two issues need to be considered here: first, whether, in each alliance, the measures proposed would strengthen the Europeans in relation to the superpowers; second, whether these measures would tend to loosen, or even disrupt, each alliance.

In itself, strengthened European influence would be a positive development, even if it were to take place only on one side. The European states, East and West, have an immediate and tangible interest in the avoidance of conflict at any level and in the furtherance of détente, and so would tend to exercise a moderating influence on the superpowers. If, however, the internal cohesion of one alliance, but not the other, were seriously disrupted, the effects on the prospects of ending the bloc system as a whole would be more ambiguous.

In NATO, it is probable that denuclearization and the reduction of US forces would go hand in hand with an increase in the influence and bargaining power of the European states vis-à-vis the USA. The actual process of removing US nuclear weapons and bases would involve the acceptance by NATO of priorities and perspectives more widely held in Europe than in the USA, and a strong assertion of these priorities by European

NATO states. This would be especially true of unilateral measures of nuclear disarmament by NATO, which the USA can be expected to resist strongly. It might be less true of certain negotiated agreements, such as one to remove all intermediate-range nuclear systems on both sides, especially if this were a step taken in isolation and not part of a broader nuclear disarmament programme. Certain European governments, after all, played an active part in the 1979 decision to deploy cruise and Pershing II missiles. However, if European governments were insisting jointly on a programme of total denuclearization for NATO, their political complexion would perforce be very different from that of the Thatcher, Kohl and Mitterand governments who in February 1985 reportedly objected strongly to any 'zero option' agreement which would have meant the removal of these weapons.[17] In such circumstances, they would undoubtedly be making the running against strong US opposition.

Any major reduction in the US contribution to European defence at the conventional level would also tend, in most circumstances, to strengthen the hand of the European NATO states. In this case, however, it is less the details of NATO decision-making that are likely to be most important than the fact that, with fewer US forces in Europe, the European states would be shouldering a greater share of responsibility for their own defence and would thus be better placed to insist that their views be taken into account in NATO councils. (This would not apply, of course, if the US reductions were part of a programme of across-the-board cuts in the conventional forces of both alliances which left the proportional contribution of the USA unaltered.)

In the Warsaw Pact, it is less likely that the removal of nuclear weapons would represent a success for East European, rather than Soviet, priorities. It is extremely improbable that this step would be taken unilaterally, though possibly, behind the scenes, individual Warsaw Pact countries, anxious to improve relations with the West, might urge the Soviet Union to reach a settlement, and in so far as any agreement were the consequence of such pressure, it could mark a certain shift in the balance of influence within the bloc.

Even a reduction in Soviet forces deployed in Eastern Europe is only likely to have a marginal impact. East European states might be assigned a more important role in combat operations but, in the absence of more far-reaching changes, the Soviet Union would continue to have wartime responsibility for the direction of Warsaw Pact forces.

More importantly, even a very considerable reduction in the size of Soviet forces would not affect the key policing function these forces have, nor the Soviet ability, should the need arise, to bring in massive reinforcements to crush popular unrest or unseat unacceptable governments. (The absence of Soviet force deployments in Czechoslovakia in 1968 was not an obstacle to Soviet intervention.) Because these functions of the Soviet forces in Eastern Europe are so important, reductions in Soviet peace-time deployments would not seriously affect the power relations in the Warsaw Pact, unless the reductions were both very large and were accompanied by guarantees that substantially reduced the likelihood of future Soviet intervention.

It therefore appears likely that European nuclear disarmament and/or force reductions, which reduced in each alliance the ratio of superpower forces deployed in Europe, would affect the internal balance of power and influence in NATO more than in the Warsaw Pact. The more important question, however, is how far these steps would tend to disrupt one or both alliances.

It is likely that the controversy would be fiercer in NATO, especially if the European NATO states were insisting uncon-ditionally on the total denuclearization of NATO strategy. Indeed, there are circumstances in which NATO might fall apart over the nuclear issue, or in which several member states might leave the Alliance. We consider these in more detail in the next chapter. Critics of any programme of *unconditional* nuclear disarmament by European NATO argue that military disengage-ment of this kind which affected the two alliances so unevenly would tend to hinder rather than promote the ending of the bloc system. We deal with this point in the next section.

b) Strategic consequences of European nuclear disarmament and superpower force reductions and their impact on the bloc system.

Although, as we have argued, political and ideological factors are probably more central to current Soviet thinking than military-strategic ones, it is clear that the latter remain important. Thus the programme of NATO denuclearization, the establishment of nuclear-weapon-free zones and the reshaping of conventional defence which we recommend should at least reduce Soviet apprehensions and encourage it to reassess its approach. The main reason why the Soviet Union might make such a reassessment would be its awareness of the political and other costs of trying to prevent political changes in Eastern Europe; but Western denuclearization could remove an obstacle to a Soviet rethinking of its policy.

The counter-argument to this analysis is that nuclear disarmament, even if carried out in a balanced way, would not affect the Soviet capacity to retain control in Eastern Europe, as this depends on conventional forces; at the same time it would weaken the West militarily.[18] With nuclear weapons physically removed from Western Europe, and perhaps with NATO's offensive conventional capability also reduced, the Soviet leadership might conclude that the balance of forces had shifted in its favour and that it need no longer act, in the Soviet sphere, with as much circumspection as before.

In reality, however, nuclear disarmament would only have a marginal effect on Soviet capability to employ military force in Eastern Europe. The West, by its past decisions (as during the Soviet interventions in Hungary and Czechoslovakia), has shown that it will not use military force, much less threaten the use of nuclear weapons, to oppose such interventions in Eastern Europe. The only real change in this respect resulting from nuclear disarmament might be a Soviet expectation that NATO would react even more cautiously, and be at even more pains than at present to avoid becoming embroiled, by accident or miscalculation, in a conflict over Eastern Europe.

It is interesting to note that some of the independent movements in Eastern Europe, such as Charter 77 in Czechoslovakia, support the restoration and strengthening of détente, and the creation of a nuclear-free Europe.[19] Clearly those who take this position do not accept the argument that a *balanced* withdrawal of nuclear weapons from Europe would increase their vulnerability to Soviet military pressure. (However, support for the idea of *unilateral* nuclear disarmament by NATO, or major unilateral disarmament initiatives, would not at present have any widespread support among the independent movements in Eastern Europe and would generally be regarded as weakening the West's position. This situation could possibly change as the dialogue between Western peace movements and independent movements in the Soviet bloc countries continues and deepens and as proposals for alternative non-nuclear defence are elaborated and understood.)

The political (and military) realities in Europe are such that, with or without nuclear disarmament, the incentives that the West can provide to induce a change in Soviet attitudes to Eastern Europe, and the disincentives to intervention and repression, are essentially non-military in character. In addition, the Soviet leadership would have to take seriously the risk that further military intervention in Eastern Europe would undermine the viability of Western governments and movements which had succeeded in removing nuclear weapons from Europe and might contribute to the restoration of governments committed to the re-deployment of nuclear weapons.[20]

In sum, there are certain risks that the changed strategic circumstances (or perceptions of such changes) following the denuclearization of Europe might lead the Soviet Union either to feel that it would be under fewer constraints in its dealings with Eastern Europe, or to be more assertive in its dealings with Western Europe. But these risks could be minimized if the action of West European states in renouncing nuclear weapons sprang from a confident sense of moral and political purpose, and was accompanied by an alternative defence system. In addition, in assessing the risks and benefits, it is also essential to give due weight to the impact of the restoration and strengthening of détente to which the programme of denuclearization and arms reduction can be expected to contribute.

c) The contribution of détente to ending the bloc system.

As already indicated there may be a tension between the short-term goals of détente and ending the bloc system. Détente as it has so far developed rests on the bloc system. The present discussion suggests ways in which détente might help to create conditions in which efforts to dismantle the blocs could prove effective.

Détente, because it brought greater economic interdependence in Europe, provided what one might call a 'background political disincentive' to aggression in Europe. It became in fact increasingly clear that any military conflict in Europe would be between states which had a strong interest in continuing cooperation.

Détente, in effect, gives both sides a stake in maintaining peace. However, the economic and other benefits have more potential significance for the non-superpower European states than for the superpowers, whose resources and freedom of manoeuvre are so much greater.

As we noted earlier, European states in the early 1980s attempted to maintain détente sometimes in defiance of pressure from the superpowers. Even conservative governments in Western Europe were anxious to maintain the improved relations built up during the 1970s. Thus in 1984, at a time when the superpowers were barely on speaking terms following the cruise and Pershing deployments in Western Europe and the breakdown of arms control talks in Geneva, there were several exchanges of visits between government leaders and representatives in Western Europe and those in Eastern Europe. Mrs Thatcher visited Hungary in February of that year, stressing the importance of achieving arms control and of bilateral cooperation between the two states, despite their different political systems and their membership of different alliances. The following October the Hungarian leader, Janos Kadar, paid a return visit to Britain. Kadar also visited France in the same month, and earlier in the year had received both President Mitterand of France and Chancellor Kohl of West Germany in Hungary.

One of the most noteworthy and lasting changes brought about by the period of détente has been the transformation of relations between the two German states. Not only the social-democratic-liberal (SDP-FDP) but even the conservative-liberal (CDU/CSU-FDP) government in the FRG have promoted government and popular contacts, trade ties and other economic cooperation between the FRG and the GDR. Though the visit by East German leader Honecker to Bonn in September 1984 was cancelled – almost certainly because of Soviet pressure – the fact that it had been arranged at all is indicative of how much relations between the two Germanys have improved since the 1950s and the early 1960s.

Between 1969 and 1976 trade between the two countries expanded at an annual rate of fourteen per cent.[21] Despite a slowing down in the later 1970s, the value of inter-German trade reached $6 billion a year by the early 1980s. This represents only two per cent of West German, but approximately twelve per cent of East German, foreign trade.[22] Jonathan Dean, a former political counsellor in the US Embassy in Bonn, has speculated that economic ties between the two German states may well become so strong in the coming decades that the GDR – though not West Germany – would be dependent on the relationship for its continued existence.

The degree of cooperation between the two German states is based in part on a sense of common German identity, and, to some extent, is a special case. Nevertheless, the development of cooperation between the two Germanys is important, not only for them but also for the possibilities it opens up for European security and cooperation in general. An example is the draft agreement for a chemical-weapon-free zone in Europe drawn up in 1985 by a joint working party of members of the ruling SED in the GDR and the West German Social Democrats. We discuss this in Chapter Seven.

Clearly the desire to maintain détente and the fruits of closer inter-European cooperation is widespread among governments in both Western and Eastern Europe. This special concern with maintaining détente provides an incentive to European states in both alliances to strive with greater vigour to restrain the superpowers from taking action that would put détente at risk, as well as to take independent initiatives to develop East-West cooperation in Europe.

Now while some of the elements in the programme we recommend would tend to affect NATO's internal relations more than those of the Warsaw Pact, there is reason to hope that détente would encourage more independent action in the Warsaw Pact, as well as in NATO.

Firstly, the USSR itself is likely to be more reluctant than during a period of Cold War to intervene militarily in Eastern Europe, as this would risk undermining détente. This fact should give East European governments greater leverage in their arguments that, in order to retain legitimacy in their own countries, or to deal with pressure from below, certain political and economic reforms are necessary. Eventually such changes could lead to the increased independence of Warsaw Pact countries. This in turn would make it easier for the Soviet Union to accept a more radical break at some later point.

Détente could also strengthen the hand of independent forces in Eastern Europe. As we argue in Chapter Three, it is difficult to ascertain whether the détente of the 1970s actually encouraged liberalization in Eastern Europe; but the Helsinki Accords did establish norms for intra-state (as well as inter-state) behaviour, and this is sometimes seen as their most innovative and potentially significant feature.[23]

In Chapter One we examined the reasons for the breakdown of détente in the 1970s; in the 1980s, in Europe, the crucial events were the deployment of the SS20, cruise and Pershing II missiles and the introduction of martial law in Poland. The most important first step towards the restoration of détente in its widest sense would be a change in the international behaviour of the superpowers: Soviet withdrawal from Afghanistan and an end to US aggression by proxy in Nicaragua would contribute more than any summit to an improvement of East-West relations and would restore some confidence in the good intentions of the two powers. The denuclearization of NATO, which would include a removal of the 'Euromissiles', would also be important. (Indeed, a positive response by Britain to the Gorbachev European INF proposals in February and March 1986 would have been a valuable contribution not only to the détente process but also to the prospect of arms control in Europe. Sadly, this opportunity was thrown away by the Thatcher government. It is possible, though, that it might occur again after a future election in Britain. Clearly, too, the abandonment by the Reagan Administration of the SDI programme, and a positive response to the Soviet unilateral moratorium on testing, would have been of immense help.)

But although détente may strengthen the hand of European states in relation to the superpowers in each alliance, the bloc system will not wither away of its own accord. As we argued earlier, the withdrawal of superpower forces from both parts of Europe and the attainment of genuine autonomy by the countries of Eastern Europe is only likely to occur in the context of a broad East-West political settlement in Europe. Before we consider the possible contours of such a settlement we look briefly at the role of Western peace movements in preparing the ground for these tasks.

Western Peace Movements and the Independent Peace and Human Rights Organizations in the Soviet Bloc

Attempts by Western governments to influence directly the independent movements in Eastern Europe are almost invariably counter-productive, may smack of political opportunism (if not outright hypocrisy), and give the Soviet Union opportunity to depict these movements as Western-inspired. Western governments, however, can draw attention to particular violations of human rights, sometimes to good effect, and continue to insist on the importance of the norms established by, and formally accepted by all signatories to, the Helsinki Accords. In addition, if Western Europe has rejected any reliance on nuclear weapons and adopted a clearly defensive strategy it would be in a stronger position to plead on behalf of independent peace and human rights groups.

Western peace movements, however, are even better placed to do this. While their main work will continue to consist in putting pressure on Western governments, they can establish direct relations with independent peace, human rights and similar groups in the Soviet bloc, provide them with moral and material assistance and raise with official and semi-official bodies the importance of such movements being allowed to operate freely.

In both parts of Europe, movements at the base have a critical role to play. In the West, the peace movements can pressure governments to adopt a non-nuclear and non-provocative defence policy. In the Soviet bloc, independent movements can bring home to the Soviet leaders the fact that reformed relations between the Soviet Union and Eastern Europe are essential for a secure peace. Both can promote 'détente from below' and co-operate at various levels, recognizing that they have compleme-tary roles to play in building a new Europe.

Moving towards the Dismantling of the Blocs

Ideally we would want to see Britain and NATO making a prin-cipled decision to move away from any reliance on nuclear weapons and taking the initiative to secure susbstantial reductions in con-ventional forces. The measures we envisage being undertaken to implement this approach include the phased denuclearization of NATO strategy coupled with systematic efforts to persuade the Soviet Union to reciprocate; a shift towards 'defensive defence'; and negotiations with the Warsaw Pact aimed at confirming by treaty any gains made as a result of unilateral initiative and recipro-cal response, and exploring new agreements.

However, even if NATO in the near future proves unwilling to adopt *in toto* a programme as radical as this, it might at least be willing to reduce its present reliance on nuclear weapons – as indeed many orthodox strategists have urged – and adopt an approach to arms control in Europe based on (limited) unilateral initiatives and serious new negotiations. In the present climate, with the Soviet union apparently looking for ways to reduce the burden of its military budget, agreements might well be possible on, for instance, the creation of nuclear weapon-free zones, and changes in conventional deployment.

The second aspect of British and Western policy should be to restore and consolidate détente and to strengthen East-West trade and cooperation, especially in Europe. This would be a long-term process which might both promote and build on changes in mili-tary deployments. In the context of promoting nuclear disarma-ment and military disengagement by the USA and USSR, Britain and other West European countries should make exploratory soundings about a wider European agreement which would cover the future of Germany, the dissolution of the military blocs and the establishment of an alternative security system.

5. The Contours of a Possible European Settlement

A necessary pre-condition of the withdrawal of the superpowers from Europe and the dissolution of the blocs is a settlement of the status of the two German states. At present, the USSR, the USA, Britain and France have, in principle, ultimate responsibility for both German states. This can only be changed by the conclusion of a Peace Treaty between the Four Powers and the two German states.

One of the positive outcomes of the détente period and Brandt's *Ostpolitik* is that it no longer seems impossible that the two Germanys might participate in a conference with the four occupation powers. Both German states have been UN members since 1973 and, as we have noted, there is increasing co-operation, especially on economic matters, between them. Moreover, at least in the FRG, there has in recent years been a growing interest in the idea of a Peace Treaty to resolve the anomaly of the German situation, an interest accompanied by a debate about an alternative security system for Europe. Public opinion polls in the FRG over a number of years show that there is considerable latent support – about 30 per cent – for West German neutrality.[25] Of course, many of those who would in principle prefer the FRG to adopt some kind of neutral status see no alternative to NATO membership at present. However, if at some point neutrality looked like a real choice, popular support for it could grow rapidly.

Several models for the solution (or further alleviation) of the German problem are currently being canvased. One envisages a neutral, non-nuclear West Germany at the centre of a revised European security system. The two alliances would continue in being and the GDR would remain a member of the Warsaw Pact; nuclear weapons would be withdrawn from the Warsaw Pact states in East-Central Europe – the GDR, Czechoslovakia, Hungary and Poland – and the forces stationed there greatly reduced; in the West, Belgium and the Netherlands would also be denuclearized and lightly armed and assume a status similar to that of Denmark and Norway. West Germany's status as a neutral state might be guaranteed by a formal treaty prohibiting nuclear weapons from being stationed there, and possibly restricting the level of other military forces. Adjacent countries might agree to accept similar military restrictions. This scheme recognizes present political realities, especially in Eastern Europe. For instance, it does not assume the possibility of a neutral GDR, and it concentrates on proposals that could be explored at a relatively early point in the disengagement process.[26]

Clearly, there are some difficulties with this approach. It would mean, for instance, that the USA, France and Britain would have to withdraw their forces from the FRG, without the conclusion of a Peace Treaty to end the formal state of occupation and, presumably, with Soviet forces still stationed in the GDR. If the demand for the USA, Britain and France to do this was made strongly enough by a future West German government, they might feel they had to accede in order to avoid making a fundamental challenge to the political autonomy of the FRG. An *ad hoc* arrangement might deal with the formal legal difficulties involved;[27] thus the actual withdrawal from the FRG of British, French and US forces might take place without changing the legal and constitutional status of the two German states, and the possibility of an eventual Peace Treaty involving both them and the Four Powers could be left open. The status of West Berlin would also have to be clarified; this would presumably require some revision of the Quadripartite Agreement of 1972.

Other proposals currently being put forward in the Federal Republic are more radical: for instance, a 'Memorandum on the Implementation of a European Peace Policy', drawn up in March 1985 and whose approximately 80 signatories include academics, trade unionists and members of different political parties, calls for a German Peace Treaty, a Confederation between the two German states, the dissolution of the blocs (including the withdrawal of foreign forces from both parts of Europe) and an all-European security system.[28]

Confederation would allow the two Germanys to maintain the main features of their economic and social systems and provides a formula for reintegration at various levels; at the same time, restrictions on the permissible nature and level of armaments – and especially the banning of nuclear weapons – would provide some reassurance to other European states in East and West which might view the reintegration, or reunification, of Germany, with considerable misgivings.

Of course, there are other possible arrangements: the two German states might remain completely separate but withdraw

211

from their respective blocs; alternatively, if a Peace Treaty were eventually signed, it could include a clause preventing German reunification for a specified period, for example twenty years, as a means of reassuring neighbouring states in both East and West. West Berlin could be internationalized and UN contingents stationed in the city.[29]

Another possible option would be for the military alliances as such to be dissolved but for some superpower forces to continue to be deployed in the two German states and perhaps also in other East and West European states. This position would be analogous to that which obtained in the post World War II period before the formation of NATO. The Soviet side has always maintained that the Warsaw Pact was formed in response to NATO (and more specifically to the inclusion of the FRG in the Alliance) and that it would be prepared to dissolve the Pact were NATO to do the same. One of the main reasons this has been unacceptable to the West is that bilateral treaties could allow Soviet troops to remain in Eastern Europe. Only if NATO broke up as a result of internal disagreements and the Soviet Union decided that the Warsaw Pact was no longer needed is it at all likely that the military alliances would be dissolved without a formal agreement.

However, one cannot altogether rule out the possibility that, at some stage in the process of demilitarization and dealignment, the West European states might feel confident enough in their own ability to defend themselves to dispense with the Alliance in its present form, while some Soviet forces would continue to be deployed in Eastern Europe. In terms of bargaining strategy, the disadvantages of taking this step without securing the removal of all superpower forces from Europe are clear enough. However, it is possible that if the USA were sufficiently unhappy about the whole denuclearization and demilitarization process in Europe it would not be prepared to continue cooperating with the Alliance and in this event radical changes in West European security arrangements would be unavoidable.

To sum up the lines of an eventual settlement which would not simply secure the dissolution of the military alliances but also the withdrawal of superpower forces from both parts of Europe: first, as argued above, there would have to be a German Peace Treaty. Whatever its detailed provisions, we suggest this should provide for the neutrality of either a reunified or a confederate German state or of the two German states if these continued to exist. (Clearly, such an agreement would require the assent of both German states.)

Second, in order to meet Soviet security needs, the present Warsaw Pact states would probably have to conclude a treaty similar to the 1948 Treaty of Friendship and Cooperation between Finland and the Soviet Union: this might include acceptance of neutral status, retention of special economic and other ties with the USSR, an undertaking to resist any foreign intervention, and perhaps acceptance, in specified wartime circumstances, of Soviet military assistance but with no Soviet forces deployed in peacetime.

Third, the present NATO countries could be debarred from forming a peacetime military alliance with the USA but be otherwise free to associate together for their mutual protection. Nuclear weapons, however, whether independent or belonging to another state, would be prohibited in Europe outside the Soviet frontiers.[30]

Numerous refinements and variations of the above proposal are, of course, possible. Thus some West European states presently in NATO might adopt a neutralist or non-aligned position, or all present NATO states might undertake not to allow the peacetime deployment of any foreign troops on their territory. The provision about no peacetime alliance with the USA could be hedged with a proviso that if Soviet forces re-entered any of the former Warsaw Pact states, it would no longer be binding. As one of the measures of reciprocation for the removal of nuclear weapons from Europe outside Soviet frontiers, one would expect that all nuclear weapons inside the USSR capable only of reaching Europe would be dismantled. (Or, if France absolutely refused to budge over the *Force de Frappe*, some Soviet deployments might be countenanced in response, as a way of avoiding the whole agreement from being blocked.)

Clearly, a detailed blueprint is not possible at this stage, but it is important to be aware that there are alternatives and to understand the dynamics in both East and West that could lead to their realization.

6. British non-alignment

1. THE CONTEXT OF BRITISH WITHDRAWAL FROM NATO

A non-nuclear British government might decide to withdraw from NATO in two rather different situations. First, assuming it had initially remained a member on a conditional basis, it might find that NATO was unwilling to adopt a non-nuclear strategy and therefore be obliged to leave. Second, it might decide at the outset that withdrawal from a nuclear-based alliance was a necessary concomitant of its rejection of nuclear weapons.

The response of the USA and European NATO states to British withdrawal could vary considerably depending on which of these circumstances obtained. If withdrawal followed several years during which Britain had patiently argued the case for denuclearization then perhaps the parting would take place 'more in sorrow than in anger'. This was an argument for the conditional approach that carried considerable weight with Commission members in drawing up the first report. It is also possible that in the process Britain would have helped convince other European NATO states of the validity and importance of NATO adopting a non-nuclear strategy, so that they would withdraw at the same time or continue to campaign within the Alliance for denuclearization.

Despite these considerations, if it appeared virtually a foregone conclusion that NATO would not accept a totally non-nuclear approach, a British government might decide that a clean break at an early stage would be preferable to embarking on a protracted bargaining process, even from the point of view of maintaining reasonable relations with former allies. Thus in the conditional approach, if NATO had acceded to some British demands, for instance on no-first-use and the withdrawal of battlefield nuclear weapons, but Britain withdrew nevertheless because the Alliance was unwilling to take further steps towards denuclearization, the resulting acrimony could be greater than if a British government stated at the beginning that on principle it could no longer remain a member of the Alliance.

Whatever the circumstances of British withdrawal, it would be most important for Britain to explain the reasons for its decision with maximum clarity. Above all it should make it clear why withdrawal did not imply a retreat into isolationism, but was a step taken on principle and in the conviction that Britain could play a more constructive role in international affairs if it rejected unequivocally any reliance on nuclear weapons.

In assessing the risks and the opportunities of British withdrawal it is the short-term, that are most critical and could be most affected by the circumstances of withdrawal and whether or not Britain gave the right political signals to its neighbours. If the immediate problems and hazards can be overcome, the longer-term prospects for a non-aligned Britain are approximately the same whether a non-nuclear government pursued conditional NATO membership first or announced from the outset its decision to withdraw.

One difficulty about considering the context of British withdrawal from NATO is that no major British political party presently supports such a policy. Even the Labour Party, which favours British nuclear disarmament, is not prepared to contemplate withdrawal from NATO or to attach conditions to continued membership on the lines the Commission has suggested. It is true that of late there has been some interest in the idea of British neutrality, an interest not confined to the Left.[1] Nevertheless, short of dramatic and unforeseeable changes the likelihood remains that no British government will take Britain out of NATO in the near future, and by the time a government might be prepared to do so, the situation in Europe, and therefore the impact of British withdrawal, may have changed.

The point can be illustrated by supposing that the Labour Party won power in Britain in 1987 or early 1988 on the basis of its present defence and foreign policy commitments. Britain

215

would then remain in NATO, but as a non-nuclear power, and at the very least it would be urging its European allies to reduce significantly NATO's reliance on nuclear weapons. If it were even partially successful in this, then by the end of the Party's term in office NATO might have taken a number of significant steps, such as adopting a no-first-use policy and reducing the numbers of short-range battlefield nuclear weapons. Conceivably, the cruise and Pershing missiles might also have been withdrawn, as a result of either unilateral NATO action or East-West agreement on intermediate-range nuclear weapons deployed in Europe. Progress might also have been made towards the establishment of nuclear-weapon-free zones or corridors in Europe. If developments of this kind had taken place then clearly the debate about a possible British withdrawal would be taking place under very different circumstances from those existing now. Although, therefore, it is necessary to take the present political situation as the starting point for the discussion, these considerations must also be borne in mind.

2. DEFINING BRITISH NON-ALIGNMENT

As indicated in Chapter Two, we have chosen the term 'non-alignment' to describe the position we would want a Britain out of NATO to adopt, to convey the idea of a country playing an active and positive role in international affairs rather than retreating into a passive neutrality. The term is associated with the goals of the non-aligned movement in the Third World, which was launched at the Bandung Conference in 1955 and sought to prevent the extension of the Cold War into new areas and to allow non-aligned countries to play a mediating role in the East-West confrontation.

Non-alignment thus need not imply lack of commitment on many of the political and ideological issues that divide East and West, nor does it preclude closer economic, cultural and other links with one side or the other. It does, however, indicate independence of judgement, and, above all, a refusal to become embroiled in the military confrontation between the superpowers.

We would expect a non-aligned Britain to maintain its commitment to parliamentary government and individual liberties and, in this respect at any rate, to remain in the Western group of nations in much the same way as most of the neutral and non-aligned states in Europe – Sweden, Switzerland, Austria, Finland and Eire. Changes in internal policy might accompany Britain's adoption of a non-aligned position, but they cannot be considered a necessary and inevitable part of the change in its international status. The important point is that Britain would be committed to remaining outside NATO and to refusing to accommodate US or any other foreign military bases on its territory.

3. RISKS AND OPPORTUNITIES ASSOCIATED WITH BRITISH WITHDRAWAL FROM NATO

The risks attached to British withdrawal from NATO were examined in our first report. These relate not only to British but also, more centrally, to European security. The most serious concern is that the USA and West Germany might strongly dominate the Alliance and that the USA might introduce even more nuclear weapons into Western Europe. The Soviet Union would clearly regard such developments as particularly threatening and this could lead to a further escalation of the nuclear arms race in Europe and a deterioration in East-West political relations.

Another possibility is that NATO would break up and the West European members enter into bilateral or regional agreements or alliances. West Germany and France, for instance, might form a nuclear partnership based on the *Force de Frappe*. In the worst case West Germany might decide to produce and deploy nuclear weapons of its own. This development seems highly improbable in view of the West German commitment not to develop nuclear weapons and since even a conservative West German government has a strong interest in maintaining good relations with the GDR, but it cannot be ruled out altogether. A further threat to Britain's own security could arise if West European countries lined up with the USA in imposing economic and political sanctions against an anti-nuclear British government to bring it to heel.

These are risks, not inevitable consequences of British withdrawal from NATO. Moreover, some of the risks would be present even if Britain remained in NATO as a non-nuclear power. Thus, if Britain served notice on the USA to remove all its nuclear bases and weapons from British territory – a step that the Labour Party is committed to if it takes office – this could lead the USA to station more nuclear weapons in West Germany and to the strengthening of the Washington-Bonn relationship within NATO. It is even conceivable, as critics of such a policy insist, that it could cause such a serious crisis that the Alliance itself would be in jeopardy. But risks are an inevitable part of any process of change – which is why such care must be taken over the process as well as the policies themselves. Moreover, a non-nuclear Britain which had decided to leave NATO could take certain initiatives to reduce the risk of a deterioration in European security, including pressing the Soviet Union to make reciprocal concessions. In fact, the most persuasive argument for the conditional British membership of NATO may be, not that the alternative is too hazardous to be seriously contemplated, but that this approach might succeed in winning the Alliance as a whole to a non-nuclear strategy – which of course would be far more significant internationally.

The USA and some Western European governments would be likely to put political, and perhaps also economic, pressure on an anti-nuclear British government to modify its commitment. Even a government attempting to change NATO from within by adopting the conditional membership approach could well find that the pressure intensified as it pressed the Alliance to move entirely from any reliance on nuclear weapons. Pressure on a British government which had decided at the outset to withdraw from NATO could be particularly severe, and if Western Europe were to act in concert with the USA in imposing economic pressure, this could present serious problems for Britain. Thus it would be important for a British government – and for an anti-nuclear party before election – to explain its approach and to seek allies in mainland Europe.

Although British withdrawal from NATO would inevitably entail some risks, it would open up significant opportunities. Thus, non-alignment can contribute to the security of neighbouring states – Sweden's neutrality (in many ways closer to non-alignment) in association with Norway's and Denmark's refusal

218

to accept nuclear weapons on their territories in peacetime, makes an important contribution to the security of the Baltic region. It is doubtful whether Finland could retain its present independence and neutrality if it were not for Sweden's stance; and if Finland were forced to accept the presence of Soviet forces and weapons, the present East-West divide in Northern Europe would be much more heavily militarized.

Of course, Britain's geographical position is not comparable to that of Sweden, and if we are to look for benefits to European security from British non-alignment it must be at a different level. The crisis British withdrawal from NATO would cause in the Alliance could be the occasion for a salutary reassessment of the whole security situation in Europe and of defence arrangements. Britain itself would be better placed to explore alternative defence options. In addition to changing the emphasis of its conventional defence, it could give due weight to defence by non-violent civil resistance.

At the non-governmental level, the election of an anti-nuclear government in Britain would give an important boost to movements for change throughout Europe, whether or not Britain withdrew from NATO. This could have a major impact on European politics. Thus the popular movements in Europe could be expected to step up the pressure for non-nuclear policies and to demand their country's refusal to join in any US-led economic and political sanctions against Britain.

4. THE PROCESS OF WITHDRAWAL

If Britain had attempted the 'conditional membership' approach this would not, of course, preclude British withdrawal within two to three years, since NATO might decline to meet its conditions. Britain would engage in intensive discussions with the North Atlantic Council and indicate what changes in NATO strategy would allow it to reconsider its decision. The next stage would be a two-year suspension of NATO membership – followed, if necessary, by complete withdrawal. Thus, there would be a continuing appeal to NATO during the period of suspended British membership for NATO to reassess its position.

If a non-nuclear British government decided at the outset to withdraw from NATO, the diplomacy of withdrawal would be even more important. Much could be undertaken by an anti-nuclear political party, before a General Election, to explain its approach both at home and abroad. After election it should seek a meeting of the North Atlantic Council to examine the questions arising for the Alliance from its decision. A minimum year's notice is required by NATO for the withdrawal of a member state but Britain could extend this to two years.

5. SIGNALLING A NEW INTERNATIONALISM IN BRITISH POLITICS

At whatever stage Britain left NATO, it would be important for it to signal that, far from retreating into isolationism, it was committing itself to a new internationalism in its foreign and domestic policies. Many of the steps suggested below could, of course, be taken by any non-nuclear government, whether in NATO or not.

A British government withdrawing from NATO, especially at an early stage, would be likely to be suspected of isolationist motives, and it would therefore be important to demonstrate its acceptance of its international obligations. Moreover, if Britain had made a definite break, not only with previous nuclear defence strategies, but also with major elements of its foreign policy, its former allies would be urgently pressing for full explanations of Britain's new stance. Finally, the break with the past could release popular enthusiasm for new initiatives on a range of current issues and for longer-term policy changes.

Below we suggest a number of steps that a British government adopting a non-nuclear and non-aligned status could take. Clearly there are other possibilities.

First, there should be a declaration of principle and intent. This would stress Britain's obligation, as a country subscribing to the ethical and religious norms of the Just War tradition, to renounce all reliance on weapons of mass destruction. It could indicate that its withdrawal from NATO was an unavoidable consequence of that renunciation. It would add that this renunci-ation, the first ever by a nuclear weapons state, was intended to strengthen efforts to prevent the spread of nuclear weapons and it would call upon the other signatories of the Nuclear Non-Proliferation Treaty to begin to make serious advances towards the reduction and abolition of nuclear arsenals.

The declaration would stress that Britain was not turning its back on Europe. Britain would continue to work through various European institutions to promote the political, economic and cultural interests of Europe – its home region. But Europe's security must not be based on the threat to annihilate millions of civilians: it must not in effect repudiate the cultural and spiritual heritage it wishes to defend.

Thus, a non-nuclear government, acting in parallel with peace and human rights movements, could become the rallying point for a renewed effort to rid the world of nuclear weapons, and could issue a call to all nations to renounce such weapons, and to scientists and indeed all people to refuse to work on them. The UN General Assembly would be an obvious forum for the launch of such an appeal, which should be combined with diplomatic initiatives to strengthen the Non-Proliferation Treaty, to secure a comprehensive test ban and prohibition of chemical weapons, and to promote arms control and disarmament along the lines discussed in Chapter Seven.

Second, a high-powered diplomatic mission could be sent to the capitals of all NATO states to meet governments, parliamentary committees, political and religious leaders, newspaper editors, and other opinion-makers and put to them the reasons for Britain's decision. The mission would preferably include people from a range of political backgrounds subscribing to Britain's new policy: religious, trade union and community leaders as well as members of both Houses of Parliament and government representatives.

Although this would be an unconventional approach, there are some partial parallels, for example the mission sent by the Wilson government, immediately after its election in 1964, to all the Commonwealth countries to discuss Britain's immigration policy. The mission would, of course, be trying to reach out to a much wider audience, though the private discussions with other governments would be of particular importance. Another approximate parallel, despite the very different aims, would be the diplomatic and public relations offensive by the Reagan

221

Administration during 1983 to try to swing West European opinion behind the cruise and Pershing II deployments. In the course of this the US Secretary of Defense, Caspar Weinberger, sent to leading newspapers in Western Europe an article explaining the US position, and Vice-President Bush toured European capitals in an effort to counter the opposition of the peace movements and of a significant section of European political opinion.

Similar initiatives could be taken at an unofficial level by the various constituencies of the peace movement. Thus, representatives of Christian CND and other religious peace groups might seek meetings with influential members of religious bodies in the USA and other NATO countries: the aim would be to engage in dialogue not only those who are sympathetic politically but more especially those who are not but might be open to the view that there are good grounds for the British stand. Other specialist groups in the peace movement, such as doctors, teachers, scientists, technicians, journalists and party-political groups, could play a similar role, by approaches to their colleagues and counterparts in different countries.

The main object of both official and unofficial missions would be to explain Britain's case to governments and populations in NATO states. At the same time, if there were threats of economic and political sanctions against Britain, particularly in a concerted way from the USA and Western Europe, the missions would seek to rally popular opinion against these threats.

Third, an announcement could be made by a newly-elected British government that it would earmark a section of the armed forces for special training as a task force to be on permanent standby to help deal with emergencies such as famines and natural disasters. Thus, instead of having forces assigned to out-of-area military operations, special forces could be trained and allocated for such emergency relief work. For example, if the need arose these could be used to deliver grain supplies to stricken areas, and put planes and lorries, and military and civilian personnel with the necessary logistic skills at the disposal of international relief agencies. The necessary caveat, as we argue in Chapter Eight, is that even in the most dire emergency any such immediate efforts need to be carefully integrated with longer-term development plans, particular care being taken to ensure that they do not undermine efforts by aid recipients to achieve greater self-reliance.

At the same time, Britain should announce a substantial increase in foreign aid, emphatically linking this to any savings made in the defence budget and stressing that it saw the alleviation of hunger as not only an evident human obligation in itself, but also as an essential contribution to global security. Clearly, in the long term, aid is not the answer to the problems of famine and the inequalities within and between nations; as we argue in Chapter Eight, radical structural change is necessary. But, given the current situation and the fact that restructuring takes time, aid and, even more importantly, trade on concessionary or indeed simply equitable terms can play a part. The cutback in Britain's aid programme and concessionary trading in recent years is plainly indefensible and has demonstrably cost lives in Third World countries.[2]

But the problems of world hunger and underdevelopment are complex. We therefore recommend that a non-nuclear government should consider setting up a body to study how Britain's trade and aid policy could best be changed and its domestic economy reorganized to promote partnership in development in the Third World. Specialist groups in Britain as well as others from Third World countries could be invited to participate in this work. A political party committed to a non-nuclear and non-aligned stance need not wait for electoral victory before re-examining the problem and coming up with a programme to put before the electorate. But an authoritative Commission with government backing and, if possible, representation across the political spectrum, might be able to produce a report with the kind of authority that the Beveridge Commission had in the 1940s when it recommended steps to build a welfare state in Britain.

Fourth, Britain should emphasise support for the UN and especially for its peacekeeping role. On leaving NATO Britain could put at the disposal of the UN a proportion of the troops withdrawn from West Germany. This would dramatize concretely the fact that Britain's military withdrawal from Europe was the reverse of an isolationist policy and was rather to be seen as a positive commitment to internationalism in a wider sense. Britain could also seek to increase the importance of the UN as a peacekeeping body, for instance along the lines recommended by the Palme Commission.[3]

This re-affirmation of Britain's commitment to the ideals and objectives of the UN and its increased support for certain areas of its work should not imply an uncritical approach to the UN as an organization. While some of the attacks on it and its special-ized agencies have been politically motivated – the withdrawal of the USA and Britain from UNESCO is particularly to be deplored – there has clearly been much waste and inefficiency in the organization. Britain's efforts should therefore have a dual character: it should commit greater resources to vital areas of the UN's work, such as its peacekeeping operations, but it should also support efforts to improve the internal efficiency of the organization.

Finally, Britain, preferably in conjunction with other European states, could table proposals, along the lines suggested in Chapter Five, to end the system of military blocs in Europe and secure superpower withdrawal. Even though there would be little immediate prospect of these proposals being realized, putting them on the table could be important as a way of reasserting the goal of a reunited Europe free of the military blocs.

6. REPERCUSSIONS ON NATO OF BRITISH WITHDRAWAL

There are three main possible effects on the Western Alliance of British withdrawal, each of which opens up several other avenues. First, NATO remains intact and continues to operate much as before but without British support; second, it continues in existence but with several other countries besides Britain leaving the Alliance; or third, it disintegrates. We will consider in turn some of the implications of these possible outcomes.

Britain Leaves NATO, but the Alliance Otherwise Remains Intact
If Britain left NATO it is possible that the USA would transfer nuclear bases and weapons from Britain to continental Europe. As we noted earlier, this risk is unavoidable once Britain serves

notice on the United States to quit the nuclear bases here, and would probably not be affected by whether or not Britain remained in NATO. However, assuming the US nuclear facilities now in Britain were transferred to mainland Europe, the effects on European security are likely to be minimal. Given the quantity of US nuclear weaponry already deployed in Europe, including cruise and Pershing II missiles, the transfer of, say, the F-111 bombers or additional cruise missiles would make no significant difference to the strategic situation. The idea that such a change would be likely to spark off a dangerous East-West crisis is not plausible. As for the Poseidon submarines currently at Holy Loch, again it makes very little difference to Soviet security where these are based; the problem for NATO would be finding an alternative European base. Norway, Iceland and Denmark would probably refuse to have them, and stationing them elsewhere in Europe, assuming a suitable port can be found, would be likely to cause a political furore. For these reasons the USA might decide that the simplest solution would be to rely on longer-range submarines based in the USA.

There would be more serious implications for the defence of Europe in a protracted conventional war, particularly because of Britain's current roles in protecting the sea lanes in the Eastern Atlantic and acting as a staging post for US reinforcements of troops and equipment. It seems to us, however, that under current conditions it is most unlikely that any conflict in Europe would take the form of a protracted conventional war. The number of battlefield and other nuclear weapons on both sides, the offensive conventional strategy of the Warsaw Pact, and NATO's declared willingness to use nuclear weapons first all suggest that nuclear escalation would not be long delayed. NATO's adoption of the Follow-On-Force Attack (FOFA) strategy, and the US army's commitment to Airland Battle, with its emphasis on counter-offensives with ground forces in response to any attack, increase further the dangers of escalation. If, therefore, Britain had withdrawn from NATO because of the unwillingness of the Alliance to abandon its nuclear strategy and there had been no major shifts towards denuclearization, the difficulties of bringing in supplies and reinforcements for a protracted conflict would probably be academic.

However, it is possible to imagine the Alliance adopting a no-first-use policy, removing battlefield nuclear weapons, and perhaps even establishing a nuclear-weapon-free corridor in central Europe, but still retaining some longer-range missiles and bombers on European soil, and having US Poseidon or Trident submarines assigned to the European theatre and patrolling off European shores. In such a situation, despite the continuing reliance on nuclear deterrence, a protracted conventional war might still occur.

If NATO had scaled down its reliance on nuclear weapons to the point at which a protracted conventional war might thus be a possibility, Britain's withdrawal from NATO would open up new problems for Europe's defence. How could Western Europe overcome the handicap of losing Britain as a staging post and an important protector of the sea lanes in the Eastern Atlantic? One possibility would be to pre-position more equipment in continental Europe and airlift in reinforcements and supplies in a war or major alert. Basing equipment on the mainland is an effective way of preparing for rapid reinforcement and does already occur to some extent. But airlifting troops from the USA would be more appropriate to meeting an emergency than to supplying reinforcements for a prolonged war. A second option would be to continue to rely mainly on shipping but to route it via the North Atlantic and North Sea to West Germany and Holland. This assumes, however, that the sea lanes could be effectively protected by other NATO states, and in the long term the answer would have to be for Western Europe to be more self-reliant in maintaining its security.

British withdrawal might thus precipitate a re-think of NATO's military strategy and push it into relying more on territorial forces to provide in-depth defence, somewhat in the manner of Sweden and Switzerland. In addition, preparations for non-violent social resistance might begin to figure more prominently in the overall security planning.

Of course, there are more pessimistic scenarios. Thus, in military circles 'raising the nuclear threshold' is generally taken to mean increasing one's capability to fight a conventional war so as to delay the moment at which one would be obliged to resort to nuclear weapons to avoid defeat. Indeed, much of the discussion of the no-first-use concept has focused on ways in which NATO's ability to sustain a conventional defence could be strengthened.[4] Faced, therefore, with the greater difficulty of successfully fighting a prolonged conventional war in accordance with current strategy and deployments, NATO states might rule out any serious consideration of no-first-use or the removal of battlefield nuclear weapons.

But there are countervailing pressures and tendencies which would reduce the likelihood of NATO responding in this way. First, there is the fact that resorting to nuclear weapons in response to a conventional attack would be suicidal; it would not prevent defeat but rather make it more devastating and final. For this reason, many orthodox military strategists question its rationality regardless of how one assesses the East-West balance in Europe at the conventional level. Second, there is the growing debate about raising the nuclear threshold in Europe. For the peace movement this can mean developing an alternative, non-nuclear defence. For more orthodox strategists alarmed at the dilemmas and irrationalities of nuclear strategy, it can mean increasing the capability to fight a conventional war and delaying the moment at which nuclear weapons would have to be used. Thus there is a greater willingness than in the recent past to consider new options, such as in-depth defence, as a major component of strategy. Finally, the peace movement has focused attention on the strategic irrationality of the threat of first use (as well as the immorality of any use) and it is likely that a victory of the nuclear disarmament campaign in Britain would give an enormous fillip to the movement throughout Europe and make it much harder for European NATO governments to resist the pressure for at least a degree of denuclearization. It would be even more difficult for them to increase their reliance on nuclear weapons.

As we have already mentioned, the European peace movement could play an important role in reducing, and perhaps even eliminating, the risk of Britain suffering concerted economic sanctions from the USA and other NATO states. Mass demonstrations and various forms of direct action could help to undermine the determination of governments to apply such sanctions;

indeed, the prospect of mass protest might dissuade NATO states from attempting to apply them in the first place.

NATO Continues but One or More Countries Join Britain in Withdrawal
If Britain were to leave NATO after a sustained attempt to persuade it to reject its reliance on nuclear weapons, a number of other countries might also consider leaving the Alliance. Indeed, the Commission recommends that before withdrawing the British government should engage in extensive consultations to try and achieve a coordinated policy by as many European NATO states as possible. The very threat of simultaneous withdrawal by several states would increase the pressure on NATO as a whole to accept the demands for the adoption of a non-nuclear strategy. At present, possible associates in such a withdrawal might be Spain, Portugal and Greece in Southern and South-Eastern Europe, and Iceland, Norway, Denmark and, perhaps, Holland in the North.

What effect would such withdrawals have on NATO and the security of Europe? Clearly, if all these countries withdrew there would be a strong likelihood of the Alliance falling apart. We consider this contingency below. If Iceland, Norway and Denmark were to leave it is difficult to predict how this would affect European security. Politically it would open up important opportunities. If a Nordic nuclear-weapon-free zone could be established, with the Soviet Union agreeing in response to dismantle at least short- and medium-range nuclear weapons, European security as a whole would be enhanced and the example could set an important precedent for change.[5] The scaling down of conventional forces in the area would be another response which could be urged upon the USSR.

The withdrawal from NATO of several other states could strengthen Britain's own position. Economic sanctions would be more difficult to impose against a group of former allies than against a single state, and if they were applied, the victims could assist each other to some degree. More importantly, there would then be a strong core of neutral and non-aligned states in Europe which could influence proceedings at the Helsinki follow-up conferences, in a possible expanded conference on force reductions, and in similar international fora, and could work systematically for the achievement of a bloc-free Europe.

Given the advantages of strengthening the neutral and non-aligned forces in Europe and the opportunities in the Nordic region, the Commission takes the view that if Britain does leave NATO it should make special efforts to persuade at least Norway, Denmark and Iceland to withdraw at the same time. Clearly this would be a turning point for Europe.

NATO Breaks Up

The security implications of a break-up of NATO would depend to a considerable extent on exactly how the break-up occurred, what new pattern of alliances, if any, replaced NATO, and how the Soviet Union responded. The most positive outcome would be the dissolution of both military alliances, leading to the withdrawal of superpower forces from the territories of their present European allies. For the political reasons discussed in Chapter Five, Soviet withdrawal from Eastern Europe is unlikely in the short term, and if the Soviet Union did carry out the undertaking to dissolve the Warsaw Pact, the probable outcome would be that it would nevertheless continue to maintain some forces in various East European countries on the basis of bilateral agreements. The USA would probably similarly retain forces in Germany and perhaps several other European states. For instance, it might be particularly anxious to retain naval bases in Italy for possible operations in the Middle East. Even so, the formal dissolution of the blocs could open up opportunities for major reductions in East-West conventional forces and weapons systems in Europe. Certainly this would be the moment for a bold initiative to achieve arms reductions.

There are, of course, a number of other possible outcomes, several of which were touched on earlier. Some of these would be quite positive in their effects on European security, some would be ambiguous, and others clearly undesirable. The substitution of a US-West German military alliance for NATO comes into the last category, particularly if it involved the USA increasing the number of nuclear bases and weapons in West Germany. A more ambiguous outcome would be a Franco-German link-up, with France replacing the USA as the nuclear guarantor of

West Germany. The transition to such an alliance would be particularly fraught, but even if it was successfully managed it could prove to be the first step in a clearly undesirable development: the emergence of a new nuclear superpower in the heart of Europe. Whether a French nuclear guarantee to West Germany would of itself be more destabilizing than the present USA guarantee would depend in part on its nature and the pattern of nuclear deployment. If the guarantee were minimal, with France undertaking to 'protect' West Germany only against Soviet *nuclear* attack, and if it relied only on submarine-based systems for the fulfilment of this pledge, then in many ways the situation might be preferable to the present one, in which large numbers of battlefield and intermediate range systems are deployed in West Germany and elsewhere in Western Europe. But if France were to deploy its own battlefield and intermediate range systems in West Germany, including possibly the neutron bomb which it is currently developing, then at almost every level matters would be worse than at present. However, regardless of the nature of any French nuclear guarantee or the pattern of deployment, it is desirable to reduce the number of nuclear armed states in the world rather than extend the functions of second-rank nuclear powers by creating new nuclear-based alliances around them. So it would be a retrograde step if British non-alignment led to a nuclear-armed West European Alliance based on French nuclear weapons.

But while the possibility that these negative developments might follow the break-up of NATO cannot be disregarded, there are factors which reduce the likelihood of their occurring. The first is the anti-nuclear sentiment in West Germany, evinced by the mass protests against cruise and Pershing II deployments, by the growth of the Greens, and by the decision of the SPD, at its conference in Essen in 1984, to repudiate its previous support for the Euromissile deployments. The SPD conference resolution was also strongly critical of the move by NATO towards more offensive military doctrines such as Follow-on-Force Attack, and called for a 'new security concept' that would 'get away from nuclear deterrence and gradually establish a defensive conventional structure'.[6] Given that we are envisaging a situation in which a British government has repudiated its own nuclear weapons and asked the USA to remove theirs, it could prove extremely difficult for any West German government, whatever its political complexion, to agree to rely even more heavily on such weapons by, for instance, allowing new US bases on its territory.

The second factor making for cautious optimism is that all the main West German political parties now seem committed to forging closer links with the GDR. It may thus be expected that a future West German government would be reluctant to jeopardize its relations with its neighbour, and with the Soviet bloc in general, by entering into new military-political commitments whose dangers are at least as obvious to politicians and governments in West Germany as they are to those in the rest of Europe, and whose advantages, if any, are extremely dubious. Finally, to stress a more hopeful possibility, the dissolution of the two blocs could conceivably set the stage for a peace treaty in which the two German states accepted a neutral and partially demilitarized status and began to establish some all-German institutions.

Other positive outcomes for Europe as a whole would be the adoption by the present European NATO states of a neutral or non-aligned status or the formation of a minimal non-nuclear defence association. The latter could involve a pledge of mutual assistance in the event of any outside aggression but might, for instance, exclude the stationing of troops outside the national territory in peacetime. In any case it would be desirable that the military policies of the countries concerned should have a clearly defensive emphasis. This is harder to achieve within any kind of alliance system since, if the pledges of mutual support are to be credible, the countries involved would have to be able to deploy forces rapidly to other states in the alliance; and forces capable of rapid deployment outside the national territory have a greater offensive capability than more static forces. Nonetheless, the mainstay of the military security system could, for example, be in-depth defence by each country, with smaller mobile forces assigned to the defence of frontiers or for deployment where necessary in support of allies. Given either a minimal defence association or the emergence of independent neutral states, the circumstances might also be favourable for the development of non-violent social defence as an important element in West European security.

7. RECIPROCATION BY THE SOVIET UNION

Obviously the Soviet leaders will make up their own minds about responding to British nuclear disarmament and withdrawal from NATO. But Britain can at least suggest responses likely to have a positive impact and to lead to further progress in demilitarizing Europe rather than to a potentially dangerous backlash.

It would be particularly important for the Soviet Union to honour the public undertakings it has already given that it would respond to British nuclear disarmament by an equivalent reduction in the numbers of Soviet nuclear weapons deployed in the European theatre. This of itself could be an important disincentive to other European states accepting additional US nuclear weapons and, if Britain left NATO, could reduce the likelihood of West Germany feeling impelled to enter into new military arrangements with the USA or France. As noted in Chapter Four, British nuclear disarmament could also facilitate an agreement on intermediate range nuclear forces (INF) in Europe, since the existence of British and French nuclear weapons has been one of the stumbling blocks to agreement. Any agreements of this kind, which moved Europe away from nuclear confrontation, would strengthen the chances that British nuclear disarmament and withdrawal from NATO would not have the negative consequences that are sometimes predicted.

Soviet reciprocation at the non-nuclear level, however, would be particularly important if Britain was withdrawing from NATO. The broad principle that Britain could urge the Soviet Union to accept is that of commensurate reciprocation. Thus the more far-reaching the effects of British withdrawal, the more far-reaching concessions the Soviet Union would be urged to make regarding the restructuring and deployment of forces. A hard-headed analysis of various possible outcomes ought to lead the Soviet Union to conclude that it would be in its own interest to respond in this way, thereby helping to sustain disarmament-oriented governments in the West.

If Britain alone left NATO but circumstances were otherwise

unchanged on the Western side, the Soviet Union could, in addition to making concessions at the nuclear level, reduce its front-line forces substantially in response to the removal of 55,000 British troops from West Germany. If it had not already done so it could also agree to a zone of disengagement in central Europe from which nuclear and other major offensive weapons would be prohibited. Soviet adoption of a more defensively-oriented strategy on the central front, as suggested in Chapter Four, could also go a long way towards reassuring Western governments and populations about Soviet intentions.

Reciprocation on the northern front would also be important, especially if Norway, Denmark and Iceland withdrew with Britain and a neutral and nuclear-weapon-free zone were created which included these three states plus Sweden and Finland. In this event it would be reasonable to press for the removal of short- and intermediate-range nuclear weapons from the Leningrad and Baltic Military Districts, as suggested above.

Withdrawal from NATO by Baltic countries would give the Soviet Union even greater freedom of access to the North Atlantic than would the withdrawal of Britain alone. It could therefore be especially important for the Soviet Union to show restraint in relation to naval exercises and the size of its surface and submarine fleets in the region. Certainly, a marked increase in Soviet naval activity in the North Atlantic would be regarded as particularly threatening by Western countries and could end any hope of non-alignment gaining momentum as a political force in Europe. At present the Soviet Northern fleet moves out into the Atlantic en masse at relatively long intervals, and it would be reasonable to expect that, at the very least, there would be no increase in the frequency of these manoeuvres. Most Soviet exercises in the region are currently focused on defending the Barents Sea, where the Soviet Union feels under threat from US forward defence strategy. But the creation of a Nordic neutral zone would substantially diminish the rationale for such exercises, and it would be reasonable to urge that they should no longer be held. It would be especially important to avoid the kind of exercise in which Soviet amphibious landings take place a few miles from Norwegian territory. Clearly, provocative submarine incursions into Swedish territorial waters, or those of other Nordic states, should also be avoided.

Restraint could also be important on the US side. For example, if US ships carrying cruise missiles were to patrol regularly in international waters close to the Nordic area, this would signal an intention to fire them over the area in wartime, and would strongly discourage Soviet nuclear disarmament measures.

If NATO were to dissolve, either as part of the immediate set of reactions to British withdrawal, or after a number of years during which the Alliance had subsequently denuclearized its strategy, the Soviet response could determine whether there would be a real political breakthrough in Europe, or whether another spiral of confrontation would develop, bringing new perils. Ideally, the Soviet Union would help prepare the ground for new political and security agreements covering both halves of Europe and including Soviet withdrawal from Eastern Europe. But, in any case, the dissolution of the Warsaw Pact, substantial force reductions, and willingness to reconsider the future of the two German states and Berlin would all be important advances.

8. NON-ALIGNED BRITAIN: THE LONGER TERM

In the longer term, Britain should seek to gain maximum benefits for disarmament and peace from its non-aligned status.

In Europe. As suggested in Chapter Two, a non-aligned Britain should adopt a positive approach to European institutions such as the EEC and the Council of Europe. The guiding principle would be to remain in these institutions and play an active part in their further development unless there were specific and overwhelming reasons for withdrawal.

The most controversial issue would probably be whether or not Britain would remain a member of the EEC, since economic factors, as well as foreign and development policies, have to be taken into account in such a decision. But, as we suggested in Chapter Two, if Britain did remain in the Community it could work for better trading terms with the Third World, increased cooperation with Comecon and individual states in the Soviet bloc, the development of a more independent European stance on major global issues and the rejection of attempts to link the EEC to NATO.

Whether in or out of the EEC, a non-aligned Britain could

further détente at the European level by establishing closer economic cooperation and seeking improved relations with East European countries. Relations with individual countries, such as Hungary, that have shown an interest in both keeping European détente alive and developing a degree of independence from Soviet policies could prove particularly important. Austria's record since the signing of the Austrian State Treaty in 1955 is instructive here. It has not only been active in supporting détente, but also greatly expanded trade with Comecon states, in particular the Soviet Union and East Germany. Thus Austria ranks second only to West Germany in East Germany's trade with Western countries, and in December 1985 the two countries signed agreements which envisage a 45 per cent increase in trade between 1986 and 1990.[7]

A non-aligned Britain should also work closely with the European neutral and non-aligned states (NNAs), who have succeeded at times in coordinating their efforts, for instance in the context of the CSCE Conference and its offshoot the European Disarmament Conference in Stockholm. At a suitable moment Britain might also sound out opinion among the European NNAs about the possibility of setting up in Europe an organization parallel to the Non-aligned Movement, which, although it includes Yugoslavia, is essentially a Third World body. The aim of the European movement would be to secure the non-alignment of the whole of Europe beyond the Soviet frontier.

Outside Europe. While it would probably not be appropriate for Britain to seek membership of the Non-aligned movement, it could take positive steps to help Third World countries seeking to avoid embroilment in the East-West confrontation. In southern Africa, for instance, it could provide economic and other assistance to countries like Mozambique or Zimbabwe which face pressure and harassment from South Africa yet wish to avoid becoming too dependent for help on either superpower.

Britain's involvement in UN peacekeeping operations, notably in Cyprus, has provided its armed forces with experience of the problems and possibilities of such operations. Thus Britain is one of a number of states that would be well placed to train UN forces for this type of work. It should offer to assist in an international training programme on behalf of the UN. We suggest that Britain should give high priority to a programme of international development work in partnership with Third World countries and international agencies. This could have implications for the domestic economy: for instance, Britain might develop a sector specializing in 'appropriate technology' for Third World development. But there could also be wider implications if Britain's aim was to move away from a parasitic relationship with the Third World and towards genuine partnership. The Commission on relations with the Third World which we proposed earlier would have as its main task the making of recommendations on Britain's future economic and trading policies. Trade with Australia and New Zealand, which has experienced a relative decline since Britain joined the EEC, could also be increased.

Defence. Here Britain would seek to develop a system of 'defensive deterrence'. We suggest also that a non-nuclear government should back research programmes on the role of defence by non-violent civil resistance, support and perhaps initiate preparations for such resistance, and give encouragement to non-government bodies engaged in imaginative programmes of non-violent direct action, such as the Greenpeace campaign against French nuclear tests in the Pacific. The open support that the New Zealand Prime Minister, David Lange, has given to this campaign provides a model of how governments can give political backing to non-governmental initiatives. The extremity of the French response, and the political embarrassment that the Greenpeace campaign has caused, is a reminder that actions by non-government bodies can have a direct political impact. Such bodies can pioneer new approaches in a way that it is often difficult for governments to do, and their potential importance in developing alternative defence needs to be emphasized. Finally, at a more institutional level, nuclear-free local councils could be encouraged to initiate programmes to accustom the population to the ideas and techniques of non-violent defence.

There is no doubt that choosing non-alignment would provide Britain with a major challenge to its imagination and resourcefulness – and, indeed, to that of other European members of NATO. Because of some of the risks involved, and because remaining in the Alliance on a conditional basis provides an opportunity for persuading NATO to adopt a non-nuclear defence policy, the majority of Commission members regard British non-alignment as a fall-back option. But it is an option which would bring opportunities as well as risks, and if NATO were unwilling to move away from reliance on nuclear weapons, it would be a challenge which a non-nuclear Britain ought to accept.

7. What Britain can do to promote disarmament

1. PRIORITIES IN DISARMAMENT

This chapter focuses on how a British government that had decided to give up nuclear weapons could implement its nuclear disarmament programme so that it would have the greatest and most beneficial impact, and on what it could do to promote arms control agreements outside Europe.

The most urgent arms control objective is to restrain the technological arms race between the United States and the Soviet Union. This is now threatening to extend the arms race into space, to block efforts to agree upon important arms constraints, and to undermine some key existing arms control agreements – above all, the ABM Treaty. Restraint would mean an agreement to halt the American Strategic Defense Initiative (SDI) and any comparable Soviet programme. It is necessary to strengthen the existing ABM treaty by preventing testing, production and deployment of new forms of ABM technology, to agree to a treaty to ban testing or deployment of anti-satellite weapons now being developed, and to devise a comprehensive agreement to prevent the offensive use of space, including the possible offensive potential of lasers.

The other most urgent and symbolically significant measure to curb both SDI and new offensive weapons developments is a comprehensive test ban treaty. Although there is no prospect of such an agreement while the Reagan Administration is in power there is a domestic and international arms control lobby for a total nuclear test ban and Britain could throw its weight behind this. As a former nuclear weapons power and participant in the trilateral test ban talks in the past, a Britain without nuclear weapons would have special authority and expertise on this issue and could exert strong diplomatic influence.

It is important to develop international political constraints on the production and use of all weapons of mass destruction. A Biological Weapons Convention was concluded in 1972, although there are fears that the USA and USSR may be engaged in research into potential new biological weapons (defensive research is allowed under the Convention, and so the dividing line is thin). The necessary complement to a ban on biological weapons is a treaty to prohibit nerve gas and other chemical weapons.

Negotiations have been conducted seriously at Geneva on the possibility of such a ban since the early 1970s, and substantial progress has been made on the detail, though on the contentious issue of verification the USA and USSR are still far apart. Prospects for a chemical weapons agreement are not hopeless, for three main reasons. Firstly, chemical weapons, like biological weapons, arouse deep-seated human fears of contamination and disease, and there is strong popular revulsion against them. Secondly, they are not easy to use in a controlled and predictable way and are likely to have especially disastrous results for one's own civilian population if used in a war fought on one's own territory. Thirdly, chemical weapons, unlike nuclear weapons, are not seen as vital strategic or battlefield arms, although there is a renewed interest in new nerve gas weapons in Washington and at NATO headquarters. The British government has played an active role in the negotiations on chemical weapons, and should continue to do so.

The importance of what can be achieved by one country should not, of course, be exaggerated. But a non-nuclear Britain would be well placed to play an active role and it does still have considerable diplomatic status. Britain without its own nuclear weapons and taking a more independent line in NATO would be in a somewhat similar position to Canada, which has often been able to take the initiative in disarmament. In one of its most positive phases of disarmament diplomacy after 1968, Canada worked closely with Sweden to influence negotiations on a comprehensive test ban and demilitarization of the sea-bed. The Canadian role at Geneva relied heavily on its technical expertise.

Canadian diplomacy during the Trudeau period of the 1970s

reflected its decision to refuse to participate directly in NATO nuclear policy, which underlines the relevance of the Canadian model to a future non-nuclear Britain. On the other hand the analogy should not be pressed too hard. Canada never had its own nuclear weapons, and when it rejected American nuclear bases it was less central to US nuclear strategy than Britain is, so its nuclear disarmament was much less dramatic than Britain's would be. It has also in the recent past made some compromises in relation to testing of American missiles and American overflights, and has never directly challenged NATO strategy. If Britain abandoned its own nuclear weapons and set out to change NATO's nuclear policies the political impact would be much greater. Potentially, Britain could have considerable influence on the course of various negotiations by cooperating with a number of non-aligned countries and with the more independent members of NATO, even though its influence on the USA might be reduced.

If a British government abandoned its defence and foreign policy guidelines of forty years it would open up possibilities of radical change in many domestic and international spheres. A government opposed to nuclear weapons, and other weapons of mass destruction, would, in terms of both strategic and moral logic, have to oppose any NATO reliance on deadly chemical weapons and any moves that would increase the likelihood of chemical warfare involving the use of nerve gases in Europe. It could also be expected to display much greater seriousness about disarmament than its predecessors, and to commit significant professional, economic and organizational resources to promoting disarmament goals. We examine Britain's potential role in both these areas in this chapter.

It is, however, at the same time worth noting that a British government which did not accept the far-ranging policies advocated in this report might nevertheless be willing to pursue some of the goals we advocate: for example, pressure for a comprehensive test ban; giving priority to an agreement on banning chemical weapons whilst opposing the US programme to produce binary nerve gas; and a strengthening of internal machinery which deals with disarmament issues. There are arguments for each of these measures which do not depend on a commitment to British unilateralism. Similarly, a government committed to abandoning British nuclear weapons could still adopt many of the approaches proposed in this chapter, even if they were unwilling to take such a radical approach to NATO as we recommend.

The primary contribution that a Britain without nuclear weapons could make, however, is in two key areas: in making maximum use of its own process of nuclear disarmament to promote nuclear arms limitation and future disarmament by the superpowers, and in using its own abandonment of nuclear weapons status to strengthen the non-proliferation régime. The 1968 Non-Proliferation Treaty did commit many countries to foreswear becoming nuclear weapon powers, but the treaty is due for renewal in 1995, at present has many loopholes, and does not include a number of countries either of ambiguous nuclear status or very close to acquiring nuclear weapons.

We begin this chapter by looking at the contribution that can be made by unilateral British action, and then go on to consider how unilateral measures and diplomatic pressures may strengthen or promote the most urgent arms control agreements.

2. HOW BRITAIN DISARMS

Perhaps the main step that an anti-nuclear British government could take to strengthen political constraints on nuclear weapons would be to ensure that Britain carried through its own nuclear disarmament programme publicly and convincingly. This programme could create many valuable precedents in techniques of disarmament and verification, and in ways of dealing with the various political, legal, and institutional problems that would arise. Provided it is handled well, this experience could help to clear the way for future arms control or disarmament measures by other states.

International responses to British nuclear disarmament would not automatically all be positive or substantial. The programme would need to be vigorously promoted. The political, strategic, and moral reasons for Britain's decision to abandon its nuclear weapons should be clearly presented to international public opinion, as should its relevance to non-proliferation and nuclear arms control and disarmament. A newly-elected anti-nuclear government would need to engage in extensive high-level diplomacy and also use every public occasion to explain its policy, for example in the Queen's Speech, in its first Defence White Paper, at the UN General Assembly, and in major speeches and radio and television broadcasts. As well as bolstering domestic support for the nuclear disarmament programme, these statements would probably be broadcast widely overseas.

Once the disarmament policy was announced, many cynics would probably claim that British nuclear forces were only being abandoned because the UK could no longer afford them, and that the new policy was simply a sign that Britain had finally accepted that it was no longer a great power. If this interpretation predominated, it would greatly reduce the international impact of British nuclear disarmament. The publicity campaigns outlined above would reduce the influence of the cynics. The fact that nuclear weapons have been a status symbol should not be avoided in public explanations of British nuclear disarmament, but the foolishness of this symbolism and its dangerous encouragement of the spread of nuclear weapons needs to be stressed. Neither should the economic pressures for abandoning an independent nuclear force be denied. But the government could signal that economic problems were not a primary motive by increasing its allocation of resources to promoting non-proliferation and nuclear disarmament. The main evidence against the cynics' interpretation would be the dramatic changes in foreign and arms control policy described elsewhere in this report, and in the British policy towards US nuclear weapons based in the UK as discussed later in this chapter.

As we argued in Chapter Four, Britain's NATO allies are, in general, more likely to be worried by the changes in Britain's foreign policy and policy towards NATO than they are by the loss of British nuclear weapons in themselves. However, its long-standing 'special relationship' with the UK would mean that the USA would have some specific concerns about the abolition of even Britain's own nuclear weapons. The important contributions made by the USA to British nuclear forces have provided the USA with powerful leverage over various aspects of UK policy. After British nuclear disarmament, this source of leverage would be removed. Furthermore, the possibility that the British might release classified information on US nuclear systems would worry Americans greatly.

As will become clear, there are several good reasons why Britain would want to avoid releasing such information, but these impose serious constraints on how British nuclear disarmament could be verified. In this section we discuss how British nuclear disarmament could best be implemented, and then consider how best it might be verified. It will, we hope, become clear that although there are real obstacles to fully reliable verification procedures, the monitoring techniques available will allow adequate verification for all of the most important objectives of British disarmament to be achieved. Some of the most demanding aspects of verification require further research. Indeed, one of Britain's most important contributions to international arms control and disarmament may be to clarify and resolve some of the outstanding problems. However, it is not essential for all of the problems to be solved before British nuclear disarmament is carried out.

In some cases, the IAEA and Euratom have a clear role to play in monitoring British nuclear facilities. This will often fit into the normal role of these organizations. Sometimes their role may be extended as they have the opportunity to devise procedures for monitoring reprocessing or uranium enrichment plants. Furthermore, after the nuclear disarmament programme is completed, it may be appropriate for Britain to have a special status as the first ex-nuclear power, in order, for example, to meet the unique requirements to monitor enriched uranium fuels for nuclear powered submarines. We also identify a potential need for inviting neutral observers from Sweden or Switzerland to monitor particularly sensitive aspects of the disarmament programme. This would, initially at least, be organized outside the framework of the IAEA or NPT, for reasons that will become clear.

Implementing a British Nuclear Disarmament Programme
Even if the incoming government had an overwhelming popular mandate to abolish British nuclear weapons, there would be serious institutional resistance to implementation of the policy.

Many in the Ministry of Defence, the armed forces and the Foreign Office would regard it as wrongheaded or dangerous in the extreme. Some groups, such as parts of the navy, the nuclear weapons laboratories, and perhaps the intelligence services, could also regard nuclear disarmament as a direct threat to their institutional interests.[1]

Ministers would therefore have to oversee the disarmament process closely to ensure that it is carried out properly and without unreasonable delays. This would require strong political will, probably backed up with expert advice from outside the ministries concerned. It also means that the issues and obstacles that are likely to arise should have been identified and prepared for before the new government came to power.

a) *Delivery systems*: The delivery systems for nuclear weapons are a more visible, and usually more expensive, component of nuclear forces than the warheads themselves. Like all of the other declared nuclear-weapon states, Britain has a range of delivery vehicles and weapons platforms such as missiles, aircraft and submarines which are specifically allocated to nuclear roles, combined with dual-capable systems that may also be used for conventional operations. One of the first decisions that would have to be taken by an anti-nuclear government is which of these delivery systems to dismantle or alter.

In some cases this would be self-evident and, given the political will, the decisions should be fairly straightforward to implement. Polaris submarines would be decommissioned, and their ballistic missiles dismantled. The Trident programme would be terminated, and the construction facilities at Barrow-in-Furness and elsewhere would be transferred to other work, probably on conventionally-armed 'hunter-killer' submarines in the short term, but hopefully transferring to non-military products in the future.

One potentially tricky issue would arise if some Trident submarines were close to completion, or finished, by the time an anti-nuclear government came to power. It has been reported that, in such a case, the Labour Party proposes to modify the Trident submarines to a hunter-killer role, in order to make some use of the investment that had been made.[2] This could be technically acceptable, provided the missile tubes were removed or permanently blocked and periodically exposed to satellite inspection to allow verification. The USA and USSR have set a precedent for this practice, when they have respectively adapted old Polaris and 'Yankee' class missile submarines to new roles in order to keep their strategic modernization programmes within the SALT II limits. However, the Commission doubts that this would be the right policy for British Trident submarines. It is unclear that such submarines would have a sensible conventional military role, and retaining them would make it easier for a later pro-nuclear British government to rebuild British nuclear forces.

British theatre and tactical nuclear weapons are carried on ships, aircraft and helicopters. These also have a conventional role, and so long as Britain maintains modern armed forces, they could not be scrapped. Any specific adaptations for nuclear weapons should be removed, as should any supporting nuclear infrastructure. British Lance tactical nuclear missiles should be dismantled, together with their launchers. The UK would inevitably retain the theoretical capability to deliver nuclear weapons. Tornado strike aircraft would be particularly easy to adapt for medium range nuclear attacks. However, although these aircraft would not have been chosen by advocates of defensively-oriented military postures, now that they have been procured they will surely remain central to the RAF for the remainder of this century.

b) British nuclear warheads: At the core of a nuclear disarmament programme must be, of course, the dismantling of the nuclear warheads and the disposal of the associated fissile material. British nuclear warheads are designed and developed at the Atomic Weapons Research Establishment at Aldermaston. They are manufactured at the Royal Ordnance Factory at Burghfield (and occasionally at Aldermaston), using tampers and other non-fissile components made at the Royal Ordnance Factory at Cardiff.

The number and types of British nuclear weapons in existence remains an official secret, and unofficial estimates vary from 185-225[3] to over 1,000.[4] If the Trident programme goes ahead, the total number of warheads would increase, though some official doubts have been reported as to whether the full complement of some 512 Trident warheads can actually be constructed.[5] (This is reportedly due to a shortage of plutonium. If so, this is hard to understand, since British military reactors should have been able to produce more than sufficient plutonium stockpiles.[6])

An anti-nuclear government would want to dismantle all British nuclear warheads as quickly as possible, and certainly within three or four years. Delays would increase the risk of a change of government before the British nuclear disarmament programme was completed. The question is, is it technically possible to meet these time limits?

Since warheads are regularly dismantled and handled in maintenance and modernization programmes, there is no technical obstacle to their being dismantled as part of a disarmament process. However, since much of the relevant information is classified, it is not possible to reach definite conclusions about the rate at which this can be achieved. Nevertheless, it is possible to make some plausible estimates (see Appendix 1, p. 297). Approximately 500 warheads, and possibly more, could be dismantled in a year using the combined facilities of Aldermaston and Burghfield. Thus, even if there is a six-month delay before the process begins and the size of the British nuclear arsenal turned out to include as many as 1,000 warheads, it would probably be technically possible to dismantle all of these warheads within three years – well within the likely lifetime of a single Parliament.

The Verification of British Nuclear Disarmament
If British nuclear disarmament is to have a positive and enduring effect on the policies of other states and on international public opinion, some form of independent reassurance that the programme had actually been carried out would be essential. Verification is therefore an issue of great importance.

Ideally, the verification procedures would provide an absolute guarantee that the UK had completely abandoned both nuclear weapons and the capability to rebuild them at short notice. It is not only foreign countries that would prefer such proof; the British public (and many members of the government itself!) might also wish for independent evidence.

However, no set of verification procedures can be foolproof. In this case, for example, uncertainty about the size of Britain's present nuclear arsenal or of its stockpiles of fissile materials means that there would always be the possibility that some warheads or materials had been secretly hidden. So long as the UK remains a nation state with some military or industrial secrets, independent observers are unlikely to be allowed unrestricted access to all facilities or potential hiding places.

This problem would be compounded by the fact that the UK would almost certainly possess the capability to redevelop nuclear weapons relatively quickly. The necessary scientific and technical expertise would remain available for a long time to come. Civil nuclear reactors and other nuclear facilities seem likely to remain in existence in the UK for decades at least. British nuclear-powered submarines, if they were retained, would require a continuing supply of highly-enriched (almost weapons grade) uranium.

These limitations on verification are often used to argue that British nuclear disarmament could never be more than a highly unsatisfactory half-way house.[7] It is said that it would lack credibility and engender cynicism that would radically undermine the intended international response. Like it or not, the argument goes, Britain would continue to be regarded as a nuclear-capable nation and potential adversaries would assume that Britain would either retain nuclear weapons or rebuild them during crisis or war.

This analysis appears to us to be unreasonably pessimistic. As we argue below, once the verification requirements are clarified it becomes clear that some of the key requirements can be met fairly straightforwardly. When it comes to verifying that the British disarmament programme has been carried through completely – establishing precedents for disarmament measures by other countries in the future – the problems become greater: intrusive monitoring procedures are required. Even here, a very great deal can be done.

We first consider what level of confidence is required for the verification procedures for British disarmament to have the desired effects. Then we discuss how these requirements can be met.

To have a strong international impact, it is probably sufficient to establish that Britain had radically changed its policy on nuclear weapons to promote non-nuclear defence and non-proliferation. The monitoring procedures required to verify this would be minimal. The reversal of declared British policy on nuclear weapons, NATO, and arms control should be sufficient to convince most observers that the change in British defence policy was both real and substantial, especially if it was combined with the termination of several highly-visible components of British nuclear weapons capability. The reality of the change would be confirmed when the UK reclassified itself as a non-nuclear weapons state under the terms of the NPT and opened itself to the appropriate inspection agencies from the IAEA and Euratom.

The Soviet Union would probably require more rigorous verification before it decided how (if at all) it would reciprocate. As discussed in Chapter Four, the reciprocal measures that the Soviet Union might consider would be the destruction or withdrawal of an appropriate number of SS20s. Thus it would require reassurance that Britain had really scrapped its own corresponding missiles on Polaris or Trident submarines. So long as the USA retained nuclear weapons, the USSR would not, of course, be expected to respond to the British actions with complete nuclear disarmament. So the question of verifying the total abolition of British nuclear warheads could not legitimately arise in this context.

Once these key requirements have been identified, it becomes clear that verification would not be as much of a problem as is often claimed. The change in policy away from nuclear weapons to greater support for arms control and the NPT would be plain for all to see, as would the establishment of IAEA safeguards at British nuclear facilities. The Soviet Union would be able to monitor the decommissioning of the Polaris/Trident nuclear forces with national technical means such as satellite observation. Similarly, once the nuclear disarmament process had finished, the closure or conversion of nuclear facilities at Burghfield and Aldermaston would be fairly easy to confirm. Thus, adequate verification to achieve international impact and promote Soviet reciprocation should be quite possible.

The most demanding requirements for verification would probably arise from the desire to establish procedures and techniques as precedents for future arms control or disarmament measures. It is in this context that intrusive monitoring procedures for dismantling nuclear warheads and missiles, for the production and storage of fissile materials, and for the operation of nuclear facilities, military installations or dual-capable systems assume their greatest importance.

Such procedures would have additional advantages. They would make it harder for a future government secretly to rebuild nuclear weapons. Since Soviet leaders would be more confident that Britain had no secret nuclear arsenal, these procedures would also reduce the risk of pre-emptive nuclear attack by the USSR in a crisis or war against potential nuclear stores or delivery vehicles in Britain.

The conversion of dual-capable systems such as aircraft, helicopters or ships would be quite hard to verify reliably. In a few cases, adaptations for nuclear weapons may be observable from the outside, allowing verification through national technical means. A possible example would be a Tornado aircraft fitted to carry long-range cruise missiles. At the moment the Tornado has not been adapted for this role, but an adapted Tornado has been proposed as a possible alternative to the Trident programme.[8] In such cases monitoring the conversion to a conventional role could be carried out from a distance. A precedent for such a step has been set in the SALT II treaty, for example in its insistence that cruise-carrying bombers be distinguishable by so-called Functionally Related Observable Differences (FRODs).

In most cases, however, any adaptations for nuclear weapons would be relatively hidden. Where their removal could be checked by international observers without serious breaches of security, this should be arranged. Otherwise, observers should be invited to inspect as much of the removed material as possible once the conversion operation has been carried out. Even though this inspection would sometimes be nominal, it is politically and symbolically important that the conversion procedure is followed for all dual-capable systems. This would be an important confidence-building measure even when the guarantees it provides are slight.

If we turn to the verification procedures for dismantling warheads or missiles, some form of intrusive monitoring is necessary for reliable verification, whether by inspectors or by the installation of tamper-proof automatic inspection devices.

The most obvious approach would be to invite international observers to monitor the process directly. There are, however, serious constraints on how this could be implemented.

Constraints on intrusive monitoring. There are at least two important constraints on how Britain should allow intrusive verification of its programme to dismantle its nuclear missiles and warheads.

Firstly, it would obviously be undesirable for other nuclear or near-nuclear states, such as the USSR, France, China, Israel, Pakistan, or Argentina to gain information from British nuclear disarmament that would help them to develop their own nuclear-weapon programmes.

Furthermore, Article I of the NPT states that 'each nuclear weapon state party to the Treaty undertakes not to transfer to any recipient whatsoever nuclear weapons . . . directly or indirectly; and not in any way to assist, encourage, or induce any non-nuclear state to manufacture . . . nuclear weapons'. Since an important part of the rationale for British nuclear disarmament is to strengthen the non-proliferation régime, it is clearly vital that the monitoring procedures neither contravene nor appear to contravene this important Treaty article. For these reasons, verification procedures must be designed so that it is clear that no militarily important information about the design or construction of nuclear weapons systems would be revealed. It should be recognized that a great deal of general information about nuclear warhead design is already available, but the UK should certainly avoid adding to this.

Secondly, the UK is bound by international treaty with the USA never to disseminate any information on US nuclear weapon systems (primarily by the 1944 Quebec agreement). US collaboration has permeated the UK nuclear weapon programme so thoroughly that this obligation would apply to practically every aspect of British nuclear forces (See Appendix 2, p. 299).

Thus, according to this Treaty, the UK should deny independent observers access to any classified aspect of the design or construction of UK warheads, missile, submarine, or military pressurized-water reactors (as used in submarines), unless the USA has given prior permission. Since US-UK relations would almost certainly deteriorate after a British anti-nuclear government came to power, the American Administration is likely to try and insist that the Treaty is strictly adhered to. Not only would it probably be deeply and genuinely suspicious of the security of US secrets with the British, but it is also unlikely to neglect an opportunity to embarrass the new UK government.

Constitutionally, the British Parliament could overturn the Treaty. However, we do not recommend this action. Government policy should aim to bolster confidence in international treaties, not to undermine it.

Furthermore, breaking with the Treaty (with the implied threat to reveal US secrets) would provide a focus for popular campaigns against the British in the USA. The consequences of such campaigns are unpredictable but they would surely be undesirable. Sticking to the Treaty could provide an important symbol of Britain's desire to continue to work with the USA, especially since, as explained above,most of its constraints would be imposed in any case by a desire to prevent proliferation.

A less serious, but still significant legal consideration is that there are precise constraints on the unilateral termination of the 1958 Mutual Defence Agreement. If the USA refused to cooperate, the UK only has one opportunity every five years to bring the treaty to an end.[9] Since this treaty and its amendments provide the legal basis for US-UK nuclear collaboration, an anti-nuclear government would want to terminate it. This would not only be consistent with its anti-nuclear policy, but would also make it harder for a future British government to restore the *status quo ante*. An incoming anti-nuclear government should therefore halt all exchanges under the 1958 Agreement immediately, and then wait until the next legal opportunity to end the treaty.[10] In practice, however, the USA may be anxious to agree to end the Agreement as quickly as possible.

Verifying the destruction of British nuclear missiles and warheads. The dismantling of Polaris, Trident, and Lance missiles (minus their warheads) could not be closely inspected by international observers at every stage of the process, for the reasons discussed earlier. However, adequate verification procedures do appear to be possible.

...rs could be allowed to count and weigh the missiles ...ney were taken into a closed facility to be scrapped. The ...p could then be monitored and weighed at the end of ...e process. The building could be placed under IAEA-type safeguards and inspected at the end of the dismantling process to check that no missiles had been secreted. Alternatively, the missiles could have their rocket-fuel removed in a closed facility (if necessary for security) and then the remainder of the missile could be destroyed in view of international observers, and hopefully also the world press. Since fairly reliable information is available on the number of missiles in British possession (mainly from US government documents), one would be reasonably confident that all the missiles had been destroyed.

Such procedures should both safeguard military secrets and allow effective verification. However, more research is required on this issue, and it could turn out that there are some stages where monitoring would be valuable, but too sensitive to allow access to representatives of hostile states or other countries that might put the information to use in their own nuclear programmes. In this case, the Commission recommends that the possibility of allowing access to vetted experts from countries such as Sweden or Switzerland should be explored.

It appears to us that such observers could play a very important role in the verification of a wide range of measures besides the destruction of missiles. The range of countries from which they could sensibly be drawn seems very limited. The countries should be neutral, so that in the future both blocs would be more likely to make use of the observers and trust their reports. The countries should be technologically developed, and should have already explored the possibility of pursuing their own nuclear weapon programmes, so that it is unlikely that they would learn anything from limited access to the dismantling process that they could not easily have discovered for themselves. Finally they should have rejected the nuclear weapons option for themselves and have signed the NPT. An independent and vetted body of experts from Sweden and Switzerland appears to be the obvious answer.

To avoid diplomatic wrangles, it would be preferable if this system was set up outside the framework of the NPT or IAEA.

However, reports should probably be published through the IAEA.

Monitoring procedures for dismantling nuclear warheads would require even more careful thought than for missiles. In this case the weight of the warheads, the masses of the fissile and other materials used, and the number of components and their configurations are all classified. Therefore these quantities could not be used for monitoring, except perhaps to a limited extent by the neutral observers. Similarly, the warhead cannot just be crushed: the fissile material and conventional explosives must be removed and disposed of separately. Nevertheless, with careful design it should be possible to provide reasonable reassurance that all warheads put through the process actually are dismantled and that the retrieved fissile material is stored in a safeguarded building or storage facility.

The process could make use of so-called Remote Continuous Verification (RECOVER) technology.[11] This technology involves remote-controlled tamper-proof detectors or cameras, allowing controlled on-site monitoring without the intrusive presence of inspectors. Establishing and developing the use of such devices could open important opportunities for a wide range of arms control and disarmament measures.

An additional measure to help with verification could be to release historical records of the size of the stockpiles of warheads and fissile materials, and of the modes of operation of military and civilian nuclear reactors. For example, the quantities of plutonium produced at Calder Hall and Chapelcross reactors and the records of warhead production at Burghfield and Aldermaston could be published. Such measures would provide experts with the information required for independent estimates of the British stockpiles, and would therefore provide additional reassurance. However the implications of releasing such information would need detailed examination.

Verification procedures clearly require further research. However, it should be remembered that it is not essential that all of the problems be sorted out before British nuclear disarmament is carried out. Even if safeguards and techniques are not well enough developed to provide very reliable monitoring, they should be sufficient to provide substantial reassurance. The experience should then be built upon to develop more satisfactory procedures for the future.

Safeguards Against Nuclear Rearmament

Even if it were generally accepted that Britain had dismantled all its nuclear weapons, reassurance against nuclear rearmament would still be desirable. The first question is what should be done with the stockpiled weapons-grade plutonium and uranium?

Once the UK had registered in the NPT as a non-nuclear weapons state, these stockpiles would naturally be placed under IAEA and Euratom safeguards. However, as the first ex-nuclear weapon state, Britain would not be typical of other non-nuclear weapons states. Not only would it possess these large stockpiles of weapons-grade fissile material, but it would also have a continuing requirement for highly-enriched uranium to power its nuclear-powered hunter-killer submarines (together perhaps with one or two converted Trident submarines).

At some stage, these nuclear-powered submarines might be phased out. However, such submarines do have a significant edge over conventionally-powered submarines for extended underwater operations. In any case Britain has made such a heavy investment in nuclear-powered submarines that, even if it chose to abandon them, it would take many years to complete the transition. Thus, such submarines are almost certain to be retained into the next century, leading to difficult choices about how to ensure supplies of highly-enriched uranium fuel to power them.

The decision on supplies depends largely on whether one is most worried about dependence on the USA or about the dangers of future British nuclear rearmament. If the former, then one (expensive) option would be to make Britain self-sufficient by building a new high-enrichment plant at Capenhurst, alongside the present civilian installation. If the latter, then the entire British stockpile of weapons-grade uranium could be diluted in civil nuclear reactors and supplies could be bought commercially from the USA (or perhaps France) under IAEA safeguards.

Since we are greatly worried about *both* dangers, we are tempted by the compromise in which no new enrichment plant is built and supplies are bought under safeguards from the USA, but Britain's present uranium stockpiles are retained as a buffer stock. However, since information on the size that this stockpile would be after disarmament is not available, it is not clear how realistic this option would be.

Small amounts of highly-enriched uranium have been transferred from the USA to Europe and Japan for civil purposes under IAEA safeguards. However the IAEA has no experience of safeguarding uranium submarine fuels, and so new procedures would clearly have to be developed. These would involve returning spent reactor fuel from the submarines to IAEA safeguards after use, when it would be compared with the original fuel to ensure that no uranium had been diverted.

As far as the weapons-grade plutonium is concerned, the stockpile should be processed and diluted so as to make it as hard as possible for the material to be re-used in warheads. It could either be blended with other elements or diluted and used as fuel in civil nuclear reactors. An advantage of the second option is that some use would be made of the material and the resulting plutonium in the fuel rods would be even harder to refine for use in nuclear weapons.[12]

A third important component of thermonuclear weapons is tritium, the fuel for the fusion reactions.[13] Since tritium decays relatively quickly, with a half-life of about twelve years, there is a continuing need for new supplies. If all British trade in nuclear materials was conducted under IAEA safeguards and if tritium production at the Chapelcross reactor in Scotland was closed down, confidence that Britain was not maintaining a secret store of warheads would increase over the years. Any future attempts to restart British thermonuclear weapons construction would also be hindered.

Once all the British nuclear weapons had been dismantled, decisions would need to be made about the future of the nuclear weapon facilities at Aldermaston, Burghfield, and Cardiff. To build confidence that the UK had unambiguously abandoned nuclear weapons production, Burghfield should be closed down. The Royal Ordnance factory at Cardiff could be adapted for work on conventional arms, but it would be preferable if it were converted to civilian production. In each case, the work-force has many skills and should be offered retraining and new work in other areas.

Aldermaston possesses a vast range of equipment and a large expert staff. Projects at this establishment should be redirected to areas such as verification procedures and devices, nuclear waste management, fusion, and other areas of high technology. If this were done, work should be available for the great majority of the Aldermaston staff. The remainder should be offered work elsewhere. Most, if not all, of the research and development carried out there should be openly published.

One area at least of the Aldermaston establishment must either be closed down or opened to international inspection – the nuclear weapons laboratories themselves. The new A90 complex, which is being built as part of the Trident programme and is due to open by about 1988, is reportedly a direct replica of part of the US weapons laboratory at Los Alamos.[14] Thus the Quebec Agreement, combined with concerns to avoid releasing information that might increase proliferation, means that the nuclear weapon facilities could not be opened to IAEA inspection before much of the equipment had been dismantled. Until this had been carried out, the facilities should be closed and access should be under international inspection, perhaps organized by the IAEA. Remote-controlled monitoring, using the RECOVER technologies, could play a valuable role here, as could the vetted observers from countries such as Sweden and Switzerland discussed above.

The Civil Nuclear Programme

Britain has eleven civil nuclear power stations, with five more under construction or due to be commissioned. Additionally there are military reactors at Calder Hall and Chapelcross which also provide some electrical power to the national grid. Associated with these are the fuel fabrication facilities at Springfields, the uranium enrichment plant at Capenhurst, and the reprocessing installation at Sellafield (Windscale).[15] This system of nuclear facilities could facilitate any future British nuclear rearmament programme. The Commission's overall position on nuclear power is outlined in section five of this chapter. Here we confine ourselves to the question of what measures should be

256

taken to guard against the British nuclear power programme being used to help with nuclear rearmament, on the assumption that this civilian programme would continue for some time at least after the election of an anti-nuclear weapons government.

As a registered nuclear weapon state, Britain currently only submits its nuclear power facilities to relatively nominal international inspection. After nuclear disarmament this would have to change. All military nuclear facilities would either be closed down or converted to civilian use, and all civil nuclear power installations would be placed under full-scope IAEA and Euratom safeguards.

Three major areas of decision remain; what to do about the reprocessing plant at Sellafield, the uranium enrichment plant at Capenhurst, and the fast-breeder reactor programme (for which facilities are being built at Dounreay in the north of Scotland).

The dangers of a fast-breeder reactor programme, with its implications for the large-scale production of plutonium and the creation of a 'plutonium economy', seem greatly to outweigh its potential benefits, and so it should be abandoned.[16] However, the issues relating to Sellafield and Capenhurst are not so clear-cut.

Reprocessing plants pose particular dangers for nuclear proliferation, and Sellafield could be used to produce plutonium for nuclear weapons. Thus there are good arguments for closing Sellafield. There are, however, some counter-arguments.

First, as the IAEA has had no real experience of monitoring a commercial reprocessing plant, procedures developed at Sellafield in collaboration with a cooperative government could be extremely valuable for IAEA operations elsewhere in the world. Secondly, Sellafield at present provides an international reprocessing service. If it were closed down, other countries might well build their own reprocessing facilities. The immediate impact would be felt in countries such as Japan, but there would soon be pressures for reprocessing facilities in places like South Korea. There is, therefore, a case for keeping Sellafield open, in order to prevent an undesirable proliferation of reprocessing facilities and also as part of a strategy to place plutonium under international control. Sellafield would provide Britain with some leverage over the operation of the international nuclear fuel cycle.

On balance, the Commission decided that Sellafield should be closed. It is questionable that reprocessing is the best approach to nuclear waste management and rather than internationalizing the reprocessing facilities, we believe that the UK should be persuading other countries that reprocessing is undesirable and unnecessary. Furthermore, although work on the new Thorpe reprocessing plant at Sellafield could and should be halted immediately, it would take a number of years for the existing plant at Sellafield to be actually closed, and therefore there would still be an opportunity to provide the IAEA with monitoring experience at the facility.

Similar arguments apply to the uranium enrichment plant at Capenhurst. Although Capenhurst only produces reactor-grade uranium, it could provide the basis for a programme to produce uranium for nuclear weapons. However, provided it was placed under full IAEA safeguards, it could also provide an international service by reducing the spread of uranium enrichment facilities and improving international control. In this case the arguments for closing the plant down appear to be weaker, and so the fate of Capenhurst would probably depend upon broader decisions about the future of nuclear power in the UK. While it remained open, it could be used to provide leverage over the conduct of international trade in uranium, through membership of Urenco and elsewhere.

Many issues remain to be resolved, but it does appear that the programme of British nuclear disarmament could be carried out in a positive way. However, there is another category of nuclear weapon systems located in Britain, on which it is also necessary to develop a policy, i.e. those of the United States.

3. US Nuclear Weapons and Bases

As submitted both here and in our first report,[17] the removal of US nuclear weapons facilities from the UK should be an intrinsic part of Britain's non-nuclear defence policy. In fact, in many ways this would have a much more fundamental impact on international relations and NATO policy than Britain's own nuclear disarmament. The type of impact it would have depends to a large extent on which US facilities would be affected and how.

It would be necessary to close the US Poseidon/Trident base at Holy Loch in Scotland, as well as the nuclear weapons stores in Machrihanish and St. Mawgan. Similarly, the nuclear weapon facilities at the F-111 bases and other US airfields in the UK would be shut down. The nuclear warheads would be withdrawn to the United States. Ideally they would then be dismantled in a verified way using similar procedures to those described for British warheads. However, there would be no way for Britain to insist upon this if the USA chose to act otherwise.

At the same time, it is part of our recommended strategy that Britain remains in NATO, and therefore a military ally of the United States, in order to denuclearize defence policies in Europe from within the Alliance. Although it would in principle be possible to do this and at the same time to insist on the withdrawal of every kind of US military presence, we do not recommend this. It would be counterproductive, and undermine Britain's prospects for influencing and changing NATO policy along the lines discussed in Chapter Four.

Thus many of the US facilities could remain, so long as they were engaged in NATO activities along lines agreed with the UK. However, Britain would have to have greater legal authority and control at the bases. The present immunities of US bases and personnel to British law should not continue. All US facilities in the UK should be placed under British legal jurisdiction. Furthermore, British officers would need to play a much greater role in the day-to-day operations of these facilities, so that the British government can be assured that the base is operating according to agreed conventional military policies and that the UK has an effective right of veto over actions from these bases.

Given these changes, the US F-111s and other aircraft could remain at their present bases provided they were allocated purely conventional roles. The same would apply to many US army or naval facilities. The US Army and Air Force could probably adapt without much difficulty to this constraint, once the political decision by the US to accept it had been made. However, it could be a problem for the US Navy, which has a long-standing policy of neither confirming nor denying the presence of nuclear weapons on its ships.

From the perspective of controlling and reducing the role of nuclear weapons in military policy, and reducing the risks of nuclear war, there would be great advantages in impelling the US Navy to abandon this policy. It would ultimately reduce the spread of tactical nuclear weapons, and reduce obstacles to naval nuclear arms control and to the declaration of nuclear-weapon-free zones over large areas of the world, such as in the Pacific and Indian Oceans. It would also increase the credibility of a no-first-use policy by NATO.

Britain is in a position to exert strong leverage on this, since British bases (together with facilities in Iceland and Norway) play a key role in US naval operations in the North-East Atlantic, and British naval forces make a large contribution to NATO naval policy in that area. The best policy would be for Britain to insist that all American ships declare that they carry no nuclear weapons before they are allowed British facilities.

A possible, but less satisfactory, approach would be to institute more informal mechanisms for ensuring that no nuclear weapons are brought to British bases, in line with present practice in Iceland and Japan.

Years of close collaboration will have provided the British with a good knowledge of US standard procedures and, combined with informal monitoring by British naval officers, it should be possible to ensure that the British non-nuclear policy would in fact be maintained. Although this would erode the US naval policy of refusing to say whether or not ships carry nuclear weapons, it would have a much smaller international impact than if the US naval policy of neither confirming nor denying the presence of nuclear weapons were abandoned altogether.

The US command, control, communication and intelligence-gathering centres pose more difficult problems, since many of them would play a key role in both conventional and nuclear operations: the installations at Croughton, Edzell, Brawdy, or Fylingdales are good examples. In general the case for allowing these bases to continue seems strong so long as the UK remains in NATO, and it would certainly cause massive disruption if they were to close. In the case of Fylingdales, however, the arguments seem to be more finely balanced. Although it does play a role within NATO air-defence systems, its primary role has been to provide early warning of ballistic missile attack against the USA. Thus the Fylingdales facility is more essentially associated with nuclear weapons policy. On the other hand, it can be argued that early warning centres are a reciprocally stabilizing factor, and that the UK should therefore allow the establishment to remain in operation.

Since ABM and SDI systems involve ground-based radars, SDI tends to undermine the last argument, and expensive new facilities are due to be installed at Fylingdales whose role is not yet clear. On balance, a compromise approach might be best, in which British personnel take over *all* operations at Fylingdales, in collaboration with US liaison officers, in order to ensure that facilities there are appropriately used and not associated with SDI.

The potential impact on the control of nuclear weapons of this British policy towards US bases is large. US forward-based systems such as the F-111 bombers have been a significant element of American nuclear forces. At various times they have appeared to be a significant obstacle to strategic arms control. If Britain achieved the withdrawal of the nuclear element of these forces, that in itself would be a major improvement, to which some Soviet reciprocation may (possibly) be forthcoming. There is, however, the possibility that the USA would refuse to maintain its air-bases in the UK under the conditions imposed upon them and seek to transfer them to mainland Europe. This might be prevented if Britain was working closely with other European countries and it underlines the importance of European countries collaborating in the effort to secure NATO denuclearization.

If the bases were to be transferred, Southern Italy might well appear the most promising location, not only on military grounds but because of the likely opposition within NATO countries in Central and Northern Europe to having the bases. In terms of East-West relations, the worst choice would be the FRG, and it would be important to make every effort to prevent such a development.

4. THE STRATEGIC DEFENSE INITIATIVE AND THE ABM TREATY

The US Strategic Defense Initiative promotes destabilizing developments in anti-satellite and anti-ballistic missile systems and obstructs progress towards a CTBT, an anti-satellite weapon ban, and a strategic arms limitation treaty. It also directly threatens the crowning achievement of the nuclear arms control process in the 1970s: the Anti-Ballistic Missile (ABM) Treaty. Although the SDI programme is, as yet, still in its research phase and is therefore permitted by the ABM Treaty, it is only a matter of a few years before the programme is expected to contravene this Treaty directly. The line dividing (permitted) research and (prohibited) development is very fine. Already the great majority of SDI projects are strongly focused on applications and weapons rather than on basic research. Thus any British government concerned to promote nuclear arms control and at least to stabilize the nuclear arms competition should aim to halt the SDI.

When the SDI programme was established by the Reagan Administration, the Conservative British government reacted very coolly towards it, in common with its European allies and most of the rest of the world. Outside the United States there was, and still is, a broad consensus on the importance of preserving the ABM Treaty. European governments were also uncomfortable with the rhetoric used in support of the SDI, with its emphasis on the immorality and risk of continuing to rely on nuclear deterrence. The British Foreign Minister Geoffrey Howe joined the chorus of criticisms of the SDI programme in a searching and forthright speech.[18] Mrs Thatcher too capitalized on her friendly relations with President Reagan by persuading him to accept four points of understanding, including an assurance that initially the SDI would only be a research project, and that any future decisions on development, production, and deployment, or on breaking with the ABM Treaty, would be taken only after consultations with its allies and treaty partners. [19] Thus the British government did make some efforts to restrain the US programme, though achieving this only on the declaratory level: the programme, with all its disturbing aspects, went forward as planned.

In the final analysis the British government's desire to avoid straining the 'special relationship' and to present a united NATO front to outside critics took priority over its concern about SDI. In spite of its reservations, Britain provided the Reagan Administration with political support at a time when the SDI programme was meeting with strong domestic and international opposition. This support was probably an important factor in getting the SDI bandwagon rolling.

Perhaps the most significant aspect of this support, both in symbolic and material terms, was the government-to-government negotiations on British participation in SDI, which resulted in a Memorandum of Understanding being signed in December 1985. British agreement to this was prompted by industrial and economic inducements as well as political concerns. The budgets allocated to the SDI project are huge, and it was hinted that as much as $1.3 billion might be available for overseas contracts.[20] For the UK, which has consistently invested so appallingly little in industrial research and development, the prospect of using US dollars to retain a toehold in R & D projects in key technologies such as aerospace, electronics, computing and optics must have been very tempting. Added to that was a fear of missing the boat – that the SDI programme would go ahead with or without British participation, leaving the UK even further behind in these key areas of technology. It rather looks as if the British government hoped to trade political support for SDI for economic benefits.

We regard this pursuit of short-term economic advantages and anxiety to avoid any disruption to the special relationship as short-sighted when the dangers of the SDI programme are taken into account. Furthermore, British hopes that participation in the SDI will improve Britain's industrial competitiveness in high-technology products are likely to be disappointed. The size of the contracts available to British laboratories and companies is likely to turn out to be much less than initial US hints suggested, and many contracts are likely to be in specific projects subcontracted from the USA in areas with little civilian potential.

Spin-off from military R & D projects to civilian products has always turned out to be very small in comparison with what could be achieved by direct civilian investment. This is almost certain to be true for the SDI programme, where over 90 per cent of the funding is going into developing specific devices and military products rather than into basic technological processes. Once the effects of secrecy and legal and institutional obstacles to technology transfer out of the USA are taken into account, participation in the SDI seems a poor strategy for improving Britain's industrial competitiveness. In fact it seems likely to absorb scarce financial and scientific resources which would be better employed directly in civilian research.

So what more could an anti-nuclear British government do to oppose the SDI project and any Soviet equivalent? Clearly it should strongly support the ABM Treaty and whatever may be needed to strengthen it and an agreement on a ban on the testing and deployment of anti-satellite weapons even if this involved open disagreement with the USA. Now that the SDI bandwagon has gained momentum, and other countries have made agreements on participation in SDI, Britain's political leverage is substantially less than it could have been in 1984 and 1985. So long as the Reagan Administration remains in power, political pressure from the UK is now unlikely to deflect the SDI programme. However, a future US president may have doubts about such an expensive and destabilizing programme, and in that context British diplomatic pressure might be much more effective, especially if it were combined with similar pressure from the FRG and other European governments.

Britain should also oppose the establishment of any European Defence Initiative, which is presently being promoted in Europe by SDI enthusiasts. Although there is a case for improving European air defences, a programme to develop defences against theatre or tactical ballistic missiles should be opposed as expensive, destabilizing, and a potential circumvention of the ABM Treaty.

As far as British participation in SDI is concerned, government laboratories and funds should not be involved, and SDI projects already begun should be terminated. To allow them to continue would contradict British opposition to SDI and reduce British political leverage on this issue. British companies should also be discouraged from participating in SDI projects, primarily by providing alternative sources of funds for civil R & D in key areas of high technology.

5. MEASURES TO STRENGTHEN THE NON-PROLIFERATION RÉGIME

One of the central aims of British nuclear disarmament would be to strengthen the existing measures to prevent the spread of nuclear weapons. How to limit the dangers of proliferation involves many contentious political questions and complex technical issues, and it is impossible to analyse them all here.[21] The general arguments for promoting non-proliferation by moves towards nuclear disarmament by the nuclear weapon states, rather than by their extending nuclear protection to countries without nuclear weapons, have been briefly indicated in Chapter One. Our focus here is on what Britain could do: through unilateral action, by exerting diplomacy where it has special leverage, for example in the European Community and the Commonwealth, and in the multilateral fora that deal with nuclear energy and the danger of proliferation.

Nevertheless, before looking at possible British government actions in detail, it is necessary to clarify some of the key problems and to establish the outlines of a general appropriate approach. The main institutions of the non-proliferation régime are the Non-Proliferation Treaty (NPT) and the International Atomic Energy Agency (IAEA). The primary goal of the NPT is to prevent the spread of nuclear weapons, but during negotiations on the Treaty, developing countries insisted on their right to have full access to the benefits of peaceful nuclear energy, an insistence reflected in the wording of the Treaty. The IAEA, on the other hand, was set up to promote peaceful nuclear energy, but it also has the duty of deterring and detecting its diversion to military uses by inspecting nuclear facilities. This regulatory function has become increasingly important.

There are a number of obvious problems facing the non-proliferation régime. One frequently cited is that two nuclear weapon states, France and China, have failed to sign the Treaty.

But this difficulty can be overstressed, since France and more recently China have both made it clear that they will act as though they had signed the Treaty, and both are now members of the IAEA.[22] A more serious gap in the non-proliferation system is the fact that there are a number of states whose position is ambiguous: Israel is generally believed to have nuclear weapons, India has conducted a nuclear explosion and South Africa is suspected by some of having a nuclear weapons capability, though its position is still obscure. Other countries appear ambitious to have nuclear weapons and to be close to developing them; recently, great concern has been expressed about Pakistan's nuclear programme.[23] None of the states whose nuclear weapons status is ambiguous or who seem close to becoming nuclear weapon powers have signed the NPT. One major flaw in the present policies is that states which are not parties to the NPT can apparently acquire nuclear technology readily adapted to producing warheads more easily than those that are parties. Brazil, for example, bought sensitive reprocessing and enrichment technology from West Germany in 1975. Moreover, nuclear suppliers have quite often been willing to make nuclear facilities available to countries outside the NPT whilst requiring less stringent IAEA inspection than NPT signatories are bound to accept (NPT signatories accept 'full scope' IAEA safeguards). Indeed, commercial competition between major nuclear suppliers has been a key obstacle to agreement on satisfactory controls of nuclear trade.

One of the basic difficulties inherent in trying to prevent the spread of nuclear weapons is that it does not appear to be possible to devise a technically foolproof method of preventing nuclear facilities being diverted to military ends. (This was the conclusion reached by the International Fuel Cycle Evaluation Programme, set up by President Carter in 1977 in the hope of discovering a less proliferation-prone fuel cycle[24].) It is generally agreed that the most that can be done is to make military use of peaceful nuclear technology as difficult as possible by preventing the spread of technologies which facilitate military conversion. Since no technical fix is available, it is important to promote political confidence that states are not cheating: this is the role that should be played by IAEA safeguards. So it is another defect of the whole non-proliferation régime that IAEA inspection procedures are widely perceived to be inadequate. There is also no satisfactory mechanism for invoking rapid sanctions against a country that does break its Treaty commitments: though the IAEA is empowered to report that it has detected cheating to the United Nations Security Council, initial findings by the IAEA inspectorate are confidential.

Nevertheless, there are grounds for cautious optimism about the future of the NPT and the system associated with it. In the months before the 1985 NPT Review Conference, there were fears expressed that it might end in the break-up of the system. But although the parties to the Treaty who have renounced nuclear weapons reiterated the need for the nuclear weapon states to start nuclear disarmament, and there were diplomatic problems in agreeing on a condemnation of Israel's bombing of Iraq's nuclear reactor, and in meeting Iranian demands for a reference to Iraqi attacks on their nuclear facilities, the Conference agreed a Final Document. Compared with the 1980 Review Conference, the tone of the discussion was generally constructive, and the Final Document made substantive and useful proposals. [25]

There is therefore quite a promising framework for further action to try to tackle some of the problems with the non-proliferation régime which we have identified. These problems have prompted a range of suggested solutions. Some proposals envisage changing the existing institutions, for instance abolishing the IAEA or divesting it of one of its main functions, since a contradiction is perceived between promoting nuclear power and seeking to regulate it. International ownership and control of nuclear facilities or spent fuel has been recommended frequently in the past. An even more radical approach, espoused by ecological groups, is to end all reliance on nuclear energy as a desirable goal in itself and as the surest way of preventing military use of civilian programmes. Many suggestions for reform, however, concentrate on more limited measures to tighten up the existing Treaty, strengthen the IAEA organizationally, improve IAEA safeguards, impose more stringent controls on nuclear trade, and to make adherence to the NPT more attractive. [26] Since the NPT is due for renewal in 1995 the intervening period may be crucial for maintaining and building on present international commitments and to avoid proliferation.

A British government that had embarked on its own nuclear disarmament could make a distinctive contribution to the cause of non-proliferation. In particular, it could directly help to extend the scope and effectiveness of IAEA inspection, could exert pressure to promote stricter controls on nuclear exports, and could prompt nuclear weapon states to live up to their Treaty obligation to reduce nuclear arsenals. Issues on which Britain should have a view include possible reforms of the IAEA and how to approach the renewal of the NPT, and we make some provisional suggestions on these issues. In terms of broad policy guidelines the Commission favours a move towards a reduced reliance on nuclear power in both the industrialized and developing countries, and stimulating research into non-nuclear alternatives. But we do not believe that an international strategy for non-proliferation can, in the foreseeable future, be based on the ending of all civil nuclear power, although in the long term we believe abandonment of nuclear power is an essential measure to create a world without nuclear weapons. We are concerned to limit nuclear technology most easily converted to military uses (our supplementary paper to our first report laid particular emphasis on the danger of fast-breeder reactors creating large supplies of weapons-grade plutonium) and are aware that new developments like laser isotope separation increase the problem of separating civil and military technology.[27] But these are highly technical issues beyond the scope of this book, and we have confined ourselves to noting briefly the case for international control of plutonium stocks. We also believe that the strengthening of political constraints on acquiring nuclear weapons is the most crucial factor.

What Britain Could Do to Strengthen IAEA Inspection
A non-nuclear Britain could undertake a series of unilateral measures and diplomatic initiatives to improve the IAEA inspection procedure. There are three major problems that have tended to undermine the credibility of IAEA inspection. The first is that individual states often impose restrictions on inspectors. Within the overall framework of the agreed IAEA safeguards (both

before and under the NPT) governments have negotiated the details, and many have limited the frequency of inspections and access to nuclear facilities or have refused to accept inspectors of certain nationalities.[28] In practice, restrictions on the nationality of inspectors appear to have caused especial difficulties, and this is illustrated by the fact that Israel lacked confidence in IAEA inspection of Iraq's nuclear reactor partly because all the inspectors came from Eastern Europe.[29] The other two issues that affect international confidence in IAEA inspectors are doubts about their expertise and the fact that their numbers have been too low: the total has grown from 48 in 1970 to 200 in 1985, but the need for inspection is also growing.

Britain could contribute to the IAEA inspectorate directly by paying more to the Safeguards Budgets of the Agency and by offering training for IAEA inspectors, since British nuclear scientists have considerable expertise. In addition, more British inspectors could be offered to the IAEA; this might be a possible job outlet for Aldermaston scientists. Inspectors from a Britain that had abandoned its own nuclear weapons might be much more acceptable to many countries than inspectors from the major nuclear powers.

As part of its larger contribution to the IAEA inspection system Britain would be able to argue strongly for another change that would enhance political confidence in the IAEA safeguards: the creation of a genuinely international and permanent inspectorate, which would be accepted as more impartial than inspectors on short-term secondment to the IAEA, who tend to be seen as purely national agents. There is already a move in this direction that could be encouraged.

The technical effectiveness of IAEA inspection could be increased by improving equipment for continued surveillance (present methods include cameras and instruments to measure streams of nuclear material passing through enrichment or reprocessing plants). The IAEA is extending the range of its equipment, and research has produced new remotely-controlled surveillance technology that could greatly increase the likelihood that cheating could be detected and immediate warnings of violations be given.[30] But there is still scope for research in this area, which could be undertaken by British scientists and might be centred at Aldermaston.

Britain at present allows token inspection of civilian plants by the IAEA because, as a nuclear weapon state, it is making a symbolic gesture under the NPT towards accepting IAEA safeguards which are only strictly imposed on non-nuclear-weapons parties to the Treaty. Once it had abandoned its own nuclear weapons its status, for inspection purposes, would change. Britain would then be in a similar position to other members of the European Community whose facilities are subject to combined inspection by the IAEA and Euratom, but special inspection of weapons-grade fissile material would be needed. When the NPT was agreed the Euratom countries insisted on negotiating a special agreement between Euratom and the IAEA, which involves Euratom inspections on behalf of and alongside the IAEA. Britain's civil nuclear facilities are subject now to Euratom inspection; once it had given up military use of nuclear power this inspection would become comprehensive.

Some experts on problems of nuclear proliferation are highly critical of Euratom's privileged position in relation to IAEA inspection under the NPT, both because it is seen as discriminatory and because it involves a considerable duplication of resources (the Euratom inspectorate has been growing). But the advantages of Euratom are: that it is seen to be more efficient; it has a very expert and permanent inspectorate; it has more extensive legal powers over its members' nuclear programmes than has the IAEA; and it can wield more effective sanctions.[31] So although there is a general case for transferring the main responsibility for inspections under the NPT in European Community countries to the IAEA, there is also an argument for making this conditional on improved IAEA safeguards and an extension of IAEA powers. Since one of the reasons why European powers insisted on Euratom inspections under the NPT was to impose an 'equality of misery' on the nuclear weapons states Britain and France, Britain's conversion to non-nuclear weapon status would be a relevant factor in possible future discussion of this topic.

There are some positive advantages in Britain's membership of Euratom, which give it additional leverage in tackling problems related to preventing proliferation, such as nuclear trade.

Strengthening Controls on Nuclear Trade

What Britain can do unilaterally in the area of nuclear trade is limited by the fact that it is not a major exporter – it is a long time since it sold a reactor – and its main trade is in nuclear materials and in reprocessing spent fuel from other countries. There is, moreover, a strong argument for giving up reprocessing, as argued above (Section 2: How Britain Disarms). But there are a number of steps it could take. As a start it would be helpful to have a government statement publicly clarifying what Britain's future policy on nuclear exports would be and how the administrative process of authorizing such exports operates. At present there are occasional statements in Parliament but the issue is generally surrounded by secrecy.

Secondly, Britain could publicly commit itself to following a policy on nuclear trade consistent with a commitment to oppose the spread of nuclear weapons. In the early 1980s Britain was engaged in a controversial attempt to try to sell a Magnox-type reactor to Chile, although the deal fell through.[32]

This proposed export was damaging to the cause of non-proliferation on two related grounds: the Magnox reactor is suitable for weapons production, and Chile is not party to the NPT. As a minimum a British government committed to non-proliferation should insist on a strict policy on exports of sensitive technology to countries that have not signed the Treaty and require they accept 'full scope' NPT-related IAEA safeguards. It should also prevent future sales of Magnox reactors since they are proliferation-prone; at present the British nuclear industry retains hopes of selling Magnox, which is suited to developing countries.

Unilateral action by one country is open to the danger that less scrupulous suppliers will step in, or in the longer run that countries buying nuclear technology will make more effort to become self-sufficient. It is also important to note that unilateral measures by the USA and Canada in the 1970s were undermined by the refusal of Japan, France, the FRG, Switzerland and Italy to support the US attempts to restrict the supply of plutonium, or to back Canadian insistence on 'full scope' safeguards for all its sales. In the case of the US initiative, political resentment by secondary powers of great power pressure, lack of diplomatic

271

tact by the Carter Administration and suspicion that the real motive was a US attempt to sabotage the nuclear industry of its competitors, all played a part in its failure.[33] Canada's attempts to impose strict controls on its nuclear exports (after India conducted a nuclear explosion in 1974 using plutonium from a Canadian-supplied reactor) met with even more unfortunate results.[34] For example, in 1979 Argentina bought a more expensive West German reactor in preference to a Canadian one, primarily because Canada was insisting on 'full scope' safeguards and Germany was not.[35] Nevertheless, the conditions affecting nuclear trade have altered in the 1980s, and political initiatives should be tried. If enough countries take principled unilateral action this increases international and domestic pressure on other governments to follow suit. A group of countries pursuing national policies designed to minimize the risks of proliferation are also well placed to press for an agreement by all suppliers to impose strict safeguards.

The major suppliers did meet and agree in 1975 on a list of items that should be exported only if IAEA safeguards were applied.[36] The Nuclear Suppliers' Group was expanded in 1978, and has continued to meet, although the Reagan Administration has not pursued the same strict non-proliferation policies as President Carter. There are, however, serious inadequacies in the Group's approach.[37] It could not agree to ban export of sensitive nuclear technology which can be diverted to military uses, or to require 'full scope' NPT safeguards on such exports. The London Guidelines published by the Suppliers' Group in 1978 only required the less stringent pre-NPT IAEA safeguards, although they specified various controls that a supplier should exercise over the subsequent use of exported technology. Although the earlier list of sensitive nuclear exports was expanded in 1984, the problem of technology with potential military uses has not been resolved. Other important problems with the Group are that it does not include all the secondary suppliers and that it cannot enforce implementation of its guidelines, which some states have breached. There is therefore a need for a stronger organization covering all nuclear suppliers.

The main obstacle to tightening up controls on supply does not for once lie in the antagonism between the USA and the

USSR. The Soviet Union has always imposed very strict controls on its own exports and, together with its allies, has pressed for international agreement on such controls. Although in the early 1980s Cold War conflicts spilled over into the Nuclear Suppliers' Group, more recently the USA and the USSR have met to coordinate non-proliferation policy and they do have a real common interest in preventing the spread of nuclear weapons. The key difficulty lies in the economic and political pressure from nuclear industries and governments in some major Western suppliers to maintain their nuclear industries and to export. At the 1985 Review Conference a recommendation to require 'full scope' IAEA safeguards on all nuclear exports to non-nuclear weapons states that have not signed the NPT was opposed by the FRG, with support from Switzerland, Italy and Belgium.[38] Commercial dominance in nuclear energy has been shifting during the 1980s from the USA to the FRG, France and Japan and these countries in particular have to be persuaded that it is in their security interests to apply a common policy of strict safeguards, and that their national commercial interests will not suffer if all abide by the same rules.

Britain can only do a limited amount to influence these countries, but it does have obvious sources of leverage. One is the European Community, which, through Euratom, has a major interest in Europe's nuclear industry and exports, and has already agreed some guidelines on nuclear exports. If the Community could agree on strict controls this would be a major step forward. Secondly, Britain could discuss problems of nuclear trade with Commonwealth members: Canada and Australia proposed the resolution urging tighter controls at the 1985 NPT Review Conference. In addition, if Britain tries to build closer diplomatic links with Japan, as suggested in Chapter Two, then it would make sense to associate Japan as a major nuclear supplier with a Community initiative. Another way of involving both the USA and Japan would be to raise the issue in the OECD.

Whether an attempt is made to expand the membership of the Nuclear Suppliers' Group, or to create a new international nuclear trade body, a key goal must be the association of China. France has been a member of the Suppliers' Group despite its

273

refusal to sign the NPT, so there is a precedent for China to follow.

Guidelines for British Diplomacy on Other Non-Proliferation Policies

As a general strategy for strengthening the non-proliferation régime we propose that the present role of the IAEA and the conclusions adopted by the 1985 NPT Review Conference be built on. The only other major institutional innovation we would suggest is the creation of an international body, under the UN, committed to developing all non-nuclear forms of energy.

The main arguments for extending the role of the IAEA, rather than totally divesting it of one of its main functions, as has been proposed, are political. It is well established, widely accepted, has accrued considerable experience, and some of the problems of the IAEA would probably reappear anyway in a new body. It is also relevant that countries that are not party to the NPT are members of the IAEA, including France, China and states with an ambiguous nuclear status like Israel and South Africa. So the Agency is one means of involving these countries in the international system concerned with controlling nuclear energy.

The most important consideration, however, is that the IAEA inspection role is assuming increasing political significance. Limited IAEA safeguards have been accepted by the USSR, which in general has been opposed to on-site inspection as a matter of principle, and by France and China despite the fact that they have not committed themselves to either the PTBT or the NPT. The Soviet Union reached formal agreement with the IAEA in February 1985 to accept a number of inspections of its civil nuclear programme, following the precedent set by the USA and the UK.[39] France has allowed IAEA inspection of selected civil nuclear plants and in September 1985 China declared that it would accept some IAEA inspection.[40] Despite the limitations of IAEA inspection – especially in nuclear weapon states – it is an important precedent for possible future arms control and disarmament agreements.

There are, however, measures that could improve the IAEA organizationally. One suggestion is to separate clearly the regulation and promotion tasks of the Agency, so that there is less danger of one approach undermining the other. There are various ways in which this organizational reform could be achieved and it would meet some of the concerns of the critics of the present IAEA role, without the drastic political readjustment that would be required by giving one function to a totally new body.[41] Internal organizational change in the IAEA, however, would have to ensure that the end result was an effective and technically well-informed committee or commission in charge of IAEA safeguards. There is also a case for the Agency abandoning its tradition of keeping reports by IAEA inspectors secret and instead routinely publishing them so that they were available to those concerned, including the parliament and the public in the country inspected. The precise form of the published reports could be negotiated if genuine issues of commercial confidentiality were involved.

The IAEA might, in addition, extend its role in areas central to reducing the danger of proliferation. It already has some responsibility in relation to nuclear trade in that the Agency is often required to impose safeguards, and initiatives by nuclear suppliers to draw up guidelines for trade in sensitive proliferation-prone technology have been communicated formally to the Agency. Even if the organization of nuclear suppliers remains outside the IAEA, it might be possible to link up the two more closely: for example an Agency committee might be given special powers to assess nuclear trade contacts with countries that have not signed the NPT, in order to give advice on possible implications from the standpoint of avoiding proliferation.

One possible development which was much discussed during the 1970s, and always supported by British governments, is to give the IAEA new powers to impose international control over stocks of surplus plutonium in various countries. The proposal for an International Plutonium Storage (IPS) system was endorsed in the Final Document of the 1985 NPT Review Conference.[42] It is quite a modest proposal – the Carter Administration in fact opposed it (despite the fact that it was a US initiative) on the grounds that it legitimizes production of plutonium. But it does avoid some of the problems of how multilateral control should be exercised, and where nuclear materials should be stored, that have hindered adoption of more ambitious schemes for multilateral control. A possible reason for favouring the IPS is that if in future any progress can be made towards nuclear disarmament, then it would be helpful to have an established system of international control to take responsibility for surplus plutonium from military stocks. It may therefore be worth diplomatic effort to see if the objections from some key suppliers like the FRG, Italy and Japan can be overcome.

One of the central problems for the non-proliferation régime has been the insistence by the nuclear have-nots that they should not be discriminated against by the countries with a developed nuclear industry. This has meant hostility towards attempts by nuclear suppliers to tighten up controls on exports, a hostility very marked at the 1980 NPT Review Conference. One way of trying to obviate this conflict might be for developed countries to put less emphasis on nuclear power and more resources into exploring other long-term energy sources, like solar, wind or wave power. There could be several advantages to this approach. Firstly, if the prestige attached to nuclear power is downgraded and the dangers and disadvantages of nuclear power fully recognized, developing countries may be less inclined to seek their own nuclear facilities. Secondly, increased research into renewable energy resources could be extremely useful for many developing countries which cannot possibly afford nuclear power, and will be of increasing importance to industrialized countries as gas, oil and coal supplies diminish. Thirdly, there is a very strong long-term argument that so long as civil nuclear power exists the dangers of more countries acquiring nuclear weapons also exist; and moves towards full nuclear disarmament would be crucially underpinned by abandoning nuclear energy.

More international prominence could be given to non-nuclear sources of energy by creating a new international body to promote renewable and alternative energy sources. One possibility which has been recommended would be to set up a World Energy Organization, under the United Nations, to promote a balanced approach to all sources of energy.[43] In its first report, the Commission favoured this idea (Supplementary Paper No 1). But this proposal favours taking over from the IAEA its promotional role in relation to nuclear energy (a role which is in fact now quite limited and which lays a good deal of emphasis

276

on problems of safety) and runs counter to our suggestion that the IAEA should not be radically changed. A new composite energy body would, moreover, run some risk of falling under the influence of the powerful nuclear lobby. So a second possibility worth examining is to set up an international body committed to developing alternatives to nuclear power. As a result of pressure by 'green' and ecology groups over the last fifteen years there is now a constituency to support this kind of move and a great deal might be accomplished by quite modest funding.

A British government that had abandoned its own nuclear weapons and was pursuing non-proliferation as a major policy goal would clearly be involved in advance discussions about the best strategy to adopt when the NPT comes up for renewal in 1995. A major contribution to ensuring its renewal would be to secure adherence to the Treaty by some of the states at present considering developing nuclear weapons. Britain could exert most influence over Commonwealth member India and former member Pakistan, whose future decisions are partly dependent on one another; encouragement to sign the NPT might in India's case be channelled through the Commonwealth. China's position is pivotal in relation to both countries, and its new concern with questions of nuclear disarmament and non-proliferation may also encourage India to avoid developing a nuclear arsenal and reduce the likelihood of direct Chinese support for a Pakistani or Islamic bomb.

One central problem for states that adhere to the NPT is to achieve legally binding and convincing guarantees that nuclear weapon states will not indulge in nuclear blackmail, or use nuclear weapons against them. The argument for 'negative assurances' dates from negotiations on the Treaty, but the USA and the USSR took a step forward in 1978 when they both made unilateral statements promising not to use nuclear weapons against countries that had renounced them, though the terms of the statements differed in detail. There are inevitable limits to the trust non-nuclear countries will place in formal guarantees. Nevertheless a joint US-Soviet undertaking never to use nuclear weapons against countries which have renounced nuclear weapons by adhering to the NPT, and refused to have nuclear bases on their territory or to ally themselves with nuclear weapon states in nuclear strategy, would encourage development of nuclear-free zones. It would be a policy consistent with the goals we believe Britain without nuclear weapons should pursue and a government embarking on nuclear disarmament could legitimately raise the issue.

The main tactical question that will arise in relation to the NPT is whether to renew it as it stands, which would in itself be a very valuable reaffirmation of international commitment to stop nuclear weapons spreading, or whether to work for desirable amendments to the text. A decision will clearly depend on the perceptions of what is possible closer to the time. But there are two issues of considerable importance, not only to the coherence of the Treaty, but also to the goal of nuclear disarmament. The first is whether the Treaty continues to allow 'peaceful nuclear explosions', which everyone is now agreed are impossible to distinguish from military nuclear tests.[44] The 1985 Review Conference took a decisive position, insisting that any future nuclear explosion by any non-nuclear weapons state would be a serious breach of the Treaty; so elimination of the clause may prove possible. Peaceful nuclear explosions have also been a complicating factor in the Comprehensive Test Ban (CTB) talks in the past, so strong international pressure to ban them altogether would be helpful. The other key issue is whether the nuclear weapons states can claim to have fulfilled their obligations under Article VI to negotiate in good faith to try to end the nuclear arms race, and how that should be interpreted. This issue could provide an ideal excuse for countries anxious not to renew the Treaty for any reason, but there are also entirely valid grounds for the impatience of the non-nuclear weapon states at the failure of the USA and the USSR to make any real progress.

The CTB has been identified for a long time as the first measure for the nuclear weapon powers to agree in order to show they are taking Article VI seriously, a view reiterated strongly at the 1985 Review Conference. In the light of its past involvement in test ban negotiations and nuclear negotiations, Britain should be able to play an important role here. It is to this issue we now turn.

6. Promoting a Comprehensive Test Ban

There has recently been renewed pressure for a comprehensive test ban treaty (CTBT), partly in the context of the 1985 NPT Review Conference, but also out of growing concern to bring the superpower nuclear arms race under control. A CTBT is high on the agenda of many US arms control advocates and has been pressed for in this country by David Owen and Denis Healey. The argument for a total test ban is that it would curb some new developments in the nuclear arms race – the USA, for example, is now testing the Midgetman nuclear warhead and wishes to test an array of nuclear warheads, including the Excalibur X-Ray laser for Star Wars. The Soviet Union has also been testing recently, but announced a unilateral moratorium in July 1985. The other strong reason for seeking a total test ban is that China indicated in February 1985 that it would be willing to join talks – a total reversal of its previous position and one which holds out some hope for a halt to the potential nuclear arms race in South Asia.

Attempts to achieve a total nuclear test ban date back to 1957 and extended negotiations between the USA, USSR and the UK began in 1958.[45] Agreement on a comprehensive ban proved impossible but in 1963, in the aftermath of the Cuba crisis, Kennedy and Khrushchev managed to sign the Partial Test Ban Treaty (PTBT) despite domestic opposition in both countries. The major powers then lost interest in a test ban, despite efforts by the non-aligned countries to pursue the question at Geneva. A largely cosmetic agreement to ban underground tests above the 150 kiloton threshold was signed by the USA and USSR – cosmetic because it gave the impression of progress in arms control without imposing any serious restrictions on the nuclear weapon testing both sides wished to pursue.

Under President Carter serious trilateral talks on a CTB were resumed in 1977. The main issue was adequate verification, which was also (at least ostensibly), the main stumbling block in the earlier talks, with the USA demanding stringent safeguards that the USSR then refused to accept. By 1977, however, techniques for verification had improved, and the USSR appeared willing to accept a degree of verification involving the placing of seismographic instruments on its territory, exchange of seismic data, and some on-site inspection by challenge. A subsidiary problem – the Soviet desire to use 'peaceful nuclear explosions' for purposes like making dams and diverting rivers – appeared soluble when the USSR offered a moratorium on use of such explosions to run concurrently with the duration of a Treaty.

Substantial progress was made in these negotiations towards an agreement. However, a number of rather minor disputes resulted in important delays. In 1978 President Carter's arms control programme was under severe pressure in the USA, and he decided to make SALT, rather than a comprehensive test ban, his highest arms control priority. The US position at the CTBT talks hardened, and after President Reagan was elected in 1980, the talks were suspended indefinitely.

At first, the US position was that a CTBT would be desirable if only the verification problems were not so severe. But following the Soviet moratorium on nuclear testing, beginning in August 1985, the US Administration declared that, so long as the United States' defence policy was based on nuclear deterrence, a test ban would be against its national interests. However, the UK has continued (up to spring 1986) to support the objective of a test ban, whilst claiming only that the technical difficulties with verification were such that it was not worth re-starting the negotiations until there is a prospect that they can be resolved.

Much of the debate about verification has clearly been a smoke-screen for political or military objections to the CTBT. In the USA, the weapons laboratories and other powerful institutions have an institutional interest in blocking a test ban. The political campaign against arms control in general, and accusations of Soviet cheating, have put all nuclear arms control advocates on the defensive. As mentioned above, warhead development for the SDI programme and other third or fourth generation warhead programmes provide an additional obstacle. The UK Trident programme, involving warhead development at Aldermaston and testing in Nevada, probably inhibits British support for the CTBT. So long as the USA and UK remain, in practice, opposed to negotiations on such a treaty, it is impossible to probe the seriousness of the Soviet commitment to a test ban. It is very likely, however, that powerful defence interests in the Soviet Union would campaign against the signing of a CTBT.

There are certainly serious problems associated with verification. From the open scientific literature, it now appears that tests down to a lower limit of between 0.5 and 1 kiloton could be monitored by placing seismic detectors in the USA and USSR, but that between ten and twenty-five such detectors would be needed for reliable monitoring.[46] Seismic verification against covert testing could, however, be supplemented by satellite observations.

There appears to be a theoretical limit below which underground tests in secret underground 'decoupling' chambers (the building of which would probably require vast, and so clearly observable, construction works) cannot be distinguished from the use of conventional explosives for underground civil engineering or mining.[47] Decoupled nuclear explosions of less than about 0.5 kilotons probably cannot be distinguished seismically from conventional explosives in hard rock.[48]

This raises the question of whether an anti-nuclear British government should aim at a comprehensive test ban or merely at a threshold test ban, set at about 1 kiloton. A good case can be made for aiming only for arms control agreements that can be very reliably verified.

Uncertainties can be used to increase suspicion and undermine the agreement. Nevertheless, the Commission continues to prefer a comprehensive test ban. The potential for cheating within such a framework is small, provided an adequate number of seismic wave detectors are installed in the territories of the two superpowers. There would also be little chance of either side gaining an advantage from carrying out the occasional test which they might hope would escape detection. A CTBT would have a crucial political significance, and would weaken the influence of the weapons laboratories; against this a threshold test ban might actually stimulate research into the development of warhead designs that only involve testing at very low yields.

Britain could play a particularly important role in promoting a comprehensive test ban. It has been active in all the CTBT negotiations, and therefore has a detailed knowledge of the issues. This would allow it to speak with authority on technical issues and to expose invalid US objections. Britain could also press the Soviet Union if the latter adopted an intransigent attitude, for instance on the issue of the number of seismic detectors to be placed on its territory. The USSR has taken an important initiative in agreeing to allow an unofficial team of US scientists to set up seismic stations at its Semipalatinsk nuclear testing site to monitor seismic conditions. The experiment began in July 1986, and scientists from the UK have since been invited to join it. Joint studies by US and Soviet scientists at test sites in both countries should help to determine the number of seismic stations needed to monitor a total test ban. A Britain without nuclear weapons could use its expertise to build on these unofficial exchanges and to resolve outstanding technical problems associated with achieving reliable verification of a comprehensive treaty, and could devote resources to this task.

7. CHEMICAL DISARMAMENT

The general case for an agreement to ban chemical weapons was explored earlier in the chapter. The question here is what Britain can do to further these goals. The first point to be stressed is that British governments have in the past taken important steps to promote these aims. During the mid-1950s Britain unilaterally dismantled all its stocks of nerve gas and other poisonous gases, and switched Porton Down to concentration on defence against chemical attack – though it did maintain right of access to US weapons. It was also the British government which proposed in 1968 a separation of chemical and biological weapons, despite opposition from the USSR and a cool response from the USA. Britain and Canada urged Washington to act, and so could claim some credit for President Nixon's unilateral renunciation of biological weapons, announced in November 1969, and for the subsequent 1972 Convention, though the final text was less stringent than Britain would have liked. British diplomacy in promoting the Biological Weapons Convention, and its contributions to the continuing negotiations on chemical weapons, have been widely seen as constructive.

The second point to make is that at the moment Britain is in danger of abandoning its commitment to chemical disarmament. Leaks to the press in 1985 indicated that some senior civil servants and government figures were seriously considering developing new stockpiles of chemical weapons.[49] These pressures arose in the context of a push by the Reagan Administration to produce new binary nerve gases, US allegations over the last few years of Soviet use of biological and chemical weapons (allegations never satisfactorily substantiated),[50] and claims of large Soviet chemical stockpiles in Europe. Although in 1985 the US Defense Secretary told Congress that Western assessments of Soviet strategy on the use of chemical weapons had altered and it was no longer believed the USSR planned to make massive use of such weapons in the event of war,[51] the Administration has continued to pressure a reluctant Congress to authorize production of binary nerve gas. By the end of 1985 the Administration had received qualified Congressional approval of funding for artillery projectiles to dispense one type of nerve gas and to build factories to produce Bigeye nerve gas bombs – but not for the bombs themselves. No funds could be spent until October 1986, and then only if Congressional conditions had been met. The key condition, was that the NATO Council formally endorsed the need for a NATO chemical 'deterrent'. Existing chemical weapons deployed by the USA have not been under NATO control.[52] In response to US pressure NATO Defence Ministers took note of the US programme as a 'force goal' on 22 May 1986, but only after protests from six countries. It was not clear by the autumn of 1986 if Congress wuld accept its conditions had been met.

Britain however is reported to have given tacit support to the US Administration in its battle with Congress, and it is probable that if nerve gas is produced it would be stored at US bases in Britain.[53] Officially, the British government held back from committing itself on the military case for binary nerve gas or stockpiling the gas, but a government statement to the House of Commons on 28 April 1986 backed NATO deployment of the new gas weapons unless a chemical weapons ban is agreed. Britain apparently supports the US programme mainly as a bargaining chip in the chemical weapons negotiations in Geneva.[54] But weapons originally justified as bargaining chips have often become central to military strategy a few years later. There has in fact been mounting pressure from NATO military quarters, in particular from General Rogers, for NATO deployment of binary weapons.

So far, the Foreign Office has resisted direct British production of chemical weapons in favour of continuing to press for a general agreement to ban them. Unfortunately the prospects for an agreement soon are not good. During the early 1980s detailed negotiation at the Geneva Conference on Disarmament resulted in considerable progress on the very complex issues involved. On the key issue of verification the Soviet Union accepted the principle of challenge inspections and of continuous international inspection at the site of destruction of stocks, although it was still a long way from agreement with the West on the amount and type of verification needed.[55] During 1984 both the USA and USSR tabled draft treaties incorporating inspection proposals unacceptable to the other side.[56] Despite progress at Geneva on matters of detail, Washington and Moscow remain far apart on key political issues.

There are a number of obvious steps a new British government seeking chemical disarmament could take. Firstly, it should reaffirm its renunciation of chemical weapons. This step could be strengthened by stressing that the renunciation is meant to be permanent (in the past Parliamentary answers have given much more categoric reassurances on biological weapons than on chemical weapons). The government could also withdraw that part of the UK reservation attached to its ratification in 1930 of the Geneva protocol which reserved a right of retaliation in kind.[57]

Secondly, Britain should publicly repudiate any suggestion of support for the proposed US binary programme, expose the dangers of 'bargaining chip' arguments in this and other contexts and refuse absolutely to stockpile US nerve gas in this country. British opposition to the binary programme might, indeed, help to revive Congressional resistance to it. Thirdly, a British Defence Minister should follow the example of the USA and the FRG and undertake a public reassessment of Soviet chemical warfare plans.[58] Finally, the British delegation at Geneva should develop its initiatives in greater independence from the USA. Strong pressure is clearly needed from third parties to persuade both the USA and the USSR to accept a reasonable compromise on the degree of verification embodied in an agreement.

An important element in British strategy should be to consult with the FRG with the aim of coordinating a position on the US binary programme and on overall NATO policy on chemical weapons. West Germany has been storing 900,000 pounds of US nerve gas in artillery ammunition, which has provoked public opposition that is indicated by court cases being brought before the Constitutional Court.[59] On the opposition side, the SPD is committed to promoting some kind of chemical-weapon-free zone in Europe. The ruling Christian Democrat-led coalition has not been enthusiastic about the binary programme, but was persuaded to back it in 1986, apparently on condition that the stocks were stored in the USA and existing stocks of nerve gas removed from Germany.

It is more problematic whether Britain should throw its weight behind proposals for a European chemical-weapon-free zone. There are three separate issues: whether such a zone has value; the scope of the zone; and how it would be achieved. These questions have to be assessed in the context of continuing negotiations at Geneva for a total ban, negotiations that appear, despite setbacks, to have some reasonable hope of future success. Proposals for a chemical-weapon-free zone have been made by the Palme Commission, by the Warsaw Pact at the Stockholm negotiations and have arisen out of consultations between the West German SPD and the East German governing SED.[60]

There are general arguments for and against chemical-weapon-free zones. The case for such zones rests on the fact that stockpiling these weapons in an area of potential conflict increases the likelihood of their use and so of appalling destruction. A recent Pentagon simulation found that if existing chemical weapons on both sides were used in Europe there could be millions of casualties in a few days.[61] Destruction on this scale could also be a trigger for nuclear escalation. A zonal arrangement might also be a spur to a wider agreement and give scope for testing verification procedures. The standard arguments against a chemical-weapon-free zone are that it simply means a withdrawal of weapons, not a decrease in the total available, and that in a war they could quickly be brought back into the battle zone.[62] Though this argument has considerable weight in the case of Europe where (except for France) the chemical weapons are those of the USA and the USSR, it is by no means conclusive.

But perhaps the most important question is whether creating a chemical-weapon-free zone in Europe would help or hinder a universal ban. The analogy of the Tlatelolco Treaty, which created a Latin American nuclear-free zone and so aided the NPT, is irrelevant, since the USA and the USSR were not directly involved in a nuclear confrontation in Latin America. The most obvious problem about a European chemical-weapon-free zone is that the USA and the USSR, already deadlocked at Geneva, would be the key protagonists. The argument that negotiations on such a zone might divert effort from a total ban clearly has to be taken seriously.

The degree of difficulty involved in reaching agreement on a European zone would partly depend on the size of the zone envisaged and on the forum of negotiation. But whatever the zone, the issue of verification would remain vital: the joint German initiative envisages verifying destruction of stocks, but does not include checks to ensure that there is no *production* of chemical weapons. Opinions differ as to whether it would be easier to verify removal of stockpiles from a specific area or to verify total destruction of stocks. The latter may be simpler than checking that new weapons are not being produced, so verification of the absence of stocks in a European zone would be somewhat easier than reaching agreement on verification for a total ban. It might, however, be difficult to create adequate confidence on the other side that stocks had been wholly removed.

Even more central, perhaps, are the political and strategic questions. The creation of a chemical-weapon-free zone to embrace the whole of Europe, though certainly attractive, would come up against major obstacles. One is the fact that France has its own chemical weapons capacity and is likely to oppose any proposal that did not include chemical disarmament by the superpowers. Second, there is the question of whether 'Europe' should be taken as embracing the USSR as far as the Urals; clearly it is exceedingly unlikely that the Soviet Union would accept checks on its territory if the USA was not obliged to have any. Most proposals therefore assume a more limited zone in central Europe which could by-pass these two stumbling blocks, but which would still leave the problem of a satisfactory negotiating forum. The prospects of a speedy and effective negotiation being conducted through a CSCE created disarmament forum or through a chemical weapons equivalent of the Vienna MBFR Conference are hardly favourable. If the degree of political will required on the part of both Washington and Moscow to reach agreement were to exist it might be better channelled through Geneva where some problems have already been resolved.

We incline to the view that efforts to achieve progress in Europe should focus on inter-German agreement. The two German states have particular leverage in relation to their superpower allies, and may be able to negotiate an agreement on a German chemical-weapon-free zone. In that case Britain might be involved at least peripherally because of its continuing role in Berlin as one of the four original occupying powers. Such an approach would be a continuation of the *Ostpolitik* policies of the Brandt government in the early 1970s. Czechoslovakia has indicated a willingness to negotiate such a zone, and if it could be included this would clearly be welcome.

Though negotiated agreements on chemical weapons are highly desirable, we believe that NATO should in any case renounce chemical warfare as well as rejecting nuclear weapons. In the first place a British government should insist on NATO's avoiding any increased reliance on chemical weapons and should strongly oppose strategies like Airland Battle that explicitly envisage the use of chemical weapons as an intrinsic part of NATO strategy. Secondly it should press the USA to abandon the binary nerve gas programme and renounce all use of chemical weapons. If this could be achieved, NATO should seek reciprocal moves by the Warsaw Pact. Both sides are already pledged in principle to no-first-use of chemical weapons by the terms in which they have accepted the 1925 Geneva Protocol, but this commitment needs to be reflected in strategic planning and supplemented by the repudiation of any retaliatory use of chemical weapons. We realize that there are potential problems in simultaneously urging unilateral changes of strategy by NATO, renouncing the deterrent role of US chemical weapons and calling for all-German negotiations to create a chemical-weapon-free zone. But as we argued in relation to nuclear weapons, unilateral measures may pave the way to formal agreements which include provisions for verification. The leverage for agreement would not be by way of 'bargaining chips' but the need of both Washington and Moscow to respond to strategically crucial allies.

8. ISLANDS OF INFLUENCE

On another level there is an area of concern where Britain could play a distinctive role. The UK retains control of, or legal rights to, islands in the Indian and Pacific Oceans, as well as to Ascension Island and the Falklands in the Atlantic. These could allow Britain some influence or leverage for naval arms control.

In the South Pacific, Britain jointly owns five small islands with the USA, administers the New Hebrides jointly with France, and administers another by itself.[63] These are of little military importance, and British policy should be to ensure that they stay that way. However, the UK presence could increase the value of British diplomatic support in the area, and could be used to bolster and extend the nuclear-weapon-free zones that have recently been agreed by nations in the South Pacific.[64]

Britain leases land on Ascension Island to the USA for military facilities, consisting of a number of communication and intelligence-gathering installations and an airfield which is periodically used as a staging base for the nuclear-capable Orion C3 and Nimrod anti-submarine-warfare aircraft.[65] The UK should insist on these facilities being run along the same lines as we recommend for US facilities inside Britain itself. This would exert greater pressure on the USA to reduce the nuclear component in its activities outside the United States.

On the Falkland Islands, British military installations have been greatly increased and improved since the Falklands War. For example, a major new airbase became operational in 1986. A clear non-nuclear policy here, combined with progress towards an agreement with Argentina on the future of the Falkland Islands, could substantially reduce tension within the area and bolster the Treaty of Tlatelolco which established South America as a nuclear-weapon-free zone.

Britain could also explore the possibility of establishing the South Atlantic as a 'zone of peace'. This would aim to prevent the establishment of US or Soviet military bases in the South Atlantic, to stop any naval arms races amongst the littoral states, and to establish the principles of non-use of force and regional cooperation. There have, as yet, been few moves in this direction, but there is no obvious reason why progress could not be made.

After the withdrawal of most British naval forces from the Indian Ocean in the late 1960s, there were moves to establish the ocean as a 'zone of peace'. These attracted a great deal of attention but, as yet, little progress has been made towards an agreement. In fact US and Soviet naval vessels are now present in the Indian Ocean in considerable numbers, and the opportunities for preventing the ocean from being another theatre of confrontation between the superpowers are fading fast.

Thirty to forty US combat and support ships are now believed to be permanently based in the area. The USA has concluded agreements with Oman, Somalia, Kenya, and Britain for the use of support facilities,[66] and in an emergency, ports in other countries such as Saudi Arabia, Australia, or perhaps South Africa, would probably be made available.

At the centre of the American presence in the region is the British-owned atoll, Diego Garcia. In 1966 the UK agreed a treaty with the USA in which the USA was granted the right to set up bases on the atoll for 50 years.[67] In the following five years the British secretly and forcibly evicted the local population of 1,151 people from the atoll. In 1971, US forces moved on to the atoll, and in 1974 Britain approved an expansion of the US facilities there. Since then the vast military construction programme has been underway to provide naval and airbases for the US Navy and the Rapid Deployment Force.[68]

The Soviet naval presence in the ocean and ports in littoral states is less than that of the USA but is increasing rapidly. The fifth operational squadron of the Soviet Pacific fleet patrols the area frequently. A major Soviet base has been established at Socotra in South Yemen. Ethiopia has given the USSR exclusive use of the port at Dahlak Island, and this, together with the nearby ports of Massawa and Assab, is being developed by the Soviet navy.[69] In the Far East, the Soviet Union has military basing rights at Danang and the vast base at Cam Ranh Bay, both in Vietnam. It is reportedly bringing pressure to bear on Vietnam to operate also from the Kampuchean base at Kompong Son.[70] Being close to the major US naval base at Subic Bay in the Philippines, these developments could increase tension significantly in that area.

Since Diego Garcia is British territory, the UK has some direct means of exerting some influence over this deteriorating situation. Although the UK has agreed to allow the US base rights at Diego Garcia until about 2016 A.D., the archipelago remains British sovereign territory, and it appears that British agreement is required for any specific construction work.[71] Thus Britain would be able either to break with the 1966 agreement or influence how the US facilities are developed or used.

The obvious approach to explore first is for the US base on Diego Garcia to be abandoned or restricted in exchange for similar restrictions on Soviet bases around the Horn of Africa (i.e. Dahlak Island, Socotra, and the smaller bases nearby). This appears to be an equitable approach and should be explored in the context of a search for a wider arrangement covering the whole Indian Ocean. Links with the Commonwealth countries could prove particularly useful in this context.

In any case, the UK should not allow Diego Garcia to be used as a base for the Rapid Deployment Force, or for nuclear forces. Furthermore, natural justice implies that the UK government should reverse traditional policy towards the islanders it evicted. Better compensation could be offered and some arrangements be made for islanders to return to the archipelago if they wanted to. However, the nature of Diego Garcia has probably been irreversibly affected, and it must be acknowledged that it would be difficult for islanders to adopt their previous lifestyles.

9. DOMESTIC MEASURES TO PROMOTE DISARMAMENT

If disarmament is to become a priority in government policy and ways of promoting disarmament are to be effectively pursued, then several organizational initiatives would be desirable. The institutional weight and economic resources devoted to disarmament by government should be increased. But at the same time public scrutiny of government disarmament policy and public debate is also needed. Thirdly, there should be more funding for independent academic research into disarmament and related issues. Finally, some form of government planning is needed to complement initiatives from trade unions and groups in the defence industry to examine problems of economic conversion.

At present the weight accorded to arms control and disarmament by government is minimal. There is a small Arms Control and Disarmament Department and Research Unit at the Foreign and Commonwealth Office, and Michael Heseltine, when Defence Secretary, created a Defence Arms Control Unit in the Ministry of Defence. Specific negotiations are conducted by diplomats with representatives from the Ministry of Defence and other relevant bodies (such as the department responsible for nuclear power) in the negotiating team. The FCO has an *ad hoc* advisory panel on arms control and disarmament that meets about once a year, and which includes academics and church representatives.

But the influence from outside is fairly minimal. There is no regular parliamentary debate or scrutiny of disarmament matters or of Britain's specific contribution to negotiations. Neither is there any official funding for academics to do research into aspects of disarmament; whereas the Ministry of Defence dispenses considerable funds to universities for its own research needs. University-based research is largely confined to the work done by individuals linked with strategic studies or international relations departments and university research units with a strong focus on disarmament exist only at Bradford and Sussex and rely heavily on Quaker trusts.[72]

There are three reasons why the low profile accorded to disarmament matters within the government process is unsatisfactory. The first is that the main contribution a country like Britain can make to multilateral negotiations is to provide technical expertise and an appropriately focused diplomacy. British negotiators have sometimes played a constructive role in the past, but if serious progress in disarmament becomes politically possible an immense amount of research and staff work will be required to resolve complex issues of verification. Secondly, unless there are institutionalized interests responsible for scrutinizing defence and foreign policy from a disarmament perspective, then disarmament requirements will continue to be largely ignored in civil service and political decision-making. Thirdly, it is necessary to recognize the importance of disarmament goals by according disarmament much greater visibility and weight in the government and political debates. The current absence of any sufficiently influential institution representing commitment to disarmament both reflects and perpetuates the extremely low priority allocated to it in practice. When the Arms Control and Disarmament Agency was set up in the United States under the Kennedy Administration it did represent a new seriousness in pursuing arms control; and though the ACDA has had a very chequered existence, often being treated with hostility or scepticism by US Administrations as well as being subject to attack from the military and the political Right, it has helped give salience to arms control.[73]

In Britain the Labour government of Harold Wilson took a faltering step towards upgrading the importance of disarmament when in 1964 he appointed Lord Chalfont Minister of State with special responsibility for disarmament and established the Advisory Panel and the Arms Control and Disarmament Unit. But since no other really significant measures were taken to raise the priority given to disarmament, and since the Labour government made no relevant changes in defence policy, the results remained unimpressive. It would be possible for a non-nuclear government to strengthen the position of a future Minister of State for Disarmament by creating a separate wing within the FCO with its own permanent secretary to coordinate research staff and a core of diplomats specializing in disarmament issues. But this would not significantly switch resources or emphasis towards disarmament, and would attract little public attention.

The most promising institutional reform would be the creation of a new Ministry of Disarmament. This would not only signal greater seriousness in pursuit of disarmament and ensure increased government resources, but also encourage the development of a specific departmental view. There is a precedent in the creation of a Ministry of Overseas Development by the Wilson government in 1964. This succeeded in expressing more urgent

292

concern about Third World development and helped to define priorities on aid policy to the Third World.

But it is important to be aware of the limitations and possible drawbacks of institutional reform. A new ministry does not necessarily guarantee adequate changes in policy, and will be constrained by the realities of bureaucratic politics. Thus despite the creation of the Ministry of Overseas Development, most of those who are closely involved in economic aid and development matters remain highly critical of the British governments' contribution and the amount of aid that is tied to British commercial interests. A Ministry of Disarmament would presumably have to draw many of its senior staff from the Foreign and Commonwealth Office and the Ministry of Defence. At best it is likely to remain a junior partner of the Foreign Office and it could be largely emasculated by traditional attitudes. If it is at all successful in promoting its aims it can expect to become a target of right-wing criticism in Parliament and the media, and is liable to be downgraded or abolished by a future Conservative government.

Nevertheless a new ministry could make a considerable impact under an effective senior minister. A possible organizational brief for it would be to give it responsibility for coordinating the work of existing arms control units in the FCO and Ministry of Defence, and of a unit in the Department of Trade and Industry to cover arms control possibilities in relation to nuclear energy. But in addition, a Ministry of Disarmament would need a core staff of its own and its own research staff. It should be designated the 'lead' department over a wide range of disarmament-related issues to strengthen its position in relation to the FCO and MOD. It could be given a number of specific responsibilities: these should include responsibility for instructing the UK disarmament delegation at Geneva and UK delegates to other disarmament negotiations; control over the transformed establishment at Aldermaston; and the right to commission relevant research and disburse funds to universities for it. It should also be accorded the responsibility for assessing the arms control impact of proposed military developments, along the lines of the American Arms Control and Disarmament Agency's 'impact statements' to Congress, though in this country such assessments should go primarily to the Minister of Defence and the Cabinet when relevant, since Parliament is seldom asked to debate specific military proposals. But a Ministry of Disarmament assessment could be submitted alongside the Defence White Paper. If the ministry was seen to have operated effectively in its early years, it would become harder to abolish it later.

The role of a Ministry of Disarmament could be strengthened by greater parliamentary involvement in disarmament issues. At present the main instrument for MPs to elicit information about the British government's role in disarmament negotiations is the parliamentary question, which is certainly inadequate. There are procedural restrictions on posing oral questions to ministers, and careful planning and good luck are required for a back-bencher to succeed in posing a question when many others are competing for the brief time available. Most questions are answered in writing, which enables the government to give the minimum of information; and the MP cannot immediately follow up with a supplementary, which is one of the advantages of oral questions in the House. In order to focus parliamentary and public attention regular institutional means of raising disarmament issues are needed. Submission of an arms control impact assessment alongside the Defence White Paper would help make arms control and disarmament part of the debate about security, but this debate only occurs once a year.

The most obvious way to ensure parliamentary examination of a range of disarmament issues is to set up a separate Select Committee. This would be a logical move to complement the creation of a new Ministry of Disarmament since there are already Select Committees parallel to the main ministries of government. Select Committees hold hearings and produce reports which sometimes elicit media attention and very occasionally warrant debate in the House. Although a pale shadow of Congressional Committees, Parliamentary Select Committees can question civil servants and begin to discover what governments are actually doing. One important by-product of a Select Committee specifically on disarmament would be that members of the Committee would acquire a reasonable degree of expertise on disarmament matters. The British Parliament has no serious research bodies attached to it to produce independent analyses of issues, as Congress does. Several Select Committee members proposed in October 1986 the setting up of an Office of Technology Assessment to advise MPs on issues like SDI relevant to defence and disarmament. We would support such a move.

In addition to parliamentary scrutiny there is a case for both defence and disarmament issues to be examined and debated in a forum independent of the government bureaucracy, in order to give genuine representation to a wide spectrum of views and to raise fundamental questions about policy as well as points of technical detail. It is not easy to devise a satisfactory way of achieving a forum which would carry any weight and attract public interest, though there are examples of quite influential Advisory Committees on Disarmament in other countries like Finland and the Netherlands.[74] It might be possible to formalize the concept of an advisory committee on disarmament representative of various social organizations and political viewpoints. A disarmament commission could be appointed to fulfil a dual role: to engage in informal discussions with those in government concerned with specific issues, and to publish reports, analyses and recommendations which would be used by the public and by Parliament. A body nominated by the Civil Service would be weighted towards establishment views, but terms of reference might require wide-ranging representation.

How to increase the amount of research on disarmament and related defence issues (for example non-provocative defence) has already been touched on. But it is clearly desirable that future research should not solely be government sponsored, but should also be pursued independently. Research funds for disarmament issues could be allocated through existing academic channels. It is also worth considering the possibility of creating a research institute funded in part by government and in part by trusts, but run as an independent institution with its own board of directors. The Stockholm International Peace Research Institute, which is largely funded by the Swedish Parliament, but is an independent body, is a possible organizational model, although it is international in its governing board, staffing and focus; research institutes in Canada and Australia might provide useful examples of the relationship between an institute and national government. An institute which focused on disarmament issues could be less inhibited about adopting political positions than university units might be, and could explicitly act as a focus for public debate on disarmament and security, and as a resource for Parliament. It could also bring together university researchers and ensure everyone involved knew what work was being undertaken in Britain, and at the same time liaise with institutes and university programmes abroad.

A government serious about disarmament has also to tackle the issue of economic conversion in relation to bases, factories and research laboratories liable to be made redundant by measures of arms limitation. Nuclear disarmament alone would not result in a major job loss in Britain, though it would require some reallocation of resources as we have already indicated. But changes in defence policy, or simply procurement strategy, have economic implications and longer-term disarmament goals would require long-term planning for a wholly civilian economy. The Commission has already published a report on the economic consequences of non-nuclear defence, and there is a body of trade unions and academic research in this area. Here we simply wish to note some organizational recommendations from our earlier report: that Alternative Use Committees (along the lines pioneered by Lucas Aerospace Joint Shop Stewards Committee) should be encouraged in every workplace concerned with defence, and that government at the national level should seek to integrate plans for conversion and wider plans for economic development.[75] A possible device for ensuring a national focus on conversion would be some form of National Industrial Conversion Commission.[76]

Appendix 1

Dismantling British Nuclear Warheads

The most critical stage in dismantling a nuclear warhead is the removal of the fissile core, consisting of plutonium or uranium. The remainder of the materials in the warhead (including the tritium or lithium deuteride, and any uranium 238 mantle) would not be radioactive, and it would therefore be fairly straightforward to take them apart. The only other potentially difficult stage is the defusing and dismantling of the conventional explosives, but this task would probably be routine for weapons specialists.

Some warhead designs reportedly allow for the fissile core to be unscrewed easily out of the weapon. In this case the removal of the core would probably take only a few minutes. The designs of other warheads and bombs do not allow such easy extraction, and larger parts of the weapons would therefore have to be dismantled before the radioactive material could be removed. It is not clear how long this would take in a fully equipped facility; probably a few hours and almost certainly not more than a day or two.

In addition to the existing facilities at Aldermaston, four new processing bays will become available by the end of the 1980s when Aldermaston's new A90 complex is opened. At least one of these bays is reportedly allocated for dismantling older British warheads to retrieve fissile materials for the Trident programme[77]. Presumably the other bays could also be used to dismantle warheads. The facilities at the Burghfield nuclear weapons factory must also be adequately equipped for taking apart nuclear warheads.

The absolute minimum number of bays at which the fissile

cores could be removed thus appears to be two – one each at Burghfield and Aldermaston – and is actually more likely to be between four and seven. If we assume the minimum number of two to be available, with all of the other facilities being used to dismantle the non-radioactive components, and allow an average of one day for each warhead (probably generously), then an estimate of the rate at which the nuclear warheads can be dismantled can be made. Allowing all of the standard holidays (ie about 250 working days a year) then about 500 warheads could be dismantled each year.

The crudity of this estimate is apparent. It is possible, though unlikely, that an average of up to two days may be required to dismantle each warhead. However, once the process is underway it is equally likely that the average time could be half a day. If the rate at which warheads could be dismantled turned out to be substantially slower than we estimate, then more bays would have to be allocated for the removal of the fissile cores. Facilities at establishments like Sellafield or at experimental reactor stations such as Harwell could possibly also be used *in extremis*.

Appendix 2

US Collaboration in the British Nuclear Weapons Programme

Although the first British atomic and thermonuclear weapons were developed independently of the United States (though based on the designs developed in the Manhattan Project), the UK became heavily reliant on American nuclear collaboration after the late 1950s. Access to US nuclear delivery vehicles, military reactors, and nuclear warhead design was secured by the 1958 Agreement for Cooperation on the uses of Atomic Energy for Mutual Defence Purposes (and its slight amendment in 1959). This Agreement also allowed for the exchange, by barter, of British plutonium for highly-enriched uranium and tritium from the USA. Since then, several tonnes of weapons-grade British plutonium has been traded under this scheme.

Since 1958, almost all aspects of the British nuclear programme have involved some US contribution. Polaris missiles were bought from the USA, the Polaris submarines were built using US designs, and the navigation systems were heavily dependent on US support. The same will apply to the British Trident programme, if it goes ahead. Shortly after the Mutual Defence Agreement was signed, Rolls Royce was allowed to buy a single example of a submarine nuclear propulsion system (and a set of blueprints) from the USA, allowing the UK to produce nuclear submarines much more quickly and cheaply than would otherwise have been possible. Since then, the British nuclear submarine propulsion system has been developed at Dounreay and Derby with frequent US assistance.[78]

After 1958, Aldermaston appears to have abandoned original work on nuclear warhead design for some fifteen years[79]. Between

1958 and 1974 the UK conducted only four nuclear tests, at least two of which were probably concerned with Polaris. As all of these were of yields below 200 kt, it seems likely that Britain has never tested an H-Bomb design since 1958. The 'Yellow Sun' H-Bomb introduced around 1961 was almost certainly a copy of the US B28 or B43 bomb, and the Polaris warhead was a direct copy of the US W58 warhead. Of the warheads presently in the British nuclear arsenal, the nuclear depth charges and the WE177 are probably copies of the US B61 and B57 respectively. Only the Chevaline warhead has been developed more independently, probably by a process in which the British design teams produce a design and then submit it to the US weapons laboratories for comments. British Trident warheads are probably being designed by the same process.

8. Britain and the Third World

1. INTRODUCTION

So far, this report has focused on the issues which a non-nuclear British government pursuing a policy of dealignment would have to confront in Europe and in its relations with each of the superpowers. The practical ramifications of British foreign policy since 1945 and the difficulties of effecting fundamental change in it justify this emphasis, but it is necessary now to consider how the policy would function in relation to the Third World, and the opportunities it would provide for new efforts to resolve pressing problems.

We begin with an assessment of the nature of those problems. But a prefatory word of warning is required: there could well be a tendency to overstate how much could be achieved by major changes in British policy, a tendency rooted in anachronistic assumptions deriving from Britain's imperial past. It is not entirely to be scorned. In some cases, it derives not from a desire to rule the waves again, but to see Britain being as active a force for good in the world as it was once for bad. The history of imperial exploitation creates in its passing a desire to expunge the guilt. Yet, whether growing from a desire to repeat history or to atone for it, it is based on a gross – if usually unstated – misperception of Britain's weight in world affairs today. This is not to say that Britain, armed with nuclear weapons or not, in or out of NATO, can have no independent role in world politics; nor is it to deny that its role can on occasion be important and, perhaps by catalysing wider action, even decisive; rather, it is to say that what Britain on its own can do is limited and that if it is to be effective it must act in concert with other states.

2. GLOBAL INSECURITY

The outstanding problems of global insecurity fall under three headings: underdevelopment; the increasing ferocity of civil and regional wars; and the nuclear confrontation between the superpowers and their respective blocs.

Underdevelopment is now on the political agenda in many advanced industrial countries in a way it has not been for several years. In 1984, public consciousness woke up to the poverty and misery afflicting large areas of the world. The dramatic impetus to this was provided by reports of the famine in Ethiopia. As a result, in Britain at least, all the major non-governmental aid agencies have recorded large increases in funds raised from public subscription; there have been the spectacular fundraising efforts of 'Band Aid' and 'Live Aid' for Ethiopia; other countries' problems have received more coverage in the media; attention has been focused on the stockpiles of food held by the EEC as part of the Common Agricultural Policy of price-fixing. The extent and generosity of the public response has shamed the meagre efforts of most governments. But the problems of world famine, malnutrition and poverty are long-term and nothing has so far happened to offer the slightest hope of permanently eradicating them.

Public concern in the industrialized countries addresses the Third World's problems only sporadically, and tends to focus on immediate disasters rather than the underlying long-term problems. In 1980, less spectacularly than four years later, it was stirred on the issue not by television pictures, but by the publication of an independent report – *North-South*, produced by the Brandt Commission.[1] Its impact was due in part to the Commission's membership – chaired by a former Chancellor of the Federal Republic of Germany, including among its members former Prime Ministers of Britain and Sweden, the Secretary-General of the Commonwealth and numerous other individuals of rank and influence – but also to the special sense of urgency with which the report was imbued. Half a decade on, the only conclusion can be that the situation has deteriorated sharply and dreadfully, that time has only made the problems more urgent.

The immediate disasters of famine upon which public consciousness has focused arise against a background of general malnutrition, inadequate health care, insufficient supplies of clean water, illiteracy and widespread poverty. Even in countries with impressive degrees of industrialization and manufactured exports, such as in South America, urban poverty grows apace. Mounting debts – some due to severe economic mismanagement, often characterized by the waste of valuable resources in the purchase of modern arms; others due to changes in rates of interest and monetary exchange entirely outside the control of national governments, in part the result of the USA's high military spending and consequent need to borrow to finance its budget deficit, in part a consequence of the steep rise in oil prices in the 1970s – have enforced a slide back into poverty in countries which a few years ago appeared to have reasonably sound economic infrastructures offering some prospect of growth. The effect has been worsened by the cold grip on many countries' economic policies exerted by the International Monetary Fund, apparently capable only of imposing austerity measures on governments in economic difficulties, whose citizens already experience an impossible austerity. In some cases, such as Argentina, Chile and Mexico, the result has been even worse: in the respite following the IMF intervention, private capital has been able to flow out of the country, leaving an even worse situation behind. Beyond these problems, all severe in themselves, several African countries face the long-term ecological disaster of increasing desertification – the permanent destruction of hitherto fertile land.

Solving these problems requires concerted international action. Apart from the continued unconcern of governments in advanced industrial countries, and the fact that so far public concern has been only sporadic, what gets in the way are the global and regional rivalries with which the world is riven. Since 1945, there have been more than 250 wars of all sorts and sizes, most of them in the Third World.[2] The nature of these conflicts has varied widely: some were part of the process of unravelling the old European empires, while others were factional conflicts over post-colonial power; some regional wars have started from territorial and other disputes in the wake of decolonization, while others stem from disputes unconnected with the colonial history; there have been civil wars reflecting unanswered yet irresistible demands for social and political change; some wars have been outcrops of the US-Soviet confrontation. According to one esti– mate, total human losses in all these wars may exceed 50 million.[3]

Continuing political instability and festering civil wars in some countries, combined with regional wars and border clashes between others, place enormous obstacles in the way of decisive action to solve development problems. Exacerbating the situation is the social and political nature of so many of the countries, in which a privileged élite holds power over an impoverished populace. All these difficulties are multiplied by the intrusion of a dispute within the developed 'North' – the US-Soviet confrontation – into the life of the underdeveloped 'South'.[4]

In the central political and economic reality of the Third World's crisis as a whole, and in the specific crises of most Third World countries, the USSR has little or no role. Ethiopia, where the government has been supported by the USSR and Cuba in its civil and regional wars, is among a few countries where Soviet influence is potentially decisive for good and ill – and it is a specific instance where the USSR seems to have done little to relieve the suffering of the victims of underdevelopment. In most countries, US or, more generally, Western influence is the decisive factor. It is an influence which derives from political, economic and military roots in any combination. International action to solve some of the most pressing problems of world poverty is a general responsibility but, while the USSR cannot stand by and claim it is entirely up to others to act, the major burden must fall on the Western countries which have the greater influence. In order to fulfil this responsibility, there must be some major changes of policy and attitude in the advanced industrial countries.

Resources

At the time of the 1973 Arab-Israeli war, the oil-exporting Arab states used oil as a diplomatic weapon in an attempt to isolate Israel politically, and followed up in 1974 with the first of a series of price increases. This not only changed *energy* into a major political question within industrialized countries, but also transformed *resources* into a far more explicitly and explosively political question at the international level.

Access to and control of natural resources has always been a major economic question and has never lacked a political importance. But in the 1970s it took on a new urgency. As the extent of dependence of Western industrialized states, and Japan, on certain imported resources became painfully obvious, the question was shoved to the forefront of strategic debate.[5] It became common, even fashionable, to suggest that the Soviet Union might seek to undermine the Western economy by preventing access to strategic raw materials and engaging in a global resource war.[6]

The alleged risk to oil supplies from Soviet interference was one reason given for the formation by the Carter Administration in early 1980, following the Soviet invasion of Afghanistan, of a US Rapid Deployment Force – a force that has been built up and armed with nuclear weapons under Reagan. It is also one of the arguments used in favour of the British and French equivalents of the Rapid Deployment Force and to urge NATO as a whole to accept 'out of area' responsibilities.

Several points need to be made here. On the issue of principle, the notion that the West has some kind of proprietary right over Arab oil – that it is 'our oil' – must be firmly rejected. In a world of sovereign states, countries have the legal right to dispose as they decide of the resources within their territory.

Clearly such decisions ought to be taken on all sides in a responsible way with due regard to the consequences of any given decision for other countries and other peoples. Moreover in an interdependent world a decision to impose economic sanctions in the form of abruptly ceasing to supply materials or commodities to a country which has come to rely on them is only justifiable in highly exceptional circumstances – for instance as an alternative to the use of military force to halt an act of aggression or, in the case of South Africa, as a means of putting pressure on the government to end the abominable system of apartheid. President Reagan's decision, for instance, in the early 1980s to halt US oil supplies to Nicaragua as part of the campaign to overthrow the Sandinista government, is indefensible. Finally there is a growing case for international co-operation in the development, management and distribution of resources to avoid famines, ecological breakdown, and the depletion of resources.

What must be rejected, however, is the notion that Arab or Third World states have some kind of second class sovereignty when it comes to the disposal of their resources, i.e. that advanced industrial nations can dispose of their resources to suit their interests but that Third World countries may do so only to the extent that Western interests are not thereby adversely affected. Even more objectionable is the proposition that Western industrialized states have the right to use military force to compel Third World countries to maintain existing patterns of trade, especially given that the terms of trade currently operate overwhelmingly to the disadvantage of the Third World.

As regards a possible Soviet threat, the chance that the Soviet Union, in any situation short of a major East-West war, would use force to cut off supplies to the West of oil or other resources vital to the functioning of its economy is very remote. The precipitate collapse of the Western economies would have catastrophic consequences at a global level and cause major dislocations in the Soviet bloc, including the Soviet Union itself.

A Soviet naval blockade to halt shipping between Western Europe or Japan and the oil-producing Arab states would be an act of war and really only conceivable if an East-West war were already under way. Nor even in that situation are Soviet naval forces sufficiently powerful by comparison to those of the West to impose a total blockade.

Another suggestion is that by means of subversion and indirect intervention, the Soviet Union may succeed in establishing radical anti-Western régimes in the Middle East and Gulf area who will then cease supplying the West with oil. This is not a genuine possibility in the near future as far as a number of key states are concerned. More importantly, even the most radical anti-Western régimes in the area, such as that of Colonel Gaddafi in Libya, are not Soviet puppets and are anxious in their own interests to continue supplying the West with oil. The same point applies to other countries which supply the West with 'strategic' raw materials. Where the installation of a radical régime has resulted in a cut off, or major cut back, in trade with the West this has usually been the result of economic sanctions applied by the US, as for instance in the case of Cuba after Castro came to power, and of Nicaragua after the victory of the Sandinista movement.

If a Soviet threat to supplies of oil and other raw materials to the West in peacetime is remote, the most likely use to which the US Rapid Deployment Force and other naval and air forces deployed across the globe could be put is to threaten or engage in interventions in countries where US or Western interests are judged to be at stake because of political developments in the countries concerned. Clearly this is an entirely illegitimate use of military force. Moreover if the aim is to ensure the continued supply of oil or other raw materials it is likely to be counter-productive. Nothing, for instance, is more likely to produce a cut off in Arab oil supplies to the West than major military action by the US in the Middle East. It is significant that the West did not attempt to break the Arab oil boycott of 1973 by force, and it is evident that any attempt to have done so would have been disastrous. Nor can the US – any more than the Soviet Union – hope to invade and occupy the main Arab oil producing states or install governments that will simply do its bidding.

The depletion of certain energy and other resources may of course present a major global problem in the future. But the use of military force to grab dwindling supplies is more likely to aggravate than alleviate the difficulty; and even where a particular country gained a unilateral advantage by the use of force, the problem would have been postponed not solved.

This is not to rule out the possibility of 'resource' conflicts, since governments are notoriously prone to act on the basis of calculations of short-term interests. The temptation to intervene, however, could be reduced if preparations for boycotts or other concerted international action made it unlikely that an intervening power would gain even a short-term advantage, or might indeed face the prospect of a severe economic crisis because of the sanctions applied.

In the final analysis, if the present economic-industrial system of the 'advanced' countries is threatening the globe with the depletion of resources and ecological crisis, the only way the problem can be solved is by cooperation at a global level, and by fundamental changes to the industrial economies in both East and West.

The Superpowers

Areas in which access to resources is a particularly sensitive issue, are often those where there is cause for particular fears that there lies the spark to detonate World War III. Everybody may have a private nightmare of how global war might start, in many cases having nothing to do with areas such as the Middle East or southern Africa. However, the increasing determination of both the USA and the USSR to develop the capability to project their power into all corners of the world creates a situation fraught with obvious peril. The development, on the one hand, of the USA's Rapid Deployment Force, together with its long-range exercises in the Middle East and its nuclear capability, and, on the other, of Soviet ocean-going and air transport capabilities, encourages uncomfortable speculation about the course of possible future crises. Fast military action by either side over an issue deemed crucially important is a recipe for an uncontrolled crisis and rapid escalation of violence. The Reagan Administration's obvious concern to play to a domestic Cold War gallery creates doubt about its ability for self-restraint in crises. But if we are left dependent on the Soviet bureaucracy's flexibility to avoid disaster, we can have no confidence about the outcome.

The world's 'hotspots', where one form or another of regional or domestic conflict has attracted the attention of one or both superpowers, are not solely the resource-rich areas. What is common, however, to Central America and the Middle East, for example, is the globalization of essentially regional and local disputes via the mechanism of Cold War and superpower intervention. The nature of the Sandinista government in Nicaragua or the territorial ambitions of Israel, Syria, Iran and Iraq may or may not be matters of legitimate concern to observers interested in peace and justice. But the US government's deliberate confrontation with Nicaragua, its military posturing and manoeuvres in the region and its support for the Contras have forced the Sandinistas to turn increasingly to the Soviet bloc for aid, and thus turned a local political issue into a global security problem.[7] Similarly, a superpower competition for influence in the Middle East has exacerbated the terrible tragedy in Lebanon, with each side's regional supporters encouraged into a series of dangerous actions. Again, a civil war is transformed into a global security problem.

Militarism

The superpower competition is not, of course, confined to those areas which are regularly in the newspaper headlines, where political disputes have boiled over into open war with the adversaries armed respectively by the superpowers. The ferocity of these wars and the dangers of the 'hotspots' are to be seen against the background of a general process of militarization. This is reflected, on the one hand, in the large number of military régimes – and of nominally civilian governments put in place by armed *coups* – and, on the other, in the scale of the international arms trade and of military spending in general. It is both self-evident and well understood that military spending represents, in any country, a diversion of resources from other uses. The starkness of the contrast between abundant military spending and the dearth of development aid from the industrial powers is similarly well known: US spending on foreign aid amounts to but 5 per cent of its annual military budget; in the Soviet case, the comparable figure is less than 1 per cent.[8] The Brandt Commission reported that a ten-year programme to meet essential food and health needs in the poorest countries would cost under half of one year's global military spending – that is, about 5 per cent of annual arms spending for a decade.[9] A list of similar examples could be given, all making the same point that the world's massive expenditure on armed forces represents a grotesque misuse of resources.

There is, however, a further point. Military spending both thrives on and helps create ambient insecurity. The process of threat and counter-threat is well enough understood to need no elaboration here. Motives for military spending in Third World countries are as varied as the nature of their governments and the political contexts in which they operate. In some cases, territorial or regional power ambitions drive the military budget up; in others, a perception of threat from another power, often well-founded, is the cause. In some, the maintenance of domestic power against a disgruntled population is the main reason; in others, the glorification of national leaders. In most cases, however, the appetite for military spending is fed by the major arms exporters of the industrial world – in order: the USA, the USSR, France, Britain, Italy and the Federal Republic of Germany. The major period of expansion of the arms trade was in the 1960s and, especially, the 1970s. In the last few years, the growth in trade has slowed, not because of agreed restraint but because the level of orders placed in the 1970s was so great that saturation of the market was inevitable. During those two decades, three major developments occurred in this field. First, the scale of the trade increased dramatically – fourfold according to one estimate.[10] Second, one effect of this was to diffuse advanced military technology at a hitherto unprecedented rate, equipping more states with the ability to wage war at ever more destructive levels. In order to assimilate and maintain the new equipment, Third World countries began to play host to thousands of technical and military advisers: even by 1976 there were an estimated 10,000 Soviet and East German technicians in Third World countries; the purchase of one relatively unsophisticated fighter aircraft by Saudi Arabia required the presence of over 1,600 US personnel.[11] Third, the market became much more competitive, first with the emergence of some Western European suppliers as real challengers to superpower dominance of the trade, and then with the creation of production and later design facilities in some Third World countries and their own emergence as weapons exporters. While the market was expanding in the 1970s, the pressure of the new competitors could be absorbed; with the relative retraction of the market in the 1980s, that is no longer true and the pressure on exporters to secure their markets has become intense.

Efforts to gather support for restraint in the arms trade have consistently foundered on several rocks. One has been the view that the sale of arms and support services purchases influence; this is more true for the superpowers than other major arms exporters such as Britain. Another has been the view that if one exporter backs off, another will take its place – probably justified, but no basis on which to construct a policy. A third has been a more philosophical objection, that arms producers have no right to dictate importers' security policies to them by withholding necessary equipment. This objection is superficially appealing, but fundamentally flawed. The fact is that supplying states do impose restrictions on actual and would-be importers' security policies. On the one hand, nuclear weapons are among those which are not for sale; on the other, exporters refuse to sell to states they regard as actual or potential adversaries – though the judgement here can be mistaken, as was most clearly shown in the 1982 Falklands/Malvinas war when Britain fought against a country whose forces were 90 per cent equipped by either Britain or its NATO allies. In any case demand in the arms trade is no more autonomous than in any other. Apart from the extensive record of corruption,[12] an impressive array of arms fairs, travelling exhibitions and diplomatic contacts are routinely used to stimulate the taste for the latest weaponry. This is supported by the supplying states as a matter of policy, in order to sustain military industrial capacity at reduced cost to the national exchequer. Estimates for the 1970s indicate that the proportion of arms production accounted for by exports in the main supplying countries ranges from 10 per cent for the Federal Republic of Germany, through 12 per cent for the USSR, 17 per cent for Italy and the USA, to 30 per cent for Britain and 55-60 per cent for France.[13] The unreliability of statistics in this field means that these estimates are extremely rough, but they make the point. Security policies in importing countries are not alone the problem. Among the exporters, the maintenance of large arms industries is seen as an element of security policy; in fact, by necessarily generating pressures to export, it helps create global insecurity.

The elements of global insecurity surveyed in this section evidently interlock with each other: underdevelopment and militarism; the inability to get coordinated action for a decisive resolution of the problems of famine and poverty; the power of the advanced countries and the disempowerment of the poor. No British government, however boldly and imaginatively it acts, can hope even to begin to solve the problems alone. What then can it do?

3. The Superpowers and the Third World

The scale of the task is increased by the active intervention of the two superpowers in Third World politics. The polarization of global politics – whether in periods of détente or of Cold War – intensifies the process of militarization and hinders any attempt at concerted action on behalf of the people in those countries. Superpower pressure and intervention also hinders, and clearly is intended to hinder, the development of a genuinely non-aligned group of nations as a force in international politics. It is therefore worth assessing the motives and record of the superpowers in their interventions.

The USA

The economic motive clearly has played an important role in US interventions in the Third World. Its interest has been not only to ensure continued access to supplies and markets for itself but to maintain the stability of a global system in which its economy and that of Western states as a whole could flourish and expand. In the restructuring of world power attendant upon the collapse of the old European Empires in the wake of World War II, the USA took the leading role in establishing a new financial system and providing military and political support to governments which favoured the new world order.

But an explanation of US actions in purely economic terms is inadequate. In Vietnam, where it pursued the longest and bloodiest war of intervention – by either side – in the post-World War II period, its direct economic stake was not a major one, though once it had become involved, withdrawal became more difficult because of the fear on the part of US leaders of a loss of US political influence in other parts of the world. The general policy of interventionism has been continued and, under Reagan, intensified, despite the crippling economic burdens and internal dissension such actions can create, and even at the risk of not being able to exploit obvious opportunities to expand trade with the USSR, China and other communist countries.

In some instances it is difficult to believe that the US Administration could ever have expected to gain either economic advantage or political influence from its interventions. The US bombing of Libya in April 1986, for instance, far from serving any US or Western economic or political interests, put these at grave risk, as most Western European governments were at pains to point out before the action took place. In this case factors such as national prestige, frustration at US inability to take effective action against terrorist outrages, contempt for a small Arab country, perhaps even the personal antagonism between Reagan and Gaddafi, overruled caution or any rational calculation of the probable consequences of the action. The attack, indeed, illustrates the fact that one cannot take for granted that political leaders will act on the basis of a careful assessment of risks and advantages, and that emotive and irrational factors may tip the balance between peace and war.

The conviction that the USA was locked in a global ideological and political struggle with the Soviet Union, and fears of Soviet expansionist ambitions (which were intensified after North Korea's invasion of South Korea in 1950) are some of the most important factors underlying the increasingly assertive and interventionist US policies in the 1950s and 1960s. In brief, once the USA had opted in the course of 1946-47 for the 'Riga Axioms' in accounting for Soviet behaviour (the development discussed in Chapter Three), it set itself upon a course that would inevitably result in military build-up, confrontation and intervention. As Daniel Yergin has put it:

'American leaders began with the Truman Doctrine [1947] to devise policies deemed appropriate to the world as they now understood it – policies based upon containment, intervention, military buildup and economic reconstruction. They thought they were taking defensive actions, but the effect would be otherwise – a great expansion of America's political, economic, and military role in the world. Such steps reversed the trend towards retrenchment, which had begun in August 1945, and instead pointed the United States towards a new confrontation not only with Moscow-directed Communists, but also with other leftists, nationalists and various kinds of progressives, some of whom, had they operated at home rather than abroad, might have fitted comfortably into Truman's Fair Deal.'[14]

The resurgence of interventionist policies under Reagan, following a retreat from this approach during the Carter years, can also be explained in part by the simplistic anti-communist view

313

of the world adopted by Reagan and his Administration. US intervention under Reagan has been particularly marked in Latin America. The region has of course been considered by the US as a sphere of influence since the enunciation of the Monroe Doctrine in 1823, and the USA has intervened aggressively in Central America and the Caribbean on several occasions in the post-World War II period – notably in Guatemala in 1964 against the democratic and reformist Arbenz government, against Cuba in 1961 when it played a supporting role in the Bay of Pigs invasion, and against the Dominican Republic in 1965. It also engaged in a campaign of economic and political destabilization against the elected Allende government in Chile which culminated in the military coup of 1973 and the installation of a particularly vicious and bloody dictatorship under Pinochet.

The Reagan Administration stepped up US military support for repressive régimes in El Salvador and Honduras, providing training and 'military advisors' in the war against insurgents, and also assisted the 'Contras' attempting to overthrow the Sandinista government in Nicaragua. In October 1983, following a coup in Grenada in which the left-wing government of Maurice Bishop was overthrown, and Bishop himself and many of his ministers murdered, the US government invaded the island. (Prior to the coup and the invasion, the USA had also done its utmost to isolate and undermine the Bishop government.) In 1983-84 it took the illegal step of mining Nicaragua's harbours, subsequently refusing to acknowledge the International Court of Justice's right of jurisdiction in the matter.[15]

Opposition from a sceptical Congress has tended to limit the aid which Reagan has been able to provide the Contras in Nicaragua, though in 1986 the Senate approved increased funding for the Contras. However, he has been much more successful in persuading Congress to release funds to assist the Mujahedin resistance in Afghanistan. Here the US is on firmer ground both legally and morally, especially in view of the overwhelming UN condemnation of the Soviet invasion in 1979. The priority now, however, must be to support the UN efforts to reach a negotiated settlement since the continuing war is having catastrophic consequences for the Afghan people.

Congress, and apparently the overwhelming majority of the

US public, supported Reagan over the bombing raids on Libya in April 1986 in reprisal for the alleged organization of terrorist attacks on US citizens by the Libyan government. Reprisal raids of this kind have of course been a regular feature of Israeli policy for several decades, but they mark a new and dangerous twist in superpower interventionism.

If there is any comfort to be gleaned here, it is the fact that so far even the Reagan Administration has been unable or unwilling to commit large numbers of US forces in a major combat role in the Third World. Despite the rhetoric, Vietnam may still serve as a warning against the hazards, both military and political, of large-scale intervention. Whether the near universal condemnation (from abroad) of the US raid on Libya will prevent a return to massive military intervention, or even curb this more limited, yet highly dangerous, form of it, remains to be seen.

The USSR

In the case of the USSR, the economic factor is less important in explaining its interventions than it is in the case of the USA. The USSR is still relatively self-sufficient in energy and raw materials, and its level of trade with the Third World, though expanding, is still minute compared with that of the USA and other Western countries. The economic advantages it has sometimes gained, for instance in the form of increased natural gas exports from Afghanistan after its intervention in December 1979, probably represent an incidental bonus rather than a decisive motivating factor.

The motivation for Soviet policy appears to be primarily political and ideological but it resulted by the 1970s in an approach that comes close to a Soviet version of the 1947 Truman Doctrine of containment.[16] Soviet activity in the Third World has been to support certain guerrilla movements and leftist or revolutionary states, but also régimes of very varying political complexion – some of them engaged in suppressing communist movements or rebellions – where this served Soviet political or strategic interests or denied potential strategic advantage to the West.[17] It has sought to extend its own military network, partly to increase its capability to support sympathetic states, partly to protect its ocean-going submarines and its

315

merchant and fishing fleets. It has also provided significant economic aid to certain chosen states.

Taking the post-World War II period as a whole, there have been many more military interventions by Western powers in the Third World than by the Soviet Union. The US researcher Ruth Sivard has calculated that the Western powers have been responsible in the period 1945-1980 for 79 per cent of direct military interventions in developing countries in contrast to 6 per cent for communist powers and 15 per cent for Third World countries among themselves.[18] There are many instances of Soviet passivity when a state, guerrilla force or political movement which it nominally supports has been threatened, and more instances of nominal support rather than military assistance and/or intervention on the scale of its involvement in North Vietnam, Angola or Ethiopia. For example, in southern Africa neither the South-West African People's Organization nor the state of Mozambique has been given the scale of assistance which might have been expected following the demise of the Portuguese Empire in the mid-1970s.

The low profile that the Soviet Union has often adopted is at least in part a reflection of the much more limited capability it has in comparison to the USA to project its forces over very long distances – despite a considerable build-up in this capability, particularly during the 1970s. The US naval air-strike power from its aircraft carriers is many times that of the USSR; the US Marine Corps is also the world's largest – 190,000 men, compared to the Soviet Union's 20,000.

One difficulty, however, about direct comparisons between US and Soviet capabilities, resides in their very different geographical location. If the USA were to be a military power in the world outside of the Americas, it could only be so by building up its naval and air forces and establishing overseas bases. The Soviet Union, by contrast, occupies a central position on the Eurasian land mass. It is, by virtue of its geography, at once a European, a Middle-Eastern (or West Asian) and Asiatic power. This makes it at once more vulnerable, and, from the point of view of weaker Third World neighbours, more threatening. One commentator pointed out that roughly 85 per cent of the world's population lives within a 3,000 mile radius of the borders of the

Soviet Union, and it is within such a radius that the Soviet Union has focused its efforts to increase its capability to project its forces.[19]

From around the mid-1960s onwards, the Soviet Union became far more involved in the Third World, especially in military terms. By the end of the 1960s, for instance, it had become one of the main suppliers of major weapons to the Third World, rivalling, and in some years outstripping, the USA in this respect.[20] Its capability to intervene, together with the scale of its military involvement in the Third World, changed markedly in the course of the 1960s and 1970s. In 1963 it became involved in a major logistics operation carrying Egyptian troops to North Yemen where they fought on the republican side in the civil war. In 1970, 20,000 Soviet military personnel helped to operate the Egyptian air defence system surrounding major cities and facing the Suez canal. During the 1970s the Soviet Union also established significant numbers of bases and military facilities in the Third World – though again not on a scale to rival that of the USA.

The commitment of large numbers of Soviet and Cuban forces to Third World countries, first in Angola from the latter part of 1975 onwards on behalf of the MPLA movement and government, and then in 1977-78 in Ethiopia against Somalia and the secessionist movement in Eritrea, marked a further stage in Soviet Third World involvement. Not only was it involved in a major military airlift of Cuban forces, but the latter fought under Soviet command to drive out the Somalis from Ogaden. Both in Ethiopia and in Angola the Soviet-Cuban intervention was decisive in ensuring the victory of the parties they supported.

The Soviet invasion of Afghanistan in December 1979, however, was the first time since 1945 that the Soviet Union committed major forces to direct combat outside Eastern Europe. Its motive is a matter of continuing speculation, but one important factor may have been fear of the consequences of a collapse of the Marxist government there and its replacement by a fundamentalist Islamic régime. Soviet leaders are likely to have been particularly nervous of the effect of such an outcome on the large Moslem population in the adjacent area of the Soviet

Union. Soviet strategy appears to have been to replace the hardline President Hafizullah Amin with a moderate reforming government under Babrak Karmal who would attempt to win popular support while Soviet and Afghan forces stepped up the military action against the Mujahedin guerrillas.

Fears that the Soviet Union saw the establishment of a major military presence in Afghanistan as the stepping stone for further interventions appear to be unjustified. There is no evidence that it has given the Soviet leaders the taste for such actions in other parts of the world. In fact, they may be learning from Afghanistan how difficult it is to impose a political settlement by military means on a Third World country where major sections of the population oppose it.

Whatever Soviet motives, the invasion cannot be justified, and was overwhelmingly condemned in the UN General Assembly at the time. The continuing war has also proved a major catastrophe for Afghanistan. Reports by the Special Reporter to the UN on Human Rights in November 1985 and February 1986 put the estimated number of refugees from Afghanistan at 4.5 million, approximately a third of the entire population. It also cites estimates that the number of Afghan casualties since the beginning of the war is around 500,000, the majority of them civilians.[21]

Negotiations under UN auspices to end the war and secure the removal of Soviet forces resumed in Geneva in May 1986 as this report was nearing completion. President Zia of Pakistan, in an assessment not shared by the Afghani opposition, apparently believes the USSR is seeking a way out of its war.[22] On the eve of these talks it was announced that Babrak Karmal had resigned as President to be replaced by Mr Najibullah, and some commentators have suggested that this is evidence of a Soviet desire to end the deadlock by replacing the leader who was directly installed by their intervention.

Despite this disturbing pattern of increased Soviet involvement in the Third World, its influence remains limited and it has suffered a number of serious reverses, notably in China, Indonesia, Egypt and Somalia. Its freedom of action is curtailed not only by the limitations of its capability to project its military power over great distances, but by the same forces of nationalism which brought about the end of colonial rule, defeated the US in Vietnam, and resulted in other reverses for the USA elsewhere. The number of Third World states which are in any real sense pro-Soviet in their alignment is far smaller than the number which are pro-Western.[23] Its continuing war in Afghanistan has also damaged its political standing and credibility in the Third World.

Intervention and Legality

We take the view that military involvement by the superpowers in the Third World is highly undesirable under almost all circumstances. However it will be clear from some of the above examples that military involvements and interventions can take various forms and occur under widely differing circumstances and that they cannot all be placed on the same level, either legally or morally. Providing military support to a government that has been invaded by a neighbouring or other foreign power may or may not be desirable, but it is different from helping a corrupt dictatorship, like the Somoza régime in Nicaragua, or the Amin government in Uganda, to maintain power by repression and armed force against the wishes of the population. At another level, there are differences between supplying arms and training to movements fighting to overthrow colonial rule or apartheid and supporting armed groups attempting to overthrow a democratically-elected government.

In broad terms the legal situation relating to outside military intervention in a country is defined by the UN Charter. The aggressive use of force by one state against another is specifically outlawed. But an incumbent government may request military assistance from other states whereas, in general, rebels do not have that right, at least until they have been accorded the status of belligerents. However, a series of General Assembly resolutions has attempted to clarify when outside support to insurrectionary movements is legitimate; these cover struggles against colonial rule, against apartheid and against foreign occupation.[24]

Clearly international law as it stands leaves many loopholes, and any intervening power will always claim that it is acting within it. Writing in 1985, one group of researchers in Holland pointed out that the world then comprised roughly twenty-five democracies, twenty communist states and a hundred authoritarian states, most of the latter in the Third World. Because these authoritarian states are frequently unstable, the superpowers, and regional powers, are likely to be invited to intervene, or be tempted to do so, either on the side of tottering régimes or the armed insurgents.[25]

Where the superpowers, or other intervening power, use their military forces directly, the UN General Assembly, and the International Court of Justice, can act to some degree as arbiters in judging whether particular cases do or do not contravene international law. It is much more difficult even to obtain any kind of international ruling in cases of indirect intervention and various forms of covert action, which may sometimes simply take the form of a massive build-up of weapons in an area, or the introduction into it of new types of weapons. Both superpowers engage in this kind of covert activity, and each also seeks on occasion to justify its own interventions as a response to the covert interventions of the other side.

Despite these legal and moral complexities, it is clear that superpower intervention or military involvement in the Third World, even in those exceptional cases where it may be possible to advance a legal justification for it, is almost always detrimental, leading to an escalation of the conflict and the introduction of East-West rivalry into the situation. The goal, if chaos and bloodshed are to be avoided, must be the elimination of military involvement by the superpowers, and other outside powers, in the Third World. This would involve not only ending military intervention as such, but closing military bases and facilities, and establishing strict international control over the arms trade.

4. Changing Attitudes

Despite differences in their policies and motives in the Third World, the superpowers share a crucial basic assumption – that the Third World is a legitimate terrain for them to compete on and over. Indeed, this is the view held about most of the world in most of the industrialized countries. In Britain and certain other countries, it can doubtless be identified as a leftover from the days of empire. In the USSR and to some extent in the USA, it may perhaps be explained as a product of the view of a global conflict between capitalism and socialism. There can be little or no progress towards solving the problems of underdevelopment unless a beginning can be made towards eradicating that attitude.

Apart from the fact that it is wrong to view more than half the world's people and the countries where they live in that way, the question may be asked – Why bother to change that attitude? Are we in the industrialized countries not doing all right at the expense of the impoverished majority of the world's population? What's in it for us?

We suspect questions like these, usually unasked, lie behind the normal lack of attention paid to Third World problems in the industrialized countries, and behind the inaction of governments even when public concern is aroused. Such questions pose a dilemma to those seeking change. Should they rest their arguments on issues of morality, respect for humankind, values of equality, freedom and independence? Or should they seek also to make an appeal to self-interest, and what would the basis of that appeal be?

The Brandt Commission appeared to believe it had found a two-fold basis. On the one hand, it argued that until the problem of the imbalance between the 'North' and the 'South' was more properly addressed and action taken to redress it, '[T]he world community can have no real stability.' On the other hand, more generally, the Commission appealed to 'hard-headed self-interest' to 'reinforce the claim of human solidarity', and recognize that meeting developmental needs in poorer countries would help expand demand to permit the re-utilization of idle industrial capacity in the richer ones.[26] We do not deny the force of these arguments, and we fully appreciate the need to do more than appeal to a 'human solidarity' which normally has little resonance for most of the industrialized countries' populations, yet there are some problems here with the way the appeal to self-interest is made. For example, the term 'stability' is notoriously elusive, too often turning out to mean the status quo, however repressive it may be. There may also be models of development which do not simply mean the complete absorption of poorer countries into a world economy in which they are necessarily the weakest competitors.

First, to return to the issue of nightmares about how a nuclear war between the superpowers might start, various of the Third World hotspots must figure strongly in any assessment of that terrible risk. More specifically, perhaps, it is areas where both the USA and the USSR are engaged in a direct, and especially military, projection of their power that the greatest risks lie. Their competition for influence and power could in crisis lead to confrontation and escalation. The exertion of power in far-flung corners of the globe is itself a major source of the perils the world now faces. More generally, in explaining how and why the period of *détente* evaporated into a new Cold War in the late 1970s, the ebb and flow of political influence in the Third World must feature strongly.[27] It is not necessary to accept the official American explanation that all the blame lies with Soviet machinations ('this game of dominoes', as President Reagan has it), to recognize the part played by US anxieties about loss of power in the Third World in bringing on the new Cold War.

Both in the general sense of the deterioration of superpower relations, and in the more specific sense of where the immediate cause of World War III may be found, the exertion of power at long range and the attitude which legitimates it are sources of extreme danger. We can add that it is not just the assumption of power over weakness which is the problem; it is also the reality of power and weakness. The ambitions of the powerful make a perilous combination with the incapacity of the weak to be more than a stomping ground for outside competing interests. This imbalance can be tackled on both sides: power can be reduced, or at least restrained; weakness can be replaced, if not by strength, at least by resilience.

A British government pursuing a policy of dealignment would be well placed to assist in the process of destroying the legitimacy and the hold of the view that the Third World is but the arena for competing superpower and allied interests. On the other hand, a British government which is not merely closely aligned with one superpower, but is its most loyal and enthusiastic ally, is not simply unable to help develop the solution; it is part of the problem. The more it is possible for Third World states to break out of the stranglehold of choosing to align either with the USA or with the USSR, the more they can opt for a real non-alignment, then the more secure our future will be. In the nexus of problems linking global insecurity and underdevelopment, a key task is to break down the polarization of world politics which has been reasserted during the first half of the 1980s.

5. CHANGING POLICIES

Much that a British government could do lies in diplomatic endeavour – persuading other states to adopt a more generous, less restrictive set of policies towards the Third World. This should not be underestimated as 'mere words'. It is a constant theme of this chapter that what any British government – or any other state of comparable size and weight – can achieve by its own actions is highly circumscribed. This does not mean that independent actions on underdevelopment and insecurity should not be taken, nor that they will be worthless. But a realistic appreciation of the scale of task and the capacity of the British state must conclude that such actions will have necessarily limited effects – limited as to the number of countries or regions which can be helped, as to the range of problems which can be addressed, as to the permanence of any solutions which can be offered. Therefore, whereas it is normal in considering such issues, and right, to call for 'action not words', in this case the truth is that action alone is not enough.

Speaking, however, is also not enough. Before that comes listening. If a British government, fired with a sense of mission, were to rush into programmes without taking into account local wishes and local needs this would represent little more than the continuation of colonialist attitudes in a new guise and would be counterproductive in terms of development. It is now widely accepted, for example, that when governments and corporations of industrialized countries acted to revolutionize the basis of agriculture in many Third World countries, there were many cases in which they ushered in disaster. The switch from subsistence farming to cash and exportable crops has too often meant that the needs of subsistence have gone by the board. It is possible to analyse that entire phase as a cynical ploy by 'agri-business' to manipulate economic development for their own advantage.[28] Yet many of the individuals who worked on those programmes did so in the enthusiastic belief that they were bringing unalloyed benefits of modernity and progress to the countries involved. Similarly, the tendency to opt for large-scale industrial enterprises has been analysed as causing a bifurcated pattern of development, in which a relatively prosperous urban middle-class emerges alongside severe urban poverty and increasing rural deprivation.[29] There is, then, a history of mistakes waiting to be repeated. It is possible that close attention to the needs of those we wish to help will permit us to provide benefits without crippling side-effects.

6. Short-Term Policies

There are four sets of problems to which immediate solutions are desperately needed: debt rescheduling, aid and trade policies, and conflict resolution. We consider these in turn, and then reflect on what independent role Britain could play in contributing to the solutions. The discussion needs to be set in a dual context: on the one hand, the need to begin by listening, discussed in the previous section; on the other, the need simultaneously to lay the groundwork for long-term policies which we discuss in the following section.

Debt Rescheduling

The debt burden in many Third World countries has reached disastrous proportions; crisis is too weak a word to describe the consequences in many cases. The background to this is a major shift in the composition of resources flowing to the underdeveloped world from the industrialized countries. In 1960, 60 per cent of the flow from OECD countries consisted of Official Development Assistance (ODA), made up of grants and loans at concessional (i.e. non-commercial) rates.[30] In 1983, the ODA share of the flow was 34 per cent, and loans at commercial rates accounted for 64 per cent.[31] This shift means that of any economic surplus generated in the recipient country, a larger proportion must be earmarked for repayments.

324

Despite the weaknesses of ODA, the general view is that it can be channelled more effectively to meet basic needs in poorer countries – programmes in which the commercial banking sector is less interested – while the concessional interest rates on that proportion of ODA taking the form of loans, together with the grants and other assistance, are more equitable. The effect is on the lines of a progressive income tax, involving some redistribution of resources from the rich to the poor on a global scale.

Three factors have combined, however, to make this issue somewhat secondary in the overall problem of the debt burden. First, the general world recession and slump in international trade have hit hardest the poorest and weakest. The result is that the economic growth which should have provided the resources for repayments has not occurred. Second, there are problems in the economic policies of many Third World countries, not least in relation to spending on armed forces. Third, and in the short term most important, the majority of debts are nominated in US dollars – some 76 per cent in 1983, compared to 65 per cent in 1974.[32] The much higher US interest rates in the 1980s compared to the previous decade and the consequent increase in the dollar's trading value have resulted in much larger real debt repayments. Moreover, this is felt in the near future – the phenomenon of so-called 'front-loading', disproportionate increases in near-term repayments compared to later ones.[33] The higher US interest rates are a result of the federal budget deficit and the need to attract loans in order to finance it; the deficit itself is in large part the result of the huge increase in US military spending since the end of the 1970s, combined with a refusal or failure to increase taxation in order to fund it.

In short, the particular intensity of the debt problem today is caused by a combination of the long-term, relative unavailability of other resources apart from loans, in combination with the global economic crisis, economic mismanagement, and militarism in both the underdeveloped and industrialized world.

It is normal practice for debts of Third World countries to be rescheduled, so that the lending banks can protect their investments. However, what is needed now is not only a more radical and generous rescheduling of the debts, but also a means of unhitching them from the ebb and flow of interest rates and the trading value of the US dollar. Doing that would effectively involve writing off part of the accumulated debts, but that is precisely what should be done. Otherwise, the underdeveloped countries will forever be trapped in the debt cycle, unable to release resources domestically for their own social and economic development, and with agriculture and industry constantly tilted towards exports, in a desperate effort to service their debts. At the same time, debt rescheduling today is often accompanied by terms demanding the imposition of austere economic policies. That practice must be ended. It is both inhumane – when belts are tightened, it is always the thinnest who suffer most – and inefficient, since it provides no way out of the debt cycle. Beyond these changes, a long-term solution to the debt problem also requires major changes in trade policies, which we discuss below.

Increased Aid

The assertion that the development problems of the Third World have worsened sharply in the 1980s will command general assent. To meet these problems, between 1980 and 1984, Official Development Assistance from OECD countries rose by just one billion dollars.[34] This represents a dramatic change: from 1970 to 1980, ODA from those countries rose fourfold; since then, it has risen four per cent. Britain is one of eight OECD countries to have reduced its ODA spending in that time, and one of five which spent a smaller proportion of national income in such a way in 1984 compared to 1980. As Table 1 shows, the declining proportion of national income spent on ODA is a British trend since 1965. The other OECD country showing a major proportional decline in ODA spending is the USA, which remains the biggest single donor of ODA. Compared to a United Nations target of 0.7 per cent of GNP to be spent on ODA, only five OECD countries meet or exceed it – twelve fall short of it (Table 2). Were the OECD countries all to meet that modest target, the result would be to double the total they spend on ODA. The Warsaw Pact countries appear to have an even worse record.[35]

The first priority for increased aid is to provide emergency food relief to those countries where malnutrition and famine are routine facts of existence. Accompanying this should be a major effort to meet other basic human needs, especially in the provision of adequate health care, sanitation and clean water supplies. Immediate increases in food and other basic aid need to be linked to long-term programmes in agriculture and the basic elements of the social infrastructure, to establish the basis for greater food self-sufficiency in the future and a generally higher level of health. Important components in all such programmes are educational and training projects, both to increase the number of skilled people able to contribute in these areas, and to broaden the general level of understanding about such fundamental issues as nutrition and health.

The second priority is to make available larger funds which are not tied to specific projects or investments, and which therefore provide the margins of flexibility which any economic or financial planning requires. It has long been a criticism of foreign aid and especially of foreign loans that they are normally tied to specific projects. This allows very uneven patterns of development to emerge within countries, distortions of allocation and distribution which could be corrected if relatively modest amounts of capital were available, not tied to other specific projects. This is not to argue that project loans and aid should be cut. It is not an either-or choice. Programme funding complements project funding and allows the latter to function more efficiently for the recipient country.

The third priority is in the field of the transfer of technology. In the 1950s and early 1960s, largely as a result of assuming the success of the 1940s' Marshall Plan aid in Western Europe could be repeated in very different economic and social circumstances, ODA concentrated on capital investment in industry and the attendant social infrastructure – roads, communications and so on. It was assumed that this would provide the motor for economic growth which would 'drag up' the rest of the country including the rural population. The failure of this model of development and aid led in much of the literature to a concentration on aid for meeting basic needs. The fact is, however, that again there is no either-or choice. While basic needs are being attended to, the manufacturing capacity of the Third World also needs to be built up both to provide exports and substitute for imports. However, experience suggests that the more ambitious the projects and the more sophisticated the technologies are, the more mixed the blessing is. Aid and investment in the poorer countries need to be at a level within their grasp, complemented by educational and training programmes, and aimed at providing reasonable degrees of self-sufficiency in those industrial and technological sectors. Experience also suggests that leaving the process to be directed by market forces alone will not work, and therefore that direct intervention by the state is required. In that way it may be possible to provide the benefits of modern technology without what has hitherto accompanied it: dependence on the foreign suppliers of technology and a bifurcated pattern of development.[36]

Trade

Changes in aid policies, even combined with the action on debt discussed above, cannot have their fullest effect without similar transformations in trade policy. For Third World countries, reduced exports and increased real debt are two sides of the same coin. Debt represents deferred trade.[37] If a given country is to pay off the real interest on its international debt, a real trade surplus is a *sine qua non*. Attempting to do this through reducing imports alone is inefficient and punitive, and ultimately holds no solution. But for exports from developing countries to increase, there must be a market for them in the industrialized world. Over the past decade, industrialized countries' trade policies as a whole have done serious damage to the economic interests of the Third World. The retreat into protectionism has hit them particularly seriously.

One avenue worth pursuing is the extension and expansion of trade preference schemes such as the EEC's Lomé Convention, currently applicable to 46 African, Caribbean and Pacific countries. Britain could take the lead in sharing 'invisible' trade earnings, especially from freight and insurance, with Third World countries. The London insurance market remains the world's largest, which gives British actions a particular role in this instance. It is also past time that the 1974 proposals on the Integrated commodities programme were implemented to provide much more stable markets for key commodities. The original proposals envisaged a package of eighteen – metals, fibres and foods – with agreements and financing to avoid wild price fluctuations, compensate countries which suffered poor harvests in particular years, and buy in buffer stocks when the market was glutted for release in later years. Despite the difficulties in such a programme, it may be a crucial element in permitting steady export growth in Third World countries.

Conflict Resolution

We live on an over-armed and constantly warring planet. The high incidence and ever-increasing destructiveness of modern warfare puts to shame any claims that we live in a civilized era. [38] Whether this record is viewed primarily as a sequence of human tragedies, as revealing potential flashpoints for World War III, or as a major obstacle to securing real improvement in the lot of the Third World, it is clear that the reduction of warfare and of conflict likely to lead to war is a major priority. In the long term the emphasis in this task must fall on both removing the sources of conflict, and on a determined programme of disarmament and demilitarization; we discuss this in the next section. In the short term, what is required is a strengthening of the international capacity to resolve and restrain conflicts, both to prevent them from turning into wars, and to terminate wars when they have begun.

The task is complicated not only by the intractability of many such conflicts, but also by a moral dilemma which lies at the heart of conflict resolution. A conflict which is resolved in the superficial sense that fighting is brought to an end but which leaves one side having to endure systematic oppression is not acceptable and is unlikely to endure. Thus although the avoidance of violence and death is always a vital goal, there are times when the would-be conflict-resolver must choose sides, when to do anything else would be to fail to address the causes of the conflict and to compromise and discredit the effort to resolve it.

South Africa is an obvious example where it is necessary to take sides and where the conflict cannot be resolved without radical structural change in the society and its political system. Continued resistance and non-cooperation by the black population will be necessary to achieve this, and encouraging them to adopt a supine attitude would be immoral, insulting and unrealistic. To expect the bulk of the white population to agree gracefully to surrender their privileges and hand over power is also unrealistic. However, in face of sustained black resistance and the consequences it is having at the internal and international level, a significant minority of whites are prepared to accept the need for majority rule and ending the apartheid system. The white business community in particular is worried about the repercussions of continued unrest on the South African economy, and, if only out of self-interest, is beginning to look for some way forward. There also exist small but courageous white groups and organizations who oppose apartheid on principle, such as the women's Black Sash movement, and the End Conscription Council. Nevertheless when all these factors and others are taken into account it is hard to be optimistic that bloodshed on a terrible scale will in fact be averted.

Clear issues of right and wrong are similarly involved in the cases of Afghanistan and Nicaragua. In the former, the USSR had no right to invade; in the latter, the USA has no right to attempt the overthrow of the Sandinista government by a variety of economic, political and indirect military means. In both cases, however, the task of conflict resolution is complicated by an additional problem – that of saving face. For the USSR to pull out of Afghanistan without leaving behind some arrangement favourable to its clients, or for at least the present US Administration to cease pressurizing the Sandinistas, would in either case amount to a total loss of face. Yet when the USA terminated its war in Vietnam, though it lost face, a fact bitterly resented by members and supporters of the current Administration, it was clear that its standing was plummeting under the weight of international condemnation of the war, and that it would have got worse. The problem of face is perhaps marginally less intractable in the US case – where a new Administration can disown the acts of its predecessor – than with the USSR. Yet it is probable that in both Central America and Afghanistan, resolution of the conflict requires finding a relatively dignified way out for the respective superpowers.

Britain, of course, has its own problem of face and its own Third World dispute to attend to before it can properly intervene in others: the Falklands/Malvinas issue. The replacement of military dictatorship by democratic government in Argentina has brought no concessions on the question of sovereignty by either side. Yet, in principle, the way towards a settlement is clearer here than in the three cases considered above. One possibility is to place the islands under United Nations authority, with treaty guarantees that the islanders' way of life will remain unchanged, or at least will change only under their own volition. A second possibility, with the same guarantee of the islanders' rights, would be to pool nominal sovereignty between Argentina and Britain. The constant repetition that it was the wishes and the interests of the islanders that were paramount – i.e. not the question of nominal sovereignty as such – might make such a compromise acceptable in Britain. The fact that the Islands would then have special status, and would no longer be a British colony, might make it acceptable also in Argentina.

In some cases much of what is involved in conflict resolution is the classic model of providing some degree of mediation between the parties to bring them to a negotiating table. Extending the process, so that mediation leads on to arbitration, seems unlikely to be acceptable to contending parties, though it might well be desirable from a global perspective. However, not all forms of conflict resolution need depend on that model. In some cases, the key may be to help create the circumstances in which the contending parties sort out a resolution themselves; to some extent, the Egypt-Israel conciliation was an example of this. Political pressure on one or both sides in a dispute can also be a contribution to ending it. Such was the case in the Vietnam war, for example.

This raises the difficult question of the extent to which diplomatic activity should be accompanied by potentially more effective means of pressure – primarily economic instruments such as sanctions and boycotts. The question is difficult because of the degree to which sanctions can be counter-productive. The issue of sanctions against South Africa stands out, not as a classic example and a model, but as an exception. Only a few states still resist the call for sanctions, and even they are being persuaded, however reluctantly, to join in. Moreover, it is the policy demanded by the organizations and spokespeople of the black majority, *pace* the arguments of Mrs Thatcher. However, when the USA sought economic and other sanctions against the

USSR over its invasion of Afghanistan and its treatment of Poland, the result was highly divisive. There simply was not an adequate level of consent to the US view – and, in the view of most Commission members, for good reasons. The call for sanctions against the USSR in 1980 was a part of the new 'get tough' policy, the new Cold War. It functioned in that context as part of the process which killed off détente, accelerated military build-up and destroyed the chances of ending the arms race and getting arms reductions. In other words, it cut across other important priorities in the relationship with the USSR. Primarily, and blatantly, it was an effort to gain political advantage over the USSR by isolating it – not an attempt to resolve conflict. Whether sanctions can resolve or restrict a particular conflict thus deserves the most serious and cautious consideration. In the case of South Africa, one can argue that, to the extent that sanctions may hasten the end of an abhorrent régime, and with wide agreement to apply them, they are a justified and potentially valuable means of possibly shortening what shows all the signs of being a protracted and bloody conflict. In other cases, even where the moral rights and wrongs are clear, there may be numerous reasons why sanctions will not be appropriate.

If a combination of efforts at mediation and political pressure appears to be the most fruitful approach to conflict resolution in the short term, it may be thought that the approach can actually bear little fruit. An observer looks at conflicts around the world and can be forgiven for despair. Yet in the midst of conflicts, their resolution never seems likely and rarely even possible. In the late 1960s and early 1970s, such a judgement would have been reasonable about the recurring Arab-Israeli wars. Whatever the criticisms which may be made about the Egypt-Israel peace agreement, it is worth recording that as an example of what can happen. Similarly, independence and majority rule in Zimbabwe were attained. Britain and China were able to resolve a potentially disastrous conflict over Hong Kong – not least because a British government for once showed it understood some of the realities of contemporary world politics. The USA was finally able to terminate its war in Vietnam, and also managed a major improvement in its relations with China – in the course of which a continuing dispute over Taiwan was simply relegated to a less important position. Even détente between the superpowers, though finally proving too fragile, is an example of how a deeply-rooted and highly dangerous conflict can be ameliorated.

Britain's Role

On each of these four decisive questions – debt, aid, trade and conflict – there is something that a British government could do. In part, as we indicated earlier, it can argue for a change of policies by many states to initiate immediate action. There are also actions it can undertake independently.

On the debt problem, persuasion has an extremely important function, aimed at governments, at multilateral agencies such as the World Bank and International Monetary Fund, and at private banks, starting in Britain. It can also ease the terms when rescheduling repayments of loans it has made itself.

Two changes can be made in aid policy. Firstly, the switch to tied aid programmes (often representing little more than a roundabout way of helping British industries) can be reversed. Secondly, despite the ailing economy, the government could increase Official Development Assistance. Raising the proportion of national income spent on ODA to the UN target of 0.7 per cent would slightly more than double the total. It is equivalent to reducing military spending by less than 10 per cent. Indeed, cuts in military spending could be a means of releasing resources for this as well as other uses. Despite the complexity of military technology, there are many alternative projects relevant to development needs available to military industrial capacity converting to other uses.[39] This relatively modest increase in ODA could be achieved, without needing any great miracles of planning or management, in two to three years. It would, if all other OECD countries' ODA remained the same, mean an increase in the OECD total ODA of just under 6 per cent. That is not a major increase by any means; it would leave most development problems untouched. But it is a greater increase than OECD members combined could manage in the first four years of this decade. A further increase of a similar size could be planned for the following four to five years.

One point of opting for such relatively modest and eminently manageable increases in ODA, rather than for a sudden and much larger surge in spending, is to create a steady flow. What is important is not just the volume of aid, but also its dependability. The Brandt Commission proposed 'automatic' mechanisms for financing aid, ones less subject to the vagaries of domestic politics in the donor countries. Over time, it argued, they could be transformed into something akin to a progressive international tax system, with countries enjoying higher national incomes *per capita* providing proportionately more aid.[40] This would provide a much needed solidity to aid funding. In the long term, it is well worth adopting it. In the short term governments can move in that direction independently. Such steps would be endangered by starting with spectacular increases which, while satisfying the appetite for dramatic gestures to help the world's poor, would raise expectations too high and could not be sustained.

On trade, Britain can act independently to accept greater sharing in 'invisibles', can use its influence in the EEC alongside other member states to extend and expand trade preference agreements, and can seek in UNCTAD and other appropriate fora to develop support for long-term commodity agreements, including generating the finance necessary for compensatory schemes and for the purchase of surpluses.

A British government could also play a particular part in resolving three of the world's conflicts and disputes. The first is the Falklands/Malvinas dispute. It is in Britain's interest to end this essentially pointless dispute. We have suggested two possible tracks for policy to follow in seeking a resolution with Argentina. The second is South Africa, where British efforts are best channelled through the Commonwealth. The first step is to stop being obstructive – the second to persuade the USA to do likewise. The third step is to take as much advantage as possible of Britain's shameful history of links with, and investment in, South Africa to persuade the government there of the inevitability of democratic, liberating change. It is possible that, in concert with other countries, a scaling down of diplomatic relations, say to *chargé d'affaires* level, could exert important political pressure on the white government. Britain should also open discussions with the African National Congress. White South Africa's *laager* mentality offers little hope for peaceful change, but it is an effort which must be made.

The third conflict – or set of conflicts – where Britain could help in the resolution is in Central America where Britain retains a military presence in Belize. This presence remains necessary and helpful to protect Belize's independence against the territorial claims of Guatemala, but Britain's efforts should be focused on securing a negotiated solution so that its forces can be withdrawn or be replaced by a regional or UN peacekeeping force. Britain's presence in the area for the time being offers a possibility – for a dealigning Britain, not for an enthusiastic exponent of alignment – to assist in the efforts of other states in the region to seek peace, and perhaps to provide some form of mediation between Nicaragua and the USA. The main emphasis, however, must be on persuading the USA to drop its hostile policy towards Nicaragua. As we argue later in more detail, British aid to Nicaragua would also be a positive contribution to regional security and stability.

There are also other conflicts – such as the Middle East – in which a British role channelled through the EEC can have a positive effect, and some – such as in South-east Asia – where merely ending the practice of obedience to US policy would be helpful. Additionally, as discussed in Chapter Seven, Britain's temporary ownership of islands such as Ascension Island and Diego Garcia may provide the UK with the leverage to make a significant impact on the superpower military presence in the Third World.

7. Long-Term Policies

Short-term action on the questions of debt, aid, trade and conflict should lay the basis for a longer-term approach to the problems of the Third World and global insecurity. This, of course, is wholly dependent on concerted action by the OECD countries, the non-market economies and the wealthier of the Third World countries.[41] Thus, British action in this context begins as a matter of diplomacy and persuasion. The considerations sketched out in this section are guidelines for the direction of that action.

The most important long-term aim is to reduce the enormous discrepancies of wealth between industrialized and underdeveloped countries. Increased aid, beyond meeting immediate disasters of famine and improving the basic conditions of life, must be directed at strengthening Third World economies. Much will depend on how world industry and trade as a whole recover from the current long-lasting crisis.

If the historical experience of long economic cycles is to be repeated, a general recovery in the next decade could be expected.[42] If other aspects of historical experience are also repeated, one effect of this will be a more efficient exploitation of the people and resources of the Third World. In that process, it is to be expected that some countries and some social groups will benefit, while others are left out of the general recovery, perhaps to slump deeper in poverty and misery.

It is, of course, possible that recovery could be hastened by the co-ordination of economic policies favouring expansion and growth. Current signs, however, are that things will get worse before they get better. The massive US budget deficit is stacking up severe problems, not only for the US domestic economy, but for the world economy in general. In Britain's particular case, the expected fall in North Sea oil revenues, combined with the decline in manufacturing output, will create great difficulties for pulling out of the current recession. But let us suppose that recovery develops sooner than the mid-1990s. The key question then is how the recovery will be managed so as to permit the poorer countries to share – and to share disproportionately – in the general increase in wealth and prosperity.

However well aid is utilized in underdeveloped countries, any improvement in their positions depends not only on domestic policy and politics but also on how the world economy functions. Specifically, except perhaps in the few cases where a more or less autarkic development path is followed, trading policies will have a major impact. If industrialized countries proceed along the road of protectionism and trading blocs on which they started in the 1970s, the result will be to freeze out manufacturers from other countries, especially the underdeveloped. One aim should be to make Third World economies less dependent on single or limited export markets for their earnings of foreign currency and less dependent on imports for manufactures; the number of countries able to adopt the autarkic development models of Albania, North Korea and China will probably be very small. The vast majority of Third World countries will need to operate within the world trading and financial system. They will need markets for a variety of manufactured goods as well as food and other natural resources.

For all the reasons advanced earlier in this chapter, it is necessary for global peace and security no less than for economic prosperity that such markets are available. This reflects primarily on the trading policies of industrialized countries, including the non-market economies, but also on technological and industrial policy. From the commercially most successful countries, it requires a degree of restraint – of not seizing every opportunity of national economic and commercial advantage at the expense of all-comers. It is comparable to the pressure exerted on Japan to reduce its balance of payments surplus in the interests of other industrialized countries. Hard as it has been to enforce in practice, the argument has been accepted in principle, because Japan's own success requires buoyant domestic economies in the rest of the industrialized world. A similar principle applies in the case of Third World economies, strengthened by the demands both of humanity and security.

Militarism

We have considered how global militarism, poverty and general insecurity form a vicious circle. Beyond short-term conflict management and resolution, and combined with a major effort to reduce the major economic imbalances, the obvious need is for a programme of disarmament, demilitarization and prevention of conflicts. Rather reluctantly, we would warn against approaching this goal *via* ambitious schemes for general and complete disarmament, or indeed *via* further proposals for restricting the arms trade at source, which seem unlikely to have any leverage in the world as it is. It is necessary to disaggregate the overall goal and, in a sense, approach it indirectly. We suggest four headings for such a process.

337

i Regional Security: – Some of the causes of conflict and the general atmosphere of insecurity could be addressed by regional security agreements – essentially, treaties of non-aggression, combined with the 'Confidence Building Measures' pioneered in the Conference on Security and Cooperation in Europe and its 1975 Final Act. Despite all the problems which have attended the Final Act, especially the human rights' clauses and their non-fulfilment by the Warsaw Pact countries, the Confidence Building Measures – notification of manoeuvres and such-like – have worked reasonably well. They can be extended to provide fuller information about military deployments and equipment. They express a concerted willingness to avoid conflict, and as such have the capacity to lead to further measures on the same basis. Such security agreements should, wherever possible, be multilateral rather than bilateral, expressing the regional interest in the avoidance of conflict, guarding against the possibility of one party wishing to protect one front diplomatically so as to be free to open military operations on another, and isolating countries which will not participate in the process. A major part of this process could be the development of the concepts of Nuclear-Free Zones and Zones of Peace, ideas which have already received wide international endorsement.

ii Internationalizing Disputes: – Despite the UN machinery, disputes between states are not effectively dealt with at the international level. A new approach to this problem could involve standing consultation to consider in turn all territorial and irredentist claims. Through either the UN or mechanisms established by regional security agreements, the aim must be to strengthen the role of international consultation and mediation in all inter-state disputes in which armed force is involved or likely to be, and perhaps also to strengthen the role of UN peacekeeping forces.

iii Non-intervention: – A means of outlawing military intervention by one state into the affairs and territory of another, or into a dispute involving two other states, is desperately needed. Drafting such a treaty would be a difficult and complex business. Obviously, the primary aim is restraining armed intervention by the superpowers and a handful of other states capable of projecting military force over great distances. One way of achieving this might be for the superpowers themselves to agree to something akin to a code of conduct which would rule out such operations. But that might have too much the flavour of a superpower condominium. Accordingly, the development of a multilateral treaty would be preferable. This would have to permit an attacked state to call on assistance – though it would be best if assistance were multinational. However, it is not clear that the right of a state to call on military assistance in a civil war should be protected, since such invitations can be bogus, whipped up by the assisting state, and in any case simply result in raising the degree of violence and bloodshed. Such a treaty would usefully address not only the direct intervention of combat forces, but intervention in the form of supplies and advisers.

iv Disarmament and Demilitarization: – The overwhelming proportion of global military spending is done by the industrialized countries, and primarily by the members of NATO and the Warsaw Pact. In the final analysis, it is their confrontation which ensures the continuation of deep insecurity, and it is the maintenance of their military industries which underlies the expansion of the arms trade since the 1960s. It is among them that the process of disarmament must begin. In this brief discussion, we cannot go over the many proposals for both unilateral and multilateral measures of disarmament which need to be taken up. Four items, however, are of major importance for the Third World.

a) Non-proliferation: Article VI of the Non-Proliferation Treaty promised negotiations in good faith to end the arms race and bring about nuclear disarmament. It is a key part of the Treaty's central bargain between the nuclear 'haves' and 'have-nots'. It has been entirely flouted. If Britain were to abandon nuclear weapons, if the superpowers were to reduce theirs, if Europe were to become nuclear-free and if a Comprehensive Test Ban were at last to be agreed, this progress towards fulfilling Article VI would make possible far stronger measures to prevent the proliferation of nuclear weapons to other states.

b) Europe: Winding down the confrontation in Europe by removing nuclear weapons would help improve the world's general security situation. If defensive military measures of the kind proposed by the Commission were to be adopted, a consequence could also be measures of conventional disarmament. To the extent that the reduction in armed forces was accompanied by a redirection of parts of military industry to other uses (whether development-related or not), one further consequence would be to reduce the pressure for arms exports by the major producers. This would do more to restrain the world arms trade than any other single measure.

c) Foreign Military Bases Alongside this de-escalation of the central military and political confrontation, and related to both the regional security agreements on non-intervention mechanisms proposed above, it might be possible to begin to reduce the overseas military presence of the superpowers, and Britain and France. This would reflect the demise of the view that the Third World is a legitimate stomping ground for great power interests, and be a necessary part of a general demilitarization. Whether effected by treaty, bilateral understandings or unilateral action, the overall result would be to reduce the ambient insecurity of Third World regions and acknowledge their autonomy.

d) With progress being made on these fronts, it would also be possible to agree international restraints on the arms trade. The NPT ban on the transfer of nuclear weapons could serve as a model for a treaty to ban the export of offensive conventional weapons such as strike aircraft, and major warships, especially assault ships and aircraft carriers. (Chemical weapons would also be included on the prohibited list if efforts to achieve agreement completely outlawing the manufacture, deployment, transfer or use of such weapons had not been achieved.) The treaty governing arms transfers could be monitored by an international authority and report directly to the UN Security Council. At the same time private arms dealers could be denied export licences.

Taken together, these measures add up to a major change in the shape of world politics. Some of the steps are relatively modest, others extremely ambitious. Only once before in world history has even one state managed a comparable transformation – Japan, where the technology of guns having arrived with the first Europeans in 1543, it was gradually but effectively abandoned through the 17th century. This absence of firearms lasted until the first Americans arrived in the middle of the 19th century.[43] Yet precisely such a transformation must be achieved over the long term if the combined problems of militarism and underdevelopment are not to explode in humanity's face at some point in the not-too-distant future.

8. THE UNITED NATIONS AND OTHER INTERNATIONAL BODIES

The world's states, or some of them, are often referred to as 'the international community'. At one level, this is a rhetorical device and has its uses as such; at another, it expresses an ideal which is far from being fully realized. Yet there is, thanks primarily to the existence of the United Nations, a certain amount of reality in that phrase. The UN functions as a permanent forum where it is at least possible to raise major issues and discuss them – even if the level of discussion often leaves much to be desired. Through the Security Council it is able to conduct debates on immediate issues which can set a framework for international efforts on the problem in question. With its specialized agencies it does much of immediate practical effect, especially in the field of development. The potential of the UN peacekeeping Forces has not been fully utilized, nor have they always functioned effectively – especially in the Middle East in the Sinai and Lebanon – but they have often played a useful role in, for example, Cyprus and the Congo. Overall, if the term 'the international community' ever has any real meaning, it is at the UN. The steady accumulation of condemnation and pressure against South Africa is one instance of 'the international community' in action (frustratingly slow as it has been) and much of that has been accomplished through the UN.

As an international body, however, the UN is incapable of

rising above the limitations of the collectivity of states represented there – nor could it be expected to be otherwise. It is capable of expressing both the best and the worst of the world system. It can be a sounding board for confrontation or cooperation, a forum for empty bickering or for identifying and enunciating solutions to major problems. In short, in a world system based on a multiplicity of independent political entities, the UN's output is as good or as bad as its input. Neither an off-hand dismissal of its importance, such as became fashionable on the American Right during the 1970s, nor an idealistic view that it can rise above the problems of the world that it represents is tenable.

Any efforts by the British and other governments to develop an adequate body of support for action on both short- and long-term goals for development will necessarily use the UN to some degree. Some proposals will require the involvement of one or another of its specialized agencies – for example, as a channel for aid – with the approval of the General Assembly. Other proposals may be best explored within a UN Committee, or even require the establishment of new committees or agencies. Certainly, if we wish to listen to the needs of the Third World, the UN and associated bodies are among the best places to do so.

However, some aspects of the policies we have outlined above will also require action and involvement by other international bodies. In the context of debt and aid, the International Monetary Fund and the World Bank cannot be ignored – neither as problem or as solution. As a member of the European Community, Britain has a role there in developing both an EC foreign policy and a new approach to development problems, especially on trade. The Commonwealth provides another forum for action, as on South Africa, and for listening and working out joint policies. In addition, much of the work of persuasion and pressure which is so important will be done through the OECD and the meetings of government leaders of the seven richest industrialized countries, and through bilateral diplomatic contacts, at summit, ministerial and other official levels.

In short, if the term 'the international community' overstates by a long way the real sense of community among the states of the world, it nevertheless expresses the reality that there is no shortage of international bodies within and through which a programme of development and demilitarization can be generated. A British government taking a new policy towards the Third World will work through all of them, as appropriate and as opportunity presents itself.

9. DEALIGNMENT

Finally it is worth returning to the problem of the Cold War which both obstructs cooperative efforts to meet the problems of underdevelopment, and presents a major threat to global security. Alongside the other goals and priorities we have outlined, British policy must be directed at resisting the growing polarization of international politics. Wherever a state is attempting to break out of alignment with one superpower or the other into the currently highly restricted space of non-alignment, Britain can be supporting it.

Two current examples show how this policy would work. Nicaragua in the first two or three years of this decade could be regarded as a genuinely non-aligned state, the views of the Reagan Administration notwithstanding. As US pressure on Nicaragua has increased, however, and as the war has taken its toll, thanks to US funding of the Contra supporters of the ex-dictator of Nicaragua, the Sandinista government has been effectively forced to turn more and more to the USSR for both political support and economic aid. As a result, it would now be difficult to assert so confidently that Nicaragua remains non-aligned. US pressure has worked to the detriment of conditions in Nicaragua and as a self-fulfilling prophecy. Yet because of the USSR's record on aid, and assuming a degree of pragmatism on the part of the Sandinistas which has not so far been lacking, it is possible that they would prefer to receive aid from other OECD countries. British aid to Nicaragua would thus fulfil both a humanitarian and a political purpose. It would help ameliorate human suffering and it would resist the stifling grip of the Cold War. It might perhaps help ward off the tendency of the Sandinista government to discard basic human rights in the name of the wartime emergency.

In quite different conditions, the government of New Zealand has taken a stand against the intrusion of nuclear arms. This has led not only to the dramatic French crime of destroying the Greenpeace vessel, *Rainbow Warrior*, in a New Zealand harbour, but also to intense political pressure from the USA and the threat of economic retaliation for having the presumption to ban US ships carrying nuclear weapons. Against that bullying, the British reaction should be unconditional support for New Zealand's sovereign right to adopt a nuclear-free policy. This could include not only political but also economic support – not aid in this case, but a readiness by Britain to give preferential treatment to New Zealand's exports and, if other members can be persuaded, by the rest of the European Community as well.

In both these cases and others, the keynote of dealignment is an active policy aimed at increasing the practical possibility for states to opt to align themselves with neither the USA nor the USSR. In this way, the space for non-alignment in world politics can be increased, the grip of the US-Soviet confrontation weakened, and one of the most important obstacles to change gradually removed.

Table 1: *Official Development Assistance*
OECD Countries Increases/Cuts in Aid 1965–84 as proportion of GNP

Increase		Cuts	
Norway	(0.16–0.99%)	Belgium	(0.60–0.59%)
Denmark	(0.13–0.85%)	Australia	(0.53–0.45%)
Netherlands	(0.36–1.02%)	UK	(0.47–0.33%)
Sweden	(0.19–0.80%)	USA	(0.58–0.23%)
Finland	(0.02–0.36%)		
Canada	(0.19–0.47%)		
Italy	(0.10–0.32%)		
Switzerland	(0.09–0.30%)		
Austria	(0.11–0.28%)		
Japan	(0.27–0.35%)		
FRG	(0.40–0.45%)		
New Zealand	(0.23–0.28%)		
France	(0.76–0.77%)		

Source for both tables:
World Development Report 1985 (Oxford University Press, 1985) Annex, Table 18.

Table 2: *Official Development Assistance*
OECD Donors in Rank Order, 1984

i) *Measured in $million*[a]		ii) *Measured as % of GNP*	
1 USA	8,698	1 Netherlands	1.02
2 Japan	4,319	2 Norway	0.99
3 France	3,790	3 Denmark	0.85
4 FRG	2,767	4 Sweden	0.80
5 Canada	1,535	5 France	0.77
6 UK	1,432	6 Belgium	0.59
7 Netherlands	1,268	7 Canada	0.47
8 Italy	1,105	8 Australia	0.45
9 Australia	773	and FRG	0.45
10 Sweden	737	10 Finland	0.36
11 Norway	526	11 Japan	0.35
12 Denmark	449	12 UK	0.33
13 Belgium	410	13 Italy	0.32
14 Switzerland	286	14 Switzerland	0.30
15 Austria	181	15 Austria	0.28
16 Finland	178	and New Zealand	0.28
17 New Zealand	59	17 USA	0.23

TOTAL $28,513,000,000   Proportion of combined OECD GNP given in ODA = 0.36%

Note:
[a] 1980 dollars

Conclusions

This report has two main themes. Forty years after World War II, Western Europe has reached a historic juncture in its relationship with the United States, and has to make crucial decisions about future relations with the Soviet Union and Eastern Europe and its role in relation to the Third World. We have analysed the historical background leading to this critical point in defence and foreign policy, and indicated the directions we believe Western Europe, and Britain in particular, should follow. In addition our aim has been to examine detailed and credible policies which could be pursued by a future non-nuclear British government committed to unilateral action, non-provocative defence and to reversing the nuclear arms race.

These conclusions recapitulate the central features of the foreign and defence policy we advocate, and focus on recommendations which we consider of particular importance, or which help to define the thrust of these proposals.

1. General Approach: Promoting Dealignment

Throughout the world, people live under the shadow of a possible nuclear war. Many in addition suffer political oppression, extreme poverty or the devastation of conventional wars. The nuclear confrontation between the USA and USSR is the prime danger, but in addition the superpowers play a pivotal role in upholding repressive régimes, instigating or escalating local wars and in intensifying the problems of world poverty. We do not argue that the role played by the USA and the USSR is identical – there are important differences in the impact of each on Europe and on the Third World. We also recognize that there are numerous causes of war, oppression and poverty and that

346

superpower direct or indirect involvement in a conflict may occasionally be intended to alleviate these problems. Nevertheless we argue that it is essential the USA and USSR reduce their nuclear arsenals, scale down the military confrontation in Europe and abstain in almost all circumstances from military intervention in other parts of the world. In the long run the goal is an end to the system of military blocs and of superpower political or economic control over other countries. But this goal can only be achieved in stages, which might include the creation of nuclear-free zones and an active policy of détente. We have used the term *disengagement* to denote the process of reducing military confrontation between the two superpowers (and between the rival military blocs), and the term *dealignment* to denote the assertion of greater independence in foreign and military policy by the non-superpower members of military alliances.

There is little immediate prospect of the USA and USSR making substantial progress in nuclear disarmament or adopting a more limited military and political role – though there is a constituency in the USA which would support these measures and some evidence the new Soviet leadership might welcome a reduction in its military commitments. We believe Western Europe is especially well placed to begin a process of arms limitation, military disengagement, and dealignment at the European level, and the peace movements active since 1980 have been pressing for moves in this direction. The former colonial powers of Western Europe also have a special responsibility to adopt a new approach to the Third World.

In this context a non-nuclear Britain could play a decisive role, by abandoning its own nostalgia for great power status, restructuring its own defence and foreign policy, and using its diplomatic leverage in Europe.

2. SPECIFIC ASPECTS OF POLICY

British Nuclear Disarmament

A British government committed to nuclear disarmament would immediately decommission Polaris and begin the process of withdrawing and dismantling all classes of nuclear weapons in service with its forces. This should be accompanied by a major diplomatic and publicity effort to explain to international opinion and to the governments most immediately affected the moral, political and strategic reasons for Britain's decision and its relevance to non-proliferation, nuclear arms control, and the development of a defensive strategy. The anti-nuclear government should use every public occasion to promote an understanding of its decision, including the Queen's Speech, its first Defence White Paper, and meetings of the UN General Assembly. Radio and television, including overseas radio broadcasts, should clearly also be used to the full. In addition to these official efforts, non-governmental bodies such as peace groups, and sympathetic trade union, professional, religious and other organizations should be encouraged to contact their associates and colleagues in other countries and to send delegations abroad to explain why they support the British government's decision.

Diplomacy at both the official and 'grass roots' level could be especially important in the case of the USA since Britain would be requiring the removal of US nuclear weapons and bases from its territory. Whether or not the USA would be required to remove other non-nuclear military facilities would largely depend on Britain's decision about continued membership of NATO.

What Britain Can Do to Promote Disarmament

It is sometimes argued that British nuclear disarmament would have no impact on the wider world. The Commission rejects this view.

Britain's greatest influence is likely to be at the European level. By confronting Western Europe with the challenge of its own decision to get rid of nuclear weapons and secure the removal of US nuclear bases, and to remain in NATO on a strictly conditional basis, it could stimulate radical changes in NATO policy. We argue that the Soviet Union has an interest in responding positively to disarmament initiatives and changes in NATO strategy, if only to prevent a backlash against non-nuclear policies in Western Europe. Britain's actions, therefore, could set in train a series of initiatives and responses that could profoundly affect the arms race in Europe – a crucial area of East-West military confrontation. The medium term objective would be to secure the elimination of nuclear weapons from

Europe and encourage both sides to move to a genuinely defensive system. If this process can be got under way major reductions in conventional forces would come within reach. We suggest that initiatives of this kind are much more likely to result in conventional force reductions than the MBFR negotiations at Vienna which began in 1973 and show no sign of significant progress.

Verification has been an important stumbling block in past negotiations. British nuclear disarmament under international inspection could provide invaluable evidence of the problems and possibilities involved. We have analysed the potential problems of effecting British nuclear disarmament and argued that verification problems can be tackled and overcome.

A nuclear disarmed Britain could help to strengthen safeguards against nuclear proliferation. Its action in rejecting nuclear weapons would do something to remove the sense of grievance felt by non-nuclear states at the failure of the USA, USSR and Britain to live up to their obligations under Article VI of the Non-Proliferation Treaty which enjoins them to make serious efforts to achieve nuclear disarmament. It would also be politically well placed to press the two superpowers to accept their responsibility under this article. It might be able to exert influence through the Commonwealth to persuade India and Pakistan, and possibly other non-signatories, to accede to the Treaty. It could use its considerable expertise in the nuclear field to strengthen the inspection system of the International Atomic Energy Agency (IAEA) – for instance by helping to improve and refine the technology used for inspection, and by assisting in the training of the inspectorate.

We recommend that a permanent IAEA inspectorate should be developed with help from Britain and other countries experienced in the nuclear field. We also recommend the creation of an international body under the UN committed to developing all non-nuclear forms of energy, partly because of the dangers associated with nuclear power so dramatically and tragically exemplified by the Chernobyl disaster in the Soviet Union in April-May 1986, partly because, if reliance on nuclear power is reduced, there will be fewer opportunities for fissile material to be diverted from civilian to military use.

In the field of chemical and biological weapons, Britain has played a positive role in the past. In the mid 1950s it took an important unilateral initiative in dismantling its stocks of nerve gas and other poisonous gases. It can also claim considerable credit for President Nixon's unilateral renunciation of biological weapons in 1969 and for the subsequent 1972 Biological Weapons Convention.

Now, however, there is a danger that Britain may abandon its commitment to chemical disarmament, both by developing new stockpiles of such weapons and by allowing the deployment of US binary nerve gas weapons in this country. Mrs Thatcher's government publicly endorsed the new US binary programme on 29 April 1986 on the grounds that it would stimulate an agreement to ban all chemical weapons and on 22 May 1986 the NATO Defence Planning Committee accepted US nerve gas modernization as a 'force goal'.

We recommend that a future British government should vigorously oppose any reliance on chemical weapons. It should press NATO to reverse its endorsement of the US chemical weapons programme. It should refuse to participate in any chemical weapons programme or to stockpile US weapons, and should strengthen Britain's present commitment by withdrawing that part of the UK reservation attached to its ratification of the 1925 Geneva Protocol which maintained the right of retaliation in kind. It should demand the renunciation of strategies, such as the US Army's Airland Battle, that envisage the use of chemical weapons. It should support West German SPD moves to achieve a chemical weapon-free zone embracing both German states and possibly some other East European countries. And it should continue its diplomatic efforts at Geneva for a global treaty on chemical weapons.

Britain could play an important role in promoting a Comprehensive Test Ban. Since it would no longer have a vested interest in opposing a ban in order to test its own weapons it would be well placed to increase pressure on the USA and USSR to enter into negotiations. And Britain's knowledge of the technical issues involved in verification would mean that it was well placed to expose fallacious arguments against a ban.

Britain's temporary control of islands in the Indian and Pacific Oceans, and of Ascension Island and the Falklands/Malvinas in the Atlantic, give it some leverage for naval and other forms of arms control in these areas. In the South Pacific it should use its influence to support and extend the nuclear-weapon-free zones that have been agreed by nations in the region.

On Ascension Island, where Britain leases land to the USA for military bases, it should tighten controls to ensure that these are not used for exercises or military operations with nuclear weapons, and should establish an effective British right of veto over operations from them. In the Falklands/Malvinas Britain should seek agreement with Argentina over the future of the islands. One possibility would be to place them under UN authority with a treaty guaranteeing the islanders' way of life; another would be joint UK/Argentine sovereignty. Moving away from a 'Fortress Falklands' policy, coupled with a clear British rejection of nuclear weapons, could substantially reduce tension within the area and strengthen the treaty of Tlatelolco which established South America as a nuclear-weapon-free zone. Britain should also support the efforts to turn the South Atlantic into a 'zone of peace'. Here the aim is to prevent the establishment of US or Soviet military bases in the South Atlantic, to stop any naval arms races amongst the littoral states, and to establish the principles of non-use of force and regional cooperation.

In the Indian Ocean, Britain has allowed the USA rights to maintain military bases at Diego Garcia until 2016 A.D. Here Britain should explore the possibility of an agreement under which US rights in Diego Garcia would be abandoned or restricted in exchange for similar restrictions on Soviet bases around the Horn of Africa. In any case Britain should not allow Diego Garcia to be used as a base for the US Rapid Deployment Force, or for nuclear forces. It should also offer adequate compensation to the islanders who were removed when the US base was established, and make provision for those who wish to return to do so.

Britain's efforts to restrict or eliminate military bases in the islands it controls should be part of a consistent effort to reduce and finally eliminate the overseas military presence of the superpowers, or former colonial powers.

At the domestic administrative level, we repeat the suggestion made in our first report for the establishment of a Ministry of Disarmament. Such a Ministry could disburse research funds to universities, and should have the responsibility for assessing the arms control impact of proposed military developments. Its assessments could be submitted annually to Parliament alongside the Defence White Paper. In addition we recommend the establishment of a Parliamentary Select Committee to examine disarmament issues.

European Nuclear Disarmament and Superpower Negotiations

It is clear that neither superpower in the foreseeable future will abandon its reliance on nuclear weapons unconditionally. However one, or both, of them might accept a doctrine of minimum deterrence. This does not represent either a morally acceptable or strategically stable basis for long-term security, but could open up the possibility of a breakthrough in controlling the strategic nuclear arms race.

Even if only one side adopted a strategy of minimum deterrence, this would reduce the impetus of the arms race. The superpower concerned would no longer be under pressure to research and develop counterforce weapons, but could concentrate entirely on ensuring the survivability of a second-strike force. It would not be in its interest to attempt to develop space-based or any other ABM systems aimed at making the country invulnerable to attack.

Since numerical considerations . cease to be decisive once minimum deterrence is adopted, the superpower concerned would be in a position to table proposals that allowed a degree of numerical advantage to the other side. This could help to build confidence and shift the emphasis in negotiations away from the sterile pursuit of equivalence.

One major obstacle on the Western side to the acceptance of a minimum deterrence strategy has been that it would be difficult for the USA to implement it and at the same time provide a credible nuclear guarantee to Western Europe. A decision by European NATO states to reject any reliance on nuclear weapons and to decouple from the US strategic deterrent would remove this obstacle.

Britain and the Third World

As a former colonial power, and member of the Commonwealth, Britain retains close trading, political and cultural links with many Third World countries. It should use the influence it has to oppose interventionism by the superpowers or others in the Third World. It should support efforts to strengthen the mediating and peacekeeping role of the UN and in some instances it may itself be able to play a mediating role, either on its own or through bodies like the EEC or the Commonwealth. It should seek to clarify and strengthen international law as a means of checking interventionism. It would of course refuse to be party to acts of aggressive intervention such as occurred when Mrs Thatcher's government in April 1986 agreed to the use of British bases for US F-111 bombers to attack Libya.

Britain should also seek international restraints on the arms trade using the Non Proliferation Treaty (NPT) as a model. Thus the NPT ban on the transfer of nuclear weapons could be used as a model for a treaty banning the export of especially inhumane weapons such as fragmentation bombs and shells, and clearly offensive systems such as strike aircraft or major warships. We recommend that Britain should work to bring about an international agreement of this kind. The ban would, of course, apply to arms transfers between all states, not simply to those between highly industrialized countries and the Third World. We propose that an international authority should be set up to monitor the ban and report directly to the UN Security Council.

Britain could do much to change the tenor of the discussion of Third World issues by acknowledging the particular responsibility of the Western industrial powers for the phenomenon of Third World underdevelopment. We recommend raising the proportion of national income in Britain devoted to Official Development Assistance to 0.7 per cent in line with the target proposed by the UN. This would slightly more than double the present total. It is equivalent to reducing military spending by less than 10 per cent.

Changes in trade policy by the industrialized West could be even more significant. Britain could promote the extension and expansion of trade preference schemes such as the European Community's Lomé Convention. It could resurrect the proposals for an Integrated Commodities Programme aimed at providing stable markets for key commodities. It could take the lead in sharing 'invisible' earnings from freight and insurance with Third World countries.

Britain should support a generous rescheduling of debts and a means of unhitching them from the changes in interest rates and the trading value of the US dollar. It should also oppose the practice of demanding the imposition of austere economic policies when debts are rescheduled.

Promoting a non-nuclear Europe
a) *As a member of NATO* – At the European level Britain could pursue one of two major approaches. It could remain within NATO in order to change it from within; or it could withdraw from the Alliance and adopt a non-aligned stance along Swedish or Swiss lines, working with other neutral and non-aligned states to change the military and political situation in Europe.

As its first report indicated, the Commission did not reach unanimity on this issue. The majority, however, support the view that a non-nuclear Britain should remain in NATO on the strict condition that the Alliance moves to a non-nuclear strategy within a limited time period. If NATO proved unwilling to denuclearize its strategy, Britain would withdraw.

The reasons for wanting to remain in NATO, albeit conditionally, have to do with consideration of Britain's security, its sense of obligation to other countries in the region and the fear that withdrawal could lead to a more dangerous and unstable situation arising in Europe. Still more important, however, is the conviction that Britain within NATO would be better placed to promote denuclearization and dealignment in Europe, and that this would have a much greater impact on the nuclear and conventional arms race than nuclear disarmament by Britain alone.

The steps in the process of NATO denuclearization were set out in *Defence Without the Bomb* and are recapitulated in the Introduction to this report. They are the adoption by NATO of a no-first-use of nuclear weapons policy; the removal of 'battlefield' and 'theatre' nuclear weapons, including Pershing II and cruise missiles; and, over a somewhat longer time span, the formal 'decoupling' of European defence from the US nuclear

354

deterrent and the progressive adoption of a strategy of 'defensive deterrence'.

This programme in its essentials is retained in this report. But we examine in greater depth the process involved in denuclearizing NATO strategy, including the potential role of unilateral initiatives. In particular we draw attention to the important links between denuclearization and changes in conventional strategy. Much of the impact of NATO denuclearization, for instance, would be lost if it continued to maintain the shift towards offensive conventional strategies, exemplified by the Follow On Force Attack (FOFA) doctrine adopted by NATO in December 1984. By the same token, one of the most significant and reassuring responses that the Soviet Union could make to measures of nuclear disarmament by NATO would be to move away from its present offensive conventional strategy on the Central Front. We reject the notion of making NATO denuclearization *conditional* upon any particular Soviet response. But we do advocate that NATO should actively seek Soviet reciprocation including not only the removal of nuclear weapons from Eastern Europe but the modification of its conventional strategy.

We also analyse the political prospects for European NATO states supporting a non-nuclear strategy. Without minimizing the obstacles, we point to the degree of political support in Europe for at least a significant shift away from NATO's present degree of reliance on nuclear weapons. In due course, especially if steps towards denuclearization led to significant Soviet reciprocation and an improvement in East-West relations in Europe, NATO might be emboldened to reject altogether any reliance on nuclear weapons. And if European NATO states were to act as a bloc in this way to promote denuclearization, a significant section of US opinion might be won over.

We put forward some more specific suggestions and refinements to the proposed denuclearizing programme. Thus we propose that NATO should take the initiative of establishing a nuclear-weapon-free corridor of at least 100-150 km width at an early stage in the process and establish a system of inspection to show that it had been achieved. The Soviet Union would be pressed not only to declare the existence of a denuclearized zone of the same width on the Warsaw Pact side but to accept verification in its turn. If it did so, the next stage would be to draw up a treaty formalizing the existence of the zone on both sides.

We also propose a complementary NATO initiative to establish a military disengagement zone in central Europe from which all major offensive weapons would be excluded. Again the process would be one of unilateral initiative, sustained attempts to achieve Warsaw Pact reciprocation, the establishment of verification, and finally the signing of a formal, binding treaty.

We suggest that a NATO review conference should be scheduled some seven years after the election of an anti-nuclear government in Britain to finalize the decoupling agreement and to arrange for the removal of any remaining nuclear systems from Europe.

The conditions and timetable, then, which we recommend a future non-nuclear British government should set if it is to remain in NATO can be briefly summarized as follows:

- the adoption of a no-first-use policy (within two years)
- the removal of all Pershing II missiles and Ground Launched Cruise Missiles from Europe (within two years)
- the establishment of a nuclear-weapon-free zone at least 100 km wide in the FRG along the East-West German border, with adequate international verification procedures to reassure outside observers that NATO had removed nuclear weapons from the zone (within three years)
- agreement to hold a NATO review conference about seven or eight years after the election of the British anti-nuclear government to review fundamentally all aspects of NATO policy
- the withdrawal of most US battlefield nuclear weapons from Europe within about four years, with the remainder being removed by the time the NATO review conference was held
- a decision to be made at the review conference to phase out the remaining US nuclear weapons in Europe within two years and formally to decouple European defence from US nuclear weapons as soon as all these nuclear weapons had been withdrawn from Europe.

356

b) *As a non-aligned state* If NATO declines to move towards a non-nuclear 'defensive defence', Britain would first suspend its membership of the Alliance for two years. This step replaces the suggestion in the first report for an initial withdrawal from NATO's Military Command Structure. Suspension would put pressure on NATO governments to reconsider their opposition to denuclearization. But if there was no change, Britain would then withdraw, and urge other NATO states to take a similar course of action. Some Commission members took the view that a non-nuclear British government should withdraw from NATO and adopt a non-aligned position from the outset.

We recommend that if Britain became non-aligned, it should continue to maintain close political, economic and cultural ties with Western Europe. If it remained in the Economic Community, it should support the efforts of Eire to prevent the Community becoming tied to NATO. It should work closely with neutral and non-aligned states in meetings like the European Disarmament Conference in Stockholm to further the cause of denuclearization and dealignment in Europe. Because of the risk of political isolation, it would be particularly important for a non-aligned Britain to devote attention to strengthening its international links. A non-aligned Britain might in fact be well placed to establish a closer rapport with many Third World countries and should seek wherever possible to work out a common approach to disarmament and development issues with non-aligned countries in the Third World.

Promoting the Dissolution of the Blocs in Europe
We argue that a stable peace in Europe requires the eventual dissolution of both military alliances and the withdrawal of superpower forces from the territory of their present allies. Any further unrest in Eastern Europe, for instance, involving Soviet military intervention could play havoc with détente and revive a wholly uncontrolled arms race.

There is little possibility of an early end to the bloc system in Europe. However, the removal of nuclear weapons from both parts of Europe (including at least INF weapons such as SS20s from the western Soviet Union), together with substantial reductions in conventional forces could, over time, create more

357

favourable conditions for dissolving the blocs. Western Europe might take a more independent position in relation to the USA; the Soviet Union might be prepared to countenance greater autonomy for Eastern European states. Pressure 'from below' in Eastern Europe, most dramatically exemplified in the 1980s by the emergence of Solidarity in Poland, may continue to play a crucial role in bringing about long-term change in Soviet-East European relations.

Whatever the changes in Soviet-East European relations, however, the bloc system as such will not fade away of its own accord. Positive steps would need to be taken at some point to deal with the political and security problems that a dissolution of the blocs would entail. Most centrally, an agreement regulating the status of the two German states, and of West Berlin, would be needed with the agreement of the two states themselves. The neutralization of the two states, which has been seriously considered from time to time, might eventually offer a way forward in a changed political and military context.

Other states in both Eastern and Western Europe might adopt a non-aligned position. It is possible that in time the Soviet Union might accept that the adoption of a neutral or non-aligned position by existing Warsaw Pact states would safeguard its security interests since it would commit these states not to enter into military alliances against it either with each other or with Western Europe. Non-alignment or neutrality might also be adopted by some states in the West. But a comprehensive East-West agreement which would be necessary when the superpowers withdrew their forces might permit a regional security alliance in Western Europe with certain provisos – for instance a ban on the deployment of nuclear weapons or the inclusion of the USA in any such alliance.

3. Postscript on Reykjavik

The Reykjavik summit of October 1986 took place after the present report had been written and a full analysis of it is not possible in this brief postscript. It appears, however, that despite the failure to reach agreement, Reykjavik could mark an important point of departure for future negotiations. Reports from both sides suggest that the two leaders came close to an agreement on nuclear arms control that went further than anything that had been seriously discussed before, and included the removal of all INF systems from Europe, and a 50 per cent reduction in strategic nuclear forces. The elimination within ten years of all long-range ballistic missiles (and even of all strategic nuclear weapons) was also discussed. The summit broke down over Reagan's insistence on continuing US research and development on SDI, including tests in space that would violate the ABM Treaty, and the Soviet insistence that no agreement on any part of the package of proposals, including those on INF in Europe, was acceptable unless the issue of space-based weapons was settled.

In the weeks after Reykjavik, opposition mounted to some of the measures proposed by the two leaders. In Western Europe, the Thatcher, Kohl and Chirac/Mitterand governments, together with both the Supreme Allied Commander in Europe, General Rogers, and the Deputy Supreme Commander, General Mack, conducted a more or less open campaign against a 'zero' INF deal for Europe; in addition, Mrs Thatcher stated that Britain would need to retain its nuclear weapons even if the superpowers achieved deep cuts in their strategic forces. There are three brief comments we would make here.

First, although there is, as we note in the report, a growing anti-nuclear lobby in Western Europe which wants to see radical changes in NATO strategy, and the creation of a nuclear-free Europe, the strength of the pro-nuclear lobby is evident. Europe has the potential to play an important role in moving the world away from nuclear confrontation; it could also be a major obstacle to progress.

Second, Reykjavik suggests that, given a degree more flexibility on both sides, an agreement to scrap INF missiles in Europe might be possible. In this report we focus mainly on a strategy of unilateral initiatives, and pressure for reciprocal responses, to achieve nuclear disarmament in Europe, while also considering how a non-nuclear Britain could contribute positively to arms control negotiations. Clearly, if a negotiated withdrawal of INF missiles from Europe were possible, this would simplify the task for an anti-nuclear British government intent on changing NATO strategy. However, the resistance of the Thatcher government to a zero INF agreement suggests that simply to promote serious negotiations the election of an anti-nuclear government in Britain could be critically important. Moreover the relapse into stalemate on arms control since Reykjavik underlines the fact that it is only by being prepared to act unilaterally that one can ensure that a commitment to end reliance on nuclear weapons will be fulfilled.

Finally, the interest of the Soviet leaders at the present time in slowing down the arms race, partly for internal economic reasons, and the greater flexibility they have shown in negotiations, makes it more likely that they would respond positively to a programme of unilateral initiatives by the West. There is, in fact, an opportunity for progress in nuclear disarmament that has not existed for a generation. It would be tragic indeed if this opportunity were not now seized.

Notes

INTRODUCTION

1. *Defence Without the Bomb*. London: Taylor & Francis, 1983. A popular and updated version of the report entitled *Without the Bomb* was published in August 1985 by Granada in the Paladin series.

2. *Defence and Security for Britain*. The Labour Party, 1984.

CHAPTER I

1. Cited by Michael Mandelbaum, *The Nuclear Question*, Cambridge: Cambridge University Press, 1979, p 126.

2. McGeorge Bundy, Special Assistant to the President for National Security Affairs from 1961 to 1966 stated in a speech in 1979 that a retaliatory strike against Soviet military targets 'would put some sixty [nuclear] warheads on Moscow.' Cited by Solly Zuckerman, *Nuclear Illusion and Reality*, London: Collins 1982, p 56.

3. In the summer of 1982 the *New York Times* published a defence guidance statement drawn up by the Pentagon which envisaged US forces 'prevailing' in a nuclear war which was expected to last for up to six months.

4. See David Cross, 'How vague Reagan words raised a storm in NATO', *The Times*, 22 October 1981, and Nicholas Hirst, 'US tries to defuse Reagan's remarks', *The Times*, 21 October 1981.

5. There is a growing literature on the theory of and possible weapons to be used in an SDI system. The aim is to attack missiles at various stages after take-off; during the boost phase, after the multiple warheads have been released, during mid-flight and as they near the target. The range of technologies

includes various kinds of lasers and particle beams, as well as missiles and electromagnetic rail guns that would fire projectiles. One method, X-ray lasers, requires the explosion of nuclear bombs, which would either orbit in space or be fired from ground or sea-based missiles when needed. See: Bhupendra Jasani and Christopher Lee, *Countdown to Space War*, SIPRI, London: Taylor & Francis, 1984; Peter David, ' "Star Wars" and Arms Control', Faraday Discussion Paper No 3, *The Council for Arms Control*, 1985.

6. Pope John Paul II said in his Hiroshima speech: 'In the past it was possible to destroy a village, a town, a region, even a country. Now it is the whole planet that has come under threat . . . from now on, it is only through a conscious choice, and then deliberate policy that humanity can survive.' Cited by Jonathan Schell, *The Abolition*, London: Picador 1984, p 3. The statement by the US Catholic bishops, *The Challenge of Peace: God's Promise and our Response* was published in Britain in 1983 by the Catholic Truth Society and SPCK. *The Church and the Bomb* was published by Hodder & Stoughton, 1982. Other important contributions to the moral debate are Paul Ramsey, *The Just War*, University Press of America 1968 and 1983, Walter Stein (ed), *Nuclear Weapons and Christian Conscience*, London: The Merlin Press, 1961 and 1981; Rev Roger Ruston, *Nuclear Deterrence – Right or Wrong?*, Catholic Information Services, 1981; Anthony King, *The Logic of Deterrence*, Firethorn Press 1985; Michael Waltzer, *Just and Unjust Wars*, Harmondsworth: Penguin 1980. For a comprehensive review of the moral/strategic debate see John Finnis, Joseph M Boyle Jr, & Germain Grisez. *Nuclear Deterrence: Morality & Realism*, Oxford & New York: OUP, 1987

7. The USA has already anticipated this phase: the Advanced Strategic Missile Systems Program is undertaking research into how to bypass SDI-type defences. Ian Mather, 'Reagan's Secret Offensive', *The Observer*, 24 March 1985. This fact alone casts doubt on Reagan's assurance that SDI will not actually be installed until after offensive missiles on both sides have been dismantled. (Reagan gave this undertaking in an interview with Soviet journalists, November 1985, *United States Information Service*, November 6, 1985).

8. See Thomas K. Longstreth, John E. Pike and John B.

Rhinelander, 'The Impact of US and Soviet Ballistic Missile Defense Programs on the ABM Treaty', Washington DC, National Campaign to Save the ABM Treaty, March 1985.

9. Alex Brummer, '100 nuclear tests may be needed', *The Guardian*, 22 April 1986.

10. See William A. Schwartz, Charles Derber et al., *The Nuclear Seduction: Why the Arms Race Doesn't Matter*, Boston Nuclear Study Group, August 1985, p 44: 'To our knowledge, no analyst has drawn a plausible connection between the state of the superpower missile balance and any major foreign policy action, by any nation, anywhere in the world, in the past 25 years. In our own extensive interviews with Pentagon and National Security Council officials, we heard over and over again that Soviet political advantages "might well" be accruing from the "window of vulnerability" produced by their prodigious new nuclear systems. But when challenged for evidence not a single one could connect Afghanistan, Central America, the Middle East or the conflicts of any other region with the nuclear tally-sheet . . . Similarly, no scholar from the left has plausibly demonstrated that American power or imperialism has concretely benefited anywhere in the world from the nuclear portion of the US defense budget'. See also McGeorge Bundy, 'The Unimpressive Record of Atomic Diplomacy' in Gwyn Prins, ed, *The Nuclear Crisis Reader*, New York: Vintage, 1984.

11. See John Lewis Gaddis, *Strategies of Containment*, Oxford: Oxford University Press 1982, pp 274–308.

12. See Ken Booth and Phil Williams, 'Fact and Fiction in US Foreign Policy: Reagan's Myths about Détente', *World Policy Journal*, Vol II, No 3, Summer 1985, pp 501–532.

13. Phil Williams, 'The Nunn Amendment, Burden-sharing and US Troops in Europe', *Survival*, January/February, 1985.

14. Conor Cruise O'Brien and Feliks Topolski, *The United Nations: Sacred Drama*, New York: Simon & Schuster, 1968.

15. For a discussion of the implications of proliferation for deterrence, see Barrie Paskins, 'Proliferation and the Nature of Deterrence', in Nigel Blake and Kay Pole, (eds), *Dangers of Deterrence: Philosophers on Nuclear Strategy*, London: Routledge and Kegan Paul, 1983.

16. On 1 September 1979 the former US Secretary of State

Henry Kissinger argued at a NATO conference in Brussels that NATO should not rely on the Americans using their strategic nuclear weapons for Europe's defence. Kissinger said: 'If my analysis is correct, we must face the fact that it is absurd to base the strategy of the West on the credibility of mutual suicide . . . I would say, which I might not say in office, that the European allies should not keep asking us to multiply strategic assurances that we cannot possibly mean, or if we do mean we should not want to execute because we should risk the destruction of civilization.'

17. Richard Perle, speaking on *Panorama*, BBC 1, 15 July 1985.

18. For evidence of Czechoslovakian and East German popular protests, see *Labour Focus on Eastern Europe*, Vol 7, No 1, Winter 1984: Oliver MacDonald, 'Sudden Growth of Nuclear Pacifism', pp 8–9 and Günter Minnerup, 'Hard Times Ahead for Peace Movement', pp. 18–20. Petitions against the stationing of Soviet missiles were circulating in Prague, and in Brno over 1,500 people signed a protest letter. For a general account of East German anti-nuclear protests see John Sanford, 'The Sword and the Ploughshare: Autonomous Peace Initiatives in East Germany,' Merlin/END Special Report, 1983. The relatively tolerant attitude of the East German government towards these protests could suggest it was not altogether unsympathetic to the anti-nuclear issue and was possibly worried that new missile deployments would upset good relations with West Germany.

19. See Alternative Defence Commission, *op cit*, Intro, note 1, and also Charles Osgood, *An Alternative to War or Surrender*, Urbana, I11: University of Illinois Press, 1962 and United Nations, Report of the Secretary General, 'Unilateral Nuclear Disarmament Measures', 5 October 1984 (A/39/516).

20. The Peace Research Working Group at the Institute of Political Science at the University of Tübingen published a detailed report (in German) titled 'Freedom from Nuclear Weapons and European Security: Possibilities and Problems of an Alternative Security Policy', 1983. Frankfurt's Peace Research Institute contributed a series of articles in the *Bulletin of Peace Proposals* special issue entitled 'Rethinking Peace and the Threat of War' (Vol 15, No 1, 1984). See especially Stephan Tiedtke,

'Alternative Military Defence Strategies as a Component of Détente and Ostpolitik', pp 13–23. See also issues Nos 1 & 2 of the international research newsletter *Non-Offensive Defence,* which carry reviews of a number of German projects and publications, especially No 2 which focuses on the German debate. The newsletter is published by the Centre of Peace and Conflict Research, University of Copenhagen.

CHAPTER 2

1. See note 1 of Introduction.

2. CENTO (more often known as the Baghdad Pact) dissolved in 1979 and SEATO in 1977.

3. The authoritative account of how Britain came to have independent nuclear weapons is: Margaret Gowing, *Independence and Deterrence: Britain and Atomic Energy,* 1945–1952, 2 vols, London: Macmillan, 1974.

4. Lawrence Freedman, *Britain and Nuclear Weapons,* London: Macmillan, 1980, gives an incisive account of how Britain became dependent on the USA for its missiles.

5. Duncan Campbell, *The Unsinkable Aircraft Carrier: American Military Power in Britain,* London: Michael Joseph, 1984, pp 27–45, covers the consolidation of US bases in Britain and early negotiations about the degree of British control; pp 306–319 covers recent illustrations and the historical record on the degree of US consultation nuclear crises.

6. 'Launch on Warning' is one option in SIOP at present. For details of SIOP see: Peter Pringle and William Arkin, *SIOP: Nuclear War from the Inside,* London: Sphere, 1983.

7. For a full description of New Zealand's non-nuclear position see: David Lange, 'New Zealand's Security Policy', *Foreign Affairs,* Vol 63, No 5, Summer 1985, pp 1009–1019.
For an account of US reactions see: Jamie Dettmer and Philip Rasmussen, 'US Challenges Anti-Nuclear Policy', *END Journal,* no 15, April–May 1985, pp 10–11.

8. For details of EEC role in defence, see: F. Gregory, 'The European Community and Defence', *ADIU Report,* Vol 3, No 5 (September/October 1981) pp 5–9; 'Now the Tank Mountain?', *The Economist,* 5 May 1984.

9. Stuart Holland, *Uncommon Market*, London: Macmillan, 1980, discusses Lomé, pp 162–6. See also Christopher Stevens, (ed), *EEC and the Third World: A Survey*, London: Hodder and Stoughton, 1984.

10. This suggestion is made by Wolf Mendl, who emphasizes the possibility of West European and Japanese cooperation as one element in a policy of partial dealignment: Wolf Mendl, *Western Europe and Japan between the Superpowers*, London: Croom Helm, 1984.

11. Peter Lyon, *Neutralism*, Leicester: Leicester University Press, 1963, examines the concepts of neutrality and neutralism; Lawrence W. Martin, (ed), *Neutralism and Nonalignment: The New States in World Affairs*, New York: Praeger, 1962, explores contemporary non-alignment.

12. A recent interesting argument for British neutralism is: Peter Johnson, *Neutrality: A Policy for Britain*, London: Temple Smith, 1985.

13. Adam Roberts, *Nations in Arms: The Theory and Practice of Territorial Defence*, London: Chatto and Windus, 1976, discusses Sweden's foreign and defence policies, and Yugoslavia's policy of General People's Defence.

CHAPTER 3

1. See, for instance, D.W. Fleming, *The Cold War and its Origins 1917–60*, Garden City: Doubleday 1961; Gabriel and Joyce Kolko, *The Limits of Power: The World and United States Foreign Policy 1945–54*, New York: Harper & Row, 1972; David Horowitz, *From Yalta to Vietnam*, Harmondsworth: Penguin, 1967; Gar Alperovitz, *Atomic Diplomacy: Hiroshima and Potsdam*, New York: Vintage Books, 1967.

2. See John Lewis Gaddis, *The United States and the Origins of the Cold War*, New York: Columbia University Press, 1972; Geir Lundestad, *The American Non-Policy Towards Eastern Europe 1943–1947*, Tromsön: Universitetsforlaget, 1978; Daniel Yergin, *Shattered Peace*, Harmondsworth: Penguin 1980.

3. There were also, of course, forces in Western Europe supporting decolonization. The hand-over of power in India and Pakistan in August 1947 was a clear statement by the Attlee

government that it wished to see Britain divest itself of Empire. Burma, which had been largely occupied by Japan during the war, became independent in January 1948. By 1950 the Gold Coast (Ghana) was largely self-governing, though it did not achieve full independence until 1957.

4. Robert J. Wegs, *Europe since 1945: a Concise History*, London: Macmillan, 1984, p 55.

5. *Ibid*, p 56.

6. Yergin, *op cit*, note 2, p 180.

7. At a time when the spheres of influence between East and West were not clearly drawn, these demands inevitably raised doubts about Soviet intentions. The Soviet demand seems to have been based on straightforward imperialist argument. 'The United Kingdom had India and her possessions in the Indian Ocean in her sphere of influence; the United States had China and Japan, but the Soviets had nothing', Stalin told the British Foreign Minister at the Foreign Ministers' conference in Moscow in December 1945. See Yergin, *op cit*, note 2, p 150.

8. See Lundestad, *op cit*, note 2, pp 136–144.

9. Francois Fejto, *Histoires des democraties populaires*, Vol 1, Paris: Editions du Seuil, p 239–240. The former Hungarian general, Bela Kiraly, claims that Stalin made detailed plans to invade Yugoslavia in 1949–50 and suggests that he abandoned them only after the US had sent forces to South Korea to resist the attack from North Korea. See Michael Charlton, *The Eagle and the Small Birds*, BBC Publication, 1984, p 78.

10. Fejto, *Ibid*, p 286.

11. Nikolai Tolstoy, *Stalin's Secret War*, London: Jonathan Cape, 1982 edition, pp 266–267.

12. *Ibid*, p 267.

13. See Lundestad, *op cit*, note 2, pp 448–465.

14. See Daniel Yergin, *op cit*, note 2, esp Chapter VII, 'The Right Attitude in Mind'.

15. Elections eventually took place in early 1947, but under conditions that disqualify them from being considered as a genuine expression of popular opinion.

16. See Yergin, *op cit*, note 2, esp pp 345–347. After the US had turned a deaf ear to an appeal for aid from Czechoslovakia in 1947, the Foreign Trade Minister Ripka is quoted as saying

in Moscow: 'Those goddam Americans. It's because of them that I've had to come here to sign on the dotted line. We told the Americans, and asked for 200,000 or 300,000 tons of wheat. And those idiots started the usual blackmail ... At this point Gottwald got in touch with Stalin who promised us the required wheat ... And now those idiots in Washington have driven us straight into the Stalinist camp.'

17. The 'deal' gave Britain (with the US) a 90 per cent stake in Greece, the Soviet Union 90 per cent in Romania, and 75 per cent in Bulgaria. Yugoslavia and Hungary would be shared 50-50. See Yergin, *op cit*, note 2, p 59.

18. Karel Kaplan, *Dans les Archives du Comité Central: 30 Ans de Secrets du Bloc Soviétique*, Paris: Albin Michel, 1978. During the Prague Spring Kaplan was put in charge of a government Commission to investigate the political trials of the Stalinist period and it was in the course of this work that he had access to secret police files and other confidential documents.

19. Kaplan's story is based on his discussions in 1968 with the former Czechoslovak Defence Minister, Cepicka, who had attended the conference, and even deplored the fact that, following Stalin's death, Khrushchev had not seen fit to put the plan into operation. Kaplan also recalls the intense militarization of Czechoslovak society in this period, and the priority given to military procurement to the detriment of other needs.

20. Milovan Djilas, *Conversations with Stalin*, Harmondsworth: Pelican Books, 1969, p 141; also Yergin, *op cit*, note 2, p 311.

21. Kaplan, *op cit* p 163.

22. The name derives from the US diplomatic mission stationed in Riga, in the then independent republic of Latvia, in the inter-war period to report on Soviet affairs. After the US recognition of the Soviet Union in 1933, the group moved to the US Embassy in Moscow where its members witnessed at close quarters the traumatic events of the Stalinist purges.

23. Yergin, *op cit*, note 2, p 169.

24. Ibid, p 148.

25. Matthew Evangelista, 'Stalin's Postwar Army Reappraised', *International Security*, Winter 1982/1983, Vol 7 No 3, pp 110–138. See esp pages 112–116.

26. Ibid, pp 114–115.

27. Yergin, *op cit*, note 2, pp 388–389.

28. Foreign Relations of the United States, 1945, Vol II, Department of State, 1967, p 83. cited by David Holloway, *The Soviet Union and the Arms Race*, Yale University (1984 edition) page 19.

29. See especially Alperovitz, *Atomic Diplomacy, op cit*, note 1.

30. Margaret Gowing, cited David Holloway, *op cit* p 20.

31. Holloway, *op cit*, note 28, p 24.

32. J.K. Sowden, *The German Question: 1945–1973*, Bradford: Bradford University Press, 1975, pp 152–153.

33. See C.J. Bartlett, *The Global Conflict 1880–1970*, London: Longman 1984, p 276.

34. On the division of Berlin during 1948 see Sowden, *op cit*, note 32, pp 212–214.

35. See especially Willy Brandt, 'German Policy Towards the East', *Foreign Affairs*, Vol 46 No 3, April 1968, pp 476–486.

36. Adenauer however had also formally renounced the use of force to bring about German unity as far back as 1954.

37. See David Barton, 'The Conference on Confidence and Security Building Measures and Disarmament', *The Arms Race and Arms Control, 1984*, SIPRI, pp 188–199.

38. Jonathan Steele, *World Power: Soviet Foreign Policy under Brezhnev and Andropov*, London: Michael Joseph, 1983, p 104.

39. See Milton Leitenberg, 'Criteria for the Conditions of Successful Arms Control: An Examination of the Decade 1970–1980', paper prepared for the conference on Evaluation of Criteria for Nuclear Arms Control, Frankfurt, December 1984.

40. An argument put by Denis Healey in his Fabian pamphlet *A Neutral Belt in Europe*, Fabian Tract No 311, p 5.

41. Gaddis, *Strategies of Containment, op cit*, Ch 1, note 11, p 190.

42. Hugh Gaitskell, 'Co-existence in Europe', Chapter II of *The Challenge of Co-existence*, London: Methuen 1957.

43. Adam Rapacki, 'The Polish Plan for a Nuclear-Free Zone Today', *International Affairs*, Vol 39, No 1, Jan 1963, p 2.

44. See *International Affairs*, Vol 34, No 4, October 1958, pp 469–476 under the title 'Disengagement and Western Security'.

45. Zdenek Mylnar, 'Relative Stabilization of the Soviet Systems in the 1970s', *Study No 2: Crisis in Soviet type Systems*, Bund-Verlag, Cologne & Braumüller, Universitäts-Verlag, Vienna, 1983, p 31.

46. *Ibid*, p 31.

47. This concern is strongly emphasized by Rapacki himself in his article in *International Affairs, op cit*, note 43.

48. *Ibid*. See also the abridged text of the plan of March 1962 on pp 36 & 168 of the same issue of *International Affairs*. Also Jonathan Steele, 'A Nuclear Free Zone in Central Europe', *END Journal* No 1, December 1982–January 1983, Special Supplement.

49. Rapacki, *op cit*, note 43, p 3.

50. The 'Prague Appeal' signed in March 1985 by leading members of Charter 77 made available by Palach Press and published in various journals including War Resisters International *Newsletter*, April 1985 and *END Journal* No 15, April–May 1985.

51. See for instance *A Nuclear Free Europe? Why it wouldn't work*, Ministry of Defence Public Relations. This was also the objection advanced at the time by President Eisenhower in the US which was cited with approval by the British Foreign Minister, Selwyn Lloyd, in a Commons debate on 20 February 1958 – See *The Times*, 21 February 1958.

52. See for instance *Arms Control & Disarmament* No 6, November 1980.

53. Field Marshall Lord Carver, for instance, argues that NATO should 'abandon the concept that it can avert conventional defeat by initiating a nuclear war' since this would 'result in an even greater defeat'. *A Policy for Peace*, London: Faber & Faber 1982, p 109. See also McGeorge Bundy, George Kennan, Robert McNamara and Gerard Smith, 'Nuclear Weapons and the Atlantic Alliance', *Foreign Affairs*, Vol 60, No 4, Spring 1982, pp 753–768.

54. *The Times*, 21 February 1958.

CHAPTER 4

1. J. Howarth, *France: the Politics of Peace*, London: Merlin Press, 1984. See also D. Johnstone, *The Politics of Euromissiles*, London: Verso, 1984.

2. Follow on Forces Attack (FOFA) is a concept for strengthening NATO's capability to attack Warsaw Pact forces, communication centres, etc, deep inside Eastern Europe through the development of conventional long-range precision-guided missiles and their associated communications and intelligence facilities. FOFA was approved by the NATO Defence Planning Committee on 9th November, 1984. See, for example, General B.W. Rogers, 'Follow-on Forces Attack (FOFA): Myths and Realities', *NATO Review*, Vol 22, No 6, Dec 1984, pp 1–9, and C. Donnelly, 'The Development of the Soviet Concept of Echeloning', *NATO Review*, Vol 22, No 6, Dec 1984, pp 9–17.

AirLand Battle is the new US Army doctrine, adopted globally as well as in Europe. It uses manoeuvre, surprise, and (tactically) offensive operations at vulnerable points in the enemy forces through combined ground and air operations. In contrast to FOFA, it explicitly calls for the integration of conventional, nuclear, chemical and electronic weaponry in battlefield operations. See US Army Dept, *Operations: Field Manual 100–5*, Washington DC, 1982.

3. See, for example, C.N. Donnelly, 'The Soviet operational concept in the 1980s', in *Strengthening Conventional Deterrence in Europe: Report of the European Security Study*, London: Macmillan, 1983. Other references include J. Erickson, 'The Soviet military system: doctrine, technology and style', in J. Erickson & E. J. Feuchtwanger (eds), *Soviet Military Power and Performance*, London: Macmillan, 1979; and P. Vigor, *Soviet Blitzkreig Theory*, London: Macmillan, 1983.

4. D. Holloway, *op cit*, Ch 3, note 28, Chapter 4.

5. Alternative Defence Commission, *Defence Without the Bomb*, *op cit*, intro, note 1.

6. G. Flynn (ed), *NATO's Northern Allies*, New Jersey: Rowman & Allanheld, 1986.

7. This is illustrated by the activity in NATO committees leading to the NATO 'dual-track' decision to deploy GLCMs and Pershing II missiles in Europe as described in G. F. Treverton, 'NATO Alliance Politics', in R. Betts, *Cruise Missiles: Technology, Strategy, Politics*, Washington D C, Brookings Institution, 1981.

8. N. Brown and A. Farrar-Hockley, *Nuclear First Use*, Royal United Services Institute, London, 1985.

9. Report of the Independent Commission on Disarmament and Security Issues, chaired by O. Palme, *Common Security: A Programme for Disarmament*, London: Pan, 1982.

10. W. Arkin and R. Fieldhouse, *Nuclear Battlefields; Global Links in the Arms Race*, Cambridge Mass: Ballinger, 1985.

11. For more details, see the articles in S. Lodgaard and M. Thee (eds), *Nuclear Disengagement in Europe*, Stockholm International Peace Research Institute (SIPRI), London: Taylor & Francis, 1983.

12. R. Wagner (Asst. to the Secretary of Defense for Atomic Energy), Hearings of the US Senate Subcommittee on Strategic and Theatre Nuclear Forces, Armed Services Committee, May 1, 1984, Government Printing Office, Washington DC, 1984.

13. P. Bracken, *The Command and Control of Nuclear Forces*, London: Yale University Press, 1984; British Atlantic Committee, *Diminishing the Nuclear Threat: NATO's Defence and New Technology*, London, 1984.

14. I. Faurby, *Public Opinion and Western Security: an Interpretation*; paper presented to Danish Strategic Study Group, Holte, Oct 19–21, 1984. See also B. Russett and D. Deluca, 'Theatre nuclear forces: public opinion in Western Europe', *Political Science Quarterly*, Summer 1983, p 179–196.

15. L. Freedman, *The Evolution of Nuclear Strategy*, London: Macmillan, 1981, describes the European influence on the evolution of NATO policy. European influence on US negotiating positions in SALT II, are described in G. Treverton, 'NATO Alliance Politics', *op cit*, note 7.

16. W. Arkin and R. Fieldhouse, *Nuclear Battlefields*, *op cit*, note 10.

17. For example, H. Kissinger, *The Times*, 18 January, 1984.

18. D. Johnstone, *The politics of Euromissiles*, *op cit*, note 1.

19. L. Freedman, *The Evolution of Nuclear Strategy*, *op cit*, note 15.

20. G. Treverton, 'NATO Alliance Politics', *op cit*, note 7.

21. For example: S. Canby 'Territorial Defense in Central Europe', *Armed Forces and Society*, Vol 7, No 1, Fall 1980, pp

51–67; H. Afheldt, 'Tactical Nuclear Weapons and European Security' in SIPRI *Tactical Nuclear Weapons: European Perspectives*, London: Taylor & Francis, 1978, pp 262–95.

22. For example, McGeorge Bundy, G. Kennan, R. McNamara and G. Smith, *op cit*, Ch 3, note 53.

23. *Sunday Times*, 13 May 1984.

24. *Financial Times*, 13 June 1984.

25. E. Den Oudsten, Appendix A, *World Armaments and Disarmament; SIPRI Yearbook, 1985*, London: Taylor & Francis, 1985. See also the references listed in note 14.

26. Resolution passed at the Annual Conference of the SPD, Essen, May 1984.

27. Statement by Chancellor H. Kohl to the Bundestag, 13 October, 1982, reproduced in *Survival*, Vol 25, No 1, Jan/Feb 1983.

28. An example of Greek and Danish reservations about NATO policy and the way in which such reservations are relegated to footnote status can be seen in the NATO Nuclear Planning Group Communiqué issued after the meeting of 20–21 March 1986 dealing with NATO nuclear weapons policy. See *NATO Review*, Vol 34, No 2, April 1986, p 33.

29. G. Flynn, *NATO's Northern Allies, op cit* (ref 6); *Strategic Survey, 1982–1983*, IISS, London, 1983, pp 48–50.

30. *Guardian*, 17 February 1986; *International Herald Tribune*, 20 March 1986; *Financial Times*, 4 December 1985; *Economist* 23 March 1985. See also G. Flynn, *NATO's Northern Allies, op cit*, note 6

31. *Strategic Survey, 1985–1986*, International Institute for Strategic Studies, London, 1986, p 89.

32. *Financial Times*, 3 February 1986.

33. Portugal-USA Azores Agreement, 1983. See A. Vasconcelos 'Portugal and NATO', *NATO Review*, Vol 34, No 2, April 1986, pp 8–15.

34. R. Rudney, 'Mitterand's new Atlanticism: evolving French attitudes toward NATO, *Orbis*, Vol 28, No 1, Spring 1984, pp 83–101; J. Howarth, *France: the Politics of Peace, op cit* (ref 1).

35. *Daily Telegraph*, 26 March 1984.

36. Statement by FRG Defence Minister M. Worner to the

Bundestag, reported in *TIME Magazine*, 29 Oct 1984, pp 26–28. This report also elaborates on the ensuing debate.

37. For example, the International Institute for Strategic Studies, *The Military Balance 1985–1986*, IISS, London, 1986, p 185.

38. Report of the European Security Study, *op cit*, note 3.

39. Described in more detail in, for example, Alternative Defence Commission, *Defence Without The Bomb*, *op cit*, Intro, note 1.

40. See, for instance, Hans-Heinrich and Wilhelm Notle, *Ziviler Widerstand und Autonome Abwehr* (Civilian Resistance and Autonomous Protection), Baden-Baden: Nomos Verlagsgesellschaft, 1984. Wilhelm Nolte is a Lt. Col. in the West German army. His paper in English 'Autonomous Protection' is included in Hylke Tromp and Klaas de Vries (eds) *Non-Nuclear War In Europe*, University of Grongingen, due for publication in 1986. See also Gene Sharp, *Making Europe Unconquerable: the Potential of Civilian-based Deterrence and Defence*, London: Taylor & Francis, 1985, and George Kennan's enthusiastic review of it in 'A New Philosophy of Defense', *The New York Review of Books*, 13 February 1986. See, too, the chapter in *Defence Without the Bomb op cit*, Intro, note 1, entitled 'Defence by Civil Resistance'.

41. S. Lodgaard and M. Thee, *op cit*, note 11.

42. B. Posen, 'Inadvertent nuclear war? Escalation and NATO's northern flank', *International Security*, Vol 7, No 1, 1982, pp 28–54.

43. C. Archer, 'Deterrence and Reassurance in Northern Europe', *Centrepiece* No 6, Centre for Defence Studies, Aberdeen University, 1984.

44. *Guardian*, 27 May 1986.

45. Press Release, US Information Service, 28 March 1984.

46. US Dept. of Defense, *Soviet Military Power*, US Government Printing Office, Washington DC, 1986.

CHAPTER 5

1. It is in a sense slightly misleading to speak of the 're-establishment' of détente at the European level, for even at the height of the 'New Cold War' in the early 1980s during President

374

Reagan's first term of office, European states on both sides of the East-West divide showed a distinct unwillingness to abandon détente and were prepared in varying degrees to defy their superpower backers in attempting to maintain it. Nevertheless even within Europe, East-West relations suffered a setback, partly due to the knock-on effect of the deterioration of US-Soviet relations, partly as a result of such things as the crisis over Euromissile deployments, and the introduction of martial law in Poland.

2. We do not, of course, overlook the fact that the Soviet Union is a European as well as an Asian power, and thus is itself partly situated in Eastern Europe. Clearly when we talk of superpower withdrawal from both parts of Europe we mean in the case of the Soviet Union withdrawal to behind its own frontiers.

3. See Harold Macmillan, 'The Anglo-American Schism' pp 89–179 of *Riding the Storm*, London: Macmillan, 1971, and especially p 164.

4. Europe's growing economic and industrial strength during the 1960s and early 1970s in relation to the US is demonstrated by the figures for steel production of the member states of the European Steel & Coal Community (Germany, France, Italy, and the Benelux countries). In 1953 output stood at 36.8 million tons; by 1974 it had risen to 132.4 million tons. In the same period US steel production had risen only from 101.2 million tons to 132 million. See Alfred Grosser, *The Western Alliance*, London: Macmillan 1980 p 295.

5. Regarding the problems that the Western capitalist and state centrist systems share, many commentators point to the considerable unemployment in the Soviet bloc concealed by the grossly inefficient use of labour; refusal of employment has also been used as a weapon against critics of the régimes, particularly in Czechoslovakia. Ecological problems, including major ecological disasters, have also occurred in the Soviet bloc. See for example Jan Kavan and Mark Jackson, 'The Czechoslovak Economy: An Unofficial View', *East European Reporter*, Vol 1, No 1, Spring 1985, pp 15–20, and Zbigniew Bujak, 'The Polish Economy Since Martial Law', – text prepared by a team of Solidarity economic advisors and signed by Bujak on behalf of

the Provisional Co-ordinating Committee – *East European Reporter*, Vol 1, No 3, Autumn 1985, pp 16–20.

6. See for instance Karen Dawisha, 'The 1968 Invasion of Czechoslovakia: Causes, Consequences and Lessons for the Future'; pp 9–25 of Karen Dawisha and Philip Hanson (eds), *Soviet-East European Dilemmas*, London: Heinemann for the RIIA, 1981, especially pp 12–13.

7. On the role of strategic considerations in the decision to intervene in Czechoslovakia see Karen Dawisha, 'Soviet Security and the Role of the Military: the 1968 Czechoslovak Crisis', *British Journal of Political Science*, Vol 10, Part 3, July 1980, pp 341–363.

8. See for instance *Soviet Foreign Policy*, Vol II, 1945–1980, Progress Publishers 1981, written by a consortium of Soviet historians, and in particular their treatment of 'Imperialist Intrigues Against Hungary [1956–57]' and the almost cursory, but highly tendentious, treatment of the invasion of Czechoslovakia in 1968 on p 328.

9. Karen Dawisha, 'The 1968 Invasion of Czechoslovakia: Causes, Consequences and Lessons for the Future' in Karen Dawisha and Philip Hanson, *op cit*, note 6, especially pp 18–21

10. Vaclav Havel, in Vaclav Havel et al, *The Power of the Powerless*, London: Hutchinson, 1985.

11. See for instance Roger Boyes, 'How the young are cracking a monolith', *The Times*, 16 October 1984, part 2 of a three-part series on Eastern Europe.

12. See the report from Hella Pick in *The Guardian*, 14 August 1985, which tells of a sharp attack on the unions in the Polish government newspaper *Rzeczpospolita*. She speculates, however, that the timing of the attack may have been an attempt to convince Solidarity supporters that the new unions are genuinely independent.

13. On this point see Zdenek Mylnar, 'Relative Stabilization of the Soviet Systems in the 1970s', *op cit*, Ch 3, note 45.

14. See Roger Boyes, 'Hungarian Reforms get stamp of approval from Soviet delegates', *The Times*, 27 March 1985.

15. For an assessment of the Gorbachev reforms which suggests that these are likely over the next fifteen years to lead to a tightening up of the rules – rather than their relaxation and the

introduction of greater social and political freedom – see Andrew Wilson, 'Gorbachev "reforms" fail to live up to the propaganda', *The Observer*, 9 March 1986.

16. See Philip Hanson, 'Soviet Trade with Eastern Europe' in Karen Dawisha and Philip Hanson, *op cit*, note 6, especially pp 97–98.

17. Michael White, 'US Retreats From Zero Arms Option', *The Guardian*, 21 February 1986.

18. Timothy Garton Ash, for instance, argues that 'the withdrawal of nuclear weapons would be most unlikely to bring about any significant increase in freedom, self-determination, legality or participation for the peoples of eastern Europe', and that the removal of nuclear weapons from central Europe 'would immediately diminish the security of western Europe, for the simple reason that the Warsaw Pact has many more conventional forces'. See 'Raising the Iron Curtain', *New Society*, 18 April 1985.

19. The 'Prague Appeal', *op cit*, Ch 3, note 50.

20. An extension of the counter-argument is the so-called 'Finlandization' argument: a nuclear disarmed Western Europe would be vulnerable to Soviet pressure and would fall by degrees under its influence. This seems as things stand an unlikely outcome given the relative vigour of the Western political and economic system by comparison with that of the Soviet bloc. Obviously, however, if NATO were to break up in disarray and this coincided with a major crisis in the Western economy and the breakdown of other West European institutions such as the EEC, the possibility that the Soviet Union could exploit the situation to its advantage would have to be taken more seriously. But if Western Europe remained economically vigorous and maintained the political will to defend its autonomy, it should be able to do so. Yugoslavia in the late 1940s and early 1950s provides an example of a country which had much more reason to fear a Soviet attack than any West European country today yet did not back off in various political confrontations with the Soviet Union.

21. Helga Michalsky, 'Détente at Work – The Record of Inter-German Relations' in William E. Patterson and Gordon Smith (eds), the *West German Model*, London: Frank Cass, 1981, p 108.

22. Jonathan Dean, 'How to Lose Germany', *Foreign Policy*, Vol 55, Summer 1984, p 67.

23. A point emphasized by Jiri Hajek, Charter 77 spokesperson and former Foreign Minister of Czechoslovakia, in an interview with the French anti-nuclear movement, CODENE, January 1985.

24. Jacek Kuron's statement, smuggled out of prison in June 1984, called for the demilitarization of Poland, East Germany and West Germany, including the withdrawal of foreign forces. See *Labour Focus on Eastern Europe*, Vol 17, No 2, Summer 1984, p 1.

25. The figure comes from the Allensbach Institute and is cited by Jonathan Dean, former Political Counsellor to the US Embassy in Bonn, in 'How to Lose Germany', *Foreign Policy*, Vol 55, Summer 1984, p 60.

26. Ulrich Albrecht, 'European Security and the German Question', *World Policy Journal*, Vol 1, No 3, pp 575–602.

27. The legal and constitutional problems are hardly more complex than those settled in an *ad hoc* way when the Basic Treaty of 1972 was signed regulating the relationship between the two German states. (See Chapter Three.)

28. *Denkschrift: Friedensvertrag: Deutsche Konfederation: Euro-paisches Sicherheitssystem*, available from Karin Hossfeld, Fritsches-trasse 25, 1000 Berlin 10. Among the signatories of the document was the historian Peter Brandt, son of the former Chancellor Willy Brandt. A parallel document drawn up by one of the signatories of the Memorandum, Richard Sperber, sets out the possible provisions of a German Peace Treaty. It is available in an English translation from Initiativkreis Friedensvertrag, Elsterweg 2, 3008 Garbsen 9.

29. Khrushchev in fact in the late 1950s floated the idea of internationalizing Berlin as part of a wider European settlement.

30. These suggestions follow broadly those of Professor Anthony Clunies Ross, in his *Guardian* article of 9 September 1985 entitled 'Iron Curtain Road to Nuclear-Free Europe'.

CHAPTER 6

1. See *op cit*, Ch 2, note 12, Peter Johnson, *Neutrality: A Policy for Britain*, and the favourable review by Enoch Powell in *The Times*, 14 January 1985.

2. See for instance *The Least Developed Countries: 1985 Report; United Nations Conference on Trade and Developmemt*, Geneva, and the review article by Christopher Huhne, 'The Human Cost of Third World Aid Cuts', *The Guardian*, 19 September 1985. Huhne points out that the 36 least developed countries had an inflow of resources worth $8.7 billion in 1983 compared to $10.3 billion in 1980, despite a dramatic worsening in their economies in the interim.

3. The Palme Commission made specific recommendations for the strengthening of UN mediation and peacekeeping in relation to border dispute or other threats to territorial integrity in Third World countries. These included the provision of military standby forces, and a concordat among the permanent members of the Security Council to support collective action 'at least, to the extent possible, of not voting against it'. See *Common Security*, London: Pan, 1982, pp 161–167.

4. See for instance the pamphlet *No-First-Use*, Union of Concerned Scientists, Cambridge, Mass., 1983.

5. The problem about deciding what would be an appropriate Soviet response to the withdrawal of NATO Nordic countries from the Alliance and the creation in effect of a Nordic neutral and non-nuclear zone, is that the adjacent military districts in the Soviet Union – the Baltic and Leningrad Military Districts – have a very heavy concentration of strategic nuclear systems. The ports of Kola, for instance, which come under the Leningrad MD, are the home base for two-thirds of all Soviet strategic submarines. Clearly one could not expect these strategic systems to be dismantled except in the context of a US-Soviet agreement covering all such systems on both sides. Thus proponents of a Baltic NWFZ have suggested that it would be reasonable to expect that at least the shorter-range Soviet nuclear systems in the area which can virtually only reach targets in the Nordic area, should be dismantled. The INF systems, SS4s, SS5s and SS20s have a more ambiguous status since they may be targeted on the Central European theatre. Nevertheless if they were dismantled, or at least withdrawn from the Baltic and Leningrad military districts, this would be a very positive response on the Soviet side.

6. 'Preventing War in the Atomic Age – Towards a New

Strategy for NATO': Resolution adopted by the Social Democratic Party of Germany's Party Conference, Essen, May 17–21, 1984. Issued by the SPD International Department.

7. *Financial Times*, 16 December 1985.

CHAPTER 7

1. See a report in *The Times* (27 January 1981) which quotes an MOD official as observing that 'every gun in the place' would be trained on a unilateralist minister. Quoted in L. Freedman, 'Britain: The First Ex-Nuclear Power?', *International Security*, Vol 6, No 2, Fall 1981, pp 88–104.

2. 'Labour Threat Delays First Trident Order', *The Sunday Times*, 9 February 1986.

3. D. Campbell, 'Too Few Bombs to Go Round', *New Statesman*, 29 November 1985, pp 10–12.

4. See J. Gallacher, 'Nuclear Stocktaking: A Count of Britain's Warheads', *Bailrigg Paper on International Security*, No 5, Centre for the Study of Arms Control and International Security, University of Lancaster, 1982.

5. Campbell, *op cit*, note 3.

6. K. Barnham, D. Hart, J. Nelson, and R.A. Stevens, 'The Production and Destiny of UK Civil Plutonium', *Nature*, 19 September 1985, pp 213–217.

7. J. Simpson, *The Independent Nuclear State: The United States, Britain and the Military Atom*, London: Macmillan, 1983.

8. D. Hobbs, 'Alternatives to Trident', *Aberdeen Studies in Defence Economics*, No 25, Summer 1983.

9. Simpson, *op cit*, note 7.

10. There are precise constraints on the unilateral termination of the 1958 Mutual Defence Agreement and its 1959 amendment (Simpson, *Ibid*). Unilateral termination is only legally possible once every five years, commencing from the last day of 1959, and then only if one year's notice has been given. Thus the next legal opportunities for unilateral termination are to give notice in December 1988 to terminate at the end of 1989. The following dates are respectively at the end of 1993 and 1994. The Mutual Defence Agreement can of course end by mutual agreement at any time.

380

11. K. Pierogosti, 'RECOVERING Verification', *Arms Control Today*, December 1982.

12. A nuclear power station would have to undergo some modifications before it could use plutonium fuel, but these are likely to be fairly minor. The arms control advantage of using this method of disposing of weapons-grade plutonium is that the isotopic composition of the plutonium in the spent fuel rods would be altered in a way that would make it even harder to use in nuclear weapons. The proportion of plutonium isotopes with even atomic numbers (Pu-240 etc) would be increased, posing more difficult design, manufacturing, and handling problems in warhead construction and reducing operational predictability. The 'problem' isotopes of plutonium would be much more difficult to separate from the plutonium 239 than would be blends of other elements.

13. Lithium deuteride is an alternative fuel for fusion reactions. It has several advantages over tritium in this context, but the UK is not known to have any facilities for producing lithium deuteride. It is likely that all or most of the British warheads are so-called boosted fission weapons, for which tritium is generally used.

14. D. Campbell, *The Unsinkable Aircraft Carrier: American Military Power in Britain*, London: Michael Joseph, 1984.

15. See P. Bunyard, *Nuclear Britain*, New English Library, 1981.

16. Alternative Defence Commission, 'Non-Nuclear Defence and Civil Nuclear Power', Supplementary Paper No 1, August 1983, p 16.

17. Alternative Defence Commission, *Defence Without the Bomb*, *op cit*, Intro, note 1.

18. Howe, G., 1985, Speech to the Royal United Services Institute, London, 15 March 1985.

19. Thatcher's Four Points of Understanding are summarized in, for example, Young, E., 'Star Wars brought to Earth', *Space Policy*, Vol 1, No 2, May, 1985, pp 135–140.

20. Edward Teller, reported in *Newsweek*, 17 June, 1985.

21. For a summary introduction to the whole question see: John Simpson, 'Ploughshares into Swords? The International

Non-Proliferation Network and the 1985 NPT Review Conference', *Faraday Discussion Paper*, No 4, Council for Arms Control, 1985. For a more detailed analysis see: J. Simpson and A. McGrew, (eds), *The International Nuclear Non-Proliferation System: Challenges and Choices*, London: Macmillan, 1984.

22. France declared at the Second NPT Review Conference in 1980 that it would behave like other states adhering to the NPT (UN document A/PV.1672). During negotiations between US and Chinese officials in June 1985 it was established that in effect China accepted the constraints of the NPT. Details of the Chinese statements were not released, but their assurances were said to satisfy President Reagan, the State Department, the Energy Department and the ACDA. (*Keesings Contemporary Archives*, XXXI, 1985, p 33923).

23. See Leonard S. Spector, *The New Nuclear Nations*, New York: Random House, A Carnegie Endowment Book, November 1985, and Chapter Eight of Allan S. Krass, Peter Boskma, Boelie Elzen, and Wim A. Smit, *Uranium Enrichment and Nuclear Weapon Proliferation*, London: Taylor & Francis, SIPRI, 1983. See also 'How Israel Got the Bomb', Special Report, *Time Magazine*, 12 April 1976 and 'Neutron Bomb Is Suspected in South African Explosion', *International Herald Tribune*, 15/16 March 1980.

24. For more detail on INFC see: Joseph S. Nye, 'Maintaining a Non-Proliferation Régime', in George H. Quester, (ed), *Nuclear Proliferation: Breaking the Chain*, University of Wisconsin Press, 1981.

25. John Simpson, 'A New Foundaton for the NPT?', *ADIU Report*, Vol 7, No 6, November/December 1985, pp 6–9.

26. See Simpson, *Ibid* and Simpson and McGrew, *op cit*, note 21.

27. Laser isotope separation is an experimental technique for separating different isotopes of plutonium or uranium (or any other element). It promises to be much more efficient than conventional processes at enriching nuclear materials for reactor fuel or nuclear weapons. Research and development into it is going on in the USA and the USSR and, to a lesser extent, in Israel, Argentina, Iraq, South Africa, India and Taiwan but, at this stage, it is far from being commercially viable. If it is successfully developed, however, it will greatly increase the risks

of nuclear proliferation: it requires a relatively small amount of space at about only one-tenth the cost of the conventional nuclear fuel processes. See: 'Laser Offers Cut-Price Nuclear Fuel – And More Proliferation?' *The Economist*, 30 June 1984, pp 73–74; A.S. Krass, 'Laser Enrichment of Uranium: The Proliferation Connection,' *Science*, Vol 196, 13 May 1977, pp 721–731; B.M. Casper, 'Laser Enrichment: A New Path to Proliferation?', *Bulletin of the Atomic Scientist*, Vol 33, No 1, January 1977; 'Laser Isotope Separation: Proliferation Risks and Benefits', Report of the Laser Enrichment Review Panel to Jersey Nuclear-Avco Isotopes, 27 February 1979.

28. See David Fischer and Paul Szasz, *Safeguarding The Atom; A Critical Appraisal*, London: Taylor & Francis, SIPRI, 1985 for extensive discussion of IAEA safeguards.

29. *Ibid*, p 64.

30. *Ibid*, pp 54–56. One important development in technical surveillance is Remote Continuous Verification (RECOVER); see K. Pieragostini, *op cit*, note 11.

31. Fischer and Szasz, *op cit*, note 28, pp 70–73. See also M.J. Wilmshurst, 'Reforming the Non-Proliferation System in the 1980s', in Simpson and McGrew, *op cit*, 21. Also Norman Dombay, 'Strengthening Nuclear Safeguards: A Role for Britain', *ADIU Report*, Vol 8, No 1, Jan/Feb 1986, pp 1–5.

32. Duncan Campbell, 'Will Britain help Chile make an A-Bomb?', *New Statesman*, Vol 105, No 2709, 18 February, 1983, p 4.

33. See Pierre Lellouche, 'Breaking the Rules Without Quite Stopping the Bomb: European Views', in Quester, *op cit*, note 24.

34. For Canada's unilateral initiatives see Michael Tucker, 'Canada and Arms Control: Perspectives and Trends', *International Journal*, Vol XXXVI, No 3, Summer 1981.

35. John R. Redick, 'The Tlatelolco Regime and Non-Proliferation' in Quester, *op cit*, note 24, pp 118–219.

36. The meeting of the Nuclear Suppliers Group in London in 1975 (the London Club) followed the drawing up of a list of sensitive nuclear items which would require IAEA safeguards if exported, the 'Zangger Trigger List', drawn up by a committee of supplier states chaired by Professor Zangger, which completed

its work in 1974. See Fischer and Szasz, *op cit*, note 28, pp 101–103.

37. For criticisms of the NSG from Third World countries at the Second NPT Review Conference see SIPRI, *World Armaments and Disarmament Yearbook 1981*, London: Taylor & Francis, 1981, pp 315–320.

38. *Arms Control and Disarmament Newsletter*, No. 25, July–September, 1985, p 19.

39. *The Guardian*, 27 February 1985, p 8.

40. *The Guardian*, 25 September 1985, p 6.

41. Fischer and Szasz, *op cit*, note 28.

42. Michael James, 'International Plutonium Storage', SIPRI, Symposium on 'Internationalisation of the Nuclear Fuel Cycle', Oct 31–Nov 2 1979.

43. Alternative Defence Commission, *op cit*, note 16.

44. SIPRI, *World Armaments and Disarmament Yearbook 1980*, London: Taylor & Francis, 1980, pp 345–346.

45. For a review of the history of negotiations on nuclear test bans, see for example *Nuclear Arms Control; Background and Issues*, National Academy of Sciences, National Academy Press, Washington DC, 1985.

46. Sykes, L.R., and Everndon, J.F., 'The Verification of a Comprehensive Nuclear Test Ban', *Scientific American*, Vol 247, No 4, October 1982. See also Legget, J.K., 'Geoscience and the feasibility of cheating on test ban treaties', *Modern Geology*, Vol 9, 1985, pp 329–357.

47. 'Decoupling chambers' are a possible means (there is no evidence that any country has constructed one so far) by which the energy of the seismic waves created by an underground nuclear explosion can be reduced. Seismic waves are generated when the blast from the nuclear explosion 'couples' with the rock around it. The energetic seismic waves that are created can be detected thousands of miles away. If a vast spherical chamber is constructed, then the blast from a nuclear detonation at the centre of the chamber would transfer much less energy to the surrounding rock. The resulting seismic waves would be much weaker and harder to detect.

48. Everndon, J.F., 1985 (private communication); see also Legget J.K. 1985 *op cit*, note 46.

49. Julian Perry Robinson, 'New Poison Gas Weapons Ahead?', *ADIU Report*, Vol 7, No 5, September/October 1985, p 1.

50. See SIPRI, *World Armaments and Disarmament Yearbook 1984*, London: Taylor & Francis, 1984, pp 331–338.

51. Caspar W. Weinberger, Secretary of Defense, 'Annual Report to Congress: Fiscal Year 1986', Department of Defense, Washington, DC, February 1985.

52. Report on Congress and binaries, *ADIU Report*, Vol 7, No 5, p 5; and Vol 7, No 6, p 13; and Vol 8, No 1, p 6; and 'A raw nerve on the Rhine', *The Guardian*, May 21 1986, and 'Inside the nerve gas Noddy suit', *The Observer*, May 25 1980.

53. 'Britain to back US proposals on chemical warfare', *The Guardian*, 29 April 1986, and 'NATO plans to deploy US nerve gas', *The Guardian*, 23 May 1980.

54. Robinson, *op cit*, note 49.

55. SIPRI, *World Armaments and Disarmament Yearbook 1980*, London: Taylor & Francis, 1980, pp 368–369 and Bhupendra Jasani and Frank Barnaby, *Verification Technologies: The Case for Surveillance by Consent*, London: Berg, Centre for International Peacebuilding, 1984, pp 20–22.

56. See Nicholas Sims, 'Chemical Weapons – Control or Chaos?' *Faraday Paper*, Council for Arms Control, 1984, on the US Draft Treaty. For an official British response to the Soviet proposal, see Richard Luce, 'Chemical Weapons: Negotiating a Total Ban', *NATO Review*, Vol 33, No 3, June 1985, p 11.

57. The Irish government in 1972 withdrew an identical reservation it had made in 1930.

58. Luce, *op cit*, note 56, refers to the Soviet Union continuing 'to accumulate an ever-greater chemical weapons capability' and says nothing about strategy. Julian Perry Robinson notes that although the West German Army Chief-of-Staff and the Commander-in-Chief of Allied Forces Central Europe had, like the US Defense Secretary, publicly re-evaluated Soviet chemical weapon strategy, the MoD had not.

59. *New Scientist* has periodically been reporting on the progress of the groups of German citizens, trade unionists and MPs challenging the constitutional right of the US to base chemical weapons at the proposed sites at Fischbach, Mannheim and

Hanau. At the time of publication none of these cases had been resolved.

60. Press Release, Embassy of the German Democratic Republic, London, 20 June 1985 gives translation of Joint Communiqué of the Socialist Unity Party and the Social Democratic Party.

61. Robinson, *op cit*, note 49, p 4.

62. For a brief look at the arguments see Jozef Goldblat, 'Nuclear and Chemical Weapon-Free Zones: Prospects for Europe', *ADIU Report*, Vol 7, No 6, November/December 1985, pp 4–5.

63. *International Geographic Encyclopedia and Atlas*, London: Macmillan, 1979.

64. For details of the Treaty of Rorotongo establishing a nuclear-free zone in the South Pacific, see Greg E. Fry, 'The South Pacific nuclear-free zone' SIPRI Yearbook 1986, Oxford, OUP, pp 499–508.

65. W. Arkin and R. Fieldhouse, *Nuclear Battlefields: Global Links in the Arms Race*, Cambridge, Mass: Ballinger, 1985.

66. Joint Chiefs-of-Staff, 'Annual Statement to the US Congress', 1981; and C. Kumar, 'The Indian Ocean: Arc of Crisis or Zone of Peace?', *International Affairs*, Vol 60, No 2, Spring 1984, p 238.

67. A.J. Day, (ed)., *Border and Territorial Disputes*, Harlow: Longman, Keesings Reference Publication, 1982, pp 146–50.

68. Campbell, *op cit*, note 14.

69. Kumar, *op cit*, note 66.

70. *Ibid*.

71. Day, *op cit*, note 67.

72. The Bradford School of Peace Studies has a strong, but by no means exclusive, focus on problems of defence and disarmament; the Arms and Disarmament Information Unit at Sussex University is mainly concerned with dispensing information.

73. For a history of the ACDA see: Duncan L. Clarke, *Politics of Arms Control: The Role and Effectiveness of the United States Arms Control and Disarmament Agency*, New York: Free Press, 1979. The ACDA was further emasculated under President Reagan, see: Charles R. Gellner and Lynn F. Rusten, 'The US ACDA: Data

on Management, Personnel, Budget, Status and Related Matters 1981–83', *Arms Control*, Vol 5, No 2, September 1984, pp 128–147.

74. Duncan L. Clarke, 'Conclusion: Giving Arms Control Greater Salience in Policy Processes', in Hans Günter Brauch and Duncan L. Clarke, (eds), *Decisionmaking for Arms Limitation: Assessments and Prospects*, Cambridge, Mass: Ballinger, 1983, p 299.

75. Alternative Defence Commission, 'Threat or Opportunity: the Economic Consequences of Non-Nuclear Defence', *Peace Research Report* No 6, School of Peace Studies, University of Bradford, September 1984.

76. *Ibid*. This proposal has been made by a researcher in this area, Bill Niven.

77. Campbell, *op cit*, note 14.

78. Simpson, *op cit*, note 7.

79. *Ibid*.

CHAPTER 8

1. *North-South*: *A Programme for Survival*. The Report of the Independent Commission on International Development Issues under the Chairmanship of Willy Brandt, London: Pan, 1980.

2. See Michael Kidron and Dan Smith, *The War Atlas: Armed Conflict, Armed Peace*, London: Heinemann, 1983, Maps 2–4. This figure is much higher – by more than 100 – than the figures usually given. This results from the definition used by the authors which differs from ones used in other studies by including as wars armed conflicts in which regular uniformed forces are involved *on at least one side*, the fighting is centrally organized *to some extent* and there is *some continuity* between armed clashes. The italicized phrases indicate ways in which this definition is more inclusive than others. In view of the nature of modern armed conflict, this wider definition is reasonable; with more restrictive definitions, conflicts in which several hundred thousand people have been killed or injured would simply be scrubbed from the record.

3. James F. Dunnigan and Austin Bay, *A Quick and Dirty Guide to War*, New York: William Morrow, 1985.

4. 'North' and 'South' are put in quotation marks because the

terms are not geographically accurate in this context. They are used as convenient shorthand (like the term 'Third World' itself).

5. In 1979, 25 per cent of US oil imports, 66 per cent of West European and 75 per cent of Japanese oil imports passed through the Straits of Hormuz. David Holloway, *The Soviet Union and the Arms Race*, Yale University Press, 1983, p 97.

6. For typical examples of the approach, see Geoffrey Stewart-Smith, (ed), *Towards a Grand Strategy for Global Freedom*. London: Foreign Affairs Publishing, 1981. Concern about resources has also been routinely expressed in successive US Military Posture Statements since the mid 1970s. It has also been evident in British government thinking – see, for example, the present government's first Defence White Paper, *Defence in the 1980s: Statement on the Defence Estimates 1980*, London: HMSO, 1980, Cmnd 7826-1, paras 402–405. It is echoed also in a popular fictionalized account of World War III and of Soviet policy leading up to it: General Sir John Hackett, *The Third World War August 1985*, London: Sidgwick & Jackson, 1978, pp 62–66.

7. See Jeff McMahon, *Reagan and the World*, London: Pluto Press, 1984, Ch 6 for a detailed discussion of this process.

8. See Kidron & Smith, *The War Atlas*, *op cit*, Map 25.

9. Brandt Commission, *op cit*, note 1, p 118

10. *World Armaments and Disarmament: SIPRI Yearbook 1980*, London: Taylor & Francis, 1980, p 57.

11. *Ibid*, pp 63 & 69.

12. Documented by, among others, Anthony Sampson, *The Arms Bazaar*, London: Hodder & Stoughton, 1977.

13. See Dan Smith. 'The Arms Trade and Arms Control' in *RUSI and Brassey's Defence Yearbook 1982*, London: Brassey's, 1982.

14. Daniel Yergin, *Shattered Peace: The Origins of the Cold War and the National Security State*, Harmondsworth Penguin Books, 1980, p 276.

15. The US did, however, obey the interim judgement of the ICJ in May 1984 urging it to desist from mining Nicaraguan harbours.

16. In 1974 Marshal Grechko, then Soviet Defence Minister, stated: 'at the present stage the historic function of the Soviet Armed Forces is not restricted to their function in defending our

Motherland and the other socialist countries. In its foreign policy activity the Soviet state purposefully opposes the export of counter-revolution and the policy of oppression, supports the struggle for national liberation and resolutely resists imperialist aggression in whatever distant region of our planet it may appear.' Compare this with part of Truman's statement enunciating the Truman Doctrine of 1947: 'One of the primary objectives of the foreign policy of the United States is the creation of conditions in which we and other nations will be able to work out a way of life free from coercion . . . I believe that it must be the policy of the United States to support free peoples who are resisting attempted subjugation by armed minorities or by outside pressures.'
See Alex P. Schmid, Ellen Berends and Luuk Zonnerveld, *Social Defence and Soviet Military Power*, COMT, State University of Leiden, 1985, p 179, who draw attention to the parallel between the two statements.

17. The Soviet Union has even provided military support to friendly governments for the specific purpose of crushing revolutionary insurrection – in Ethiopia, for instance, in the war against the Eritrean liberation movement, and in North Yemen in the 1980s against a revolutionary movement which it had previously supported when President Nasser of Egypt had intervened on its behalf in the civil war of 1962–1970.

18. Ruth Sivard, *World Military and Social Expenditures 1981*, p 81.

19. Dennis M. Gormley, 'The Direction and Pace of Soviet Force Projection Capabilities', *Survival*, Vol XXIV, No 6, November/December 1982, pp 266–276.

20. SIPRI *The Arms Trade with the Third World*, Harmondsworth: Pelican Books, 1975 p 99.

21. The report to the General Assembly dated 5 November 1985 is numbered A/40/843, and that of 17 February 1986 addressed to the Economic and Social Councils, E/CN.4/1986/24. The estimated number of refugees appears in para 31 of the 1986 report; the estimate of total casualties appears in the November 1985 report, paragraph 82. The 1986 report in paragraph 87 gives the following description of some of the weapons being used by Soviet forces:

'The liquid fire is described as a black, tar-like substance dropped from aircraft in canisters, which open in the air spraying the ground with the substance, which remains effective for months and ignites upon contact producing gas. The fuel-air explosive cratering bombs are dropped by fighter planes and explode near the ground making craters 10 metres across and 6 metres deep ... A fire stick is 30 centimetres long and 18 centimetres thick, a canister contains several thousand fire sticks and is detonated upon contact with the ground.'

22. See 'Zia predicts an Afghan pull-out', *The Observer*, 6 April 1986.

23. See Kidron & Smith, *The War Atlas, op cit*, Map 16.

24. See the discussion of the problem in Neil Macfarlane, 'Intervention and Regional Security', *Adelphi Paper No 196*, IISS, 1985, pp 23–24.

25. Schmid et al, *Social Defence and Soviet Military Power, op cit*, note 16, p 179.

26. Brandt Commission, *op cit*, pp 30, 77, 254 and 280.

27. See especially F. Halliday, *The Making of the Second Cold War*, London: Verso, 1983 and 1984.

28. Susan George, *How the Other Half Dies*, Harmondsworth: Penguin, 1976.

29. Frances Stewart, *Technology and Underdevelopment*, London: Macmillan, 1977.

30. Brandt Commission, *op cit*, note 1, p 222.

31. *World Development Report 1985*, Oxford University Press, for the World Bank, 1985, Table 2.3.

32. *Ibid*, Table 2.5.

33. *Ibid*, p 25.

34. *Ibid*, Annex Table 18.

35. The Brandt Commission reported OECD estimates showing that the USSR and other members of the Council for Mutual Economic Assistance spent on average 0.04 per cent of their GNP on aid; Brandt Commission, *op cit*, note 1, p 225.

36. For a discussion of the problem of dependence on the suppliers of technology, see Dieter Ernst, (ed), *The New International Division of Labour, Technology and Underdevelopment*, Frankfurt/New York: Campus, 1980, especially the editor's own

contribution: 'International Transfer of Technology, Technological Dependence and Underdevelopment: Key Issues'. See also Stewart, *op cit*, note 29.

37. See Martin Wolf, 'Two Faces of a Coin: International Trade and Debt', *IDS Bulletin*, Vol 16, No 1, January 1985.

38. Difficulties with data and the definition of war make comparisons about the incidence of warfare difficult. A rough attempt, however, can be made. Lewis Fry Richardson identified 315 wars in each of which more than 1,000 people were killed in the period from 1820 to 1952 (cited in D. Wilkinson, *Deadly Quarrels*, University of California Press, 1980). Even if the high figure of +250 wars of all types and sizes since 1945 is not taken for the purpose of comparison (see note 2 above), and a lower figure of say 150 is used, the comparison still tells a graphic tale: 315 wars in 132 years (2.4 per annum) in the earlier period, against 150 wars in the past 40 years (3.75 per annum).

39. See Dan Smith and Ron Smith, *Military Expenditure, Resources and Development*, Discussion Paper 87, Birkbeck College, London, 1980.

40. Brandt Commission, *op cit*, note 1, pp 244–245.

41. The record on aid of the wealthiest of the OPEC members is proportionately more generous than the OECD record, even though both Kuwait and Saudi Arabia, the two largest OPEC ODA spenders, have both trimmed their aid in the 1980s – Kuwait by about 13 per cent, Saudia Arabia by 34 per cent. The sharpest cut, however, is by the United Arab Emirates – by 89 per cent (*World Development Report 1985* Annex Table 18).

42. While the statistical evidence for (and, for that matter, against) the Kondratiev thesis of 'long waves' is necessarily weak, the attractions of the model as a mode of understanding long-term trends in the world economy are strong. See Andrew Brody, 'Growth, Cycles, Crisis', and Carlotta Perez, 'Long Waves and Changes in Socioeconomic Organization', *IDS Bulletin*, Vol 16, No 1, January 1985.

43. Noel Perrin, *Giving Up the Gun: Japan's Reversion to the Sword, 1543–1879*, Boulder, Co.: Shambhala, 1980.

Index